TWO RENAISSANCE BOOK HUNTERS

Records of Western Civilization

RECORDS OF WESTERN CIVILIZATION

A series of Columbia University Press

TWO RENAISSANCE BOOK HUNTERS

THE LETTERS OF
POGGIUS BRACCIOLINI TO
NICOLAUS DE NICCOLIS

Translated from the Latin
and annotated by
Phyllis Walter Goodhart Gordan

COLUMBIA UNIVERSITY PRESS
NEW YORK

Columbia University Press
New York   Chichester, West Sussex
Copyright © 1974, 1991 Columbia University Press
All rights reserved

ISBN 0-231-03777-5

ISBN 0-231-09633-X (pbk.)

c   10 9 8 7 6 5 4 3 2 1
p   10 9 8 7 6 5 4 3 2

Records of Western Civilization is a new series published under the auspices of the Interdepartmental Committee on Medieval and Renaissance Studies of the Columbia University Graduate School. The Western Records are, in fact, a new incarnation of a venerable series, the Columbia Records of Civilization, which, for more than half a century, published sources and studies concerning great literary and historical landmarks. Many of the volumes of that series retain value, especially for their translations into English of primary sources, and the Medieval and Renaissance Studies Committee is pleased to cooperate with Columbia University Press in reissuing a selection of those works in paperback editions, especially suited for classroom use, and in limited clothbound editions.

PREFACE

This book represents only the proverbial tip of the iceberg. Poggius, whose contemporaries greatly admired his literary style, left almost six hundred personal letters, addressed to one hundred and seventy-two correspondents, as well as an immense number of official letters written for the popes whom he served as secretary; some of his official letters are written to dignitaries who appear in his personal correspondence as well. Only ninety-three of his letters are included in this volume, those to Poggius' dearest friend.

I first became aware of Poggius and his letters in November 1933, when Professor Lily Ross Taylor of Bryn Mawr College suggested that I write a paper on the rediscovery of lost classical texts. I found that Poggius had been a leader in the search and had described his adventures vividly in letters to his friends. I thought then that it would be rewarding to translate his letters and along with them as many answers as I could locate and to identify all the correspondents and the friends mentioned in the letters. This simple-sounding enterprise has taken me forty years.

Many people and many institutions have been good to me during this time and I am most grateful to them. Some of them, in foreign libraries, I have never known by name. Others have become very close friends. Chief among them, for constant support and good advice, has been Professor Berthe Marti, formerly of Bryn Mawr and now of the University of North Carolina.

Poggius' letters, although published in the nineteenth century, were until 1964 almost as rare in print as in manuscript form. Volume I of Tonelli's edition is not particularly rare, but Volumes II and III exist in only five or six copies, one of which miraculously turned out, in 1935, to be in the stacks of the Harvard University Library. It was a set which had belonged to the director, in the 1870s, of the Biblioteca Medicea-Laurenziana in Florence and was heavily annotated by him. After I had had it completely photostated, it was moved into the Upper Treasure Room and is now in the Houghton Library. The Lower Treasure Room in the Widener Library provided me with some of my most rewarding hours; its shelves contained the catalogues of all the manuscript collections in European libraries which by 1938 had printed catalogues, and from them I was able to compile a list of the letters and dedications by Poggius' friends which might pertain to his correspondence. The Widener Library's vast holdings in Renaissance History were also invaluable in preparing a bibliography of biographical material on the correspondents. When I moved back to New York in 1940, I found most of this material also in the Research Libraries of the New York Public Library, whose holdings particularly of Italian learned journals have never failed me. When I have needed a particularly obscure book not in the stacks of the New York Public Library, it has always turned out to be in the British Museum. This book would never have even been started without these three institutions.

Poggius' correspondents are often difficult to identify. Sometimes he does not give their full names and sometimes he addresses them only by their title. I was most fortunate, in 1947, to meet Professor Mario Emilio Cosenza, who had devoted the leisure hours of his very busy academic life to making a card file on the Italian humanists, which came to well over a million handwritten cards. He and Mrs. Cosenza were most generous and hospitable to me, and I paid many visits to their home in Rockville Centre and gleaned great quantities of necessary information.

In 1949 it became possible to go to European libraries once more to seek out some of the letters which I supposed were waiting there. Laurance Page Roberts, then director of the American Academy in Rome, allowed me to stay at the Academy while I looked for material in the Vatican Library. The splendid card catalogue of the Vatican's manuscript collection saved me many years of wasted labor because it lists the books and journals in which its manuscript material has been published. During that visit I also discovered that immense amounts of biographical material relating to Poggius and his circle were contained in the many volumes of the Vatican and Lateran

Registers preserved in the Archivio Segreto Vaticano, whose prefects, especially Monsignor Angelo Mercati, have helped me with much explanation and generous extension of reading hours.

During the first eighteen years of my research, my father, Howard Lehman Goodhart, was collecting incunabula which he made constantly available to me and which frequently contained humanist texts not to be found elsewhere. Furthermore, his friendship with many antiquarian book dealers made it possible for me to find material for work at home during hours when even the most generous libraries would be closed. Notable among my sources of research material have been the late E. P. Goldschmidt of London, the Studio Bibliografico Antenore of Padua, and William Salloch of Ossining, New York.

In 1953, Professor Paul Oskar Kristeller of Columbia University became the *deus ex machina* of this work. He introduced me then to Dr. Walter Ruegg, who had been loaned the vast archive of research material on Poggius assembled in a lifetime by Professor Ernst Walser, Poggius' learned and indefatigable biographer. Professor Kristeller introduced me at the same time to Mrs. Marguerite Walser-Escher who had worked steadily on Poggius with her husband; indeed most of his notes are in her handwriting. Her friendship and her enthusiasm for Poggius made the work a constant delight. I soon learned from a study of Walser's notes in Dr. Ruegg's possession that my fifteen years of research had not uncovered a single letter from any of Poggius' correspondents which was unrecorded by Walser. Dr. Ruegg has been immensely generous in allowing me access to the archive. It was also he who advised me to select the letters included in the present volume and to annotate them in the way in which Remigio Sabbadini annotated the correspondence of Guarinus Veronensis. Professor Kristeller has been willing to read and criticize the manuscript of this book, for which I am most grateful.

I have the most emphatic reasons to be grateful also to Sir Roger Mynors of Oxford University and to Professor W. T. H. Jackson of Columbia University for the care and attention they devoted to improving the text of my translation. Miss Edith

Wright of Bryn Mawr had already checked it and saved me from some woeful errors, Miss Diane Hatch of Mary Washington College has been dedicated and accurate in checking my large quantity of footnotes, and Mr. Edward Michael of Port Huron, Michigan, has given me great assistance in identifying classical quotations scattered liberally throughout the letters but not identified in any way by Poggius.

I cannot complete this note without expressing my appreciation to two people who have patiently and devotedly typed both what is in this book and much besides. Miss Ruth Brooks for many years typed thousands of pages of notes and hundreds of pages of translation, reading my handwriting flawlessly. Mrs. Julie Merwin typed the manuscript of this book with unbelievable patience and accuracy.

My husband and my children have shown extraordinary sympathy and good will in accepting Poggius as a member of the household. My husband never grudged the time spent on translation and research and generously adapted his vacations to visits to European libraries. My children became so accustomed to Poggius' circle that in Italian churches they would ask: "Which of your friends is buried here?" This book belongs to them too.

New York City   PHYLLIS WALTER GOODHART GORDAN
February 11, 1974

CONTENTS

INTRODUCTION

The first half of the fifteenth century was a time almost as full of change and upheaval as our own. Wars and social change were going on everywhere. Values were being questioned, and established governments all over Europe were faced with rebellion. In Eastern Europe the menace of the Turks was so serious that the Byzantine Emperor traveled from Constantinople to Italy, France, and England from 1399 to 1402 seeking financial and military help. He found none because the rulers whom he visited were themselves in a precarious position. The Hundred Years War had already lasted for over sixty years. The rightful king of England, Richard II, had been dethroned by a rebellious nobleman, his cousin Henry Bolingbroke. A great area of France had fallen into the hands of the English, and the king of France was at odds with his most powerful vassal, the duke of Burgundy. The emperor of the Holy Roman Empire was kept out of his capital by the Hussites for sixteen years. In Italy in many cities the families which had ruled during the fourteenth century had been overthrown and exiled by new groups of citizens who derived their power from the guilds and from the increasing strength of the artisan class.

Nowhere was government at a lower ebb than in the papacy. In 1377 Gregory XI returned to Rome after the popes had spent nearly seventy years in Avignon. Within two years of the Pope's return to Rome, two factions of the College of Cardinals elected popes or anti-popes and the schism so begun lasted for almost forty years.

It is difficult to say whether the spirit of questioning, research, and political debate which characterized the Italian humanists of the early fifteenth century was the cause or the result of the disturbances around them. Humanists became passionately interested in historical accounts of ancient times and devoted to the study of ancient political theory. They studied the texts which were available to them and argued about their own systems of government in the light of their knowledge of Cicero and Caesar. As they grew more concerned with their own responsibilities as citizens, they became ever more eager for the works of Livy and Tacitus, for the lost orations of Cicero, and for translations from the Greek of the works of Plato, Aristotle, Xenophon, Demosthenes, and Plutarch.

The humanists of the early fifteenth century built on the work already done by Petrarch and Boccaccio to revive the knowledge of Latin literature and history. By 1400, through such successors of these great men as Coluccius Salutatus, Chancellor of Florence, a start had been made on locating and copying lost classical texts.

The next generation of humanists, many of them his friends and pupils, were surprisingly successful in finding texts which had been lost for many centuries and were known only through quotations and anthologies. Among the humanists most devoted to the search for manuscripts and most eager to apply the ideas of ancient authors to the problems of their own time were two of Salutatus' pupils who were much later his successors as chancellor of the republic of Florence: Leonardus Brunus Aretinus and Johannes Franciscus Poggius de Bracciolinis.

Poggius (1380–1459) left a total of five hundred and fifty-eight letters, addressed to one hundred and seventy-two friends, foes, acquaintances, and strangers. By far the largest single group of letters, ninety-two in all, were written between 1406 and 1436 to his dearest friend, Nicolaus de Niccolis of Florence. These ninety-two letters are the collection which Poggius himself first chose to gather into a volume, with the help of the recipient, and to circulate among his friends and admirers. The present book contains Poggius' letters to Nicolaus, translated from the Latin into English, unabridged, and annotated to explain all the personalities and events mentioned.

Although Poggius himself chose this particular collection, it gives a very incomplete picture of his correspondence. In it he deals largely with his personal affairs and with the discovery and copying of lost classical texts. This enterprise was a major interest of both Poggius' and Nicolaus'. To them we owe a very sizable fraction of the classical Latin literature which has survived to our era. Before the discoveries made by the Italian humanists and predominantly by Poggius, and fostered, supported, and copied by Nicolaus, as well as by the searchers individually, the authors of ancient Rome were known by name, but their works had in large measure not been seen for centuries. It is extraordinary that Poggius and a few other humanists should have had sufficient knowledge and the quick-witted percipience to recognize the texts of Quintilian, Lucretius, Vitruvius, Petronius, and Cicero, as well as many lesser authors, when they explored the monastic libraries of eastern France, the Rhineland, and Switzerland in the decade of 1410–1420. Once he was established as the chief literary scout of his period, Poggius became the focal point of the literary discoveries made by others; they were reported to him and offered to him for purchase or for copying. His letters to Nicolaus are primarily concerned with this shared occupation. Because some of the most exciting letters about the rediscovery of classical texts were written by Poggius to friends other than Nicolaus de Niccolis, or by them to him, or even by them to each other, and so do not properly belong in this series, they are included in an appendix.

"Poggio, the son of Guccio Bracciolini, was born on the eleventh day of February, in the year 1380, at Terranuova, a small town situated in the territory of the republic of Florence, not far from Arezzo." Poggius received his early education in Arezzo. When sixteen or seventeen years old, he moved to Florence to study the profession of notary. There he came under the influence of the distinguished and famous chancellor, Coluccius Salutatus, himself a pupil of Petrarch, who was noted for his splendid Latin style and his interest in the revival of classical studies, both Greek and Latin. During Poggius' early years in Florence, Salutatus introduced him to the search for lost texts. Salutatus also trained Poggius in the copying of newly found texts. He encouraged Poggius to study Greek, which was taught in Florence in 1397 by Manuel Chrysoloras under the auspices of Salutatus and Nicolaus de Niccolis.

In 1403, Poggius followed another distinguished and successful pupil of Salutatus, Leonardus Brunus Aretinus, into the service of the Papacy in Rome. He and Leonardus became lifelong friends and had similar literary and civic careers, Poggius following in Leonardus' footsteps most of the way. Poggius was very successful in his service at the Curia, as is attested by the letter of congratulation written him by Salutatus in February 1404, and quickly became an apostolic secretary. He served in that capacity for fifty years, except for an interlude of five years in the service of Henry Beaufort, Bishop of Winchester and later Cardinal of England. This interlude, 1418–1423, is copiously documented in the letters in this volume. Poggius left the Curia in 1453, for the sake of the future financial welfare of his young children. He left his lifelong position because he was invited, at the advanced age of seventy-three, to become chancellor of the republic of Florence after the death of his friend Carolus Marsuppinus Aretinus, who is frequently mentioned in his letters to Nicolaus.

It must be remembered that Poggius worked in the Curia in a very disturbed and stormy period. Between 1403 and 1417, when Martin V was elected Pope at the Council of Constance, there were three anti-popes. Poggius belonged to the Curia during the reign of the anti-pope John XXIII (Baldassare Cossa) and accompanied him to the Council of Constance, where he was deposed. It was this period of turmoil for the Church which gave Poggius his great opportunity to visit the monasteries of Langres, Cluny, Fulda, and St. Gall and to make the great textual discoveries that made him famous and gave his letters value.

The reign of Martin V was relatively tranquil in regard to factions within the Church, but Poggius' letters testify to the ruined condition of Rome, physically and financially, in the early 1420s. During the first two years of his reign, conditions in Rome and in the Papal states were so disrupted that Martin V was forced to stay in Florence, where he was mocked and made to feel unwelcome. After he reached Rome in September 1420, his government was in constant danger of attack by the mercenary general Braccius de Montone, who was in the pay of Naples. He remained a danger to the Pope until he was killed near Aquila in May 1424. Martin was also in danger from Alfonsus of

Aragon, who wanted to become king of Naples, and from Philippus Maria Vicecomes (Visconti), the duke of Milan, who frequently changed sides and attacked states thought to be his allies. Numerous cities which belonged to the papal states and were governed by papal legates rebelled during the 1420s, notably Bologna and Perugia. By the tenth year of his reign Martin V, by a combination of diplomacy and severity and a skillful use of the soldiers in his family, the Colonna, had overcome most of his rebellious subjects and belligerent neighbors. His financial troubles did not grow less. His military costs were high and he had great difficulty in persuading the churches of England, France, and Germany that he should receive the taxes, such as the annates, which he expected from them. His troubles were compounded by the Hussite heretics in central Europe, especially Bohemia, who believed in national and local control of the church and had so little intention of obeying the rule of Rome that in 1426 Martin V sent a crusade against them.

Shortly after Martin's death, in the reign of Eugenius IV, the troubles worsened. The controversy about where the real and ultimate power belonged (to the pope or to the council of cardinals, bishops, and other churchmen) had been only apparently settled at Constance. The dispute had already revived early in the reign of Martin V and was a matter for discussion at the Council of Siena in 1424. It had split the Church during the great schism of 1378–1417 and split it again, though less dangerously, in the reign of Eugenius IV, for the duration of the Council of Basel, sixteen years, 1431–1447. During the long years of the Council of Basel, the wanderings of the Pope and his entourage began again when he escaped in disguise from Rome in 1434. Indeed the last letter in this volume was written from Bologna, where the Curia was temporarily settled after two years in Florence; they returned to Florence for the Council of union with the Greek Church in 1439 and were absent from Rome for almost ten years.

All these matters and anxieties are covered in letters which Poggius wrote to other friends, both lay and clerical, in the years when he was writing to Nicolaus. From the period before the end of his correspondence with Nicolaus, who died on 4 February 1437, we have about one hundred letters to other friends. Some three hundred and fifty letters exist which belong to the twenty-two years between the death of Nicolaus and Poggius' own death in October 1459.

These letters cover literature, politics, religion, domestic felicity and his marriage very late in life, child-raising, quarrels, scandal, and catastrophes of nature. Some letters are particularly interesting for the view they give of the problems of the Church in the fifteenth century which led to the Protestant reform movement of the sixteenth. Poggius was never in holy orders but was a papal bureaucrat. It was in his interest for the Church to have temporal, military, and financial security and his letters reflect that. Yet they also reflect his concern that the material prosperity of the Church and its hierarchy was contrary to the religious principles upon which it was founded. The letters in which he rather fumblingly discusses his anxiety over this contradiction make very interesting reading in the twentieth century.

Poggius wrote letters very widely, in Italy and abroad, to men of all ranks of society. Some of them he met at the Council of Constance and addressed with familiarity thenceforth. This is true of Cardinal Beaufort and two other English clerics. We still have a letter (IX, 7; Vol. II, 308–315) written by Poggius to Beaufort in 1446, seeking money for a crusade against the Turks, which contains all the cliches used in a fund-raising letter today. The letter which Poggius wrote to Prince Henry the Navigator, whom he never met, is much more in the spirit of a modern letter to the press. Poggius, by then a recognized stylist and influential member of the papal bureaucracy, wrote to Henry in praise of his expeditions to Africa, to encourage him to spread Christianity, by force or by peaceful means.

This accounts for Poggius' personal correspondence, selected by him or by his surviving friends to be preserved for posterity. There is also the vast bulk of Poggius' official correspondence preserved in the Vatican Archives, which has scarcely been studied at all and certainly not in relation to Poggius and his

other activities. This consists of hundreds of the Vatican and
Lateran Registers which contain copies, very often in Poggius'
well-known hand, of his official correspondence for the popes
whom he served. These letters were written to kings, princes,
bishops, abbots, and even lowly clerics, and to secular civil
servants all over Europe. They cover everything from far-reaching
moral pronouncements to individual safe conducts for travel in
papal territory. For instance, Poggius wrote the documents per-
mitting Henry VI to found Eton College, which began its existence as a religious foundation of the Roman Catholic Church.
There are even registers wholly in Poggius' own hand, which is
easy to recognize if one is familiar with the copies of classical
texts written by him and preserved in the Vatican and the
Laurentian libraries. These official letters and any letters which
may have survived in the Florentine archives from his short
tenure as chancellor would certainly reward further and extensive study.

Poggius' letters have come down to us mainly through three
great manuscripts: Cod. Riccardianus 759, Cod. Laurentianus
47,20, and Cod. Pragensis 94 (Prague: University Library Cod.
I.C.3). These manuscripts contain the letters which were
originally collected on three separate occasions. First there are
those in this volume, "published" by Poggius himself in 1436.
Then there is a second collection which he first made in 1438
comprising letters to his many other friends, which he dedicated
to the Archbishop Loisius, identified by Wilmanns as Ludovicus
Scarampus-Mezzarota. Poggius himself revised and augmented
this second collection in 1445. The third collection of letters was
put together by Poggius in six "books" in 1455. After Poggius'
death, his friends added a seventh book, his letters of 1455–1459.
Items 87 and 88 of the inventory of Poggius' books made when
he died are the first and second volumes of his own letters,
written on paper, and the first volume bound in green leather.
Some of Poggius' letters, included in these three major manuscripts and forming part of the three collections, appear in
numerous manuscripts with letters of other humanists. This is
particularly true of Letter III in this volume, which describes his

visit to the baths at Baden, and of his famous letter to Leonardus
Brunus Aretinus from Constance, describing the trial and execution of the Hussite, Jerome of Prague. There are a few letters
which have been located individually or in groups in isolated
manuscripts; the most rewarding of these is the three-way correspondence between Poggius and Philelphus, who were at each
other's throats for many years, and the man who succeeded in
reconciling them, the Venetian physician Petrus Thomasius.
These letters were unknown until found by Ernst Walser in
Bergamo in Cod. ΛII,32.

Poggius' practice of issuing his letters, long after they were
written, in book form has created considerable controversy about
their authenticity. Some modern critics have gone so far as to say
that none of his letters were actual correspondence but were all
written purely as examples of stylistic effect. This seems im-
probable because of their great number and great variety of content and recipient as well as the fact that so many of them deal
with matters that were of immense importance to him. The
opinion of his very thorough and inquiring biographer, Ernst
Walser, seems more reasonable: that the letters were indeed
written by Poggius originally and primarily for the eye of his
particular correspondent but also written from the outset with
deep concern for style and then much revised when Poggius
prepared them for publication.

Long after Poggius' other writings were available in print and
reprinted in nearly every century, his letters were mysteriously
a rarity. They were edited in the nineteenth century by Thomas
de Tonellis of Florence from the manuscript in the Riccardiana,
and printed in three volumes: Volume I in 1832, Volume II in
1859, and Volume III in 1861. Volume I is moderately available
in the big libraries of the United States and Europe, but Volumes
II and III inexplicably vanished, except for three sets in the
Vatican, a set reported before 1914 to be in Berlin, and a set also
then reported to be in Florence, which in 1935 was found at
Harvard. The rarity of these volumes made it necessary for everyone working on Poggius' letters to use photostats or microfilm
until these three volumes were reissued photomechanically by

Riccardo Fubini in his edition of Poggius' complete works, as Volume III, in 1964.

Poggius circulated his letters with no biographical intent, apparently, but because his contemporaries wanted them for the study of rhetoric and style. They have not come down to us copied in chronological order, though we cannot be sure that Poggius did not originally intend that they should. Our only explanation of their utterly jumbled order in the Codex Riccardianus, from which Tonelli derived his text, is an interpretation of Poggius' letter, VI, 7 to the dedicatee, Franciscus Marescalcus. In it he says: "If you want the gatherings, unbound as they are, I shall arrange to have them sent to you; but if you want to wait for the volume to be finished and bound, do as you please." Tonelli did a masterly job of dating a great mass of undated and even, occasionally, quite clearly misdated letters which he published in chronological order. In a very few instances his dating seems to be wrong, and a different date, derived from internal evidence, is supplied in this edition. For that reason this volume has a concordance of its order with Tonelli's.

It may seem strange, in an English translation of Latin letters, to annotate the many phrases quoted from classical authors, especially since sò many of them are embedded in the text without any indication of being quotations. That is the very reason for their being annotated: they were so much a part of Poggius' mental furniture. They indicate what came most readily to his mind, what he had most recently and frequently been reading, what he had been copying. He quoted constantly from Terence, with whom it is natural for the author of the *Facetiae* to have had an affinity. He quoted a great deal from the various orations of Cicero which he himself had found at Langres and Cluny. In times of special adversity, he quoted from the Bible and the Church Fathers. In a few of his letters there are sentences or paragraphs which are a veritable mosaic of quotations (see Letter III, notes 18–21; Letter XLVIII, notes 11–14; and Letter LXXXIII, notes 10–13, 15) from three or four Latin authors in succession. One wonders whether he wrote this way because the phrases flowed so easily into his mind or whether these sentences are

careful constructions to dazzle his correspondent with his extraordinary literary knowledge.

The emphasis here on Poggius' letters and his profession of
writer of official letters for the Pope suggests that he did nothing
else, but this is not so. The count of letters given at the beginning
of the introduction does not include dedicatory epistles to published works, nor does it include any of the works that are sometimes listed as letters and sometimes as orations. There is another
class of Poggius' works that are often counted among his letters,
but not here, namely, his invectives. The invective written
against Guarinus deals with the superiority of Scipio Africanus to
Caesar and was written more in competition than in anger.
Other invectives, against Franciscus Bianchi de Vellate, and
against the anti-pope Felix V, Franciscus Philelphus, Laurentius
Valla, Nicolaus Perottus, and several little-known scholars were
written with great venom.

In addition to his letters, offical and personal, Poggius left a
considerable number of literary works. He was recognized early,
at the Council of Constance, for the eloquence of his funeral
orations. His first moral tract, *De avaritia,* is discussed at some
length in his correspondence with Nicolaus, and was published
in 1429. In the course of the next thirty years he produced eight
more such essays: on gratitude, on the superiority or otherwise
of medicine vs. the law, on the origins of the Latin language, on
nobility, on human misery, on hypocrisy, and on the unhappy lot
of rulers.

In 1437 Poggius wrote a work which was very personal to him
and which he published in 1439. It is *An seni sit uxor ducenda
dialogus (Should an old man take a wife?).* He wrote it to justify
his marriage, at the age of fifty-six, to an eighteen-year-old girl of
wealth and good family, Vaggia de Buondelmontis. All his
friends, even Pope Eugenius IV, took a dim view of his behavior
and prophesied the worst. Poggius seems to have been very
happy with a wife whom he molded to suit his every whim. The
dialogue is a discussion between two of Poggius' greatest friends,
with Carolus Marsuppinus Aretinus taking the affirmative side
and Nicolaus de Niccolis, who died in February 1437 and who is

reported by his biographer "never to have married so that no woman would distract him from his studies," taking the negative. He wrote a number of letters as well as the dialogue describing his surprise at his happiness and giving advice on how to choose a wife. The letters are extreme examples of male chauvinism but perhaps refreshing in their outspoken selfishness.

Poggius continued the *History of Florence* begun by Leonardus Brunus Aretinus. His most interesting book is the *De varietate fortunae,* in which he has a chapter on the ruins of Rome as they were in his time, two chapters on the decline in fortune of some of his famous contemporaries, such as Richard II of England and Joanna, Queen of Naples, and on the vicissitudes of the popes under whom he served. The last chapter is an account of voyages to Africa and to the East. The work by which Poggius was best and very widely known for centuries was his *Facetiae,* made public in 1451. It is a collection of two hundred and seventy-three very short, somewhat pornographic, nearly always funny and vulgar stories, belonging to the ancient and medieval traditions of coarse humor. Not many decades ago it was considered most improper; now it seems rather mild and quaint. It is also rewarding in connection with his correspondence because many of the clergy and the officials of various governments who are addressed or mentioned in the letters with the respect due to their rank are portrayed in very questionable or undignified circumstances.

Fubini credits Poggius with yet another work which was not ascribed to him by Walser: a short tract published three times during the fifteen century, the *Libellus de modo epistolandi.* Its author is really unknown, but there is no one to whom it can be more suitably ascribed.

Poggius was internationally known because of his discoveries, his travels in Northern Europe, and his official position at the center of the religious world. Nicolaus de Niccolis was known widely too for the splendor of his collections of books and antiquities and for his generosity in making them available to all visitors and scholars. He was a great eccentric, very quarrelsome, very fastidious, very religious, who seldom left Florence and

whose letters and other writings have not been preserved except
for one short text. He corresponded at least as vigorously as did
Poggius with all the contemporary humanists; his character and
interests can be reconstructed from their letters to him. His claim
on posterity derives from the many classical texts which he
copied in his beautiful handwriting. This was the ancestor of,
though not the direct model of, Aldus' italic type. It also derives
from the enthusiasm with which he sought, rescued, and preserved classical texts, and from the generosity of his will: he left
his books to be established as a public library in the monastery of
San Marco in Florence, with a board of twelve trustees, of which
Poggius was a member. A large proportion of Nicolaus' library
is still preserved in Florence in the Laurentian and National
Libraries.

Poggius' correspondence with Nicolaus mentions nearly all
the contemporary humanists who were engaged in the same pursuits as they were. Some were, like Poggius, attached to the
Curia; among his colleagues there were Antonius Luscus,
Cincius de Rusticis, Rinucius Aretinus, and Bartholomeus de
Montepolitiano. All of them were engaged, either through
searches in libraries or through editing and copying, in the dissemination of classical texts. From time to time, in the early
years of Poggius' career in the Curia, Leonardus Brunus Aretinus
served there with him; in 1427 he, in his turn, became Chancellor
of Florence. His scholarship, both his original treatises and his
translations from the Greek, set a high standard for Poggius to
emulate.

Other humanists who were friends of both Poggius' and
Nicolaus' were scattered through the other city-states of Italy:
Franciscus Barbarus in Venice, Guarinus in Verona and then in
Ferrara, Petrus Candidus Decembrius in Milan, and the two
questionable characters, Johannes Aurispa and Antonius Beccadellius Panormita, who had great difficulty in finding settled
employment. Two devoted friends of Nicolaus' at home in
Florence were among the leading humanists: Carolus Marsuppinus Aretinus and the Camaldolese abbot Ambrosius Traversarius. Nearly all of them left letters, to Poggius, to Nicolaus, or

to one another, which corroborate the statements made by Poggius in his correspondence.

No account of Poggius and Nicolaus would be complete without a reference to their two great friends, Cosmus and his brother Laurentius de Medicis. They were as devoted to the search for classical texts and antiquities as if they had no other responsibilities. They admired the texts that were found; they examined ruins and read inscriptions with the greatest enthusiasm. Their bank facilitated payment for books found all over Europe, and they financed purchases and copyists at home. When Nicolaus bequeathed his library to the people of Florence, Cosmus was the leading trustee and took the major responsibility for its establishment; after a few years his fellow-trustees turned the entire management of it over to him. Not only did he see to its being beautifully installed in a building designed by Michelozzo but he added constantly and generously to its holdings.

Poggius' letters abound also in references to the clergy, both highly placed and simple. His early letters often mention his English employer, Henry Beaufort, Bishop of Winchester, who was extremely rich and powerful, given to promising much and delivering little. There are also many references to Cardinal Pisanus and Cardinal St. Angelus, both of whom could, and he hoped would, help Poggius in his official career if he returned from London to the Curia. In later letters there are many bitter comments on Cardinal de Ursinis and his selfish concealment of the manuscript containing twelve lost comedies of Plautus brought to him by Nicolaus Cusanus. Some of the other churchmen mentioned were themselves book scouts or collectors: Bartholomeus Capra, Bishop of Milan; Gerardus Landrianus, Bishop of Lodi; Franciscus Piccolpassus, Bishop of Dax and later Archbishop of Milan; and Petrus Donatus, Archbishop of Crete.

The letters contain remarkably few accounts of the activities of the two popes of this period, Martin V and Eugenius IV. Poggius seems far from devoted to either one of them and thoroughly aware of all their faults and frailties.

Since the letters to Nicolaus concentrate on literary matters,

they do not dwell long on the lesser clergy. A few letters refer to
the papal envoy to England, Simon de Teramo, and his advice to
Poggius about conditions in the Curia. Later there are references
to Nicholas Bildeston, an envoy to the Pope from Cardinal Beaufort, to represent English interests in Rome. Poggius had known
him well when they were together in Beaufort's service and
eagerly urged Nicolaus to help Bildeston to acquire a library
while in Italy. Since Nicolaus was very devout, he was interested in furthering the cause of the Observants, the order to
which St. Bernardinus and Albertus Sartheanensis belonged.
Poggius was more hostile than sympathetic but seems to have
grown gradually more willing to allow the monks their new
buildings. Poggius was also involved with the Franciscan,
Brother Franciscus de Pistorio, who agreed to go on a mission
for the Pope to the Sultan and in the course of it to collect
antique coins and works of art for Poggius and other humanists.

There is an aspect to Poggius' correspondence that is rewarding if not immediately related to the text. It is related to the
personalities of the correspondents and to their period and the
places where they lived. Of his one hundred and seventy-two
correspondents, thirty-six are closely connected with one or
more excellent examples of the art of the Renaissance. Florence
is still full of works of art: painting, sculpture, and architecture,
which it owes to the taste and energetic patronage of Cosmus de
Medicis. Pope Nicolaus V was responsible for bringing Fra
Angelico to paint a chapel in the Vatican. Pius II left almost as
many monuments as the Medici: his own town of Pienza and the
series of paintings by Pinturicchio depicting his life and commissioned as a memorial to him in Siena by his nephew. Eugenius
IV commissioned the central door of St. Peter's, designed by
Filarete. The Vatican and the Castel Sant' Angelo owe much to
the works of art commissioned by Rodericus Borgia, Pope Alexander VI. The popes whom Poggius served and many of the
bishops whom he knew lie buried in memorable tombs, as do
many of his fellow humanists. Others are remembered because
Pisanello did portrait medals of them. Some built churches and
some built palaces; some dedicated altars and others contributed

altarpieces; three of Mantegna's paintings were done for correspondents of Poggius'. The artistic legacy of Poggius' friends is to be found in churches, city squares, and museums all over Europe and even in the United States, from Urbino to Winchester and Lisbon and on to New York and Washington. This would not seem strange to Nicolaus, who ate only from "the finest antique vessels," or to Poggius, who filled his farm property in Terranuova with ancient statuary approved by Donatello to keep his books company.

Poggius is in a curious way a man of our time as well as of his own. His immensely successful research spirit and his love of communication are very like our own. He lived in a time when new technologies, especially printing, were about to change many established methods and habits of thought. Poggius lived at the beginning of the great age of exploration and gave evidence of his awareness of it both by his letter to Prince Henry the Navigator (*Poggii Epist.* IX, 35; Vol. II, pp. 379–382) and by the fourth book of his *De varietate fortunae*, which is devoted to the merchant Nicolò de Conti's twenty-five year long voyage to India and Java. He lived also in a time of great political and international danger. His letters about the rescue of scholars and books in Greece and Constantinople from the onslaught of the Turks and the desire to establish them in the cities of Italy read like accounts of the flight of scholars and libraries before the attacks of Nazi Germany. Poggius' attitude toward book collecting has at times an extraordinarily modern ring. Like collectors today, he deplored the disappearance of books from the collectors' market into permanent collections in, for instance, the Badia in Florence. He also, surprisingly, discussed some of his purchases, as modern curators do, according to the price per page.

Poggius is hidden from many readers today who would appreciate his wit, his humor, his enthusiasm, and his devotion to scholarship by their lack of knowledge of Latin. They would find him congenial, as did his contemporaries who wanted to read his letters. In the fifteenth century, his works were spread over Europe by a process that was developed in the last years of his life; they were printed in Italy, Switzerland, France, Germany, the Low Countries, and were even represented in England by a few "Facetiae" added by Caxton to his *Aesop*.

In 1483 Caxton wrote of Poggius in his introduction to *The Book Called Caton*: "There was a noble clerke named Pogius of Florence and was secretary to pope Eugenye and also to pope Nycholas whiche had in the cyte of Florence a noble and well stuffed lybrarye whiche alle noble straungyers comynge to Florence desyred to see. And therin they fonde many noble and rare bookes. And whanne they had axyd of hym whiche was the best boke of them alle and that he reputed for best, he sayd that he helde Cathon glosed for the best book in his lyberarye. Thenne syth that he that was so noble a clerke helde this book for the best, doubtles hit must folowe that this is a noble booke and a vertuous." Caxton seems to have combined the characters of Poggius and Nicolaus in his anecdote, but Poggius would have been happy that sixty years after he had left England his praise of the *Disticha Catonis* was used as the strongest recommendation that could be given a book.

CONCORDANCE

LETTER	TONELLI	WILMANNS
I	Praefatio, p. x	
II	Praefatio, pp. xiii–xvi	
III	I, 1	
IV		pp. 302–304
V		pp. 300–301
VI	I, 6	
VII	I, 7	
VIII	I, 8	
IX	I, 9	
X	I, 10	
XI	I, 13	
XII	I, 14	
XIII	I, 15	
XIV	I, 16	
XV	I, 11	
XVI	I, 12	
XVII	I, 17	
XVIII	I, 18	
XIX	I, 19	
XX	I, 20	
XXI	I, 21	
XXII	I, 22	
XXIII	II, 2	
XXIV	II, 3	
XXV	II, 4	
XXVI	II, 5	
XXVII	II, 7	
XXVIII	II, 17	
XXIX	II, 20	
XXX	II, 22	
XXXI	II, 23	
XXXII	II, 24	
XXXIII	II, 25	
XXXIV	II, 26	
XXXV	II, 27	
XXXVI	II, 28	
XXXVII	II, 29	

LETTER	TONELLI	WILMANNS
XXXVIII	II, 30	
XXXIX	II, 31	
XL	II, 32	
XLI	II, 33	
XLII	II, 34	
XLIII	II, 35	
XLIV	II, 36	
XLV	II, 38	
XLVI	II, 1	
XLVII	III, 1	
XLVIII	III, 5	
XLIX	III, 12	
L	III, 13	
LI	III, 14	
LII	III, 15	
LIII		pp. 305–306
LIV	II, 9	
LV		pp. 307–309
LVI		p. 310
LVII	III, 17	
LVIII	III, 18	
LIX	III, 19	
LX	III, 20	
LXI	III, 21	
LXII	III, 22	
LXIII	III, 25	
LXIV	III, 27	
LXV	III, 28	
LXVI	III, 29	
LXVII	III, 30	
LXVIII	III, 31	
LXIX	III, 32	
LXX	III, 33	
LXXI	III, 34	
LXXII	III, 35	
LXXIII	III, 37	
LXXIV	III, 38	
LXXV	III, 39	
LXXVI	III, 40	
LXXVII	III, 41	
LXXVIII	IV, 1	

LETTER	TONELLI	WILMANNS
LXXIX	IV, 2	
LXXX	IV, 3	
LXXXI	IV, 4	
LXXXII	IV, 5	
LXXXIII	IV, 11	
LXXXIV	IV, 12	
LXXXV	IV, 13	
LXXXVI	IV, 16	
LXXXVII	IV, 17	
LXXXVIII	V, 6	
LXXXIX	V, 8	
XC	V, 11	
XCI	V, 3	
XCII	V, 4	
XCIII		p. 290

Poggius Bracciolini to
Franciscus Marescalcus Ferrariensis [1]

In the past, in various places and at various times, I wrote many
letters to Nicolaus de Niccolis,[2] who was the most learned citizen
of Florence and connected with me from my youth in the closest
intimacy and devotion. I wrote them on all sorts of domestic
matters and on our private concerns, whenever a favorable
moment and the state of our affairs made it possible. For I used
to put into the letters whatever came to the tip of my tongue,[3] so
that sometimes even the vernacular[4] is mixed into them, though
for amusement. I entrusted to the letters not only what I was
doing or saying but even my worries and reflections, as if I were
writing to my own other self. I wrote them for the most part on
the spur of the moment and quickly so that there was neither the
leisure nor the intention of recopying them, with the result that
no version of them remained with me.

I have never made nor do I make a great deal of my writings,
for I am never so conscious of how trifling is my ability to express
myself as when I take pen in hand and settle my mind on the
effort of writing. In this matter I am very often such a failure in
my own eyes that I seem to myself ignorant and without talent
in writing since sometimes not only matter but even words fail
me, although I have spent a long time searching for what I
should say. But when I learned that quite a few people,[5] either
stirred by good will or induced by an eagerness to pursue some
trifle, were not only diligently seeking my letters, such as they
are, but were reading them for pleasure and with enthusiasm,
and when I was frequently asked to locate them and to assemble
them in a volume for the general good of the uneducated, I com-
plied, at least in part, with the requests of my friends, not because
I thought that the letters would have any future value among
scholars but so that I might not deny my petitioners what could
be fulfilled with little trouble. And so when the Pope[6] was recently in Florence I seized the opportunity and requested of

Nicolaus, who up to a point had carefully preserved them somewhere, some of those letters which I had formerly sent to him
and arranged to have them transcribed by my secretary. Granted
that many were missing which I remembered having written
long ago and which could have seemed a little more elegant, still
I did not want the recollection of those which I had found to be
so quickly effaced because of the loss of some others. Thus I put
together a small collection out of these letters so that it might be
the source from which those who wished either to read or to
laugh at leisure might select their material. This book, although it
may seem to represent a man who is unlearned and of no great
account, still such as it is, dear Franciscus, I have determined to
send to you because you are both a scholar and a dear friend[7] of
mine who have greatly enjoyed my letters, so that you may increase your affection for me[8] and so that this may be, as it were, a
sort of incentive to reading by which you may be stimulated to
greater endeavors, that is, to imitating the literary style of the
ancients[9] from which I am very far away. Therefore read when
you find time free from more important business and, if you are
offended by anything in your reading, be generous either to my
ignorance or to my wordiness. Farewell. [Bologna, 1436.]

Poggius to Nicolaus de Niccolis

LETTER
II

I have received[1] a painful and sad piece of news, dear Nicolaus,[2] and one which hurts me deeply: that is the death of our
father Coluccius,[3] the most eloquent of men and the best. I have
paid my respects to him with many tears[4] and with heartfelt grief.
For the death of such an unusually admirable man cannot be
allowed to pass without great pain and sorrow, unless we want to
be men with hearts of stone or forgetful of the many important
benefits[5] which he conferred on us while he lived, through his

kindness and culture. His reputation has spread among many men, some of whom he sustained with the most generous of words and others he helped with the most benevolent of deeds.

But there is something else which forces all of us who are devoted to the Humanities to be in the depths of sadness and grief. For we have lost a father[6] who will be hard to find again; we have lost the haven and refuge[7] of all scholars, the light of our nation,[8] the glory of Italy. We have known many men and we have read a great deal about any number of famous men; but surely you can never again find so many natural gifts, such power of knowledge, and finally such qualities of character combined in one man. In what man, even if we ignore how much he excelled in wisdom and eloquence, in what man, I repeat, will you find as great polish, friendliness,[9] kindness, and humor as in this best of men, for we cannot otherwise describe him? Although these qualities were based on solid learning and the authority[10] of his old age, nothing could have been more delightful than his company[11] and his conversation with us. How can I fail to mention that he was a father shared by all and a friend of good men; all those in whom he perceived some gleam of intellect he not only fired with a zeal for virtue by his words but actually helped them far more with his resources and especially his own books,[12] which he wished to be a cornucopia for other men's use as much as for his own. But I'm teaching my grandmother.[13] I am telling you things which you have observed earlier and know much better than I. But it is a pleasure for me to dwell on the subject of our beloved Coluccius, whose great qualities and unusual devotion to us, whose generosity and holy habits of life, and in fact whose whole career I shall describe[14] more fully elsewhere, if I live to do it. Now let me write that I am deeply affected by the loss of such a father, a situation which might perhaps have been a bit more bearable if, after I came to Rome, I had been able to see him just once alive.[15] That is the reason why I consider all of you there fortunate; you could be with him and breathe his last breath with him and hear and answer his well-known voice.[16]

I do not believe that you can possibly hold back your tears

when you visit the part of the Palace[17] where he used to live and where we listened to him so often. But enough of this. May God help me, for I cannot restrain my tears while I write these words. I hear that he was given a splendid funeral, and I want you to tell me all about the ceremony and its magnificence, and about his death, the cause of his illness, and everything else that relates to him, and I want you to write me all of it[18] in detail. Express my sympathy to his sons and tell them that I am plunged in grief. This too I want to find out from you: what you think will happen to his books[19] and likewise for what friend, as I learned from Muiginus Loyisius, did you have a portrait[20] modeled of him. Cherish the memory of a man of such stature with veneration and cherish his works with care, but take care of yourself and praise him as long as you can. I hear that there are many candidates[21] competing to succeed him in office. In this matter work for our friend Leonardus[22] for the sake of his honor, as you always do. Farewell. May the fifteenth, Rome [1406].

LETTER

III

If you are well, all is well; for I am well too. Through a relative of mine, I sent you a letter from Constance on February the twentieth, I believe it was, which, if you have received it, ought surely to have made you laugh for it was quite a production, full of wit and humor. I said a good deal about the Hebrew language, which I was studying, and I made even more jokes at the expense of my teacher,[1] since he has the mental capacity of a typical convert from Judaism to Christianity. He is a trifling sort of man, with no sense of humor or stability. I made fun of his literary ability and his learning as being crude, rude, and rustic. But I am afraid that that letter and the other, which I wrote to Leonardus,[2] did not reach you. For most certainly considering the careful attention which you devote to letter writing, you would have sent some answer right away or at least congratulated me on this new study of a new subject which you had often urged me to master.

Although I see that this study is of no use in increasing our
wisdom, it adds something to our study of the Humanities, particularly in this respect, that I have learned Jerome's method of
translation.

But I wrote you this letter from the Baths,[3] to which I had betaken myself to cure the rheumatism in my hands, because I
thought it worthwhile to describe to you what a delightful place
it is and the habits of the people there and their customs at bathing. A great deal is told by writers of antiquity about the baths of
Puteoli,[4] where almost the whole Roman population congregated
for pleasure, but I hardly think that the Roman baths could have
approached the charm of these and were not at all to be compared
with ours. For the pleasantness of the situation and the magnificence of the villas contributed more to the pleasures of
Puteoli than did the gaiety of the people or the use of the baths.
But although these places offer little or no rest to the spirit, in
every other way they afford tremendous amusement, so that I
often think that Venus has removed from Cyprus and that whatever pleasure there is anywhere has come to these baths, so
carefully do they observe her customs and display her wanton
habits. Although they have not read the discourse of Heliogabalus,[5] they seem sufficiently learned and proficient in it by
their very nature.

But since I am going to describe these baths to you, I must not
fail to tell you the route by which one goes there from Constance,
so that you can guess in what part of Gaul they are situated. On
the first day, by boat on the Rhine, we traveled twenty-four miles
to the town of Schaffhausen;[6] then since the journey had to be
made on foot for ten miles because of the tremendous drop of the
river over a steep cliff and rocks, we approached the castle, which
stands high above the Rhine and is called Caesarstul; this in their
language means Caesar's throne. I think that this place, to judge
by the name, must once have been a Roman camp from the apt-
ness of the site, for it is on a high hill overlooking the river,
which here joins Gaul to Germany by a narrow bridge. On this
walk we saw the falls of the Rhine[7] from a high cliff over scattered
rocks, full of sound and fury, so that you might think the river

itself was complaining and lamenting about its fall. Then I remembered those well-known stories about the steep fall of the Nile,[8] and I do not wonder that those who live near it are thought to be deaf because of its remarkable roaring and crashing, since the noise of this river, which can be considered the image of the Nile, can be heard almost three-eighths of a mile from the falls.

Then comes the town of Baden, which means Baths in the German tongue, quite prosperous and situated in a valley surrounded by mountains, near a wide, very swift river which flows into the Rhine six miles from the town. Half a mile from town beside the river a very handsome villa has been built for the accommodation of the baths.[9] There is a large court in the middle of the villa and around it are elaborate suites for the reception of many nations. Each house has its own bath inside where only those people bathe who are lodging there; then there are both private and public baths, about thirty in all. But there are two public baths, one on either side of the court, the baths of the lower classes and common people to which come women and men and boys and unwed maids[10] and the dregs of the surrounding population. In these a sort of open fence like one between peaceful neighbors separates the men from the women. It is comical to see decrepit old women as well as younger ones going naked into the water before the eyes of men and displaying their private parts and their buttocks to the onlookers. I have often laughed at this extraordinary sight, calling to mind the carnival,[11] and I have privately wondered at the simplicity of these people who do not stare, suspect evil, or speak it. But the baths in private houses are very clean and are used by men and women;[12] a sort of lattice separates them, and in these there are many low windows, through which the bathers can drink together and talk and see both ways and touch each other as is their usual custom.

Above the pools there is a walk all the way around on which people stand to stare and gossip, for anyone who so desires can go to other people's baths to visit, gossip, joke, and relax, and can stay there, so that when women go in and out of the water, they are seen virtually naked. No guard keeps watch at the door and no one is forbidden entry; there is no suspicion of impropriety. In many places, the entrance to the baths is the same for men and women, so that it often happens that a man and a half-naked woman or a woman and a naked man come face to face. The men wear nothing but a leather apron, and the women put on linen shirts down to their knees, so cut on either side that they leave uncovered neck, bosom, arms, and shoulders. They often have picnics by subscription in the water, with the table set floating on the water, and men are usually present at these. We were once invited to join in this practice in the house where we bathed. I paid my share but did not want to participate though asked again and again, not that I was moved by any undue modesty, which is considered cowardice, or provinciality, but by my ignorance of the language. For it seemed to me ridiculous that a man from Italy,[13] ignorant of their language, should sit in the water with a lot of women, completely speechless, while the day was wasted by everyone's drinking and nibbling. But two of my companions went to the baths and had a very good time. They were there with women, touched them, drank with them, and ate with them, even talked to them through an interpreter, all the while making a little breeze with a fan;[14] all we needed was that picture of Jove appearing to Danaë in a shower of golden rain and the rest. But the men wore linen shirts, as is their custom when they go bathing with women.

I watched all this from the gallery and observed their habits and customs, the gaiety of their lives and the freedom and lack of restraint in their way of living;[15] it is wonderful to see in what simplicity and trust they live. Men watched their wives being handled by strangers and were not disturbed by it; they paid no attention and took it all in the best possible spirit. Nothing is so difficult but that it is made easy by habit. Obviously they would have been home in Plato's Republic, where all property was held in common,[16] since even without his teaching they are found so ready to adopt his methods. In some of the baths, the men live freely with the women,[17] to whom they are related by blood or by friendship. They go into the pools three or four times a day, spending the greater part of the day there, sometimes singing,

sometimes dancing for they play instruments while squatting in
the water. It is very pleasant to see girls already ripe for a husband, already of marriageable years,[18] good looking and well-
born and in manner and form like a goddess; for when they play
on instruments, they draw their clothes slightly behind them,
floating along the top of the water, until you might think they
were winged Venuses. It is customary for the women, when men
gaze down at them, to ask the men in fun for alms. And so the
men throw down pennies, especially to the prettier women,
which they catch sometimes in their hands, and sometimes in
their outspread clothes, pushing one another, and in this game
they even sometimes uncover more hidden parts of their bodies.
They also throw down wreaths of different colored flowers, with
which the girls decorate their heads while they bathe.

Lured by this extravagant gaiety and entertainment, since I
bathed only twice in a day, I spent the rest of the time visiting
other baths, where I often threw pennies and garlands according
to the custom of the rest. For there was no time for reading or
philosophy in the midst of all the bands, flutes, zithers, and songs,
resounding all around me, where only to wish to be wise would
have been the height of folly, especially to anyone who is not a
very Menedemus the self-tormenter[19] and who is a man who
thinks nothing that is part of men's lives is foreign to him. What
was needed for the fullest satisfaction was a knowledge of the
language,[20] which is the prime requisite of everything. "Nought
else remained to do save feast my eyes, pursue her, follow her to
school and back";[21] besides which there was space to wander
around and it was so freely permitted that I had no fear of the law
of trespass. Besides these numerous amusements, there is another just as good. There is a big field behind the bathhouse,
beside the river, shaded by many trees. Everybody comes there
after dinner from all around to play all kinds of games. Some enjoy dancing, some sing, a great many play ball. They do not play
the way we do at home, but men and women throw a ball full of
bells to one another and especially to the one they like best, and
then everyone rushes in to catch the ball, and the person who
gets it is considered the winner. The winner throws it again to

the person he prefers, although many people reach for it with out-
stretched hands, and he pretends that he is going to throw it[22]
now to this man, now to that woman. They play many games beside these, which would take a long time to describe. But these
I have described so that you may understand from a few examples what a great center of the Epicurean way of thinking[23]
this is. And I believe that this is the place where the first man was
created, which the Hebrews call Ganeden or the garden of delight.[24] For if pleasure can make life happy, I do not see what is
lacking in this place for complete and perfect happiness. But if
you ask, what is the power of the waters?[25] It is not only various
and manifold, but also the quality of the waters is truly marvelous and almost divine. I think that nowhere on earth are there
baths more adapted to fertility in women. And so since many
barren women have come here because of sterility, they find out
the marvelous quality of the waters; for they follow the prescrip-
tions carefully, by which remedies are applied to those who cannot conceive. Among other things, this is worth recording: there
is a vast multitude of nobility and common people who come two
hundred miles to this place, not for health but for pleasure. They
are all lovers, all suitors, all men for whom life is based on fun,
who come together here so that they may enjoy the things for
which they hunger; many pretend to have bodily ills, when they
are really troubled in mind. So you will see many women of outstanding beauty, without husbands, without relatives, with two
maids and a valet, or with some elderly female relative, easily
supported and still more easily deceived. Each one, however,
comes decked out in her best in gold, silver, and jewels to the
limit of her ability; you would say that they were going not to the
baths but to a most fashionable wedding.

There are Vestal Virgins[26] here too or, to express it more accurately, Floral virgins, and here abbots, monks, friars, and
priests live with greater freedom than the other men,[27] bathing
sometimes right with the women and dressing their hair with
garlands, all their religion thrown to the winds. They all have
only one purpose: to flee from gloom, to seek amusement, and
to think of nothing except how to live happily and enjoy their

pleasures. It is not a question of separation of common assets
but of putting separate assets to common use. Strange as it may
seem, in all that vast crowd, for there are nearly a thousand
people, of very varied backgrounds and all drinking very freely,
no quarrels ever arise, no grievances are aired, and there is no
bickering, no grumbling, no cursing. Men see their wives
handled; they see them flirt with strangers, even *en tête-à-tête*,
and they are unmoved by it. They are not surprised; they think
it is all done with the best and most home-loving intentions. And
so the name of a jealous husband, which weighs upon nearly
all our husbands at home, has no place among them. The word is
unknown, unheard, they do not know this kind of disease; they
do not even have a name for this ailment and it is no wonder that
its name does not exist among them when its substance is not
there. For no one has up to now been found among them who is a
jealous husband. Oh how different their customs are from ours!
We always take the worst view of everything; we delight to such
an extent in scandal, and in disparagement, that if we see anything in the least suspicious, we immediately regard it as an
obvious crime. I often envy them their calm and I hate our per-
versity of spirit, for we are always searching, always hunting,
always turning sky, earth, and sea upside down in order to make a
fortune, content with no gain, appeased by no money. We are
terrified of future catastrophes and are thrown into a continuous
state of misery and anxiety, and for fear of becoming miserable,
we never cease to be so, always panting for riches and never
giving our souls or our bodies a moment's peace. But those who
are content with little live day by day and treat any day like a
feast day. They do not seek wealth that will do them little good
but enjoy their own property and do not worry about the future;
if anything goes wrong, they bear it optimistically. And so they
are enriched by this saying: "He has lived, as long as he has
lived well."[28]

But let us stop this, for I do not intend either to praise them or
to criticize us. I want this whole letter to be full of amusement so
that even far away you too may get from it a small part of the
pleasure I have derived from being at the baths. Goodbye, dear-

est Nicolaus, and show this letter to our friend Leonardus,[29] since friends have all things in common,[30] and give my greetings to Nicolaus[31] and to Laurentius[32] and give Cosmus[33] my best wishes. From Baden, the eighteenth of May[34] [1416].

LETTER

IV

I see that one of two things will happen about which I had written to you on my journey. For I wrote,[1] if you remember correctly, that I would by all means bring back something useful from these travels of mine, either by adding something to my money or by learning that I ought to be satisfied with my own holdings, that is with little. Therefore I see and clearly perceive that not in the future but rather at present the only gain I shall be able to record is a lesson that moderation is healthy and that to acquire superfluities requires hard work, and surely, dear Nicolaus, I have gained enough. If, as Demetrius says, you want to make Pythocles rich, you must not increase his money but decrease his greed.[2] This is what drives us headlong, since it sets itself no bounds. Of this bad habit, believe me, I am almost free. For what is the reason why what I now have should not be enough? And yet, as you know, there was a time long ago in my youth when I made a vow not to strive further if I had reached this far. But now, when I have exceeded the goal in my avidity for wealth, I am properly punished by God for wanting to escape from my insignificant status. But I have reproved myself a little and checked myself, considering how much effort and trouble I should endure for something that will not succeed. For since I am in my thirty-ninth year,[3] when I take count of these external things, I see that to this day I have received nothing from this great mass of goods except food and clothing, two things which would never fail us, if we kept a limit on our holdings.

Hunger and thirst should be controlled, the body should be protected from the cold; whatever is more is of evil origin. Since God gave me these things even if with shame, what is this fool-

ishness of mine to have left my native land, my friends, my relatives, and the other things which ought to be sweeter to us than
life itself, without which, indeed, life cannot be sweet at all, to
sweat and to freeze to acquire those things which will be more of
a burden than a benefit?⁴ In my madness I wanted to establish a
life for myself so that I could live without working, as priests are
accustomed to do; as if in this life we could have any part of
peace, when it is firmly fixed between floods and the most violent of storms or as if the work of a priest is trifling, if we want to
fulfill our duty faithfully. Though I am but a little man, I refused
to write a little to earn my keep, although Jerome himself, that
extraordinary luminary of holiness and wisdom, in a letter to the
priest Marcus, testified that he earned his bread every day by the
work of his hands and by his own sweat.⁵ And yet it was written
by the apostle: "He who does not work shall not eat."⁶ But I was
drawn, as many others are, into a dangerous habit, so that I kept
thinking not of what was right for me or what was enough for me
but how much others have, especially those unworthy men who,
according to the capacity of men of our time, are always preferred to their betters. For such is our custom of thrift that we
have always before our eyes not whence we come but whither
we are going;⁷ and so if we fail, if we fall, it is no wonder, since
one man pushes the next and no one holds back. I was driven not
by envy but by sorrow and indignation,⁸ when I saw many men
preferred to me, to make this decision; but if my mind, if my
reasoning power, had been strong, I ought to have considered it
the greatest blessing that I did not have the ability to do wrong.
But I have corrected myself and if the means of meeting you is
given to me, as I hope, I shall discuss with you more at length
the organization of my future life and I shall follow your advice.⁹

Nothing is steady, dear Nicolaus, nothing is fixed except virtue.
Everything else is transitory and in someone else's power.
Virtue is our own. I have pursued virtue long since in my mind;
but in performance I am far from it. I am like a dreamer: they
seem to do much and do nothing and there is nothing in my way
but me myself,¹⁰ who wish to reach virtue but not by the gentle
path, that is, by getting rid of those things which prevent the

genuine possession of virtue. I praise you for having held an
auction in order to be freer.[11] Some quiet spot must be chosen
which will not stir up desire, for these famous places are suspect.
They fire the mind with greed; they spur us to competition until
each man yearns for what he sees. Long ago, when I read
Horace's satire, I noted these verses, for he speaks with hate and
disgust of the city:

> "Oh countryside mine when shall I see you again?
> Read my favorite classical authors, and then
> Get some sleep and get back to my lazy routine of life,
> Of pleasure mercifully free from worry and strife?"
>
> Those nights and feasts of the gods, when friends and I sup
> In *my lar's* presence.[12]

This, dear Nicolaus, is to me the sweetest life. If you should
want to pursue it, I shall never desert you. But of these matters
more when we meet; now of domestic matters. I have already
obtained from my master leave to go home, but it pleases him to
have me wait for spring[13] and he said he would give me my passage. Besides, I send you thanks for your very generous offer.
You behave like a devoted friend but I hope there will be no
need of it. I cannot find leisure for a search for books[14] as I
promised in my letter; this is the fourth month in which I suffer
from hemorrhoids,[15] which trouble me severely, and although I
have tried many remedies, I cannot get rid of them because they
are inside. I had however improved a little and only in . . . .
[London, winter 1419–1420.]

LETTER

V

Although I have nothing new to write to you, I want to scribble
a few trifling lines[1] because I am longing to talk with you. But I
do not know what to say, being short not only of subject matter
but of words. You want to know what I am doing. I devote myself
to church literature and that entirely. I have run through a few
volumes of Jerome and quite a few of Augustine, of which I have

in hand the *Contra Faustum Manicheum,* a huge work and wordy though admittedly so because of the requirements of the subject.[2] In these I learned a lot so that I now seem to myself halfway to being a theologian.

Moreover I have carefully made note of this: it is by no means proper for a priest to take anything from the altar except his food and clothing.[3] But if he takes more, they say he is a thief and a temple robber. Therefore all this searching for benefices, if we are to believe what the Book says, looks to the destruction of the soul, for it is not right for anyone to take even food and clothing unless he labors in the Gospel. The apostle says: "He who does not work shall not eat."[4] Therefore I suppressed my greed a little, counseled by the greatest scholars that these things which men treat as hereditary belong not to us but to the poor, and what I used to consider of the highest importance I now set at the lowest level. This regular reading profited me much not only in learning but even in life.

I have written this to you because I know that these studies please you greatly and that it will be no small pleasure to you that I too am giving them my attention. You see that I am not allowing this time which I have free of business to slip away through laziness but that I am doing something worthwhile. For I devote the greater part of the day to books; the rest I use up by walking around, seeking and turning over bundles of books in case I should find anything good. But so far I have found nothing of interest to you except the small word book about which I had written before, which is by Nonius Marcellus like the rest.[5] Besides I bought an ancient codex of the *Historia Tripartita*[6] for three gold crowns. But you will ask where the money came from to buy it. There is someone who will lend it, and I do not think it wicked to incur a debt in an honorable cause even if it has to be paid through a new loan. But I hope God will be favorable to me sometimes, especially when I undertake the right sort of thing.

Now I want to know what you are doing and in what state of mind you are, what you think about the future, whether your quarrels with your brothers have ceased, and whether you have resumed affectionate relations with our friends?[7] I beg you to write me everything, for there is nothing that I would see more gladly than your letters, which are the more delightful the longer they are. For I want to hear from you what house you are living in and whether Sibilla, about whom so many quarrels arose, is still with you. I do not doubt that the names of the virtues and felicities of our men which are on everybody's lips please you immensely especially when the words harmonize with the facts.

And so write me something also about these things, as you have been doing, for it pleases me immensely that you are so charmed with the customs and the quality of the Curia that you too want to become a member of that body.[8] Persevere and

"My son, from my example learn the war,
In camps to suffer and in fields to dare."[9]

Democritus could feed his spleen, and shake
His sides and shoulders till he felt 'em ache
Tho' in his country town no lictors were,
Nor rods, nor ax, nor tribune did appear,
Nor all the foppish gravity of show
Which cunning magistrates on crowds bestow.
What had he done, had he beheld on high,
Our praetor seated, in mock majesty?
His chariot rolling o'er the dusty place. . . .[10]

I say to you:

"Now let Rome be ashamed
The third Cato too has fallen from the sky."[11]

But farewell; my poor scrap of paper[12] has run out, for I took only a small sheet thinking I would not find anything to write. But in the course of talking the flow began. And so farewell and write back. London, the twenty-ninth day of January [1420].

LETTER
VI

I keep longing for a letter from you because I am so anxious to know what you are doing or whether you are just resting and whether you have received my letters. I have written you a great many since my return. It is a funny thing about you: when I do not write to you, you write to me assiduously; but when I not only challenge you but actually bombard you with letters, you say nothing. If you keep on in this way you shall find me both deaf and speechless in the future; for I do not want my chattering to deprive me of your letters, which are the only things that relieve me of my worries.

A little while ago I saw a catalogue of a number of books from some monastery or other;[1] I took down the titles of several of them bearing on religious subjects, and I hope with the help of a friend of mine to have them brought here. If they get here, I shall write you what they are but if not I do not want to raise your hopes in vain.

I have been reading Augustine and just now I have John Chrysostom[2] in hand; I have read some of his Opuscula, and his sermons, translated with the greatest elegance. Now I am going through some others of far inferior style, according as the translators vary, for there are twenty-five homilies on Paul's Epistle to the Hebrews[3] and seven homilies in praise of Paul the Apostle, of which Anianus[4] was a fairly skillful interpreter. The most important are the eighty-eight homilies on the Gospel of John;[5] and if their translator had been good, you could not have read anything more learned, more seriously considered, or more magnificently written. But the translator was some Pisan fellow[6] who confesses in the Prologue that he translates word for word; and yet the translation is not so awkward as to prevent the author's eloquence from coming through.

You see me accomplishing something by doing nothing, and counting something as gain,[7] actually from those very things whose possession truly is gain, for it is certain and stable. Please believe me, I have gone through this time without any illness, concentrating on literature alone, so much so that if I should lack money, it would not inconvenience me much and I would not worry about it.

My master[8] is away nearly all the time, as nomadic as a Scyth-

ian; but meanwhile I live here in quiet and wrap myself up
in my books. My food and clothes are provided and that is
enough; for not even the king[9] has any more with all his pomp
and state. But I shall come back to you next summer, for I am
putting off my return until I find out to what place the Curia is
going. I am unwilling to leave here while the Curia is with you,[10]
because I should not wish to be there for a number of reasons.
But if my master should cross the sea to join the king, then I too
shall cross it, but not by the same route; for he would go to
France[11] and I to Italy. Commend me to my lord the Cardinal
of Pisa[12] and greet Nicolas[13] for me. Farewell. At London, the
fifth of March [1420].

LETTER

VII

I was a bit angry with you, because you were not answering[1]
my letters; so, since I do not know the reason for your silence,
I am going to keep quiet too and make it all even. And as I
remember that in the past I used to write to you fairly often I
wished you would write me frequently, even if only a few lines,
rather than send me volumes once in a while, as you have been
doing. For news does not bring so much pleasure all rolled up
in one bundle as it does spread out and bringing pleasure day
by day. Besides, to keep silence for a long time does injury to
a friendship; for it evaporates when friends are separated, or
at least cools off, unless it is kept up by frequent letters and com-
munications on the part of both friends. But the love between
us[2] is of such a kind that it could not come to any harm from even
the longest silence; even so the rules of friendship must be
preserved.

I have written all this for one reason: so that you will understand that your letters are very dear to me and that it saddens me
not a little when they are brought to me so rarely. For deprived
as I am here of every amusement I am refreshed by my friends'

letters[3] though I must admit that except for you none of them write to me. I have been relegated to oblivion[4] as though I were dead. Truly I found out yesterday how much your letters help me; for I felt as though I had recovered from a long sickness in which I had been forced to linger and I feel free of all my uneasiness and can fix my mind intently on what you write, and answer it briefly.

First of all, as to what you say near the end of your letter, that you have made friends with a man who, as you say, is learned and good: namely, the Cardinal of St. Angelus.[5] This gives me the greatest pleasure. If he is as you describe him, he is not merely likable but should be loved and honored both for his own good qualities and on account of the scarcity of such men. For you see that he is "a rare bird on earth, very like the black swan."[6]

You see others of the same rank, with few exceptions, what a holy life they lead, how cautiously and honorably they live. I shall leave out all discussion of their theology; even that now is banished and so is every kind of virtue. The idols of the nations are silver and gold, and the nations are dedicated to belly and bed, and so swollen with pomp and pride that if a man does not worship the image of the beast, he is put to death. The principles of the good life[7] they have turned into mere display of rhetoric, and what merit they do not gain from their religious devotion, and their good behavior and holy living, they wish to gain through intimidation and pride and superstitious practices. As you write most correctly, if it were not that the words and deeds of our ancestors help us more than the dissolute example set by our contemporaries, through the examples we mentioned, Faith would undoubtedly perish. Our contemporaries know only one thing: that they can do everything for the sake of appetite and greed, to which they subordinate everybody. For very few fight for the Gospel, but many fight for their ease and their wealth.

And so all the more should you appreciate this man and also be grateful to the noble and renowned Cardinal of Pisa, as he is good, he has been willing to admit you too to the friendship

of a good man.[8] I do not know whether in conversation you have
made any mention of me; I wish you would for several reasons.
What you write about future travels abroad pleases me greatly,
provided the man is really what you say he is.

You know that loyalty is rare;[9] and I know that you are quite
free from the fault of flattery, an affliction which generally is
useful to those who live in the houses of the powerful. Yet I
believe that you would rather trust in your own abilities than in
those of others to undertake this duty. I wish I might have an
opportunity to go with you;[10] there is nothing that I would do
more happily with my time, which I spend unhappily in the
Curia.

But you know how little money I have; and to undertake a
trip with the hope that someone else will pay the expenses seems
to be the height of folly. I have had enough experience to know
how much trust to put in promises. But if there were any way in
which I could conveniently go with you, I should like to. And
so you sniff sagaciously and find out if there is any way for me
to come, for I shall follow your counsel. You might see what
the Archbishop of Crete[11] thinks about it; there is enough time
to consider the matter and in the meantime I shall see you.

I would have come home already except for the Pope's being
in Florence; but I have decided and mean to stand by my decision not to leave here until I have heard that the Pope has
left you or is on the point of leaving. But if as I hope above all
things our friend Guarinus[12] should come there, I shall be with
you this next winter and forget about the Curia, so that I may
have time to study Greek, which I burn to do[13] more and more
every day.

As for what you write about the Bishop of Bologna,[14] whom I
consider a very saintly man, I do not know whether to be pleased
or displeased. I feel very bad about his troubles although I
realize that it does not distress him to lack something he never
wanted; for men who desire to be great but not to do good should
not, as Augustine[15] put it, be considered bishops. But this man,
who really wished to do good, when he found it impossible,
went away, as I see it, from his senseless flock. For I know that

it is by virtue of his strength of mind that he cares little for the things that other men pursue with such intensity and that he takes more interest in the health of his soul than of his body. One thing has he asked of the Lord, and this he implores, that he may dwell in the house of the Lord,[16] and the rest is nothing to him. Thinking it over from this point of view, I rejoice that he should have had a chance to show what sort of man he is.[17] For strength, as the Apostle says, is made perfect in weakness.[18] John Chrysostom, whom I prefer to every other author that I ever read, when he was driven into exile from his church, said in a sermon to the people before his departure: "Let the sea rage, let the floods sound in fury against me, etc., my heart shall not fear, for I stand upon a rock";[19] and that rock, as you know, is Christ. This too can be said of the Bishop of Bologna, whom, because of his holiness, the mob could not bear; and no wonder; for only the people who displease Christ please the world, as Jerome says in one of his letters.[20] But I beg you again and again to visit him once in my name and give him my respects; and do not regard this as a chore, even if it is summer.

What you tell me of your life and worries distresses me very much, as God is my witness. I thought that you had escaped all these storms into some safe harbor; but I see that you are dragged hither and yon by the currents and have no peace of mind. The wilder the storm grows around you, the more you must stand your ground and prove yourself a man; pull yourself together and try your strength against adversity.[21] This is the trial, this the effort;[22] for any spoiled darling can easily bear good fortune. Virtue is recognized in times of trouble, and you must not look upon it as strange if you are beaten and shaken hither and yon; this is the play of human affairs. So says Naevius in this verse: "Pati necesse est multa mortalem mala." "Man must suffer many wrongs."[23]

I am sorry that you have been threatening those who caused your troubles; in that regard I wish that no threats had come from you; for you know that it is unseemly for a Christian to exact or even to hope for revenge. Forgive, He says, and you shall be forgiven,[24] and this sentence is in the mouths of all the doctors of antiquity, who give you so much pleasure. So since you too need forgiveness, you must pardon others; and the more is owed to you, the more freely must you wipe out the debt: for God loves a cheerful giver.[25] But since you know these things better than I do, see to it that what you have read is useful to you; otherwise your past life would seem to have been lived in vain. For you know that divine or human philosophy can bring us only one good thing: that through contempt for earthly things we may achieve something better. But if you consider these things, you will despise both what happens to you and those who contrive it and will think nothing of them. And in all friendliness I urge this on you; for injuries are wiped out more thoroughly by forgetting them than by avenging them.

Since you say that my thoughtfulness pleases you, and also my way of life, and the study of sacred literature, you ought to recognize that it is just as I said and you will see it proved by the facts. Believe me, I shall be content with my small office and in it end my desire for gain. For whoever obtains what is enough, let him, as Flaccus said,[26] want nothing more; for what is more, comes from evil and has no business with us. Let other people strive after rank or after wealth but I shall wrap my poverty around me, by my disdain richer than them all.

For I believe Jerome when he says that all riches derive from iniquity,[27] hence the well-known saying is self-evident: "A rich man is either a scoundrel or heir to a scoundrel."[28] It seems to me that nothing truer could ever have been said, if you examine the lives of those who concentrate on their wealth. For they have to be covetous; but a man who is covetous has to be vile, for covetousness is, as the Apostle said, the slavery to idols.[29] And so Augustine was in doubt as to which sinned more grievously: the man who ignorantly fell into heresy or the man who with his eyes open did not recoil from avarice, which is idolatry, for he says that the man who is covetous is guilty of the sin of idolatry.[30] When I had thought over these and many other things which I found in the Holy Scriptures I set a limit on myself, that is, on my ambitions, and decided that the small amount of leisure which I had left, after I had attended to my trivial affairs,

I would devote to the study of literature and especially of sacred literature, in which lies the foundation of all honorable and just living. And in this I hope you will help me by sending me a lot of your books to read.

This is not at all a good time for the trip you urge me to take to look for books. Nearly the whole island is sick with plague,[31] and besides it is not possible here to find the great things which you expect. I have obtained the catalogues of several monasteries[32] which are considered famous and old. There is nothing of value in any of them. In the past many barbarous nations seized this island and pillaged it.[33] As for what you want to know about Petronius Arbiter and what he wrote: read the beginning of Macrobius on the dream of Scipio,[34] where, listing the various kinds of stories, he says that among them are stories of the imagined misfortunes of lovers and that these were a favorite subject with Petronius. Moreover he is a man who was serious in verse and consistent in prose, and lived, I guess, a little after the time of Augustus.[35] Look what a wordy letter you have. I beg you to commend me to my lord of Pisa.[36] Farewell, my dearest Nicolaus, and write to me. London, the thirteenth of June [1420].

LETTER

VIII

I have nothing to say except that I wish the Curia would leave[1] your city so that I could return there as soon as possible. This friend[2] of ours, who is a craftsman in words, promises a lot of things, more and more every day; but they carry no weight with me. I see well enough that I am delaying in vain; for I do not see what there is to keep up hope, since I have rolled this stone so long without any reward. One thing consoles me: this time has not been altogether wasted. I have even added a little to my hoard of gold, that is, to my knowledge of literature to which I apply myself every day, for I have plenty of time to read. For my master is abroad like the Scythian and I wait quietly here

and am not at all busy. Truly wherever on earth you live is
adequate if you live comfortably; for if I were at home with you,
I should honestly have very little more chance to read.[3] Here I
lack the pleasantest thing, the company of my friends and especially yours. This bothers me more than anything else; the other
things are practically universal. For I hardly miss my homeland.
Indeed I have always considered this a very true statement:
one's home is where one feels at home.[4]

I have written thus for this reason: so that you will know that
in the midst of my disappointments I have a certain amount of
profit, of what can really be called profit. For I have already been
able to devote three months to Aristotle, not so much for the sake
of learning at present as of reading and seeing what is contained
in each work.[5] But this reading of mine is not altogether fruitless.
I learn a little something every day, even if only superficially,
and this is the reason why my love of Greek literature has come
back so strong:[6] I am becoming acquainted, in his own language,
with an author who is practically speechless and ridiculous in
translation.[7] For a commentator I have Thomas Aquinas,[8] a great
man and a good scholar, as the seriousness of the subject demands. But I have neglected theology because the man who
provided me with books has been away for several days. And so
in order not to be idle I turned to this one. Nonetheless I shall
soon go back to Chrysostom and Augustine, for there are still
some more of their writings on certain of the Epistles of Paul
and on Matthew which I want to read; for, begging the pardon of
all others, Aristotle stands head and shoulders above them. In
all the others put together there is not so much dignity of style,
so much substance, so much weight of aphorisms as in this one
man alone. And although the ignorance of those who translated
him was very great, the vigor of his style comes through and his
light shines in darkness and his translators do not so sink him
under their mistakes that he cannot raise himself and the dignity
of his opinions elevates him.

I have written you two letters about your trip to Greece,[9]
adding a good deal about myself. I beg you to answer everything and especially whether Guarinus is going to be with us.[10]

Now as for the note which I enclosed in my last letter, I see that nothing will come of it and yet answer, please, and take care that that letter is taken to Terra Nova.[11] Goodbye and remember me to my lords of Pisa[12] and of Piacenza,[13] whose doctor was here and has gone to the king.[14] London, the seventeenth day of July [1420].

LETTER

IX

As the plague was very severe[1] and I had been seized with an awful fear of it, I went away to a country house with the Bishop and stayed there two months. Every day I waited for letters from you to find out what I was to do; and when none came, I was irritated both at myself and at you because you did not answer. But when the plague had for the most part died down,[2] I went back to the city, four days ago now, eager to hear the news. As I was getting down from my horse, a small package of your letters was handed to me, of which the greater part was taken up with the story of your tribulations and worries.

I am very sorry for you, seeing that you are having such a hard time and that you have reached the highest state of hostility with your friends.[3] What disturbs me most of all is that Laurentius,[4] whom I had always considered an upright man, has written an invective against you; that bothers me very much. I shall not hesitate to impress upon you very often that you are a Christian and that *evil must be repaid with good;*[5] for if you return good for good, are you not doing what the Gentiles do? Follow the teachings of Chrysostom: despise what is written against you if it is false;[6] but if it is true, correct yourself. This advice is very holy and of the best, and if you follow it, you will be preparing your own salvation.

Still, you must know that I lose no love on talebearers and I am sure that if he has spoken evil of you, he has written falsely.[7] I do not mean to act the philosopher with you; such behavior requires one's bodily presence and conversation. One thing I do say: even if everyone else has abandoned you, I shall remain faithful[8] and shall never fail you or your honor.

I take pleasure in what the Cardinal of Pisa[9] discussed with you about my affairs: I shall follow your advice and come home at the first opportunity. After tomorrow my master will be here;[10] I shall ask for permission to leave and shall get ready for the journey, and I shall not wait *ad infinitum;* for he promises a lot and performs nothing. I believe I shall be with you in time for Christmas or a little afterward; and I shall either be in the Curia or I shall go with you if you can contrive the means.

I understand all about Guarinus;[11] we must bear it with good humor[12] as long as we have to. I have written to Nicolaus what I think of your quarrels and of Laurentius' invective.[13] Do look over my letter, which I have written very hastily. I am not writing you a long letter, because I hope to see you shortly. I have forwarded all my things, some to Venice[14] and some to Pisa. Goodbye and do not forget me; give my greeting to Cosmus.[15] London, the twenty-fourth day of October [1420].

LETTER
X

On the first of the month I wrote you just a few words because I was worn out with having to write at greater length to the rest of my correspondents.[1] Yesterday I received a letter from you, in which among other things you discussed the Roman Curia and the trouble you think is in store for it, in such a way that you filled me with fear of coming back. I had sought permission of my master who has come here;[2] but I began to cool off when I read your letter. For if the Curia is in such straits, I do not want to stay in it; I do not know what to do. Shall I go home or shall I wait a little for a chance to think it over? May God direct my decision.

I am oppressed by difficulties on all sides. Even from home my mother asks me for money; another has taken the place of my dead father; my brother wants to live in idleness by the sweat of my brow;[3] and so I cannot decide what is most important to do. The best life would be for the soul to forget all the earthly miseries and cleave to God; but I am weak and my reason is overcome by my senses. For twenty years now I have been toiling,[4] so that I might prepare some sustinence for this our earthly pilgrimage; and now I seem to be starting a new game, piling one uncertainty on top of another. I used to think that I was going to have peace away from home; and now up jumps my brother to vex me, as though what I suffer here were not enough without adding something new to it. But enough of these complaints of mine.

While I was fleeing from the plague, I saw the cathedral of Salisbury[5] and I hunted for the books about which you have written me so many times. What Manuel[6] saw long ago I cannot imagine; I know only this, that there are no books of Origen there now. I did not make a careless search, but there was no one who could say that he had ever seen them. We can find plenty of men given over to gluttony and lust but very few lovers of literature and those few barbarians, trained rather in trifling debates and in quibbling than in real learning. I saw many monasteries, all crammed with new doctors, none of whom you would even have found worth listening to. There were a few volumes of ancient writings, which we have in better versions at home. Nearly all the monasteries of this island have been built within the last four hundred years[7] and that has not been an age which produced either learned men or the books which we seek; these books were already sunk without trace. As for the monastery of Corvey,[8] which is in Germany, you have no grounds for hope. There are supposed to be a lot of books there; I do not believe the tales of fools but even if what they say were true, the whole country is a den of thieves.[9] Even those natives who stay in the Curia do not go back safely to their own country. So give up that idea. As for the other things, when I get home I shall attend to them as carefully as I can. I did not see Oxford,[10] for it requires more than the mere inclination to go there.

Although I believe that I shall see you before you go to Greece, yet since I am still away I want to tell you by letter what I would

like to tell you face to face. I certainly praise you for your desire
to see Greece, for the sake of study and of travel; but thinking
over two aspects of it, I have reason to hesitate a little and I
should not dare to urge you to undertake this effort. First of all
there are your age and your habits and your way of life;[11] and
then, much more important, there is the nature of the priests[12]
and of those of high rank. Familiarity, as you know, breeds contempt. You do not know what will become of you on such a long
journey: you know how hard it truly is, and difficult, to take a risk
about friends.[13] Now many things are pleasant in the telling,
which, if you went through the experience itself, would be very
unpleasant. Study yourself and consider to what extent you can
bear so many discomforts and the thousand obstacles which you
will have to meet on your way. In a war ship, as you know, there
are few private cabins,[14] and those few will be occupied mostly
by high officers; things which now if seen once a month seem
agreeable, will be unpleasant when seen every day. Listen to
what I say: you are, besides, a man in poor health,[15] and if anything inconvenient should happen, consider whether you could
endure it. Therefore, think everything over at the right time,
before you start off; do not undertake a plan which you cannot
give up without discredit. Investigate each point that I have
made, for they are few, and see their force. I am telling you all
this for the love I bear you, for I like to use forceful language.
I pray God that what you decide will be for your good.

Today I again asked permission to leave, for I have been
rolling this stone too long,[16] here and always in vain. And so I
hope that in a fortnight's time I shall set off to join you, if he lets
me, that is, if he gives me the money to travel; but be sure not
to tell anyone. As for Chrysostom on Matthew,[17] I am not sure
how much there is or how good; but before I leave I shall see
the library of the Preaching Friars,[18] where it is, and if there is
any text that is missing in your copy I shall have it transcribed.
I shall give you my answer about the other matters when I see
you. Farewell, my dearest Nicolaus. This has been written, as
you see, hastily, because I have had to write a number of letters.
The twenty-ninth day of October [1420].

LETTER
XI

For a long time now I have been a little slower in writing to you, both because I had no letters in the meantime from you and because I kept thinking each day that I was going to leave the next. For as I wrote you before, I have taken leave of my master and I should be with you already if the winter weather had not held up my trip, for it is completely against me. But just lately, when I was on the point of starting on my trip, the arrival of the King and Queen kept me back and, since her coronation is approaching,[1] I decided to see the ceremony, which, I think, will be very impressive. Then I shall leave as soon as possible and I hope before Easter.

And yet I would not be writing to you now if I had not been spurred on by your letter written on November the twentieth which gave me the utmost pleasure, both because it is so kind and because I see that you alone of all my friends have not forgotten me. As to the rest, I do not know what to think, either they cannot or they will not.

I, as I wrote you elsewhere, went traveling with my master, at the time of the great plague here; but the trip afforded me no pleasure, for a number of reasons, but particularly because I found no books. The monasteries here are very rich but only newly founded, for they have been built by the kings for the most part, within the last four hundred years.[2] But if there are any older, they have no secular books but are filled with recent authorities, and especially with those of the church. I saw some catalogues as well, very carefully made, in which there was nothing worthwhile for the study of the Humanities and no wonder. This island was for a long time invaded by foreign nations,[3] so that there were many different kings in it, all attacking one another. Not only will you not find old books but not even one trace of ancient times. I have not seen Oxford and I have no hope of seeing it. My money is hardly sufficient for my voyage home, even if I hurry; and so you had better give up hope of books from England, for they care very little for them here.[4]

If you want to know simply how many courses to prepare for a banquet[5] or the art of making sauces, you could perhaps find some pretty good authors here, well trained for that kind of game. But I, Nicolaus, have somewhat cooled off in my enthusiasm for searching for books that are new to us.

Now it would be high time to awake out of sleep[6] and pay attention to getting some benefit for my life from those habits which I have and those which I read about daily. For to be constantly collecting wood, stones, and cement can seem to be very stupid, if you never build anything with them. But this building, which we ought to build for a good life, is so much work, so strenuous and demanding, that it can hardly be finished, even if we begin at the beginning of our lives. As far as I am concerned, I have the will to build it, but not the ability to finish it. I see and recognize a lot of things that are for my own good but I never do any of them, just the contrary. Perhaps in my declining years the desire for improvement will grow and then, if I live, I shall begin to do, when I am not able to, what I ought to do now. But who knows when the hour of the Lord will come?[7] Therefore it would be good counsel to begin as soon as possible. I should begin now, if I could, or rather if I would; but it will be difficult for a man belonging to the Curia, or rather impossible. I cannot be anywhere else. For I am not one of those perfect men, who are commanded to abandon father and mother and sell everything and give to the poor;[8] that power belonged to very few people and only long ago, in an earlier age. I should be happy if I were one of those first-class people who could begin to give up those vices which deprive us of the kingdom of God and to live sparingly and soberly.[9]

Do not think that I am writing this way to censure your interest and desire for books but to urge you, if what you want you cannot have, to want what you can have.[10] Please believe me. The sacred books which I have read and which I am reading every day have cooled off my former interest in the Humanities,[11] to which as you know I have been devoted since childhood. For the sources of these studies are vain and partly false and all worthless. But the source of sacred eloquence is truth and, when

that is lost, we can hold nothing to its true course, we can accomplish nothing.

Perhaps you think that because of what I write you in a phi-
losophizing mood, I have reformed my former ways. That is not
so and it causes me the greatest sorrow. I am worse than I used
to be and although I know my faults, I do not counteract them
but, seeing them, knowing them, conscious of them, like a man
rushing headlong to his ruin, I fear that my sins will abandon
me before I abandon them. Therefore I am eager to see you as
soon as possible, to use your advice and help in settling my life.

I heartily praise and approve your changing your mind about
going to Greece,[12] as you have written me. I never liked that
plan; I wrote you my opinion of it before, urging you and begging you not to go. You do not know what discomfort there is
in sailing, especially with that sort of people; and you would
not want to try it with your disabilities. You are in bad health[13]
and you can hardly keep well in your own house, where you live
as you want to. What would happen in the open air, where discomforts are always lurking? Please stay home and, if you cannot
enjoy the company of the living, at least enjoy the dead, of whom
you have a tremendous number.

What you say about my brother, that he is a scoundrel and a
nuisance to my mother, I have heard from people at home. Would
that God would set him straight, which I should prefer, or else
destroy him.[14] He is a chatterer and a liar; for I do not believe he
has changed his habits and he spent many years in the most
corrupt country in the world. But we shall attend to him when
I get home.

As for the other things you mention, we shall discuss them
more freely when we meet. But be prepared to find your friend
a little more voracious than before. You have heard of the customs of those whose God is their belly.[15] Your friend has caught
some of that contagion and has stretched his skin because of
his appetite. But this is nothing you need fear; he does not
desire things bought at a high price, just stuff him with greens
and he will be happy. Goodbye, my dearest Nicolaus. Greet
Nicolaus[16] for me. London, the twelfth day of February [1421].

LETTER
XII

If I had believed that I was going to stay here so long, I would have written to you oftener; but because I thought that from one day to the next I would be on my way to you, I kept silent, expecting that I would soon be conversing with you not by letter but in person. But new promises and the sad state of the Curia have kept me here until today and will hold me up a little longer. For the emoluments of my position are so small that no one can live on them;[1] but if I have to earn my living in service, I prefer to serve here rather than elsewhere, for here serving is less trying and less of a dishonor. Add to this that I have not completely lost every hope; one man makes many promises,[2] though I take little stock in them, and another says that he will do something for me and I have more confidence in him. Moreover to be at home is very hard when there is no livelihood and no place to find one; but it is a point of honor to tell me there is nothing for me.[3] My disgraceful and idle brother also causes me suffering even in these matters for I think his company is to be avoided like a contagious sickness. And so I have decided to follow the advice of some of my friends to wait here a few months longer and to try every possibility to avoid going home to a mean and uncertain livelihood. But if the Curia were what it ought to be and as I remember it, I should have been back with you long ago. Stinking jaws and a more than tumbledown wall;[4] who would have believed it?

I wrote you another letter about a number of things which lately I had sent to Venice[5] to be delivered later to Nicolaus and also about other possessions, which I sent by a ship which, I hear, put in at Pisa. These were directed to Gherardus de Canigianis.[6] I believe that you have had everything delivered to my house, as I wrote you. Ask Nicolaus to write to me, especially about the expenses he paid for carriage on the things that came to Venice.[7] I have heard that the plague[8] has started at home and that many are fleeing. Write me in detail what you are doing. Farewell, in great haste. London, the fourth day of June [1421]. Remember me to Nicolaus[9] and write to me again.

XIII

I have written you in several letters to take care of certain things which I had sent to Pisa by a ship that surely docked some time ago. But still I have no idea what has happened to them; for neither you nor any of those to whom I wrote has answered me.[1] It is extraordinary how everyone either despises me or puts me off in this way. Do not you be one of those yourself who express their friendship only in words; but I wish they would at least give me some satisfaction in words, for it would be a sign that they remember me somewhat. Sometimes it would be kinder to satisfy with words than with deeds, as it is for me now, for it would please me very much to have some news from you about my things. For even if you have done as I suggested well and carefully, yet what you have done has no taste, lacking the spice of a letter to tell me what has really happened. Therefore I ask you again and again to let me know whether everything has arrived and where it is and in whose care. For I had sent my things to Chellus,[2] my kinsman, to keep so that they might not fall into my brother's hands, for I understand that both his life and his habits are dissolute. Likewise, do write to me about each sum paid out[3] and to whom I am in debt, so that I may repay them.

As for my return, I can hold out no hope now, especially on account of the bad condition of the Curia, which is said to be more or less on the verge of collapse. Therefore I have no idea what I could do there.[4] For the job would not pay for my food; besides, I prefer to be in service here than there, where the conditions of service are worse. Still, I have not given up all hope. That man[5] promises me each day that he will not forget me and, while I do not trust him much, I want to test him a little more, not of my own free will, but because I am forced to by the cruelty of circumstances, which are wearing out the Roman Curia.

The Cardinal of Pisa[6] is urging me again to come back. Indeed I should like to; but when I hear of the state and the apprehension in which the members of the Curia are living, I am a little discouraged and I do not see what purpose there would be in going to a place that everyone else is leaving, as I hear. That very learned man, my great friend, Simon de Teramo, the treasurer of this province, is coming to the Curia;[7] he will have a more thorough discussion of my affairs with you, and after he has been to the Curia he will send me word what he thinks I should do.

I wish you would send me the invective that Laurentius[8] wrote against you; for perhaps at my leisure I shall think up something in answer[9] to it. Please keep the engraved gem you have got for me to use as a seal. Farewell, at London, the nineteenth day of July [1421].

LETTER

XIV

I have been traveling around England for some time with my master, who went to the remotest parts of it because he was on a pilgrimage.[1] I reached home only yesterday, after two months and more, and found letters from you and from my kinsman[2] which were most precious to me, especially yours. For the rest brought me more annoyance than pleasure on account of the wickedness of my brother, who is amazingly dishonest and unregenerate; but if I ever come back, I shall remove the cause of all discord by holding a public sale of everything I have acquired[3] by the sweat of my brow.

Thank you very much for the trouble you took to see that the things that I had sent to Pisa were brought home; I send you thanks, not the "sincere" kind one gives a stranger, but as friend to friend. But there are two things in which I could prove carelessness on your part or on somebody else's. First, someone was so careless that the tin and bronze were taken to Florence, as a result of which I had to meet huge costs which would not have been necessary if a little care had been taken. The other is that you make yourself out to be so inexperienced in things and so inefficient that you did not know how to find a way in which three little pieces of cloth[4] could be brought to my home from Pisa. A long time ago, on my way back from France,[5] I brought home a piece of foreign cloth made from different materials, which was made into a sort of coat. Lately with the things I sent to Nicolaus, I again packed in a piece of foreign cloth and it was delivered to my family. With all the citizens who come and go every day on public and private business, why did you not have sense enough to find one who could take along one piece of cloth by itself? Officials and captains and many other people go there,[6] and you could safely have entrusted the business to one of them and it would have been brought in unnoticed with the other things. All you need to do is to use some sense and to pay attention. Just pretend they are books[7] and all will be well.

Dear Nicolaus, imagine that my property were yours and furthermore that I am very poor, for I have plenty of sense, and then you will understand how even the smallest loss is grave for your friend Poggius. If I could have foreseen this, I would rather have kept the money than have mixed myself up in all the mazes of this labyrinth. Please take care to have my cloth taken away from there secretly and carried to my home so that it does not stay there longer and either rot or get eaten up by grubs.

As for your urging me to come home, I see that you do it in a friendly spirit[8] and from sincere affection. Do not think that because I am here, I like being here; but I must try everything, so that I may achieve something, and so stop being a servant to men and have time for literature. My master here has promised me in the presence of Master Simon de Teramo that he will give me the first benefice that falls vacant. If he does this, it will be enough for me; for I do not want a lot, and to accomplish what I do want will not take a long time if he keeps his promise, for something falls vacant every year. And so because of the Collector's advice I have decided to be patient still, while I try it out. This I expect the Collector himself has already told you, for some time ago when he left I asked him to discuss everything with you.[9] As to the Cardinal of Pisa's writing to you that I would find the door closed if I delayed, I see what he means. This confirms me in the feeling that I should wait. If I get something here, I shall care less about the things which I have seldom desired; for to stay in the Curia and in that position is not my ambition. For I wish some time to free myself from service and from that place where I perpetuate the principle of service. Nevertheless, as you write, these things cannot be properly looked into from a distance. Time, on which everything depends, will counsel us.

On this trip of mine I visited a monastery that is older than all the others in England and more magnificent. I inspected the library thoroughly: there are many books but none for us. I saw other libraries besides in many places, all full of nonsense, as I wrote you before; there is no supply of good books here for reasons that I explained to you. I shall go to Oxford[10] as soon as I can, and before I go home, and if there is anything of value I shall let you know.

I wrote to Nicolaus[11] myself, before I started on my travels, reproving him for his laziness in writing. If he corrects himself, I shall rejoice that I have roused the man; but if he keeps his usual silence, like the kind of man he is, I shall humor him and let him be silent as long as he likes. Give him my greetings. As to the Canigiani,[12] they had been commissioned to give the boy half a florin, not a whole one. When I was young, I used to come to Florence from my home with five soldi;[13] that they gave him so much was contrary to my instructions. Farewell and love me as ever. London, the third day of October [1421]. I am writing to Chellus[14] to go to Pisa for my cloth, after he has discussed it with you and with Nicolaus; please direct him and help him.

LETTER
XV

If you are well, good; so am I. Although I had already explained to you in an earlier letter what purpose I had in staying here all this time, I see from the letter which I received from you two days ago that you along with others are much astonished that I am still here so long, as if I had changed my former plan.[1] At the same time some people, as is their habit, are putting it in a worse light and so I have decided that I must write to you again and on the same subject. If perhaps in my former letter I used fewer words than was desirable and did not know how to make my intentions clear to you, now I shall try to see whether I can prove to you that I have not been moved by frivolity, or by a discreditable motive, but by deliberation that was conscientious enough, though human and fallible, to stay in this region.

As you know, influenced both by disgust and by the pay which looked very generous, I left the Curia[2] in the hope that, through a short period of work and service, I might achieve in the future the leisure and liberty which I particularly desire.[3] Therefore I came here, trusting not so much in my own opinion as in that of everyone else, because everyone was urging me to it. Indeed no one doubted that he could perform the things he promised if he wanted to; but they all thought he wanted to, since he was so generous in promising of his own free will.[4] It was his failure to deliver, not mine, which ruined the plan. He did not keep the promise he had repeated a hundred times. I never was fooled for I saw that I was rolling this stone too long in vain. That is why I had decided to go home, and I would have been back a year ago, if the bitter winter weather had not kept me here.[5]

Truly my soul hungered for the Curia, so that satisfied with my little job I could earn my living by writing as I once used to do.[6] Meanwhile the Pope has gone to Rome contrary not only to the will but to the expectation of all; everyone with one voice foretold the worst for him and for those who were his followers. The war with Naples broke out to the horror of everyone attached to the Curia.[7] Out of it have arisen famine and scarcity of everything and such despair in good men that a number of them have left the Curia.[8] The pay is so small that no one could live decently on it. This news has come to me in letters along with rumors, which always make a situation worse. Everyone deplored the many difficulties of the Curia and prophesied still worse ahead.

Travelers returning from it announced that the Curia was at its end; that there were riots in Rome; that there was fear that the Curia would have to flee as they had done long ago. One of my friends even wrote to me in jest that he hoped I would come back soon, so as not to miss the ills from which others were suffering.[9] Then the plague descended upon Rome; the Pope went off traveling in those splendid and highly civilized places in which he was brought up. Those who were in the Curia fled here and there, east and west.[10] When we were told that all this had happened, what do you think I should have done, dear Nicolaus? Put yourself in my place. I wanted to leave here for this purpose: to be in the Curia. But the Curia was in such a state that not only was it not there to go to but, if anyone had been there, he would have had to leave.[11] I could not stay long in my own country because of poverty; moreover to earn a living by spreading my nets for some other bird[12] is easier said than done. What is, not harsher, perhaps, but more wretched than to be always starting life over again? And so after considering my reasoning, such as it was, although I was ready for the journey, I held back a little while, hesitating lest I be acting rashly if I left here in a hurry when there was no place where I could stay without great inconvenience.

There was also a certain hope in a friend, whom I have not named to you, who, when he wanted me to be with him, made me many promises of his own accord which he has not kept; also, although he had so often broken his promises, he kept encouraging me to be with him, offering to do a great many things.[13] Though I did not really believe him, he had some influence with me because I saw that he could easily accomplish what he was promising if only he would stick to it. But then, looking back to what had already happened and having little confidence in it and wondering what I should do, I was carried hither and yon as though on waves; and of the many things that were troubling me, I could not determine what was the most important to do. Believe me, that boy in Terence's play was not wavering any more than I when he said, "What then shall I do?

Shall I go? Not even when I am sent for?"[14] and so forth. I wanted to leave. To go to the Curia when its condition was reported to be the very worst seemed stupid. Yet I judged that it was neither convenient nor to my credit to stay here any longer. But as long as the slightest hope was held out to me here, while elsewhere the outlook was hopeless, I thought it was wiser to wait for a hope, however uncertain, rather than go forth to meet certain disappointment.

While I was still undecided, for I had not yet made up my mind to stay here longer, the Collector,[15] who had come here, gave me many reasons for staying here, not indeed forever but at least long enough to find out whether the promise that had been made, not only to me but far more to him, would be carried out. So I yielded to his exhortations, not for the love I bear this country, for I do not like it much, but because of the desire of getting some way of supporting myself quietly and having time for my literary occupations.

As to what the Collector said to you about the priesthood, you have both misunderstood me. For I am not withdrawing from my former decision nor have I changed as you think; I do not think of the priesthood as liberty, as many do, but as the most severe and oppressive form of service.[16] And you must not think me so silly that I am willing, for the sake of a very trivial thing, which could be taken away from me at any moment, to undertake the heaviest of burdens and one which can be given up only with life. But there are certain limited benefices which are not demanding and which can be held with an easy conscience. If I had got one, however small, I should have come back to you at least in time for the next council.[17] Truly the Collector was the most potent cause of my delay, for I expected a great deal from his being here. If I had known from the beginning that he would go away to the Curia, I would not have waited even one more day. For after he left, you need not think that it was the round of gaiety that kept me here; I have tried every means of finding a way of leaving at someone's expense. Because I have not yet found it, here I stay, discouraged and worried. But as soon as the opportunity comes (that is, when I can go away as I am always striving to do, at someone else's expense) I shall not put it off any longer. There is no one who hates this life more than I; and I should have left two years ago if the Curia had had the importance it used to have, but I do not know how commendable it would have been to flee from toil into sorrow. To establish an entirely new way of life would have been not only irresponsible but idiotic. It is an extremely serious matter to determine the whole of one's future life,[18] since if one fails, as often happens, one abandons what one has begun not without disgrace. Therefore, secondly, one must act rather cautiously and to persist in a course which one has not chosen rightly seems to be complete insanity.

These considerations, so different and contradictory, kept me so hung up and worried that, poised as I was between hope and fear, I stuck here as in a morass, not knowing how to choose the right path. Now you have the reasons for my delay though I do not know whether they sound plausible to you. One thing I do know, that the circumstances, both the time's and my own, were such that anyone placed in such perplexing positions would not easily come to a right and convincing decision.

As for the Sirens which you mention, I do not pay much attention to them; let each one judge as he wishes; he must be judged too. But if you think that I have less sense now at my age than I used to have in my youth, you are absolutely wrong.[19] As you know, I have never been averse to such things, for I am a man; but I never, on that account, turned away from my own advantage. Like a man who is traveling abroad, if any provision was offered to me I accepted it without straying from my direct path, but I never sought such things. Therefore it is ridiculous to think that in a matter so important as making a decision affecting the pattern of the rest of my life, I would undertake to decide on a very trivial and damaging basis. Do not think me so crazy and so irrational that, moved by a siren's song, I should turn off my true course. These passions indeed have agitated me but never have overcome me.

As for what the Collector says: that there are very ancient monasteries in this island, that I have seen nothing, that the books are countless, and that you have some reason for suspecting sirens, I had a good laugh, I must say, both at his love of showing off and at your credulity, which I have so often criticized. For to be so easily convinced by a word here and there from a storyteller is reprehensible not only in so well-educated a man as you, who have heard these ridiculous stories so often, but even in a child. But you will say that you had to take the word of a man of great influence with you. So what? You are believing a blind man's judgment of colors. The man is well trained in the law; if he presumes in other things, you who have known him ought not to believe him.[20] You know that once upon a time Apelles,[21] I think, when some man had criticized the shoes which he had painted in a picture, asked him of what art he was master; and when he said he was a cobbler, Apelles corrected the shoes, because he thought that a man who knew his craft had rightly judged what ought to be corrected in a shoe. But the man, elated because such an eminent painter had corrected part of his picture at a word from him, presumed further, asserting that the dress was wrong too; but Apelles said: "That is not your province." Why do you, in these matters that are in a certain way our specialty, trust another rather than me? Have you ever up to now found me a liar or careless? Have you ever found anyone more thorough? You will find many more learned than I but I will not admit that anyone is more enthusiastic in his search for knowledge than I am. The Collector was here four months and he never went out of London;[22] he did not see a single monastery; he read no books that would have told him the age of the monasteries or the story of their founding or the number of books in them. Therefore he must have learned all that you mention from hearsay and from people who are entirely untrained in such matters and from whom I have heard the same statements a thousand times myself. Will you therefore put faith in a man without any learning and on subjects about which he may say what he has heard from others more ignorant than himself? How stupid it is of you to be in the least influenced by everything you hear.

I wrote you in my last letter that I had recently seen an older and richer monastery[23] than the others in this island and yet had found nothing there worth my effort. Are you not therefore doing an injustice to me and to our friendship by having so little faith in me and by being blown about by every breeze? It scarcely consorts with your dignity to be so carried away by any man's report that you constantly underrate me and put more confidence in another man's guesswork than in my research. When he comes back to England,[24] he will show his diligence and without any assistance from me; for, as I think, unless the sky falls and the earth evaporates, before he comes here again, I hope to have left. I shall come to you even on foot, if necessary; for I do not wish to be wiser than all of you.

As for the things which I had sent, I heard from you on another occasion what was done about them. I am sorry that you or the other man paid so little attention that those pieces of cloth, which cost me a lot of money, have not been sent along with the other things; for the things I had sent to Pisa could have been handled in the same way as those I sent to Nicolaus; they can be taken away from there as if they were being sent to Rome or Siena or elsewhere. For there was the greatest negligence about the trunk, so that only because of someone's carelessness, or as I see it, everyone's, I have been put to unnecessary expense. But what is done cannot be undone. Take care, I beg of you, that in some way my cloth may be retrieved safe from Pisa,[25] as I wrote you in another letter. There are many ways in which the matter can be arranged.

As for our Nicolaus[26] your saying that he is very fond of me is entirely superfluous. It would go ill with me if I were only now beginning to know him. I was long ago persuaded that he was my other self[27] and that everything we had, as is proper in close friendship, we shared with one another;[28] for when I have need of it, I use his property as if it were my own. May God preserve him to us; for he is a man rare among men. I have tried many but I have always found him a true friend, as they all should be. For when I need his help, there is never any need to use that tiresome and annoying word "Please," with a submissive look; he offers himself of his own accord[29] and does not wait to be asked. I have nothing to criticize in him except a certain thought-lessness and carelessness about writing, and as he behaves that way in his own affairs I must not demand that he should show himself more careful in mine. It would please me very much if he would even answer my letters, for in the duty of friendship he not only returns tit for tat but far outdoes and surpasses me. Therefore, since he is so far ahead of me in more important things, he is determined to lag behind me in more trivial ones, and out of his kindness he. defers to me in this so as not to surpass me in everything. Give him my greetings, please, and tell him not to worry about the money I owe him for I shall give him a quick answer whether I see him or not.

I am glad to hear about the Greek books[30] which you tell me have been found lately. I understand that Guarinus has married a very beautiful young wife who has a large dowry, which is the most important thing.[31] Now he is peacefully at home and happy, which pleases me tremendously. Franciscus Barbarus has also taken the advice of his own little book in choosing a wife;[32] he has imitated good doctors, who give proper advice not only to other people but also to themselves on the subject of recovering their health. You will understand what I mean if you know what sort of man he is; for his eloquence will flourish not only in his learning but also in his offspring. All that we need now is that you should get married too;[33] it is all over with me, for I cannot satisfy myself, much less anyone else.[34]

That you think my brother is not actually wicked relieves my mind; but I am surprised that he has so long remained lazy and out of work, without taking up any profession in which he might get ahead. It is hard enough for me to support myself without supporting him in idleness. But I hope that I shall soon know the whole story. I shall be ruled by your advice, since you have fought the same battle for a fairly long time.

I am awaiting the Collector's letters from the Curia,[35] for I asked him to let me know about its condition and at the same time to communicate with my lord of Pisa[36] and to write back to me what he thought I ought to do, for my heart is set on coming back. I am waiting for his letters; and if he still writes to me not to come back, I shall do the opposite and I shall assert to him that he wrote to me about my return. And so you can certainly write to my lord of Pisa that I shall wait a further two months at the very most and that I am only investigating the chances of coming back at someone else's expense; but if that fails I shall do the best I can. I have always intended to come home, but now your letters have added a stimulus so that I think of nothing but my return home, since it seems possible to you.

I am worn out with writing. If my letters are rougher in style than they used to be, put it down first to my haste in writing and then to my reading of the works of Aristotle,[37] on which I have been working for a long time, though making little progress. Farewell and love me as ever, and please forgive the length of this letter. Because Nicolaus[38] perhaps belongs to those who suspect me of something or other, as you have told me, please share this letter with him and with those who are of his opinion, so that they may not form a false judgment of their friend. London, November the thirtieth [1421].[39]

LETTER

XVI

Lately when I had written you at greater length why I was staying here longer than either you or I had expected, I added that I was going to come home just as soon as I had the opportunity to do it at someone else's expense. In this letter you will see me hanging like a pendulum, and that not groundlessly, for I have great difficulty in choosing what is best to do. For since I had either to belong to the Curia or somewhere else when I left here and since, on the other hand, the Curia was so weak that it could hardly support itself but elsewhere there was no place in view to stay, not even a modest one, it does not seem to me to have been entirely senseless, since I was in doubt about things still so uncertain, not to go home. And indeed I shall follow the advice of others, for I myself do not know how to work out an adequate solution; for the more I dwell upon the subject the more I become involved in it, like a bird caught in a net.[1]

After I wrote to you the last time, I received a letter from the Curia from a man named Bartholomeus de Vincio,[2] whom I think you know as a person of fairly good judgment. Now listen to what he writes at the end of his letter in the language of the people: "Ben ti prometto, che qui si fa degli stentolini. L'ufficio valse il mese d'agosto IIII fiorini" ["I assure you that there is all sorts of trouble here. The position was worth four florins in the month of August"]. In another letter he was considering leaving the Curia.

These things disturb me, Nicolaus; even you admit that it is not to my advantage to be in the Curia. What then shall I do? But, you say, there are many ways by which you can come to the right decision, when you are with us; but those schemes of yours are also uncertain and you do not tell me anything that is dependable. If you had reported to me some definite offer, I should have seized upon it with avidity.

I do not say these things as if I were not determined to come home, just as I always was, but so that you may see that I have not remained in this state of indecision up to this very day from some futile whim, as you say many people believe. I wish that those who hold such a suspicion of me might be in this same maze, if it were a question of their affairs too. I do not mean to invoke a curse upon them and indeed it happens to many men, that what they cannot accomplish by deliberation they denigrate by guesswork.

There is a young Venetian nobleman here, who was a pupil of Guarinus'. He is very well educated and so well read that one is bound to like him. We have built up a great devotion and are so bound together by ties of affection that one of us cannot exist without the other. His name is Fantinus Georgius,[3] and I think that he is very fond of me. I have often confided my indecisions to him. He has promised me that as soon as he reaches Venice, he will take action for me and that without any doubt he will find something worth my while; and he has also told me what he intends to do. I shall write to Franciscus Barbarus,[4] for Fantinus is leaving here soon, to get in touch with him and help him. If there should be any result, I shall not be caught napping.

I am hunting everywhere to find some means of leaving here at someone else's expense and I hope to find a way. For some-one intimated to me today that he was on his way to the Curia and that he would willingly pay my expenses on the trip to have me with him. If I find nothing better, I shall seize upon his offer; but it means staying here till the Feast of the Purifica-tion. Goodbye, for I have run out of paper. In London, the twelfth day of December.

After I had written this, I received a letter from the Collector, that is, Simon de Teramo,[5] whom I had urgently asked to let me know about the state of the Curia, and at the same time, when he had discussed his plan with the Cardinal of Pisa, to advise me what to do, whether to stay here or to leave, and to let me know not only what state things were in at present but how he guessed they were going to be. He writes me that I have so far chosen the wiser course by staying here and urges me not to return, declaring that the Curia is very much desolated. About my lord of Pisa, with whom I ordered him to consult, he says not a word, from which I conjecture that my lord is either away or of the same opinion. But you who love me are the only person who advises me to come back, not that you have any confidence in the resources of the Roman Curia, in which you think I should by no means tie myself up, but because you hope that I will find something else in which I could use my talents, and not without a salary.

All this troubles me very much, Nicolaus. For placed as I am between lines of advice, not merely various but diametrically opposed, I do not see what course I should take. To return to the Curia, where I can no longer make a living as I used to by writ-ing, seems ridiculous; but to wait here for a chance, which has failed me I know not how many times, is absurd.[6] But truly to turn from a hope, however uncertain, to an empty guess I con-sider the height of folly. I wish that you had outlined something to me, on which I could more confidently have based my decision. For I do not know what I can do outside the Curia except teach boys or work for some master or rather tyrant. If I had to take up either one of these, I should think it utter misery. For not only is all servitude a dismal thing, as you know, but especially so is serving the lusts of a wicked man. As for school teaching, may I be spared that![7] For it would be better to be subject to one man than to many.

I imagine you will make fun of me, Nicolaus, for battering at your ears so often and so lengthily about the same thing, and such a trivial one at that. But I do this first of all from a desire for conversation with you and for a discussion of my affairs just as if we were together and then particularly so that you may not wonder or ascribe to lightmindedness the fact that I seem to have changed my mind so many times. For it seemed right to submit to circumstances[8] and, since they do not always remain the same, it is fitting to change my plans as circumstances change. But because it very often happens that we are better judges of another man's affairs than of our own, since, as Terence says, we are by some sickness[9] hindered in the care of ourselves, therefore I ask you to investigate everything I have written from every angle; and if in every respect it seems to you advisable for me to come home, I shall follow your advice.

One thing I want you to know: I have not changed my intentions an iota since my earlier letters. I had left out what gave me the most powerful inclination to stay here. For a long time ago you wrote to me that the Cardinal of Pisa[10] had written to you that I would find no openings there because I had been away so long. I understood that he meant the post of secretary, about which he had written himself.[11] Then I did not want to shut every door to myself and especially not the one which had up to now been open to me. Please write me again what you think I ought to do. Truly I want you to believe that I am here against my will. The Venetian[12] whom I mentioned to you encourages me with his promises daily; I hope something will come of it.

I ask you more particularly that you and Nicolaus will undertake the care of my cloth, which is at Pisa, and see to it that it is taken away from there, so that it does not rot: *che mi costano troppo caro* [for it cost me too dear to lose]. Give Nicolaus my greetings.[13] Farewell and love me; and if I seem to you more rustic than usual, do not be surprised for I have read nothing since I left you that is conducive to a good style. London, the seventeenth day of December [1421].[14] Write me what Leonardus Aretinus is doing and whether you are friends again.[15]

LETTER
XVII

Two days ago I received two letters from you and with them one from Pier Lamberteschus,[1] which I read thoroughly from beginning to end. To put it briefly, I like what Pier pictures and what he offers; and, I think, I shall follow your advice. He writes that he will see to it that I have 500 gold pieces as a three-year salary; let him make it 600 and I shall accept.[2] He holds out great hope of a lot of things and though I grant you that they may come true, it is more satisfactory to make a sure contract than to depend on hope alone. Read the letter which I am writing to him, for it is not sealed.[3] If he is with you, settle it with him as you think best; but if he has left, send the letters after him, both mine and yours.

I have decided to leave here for home in May and then to go to Rome, where I shall wait for his answer, for there is no sense in going there on nothing but hope, but only after he has come to some decision with his friend and made arrangements for me to get there.[4] The job which he urges me to take pleases me and I hope to do something worth reading. But as I am writing to him, I shall need quiet for this and time to study.[5] You read my letters and, if there is anything in them that you think should be changed, do as seems best to you; for I put myself and my affairs in your hands. I shall be glad to live with Pier unless we are to be Scythians, for I want to rest.

My master has finally given me something; for the mountain

labored and brought forth a mouse,[6] which gnaws at my ears.
He has given me a tiny little benefice and a big burden. It is
a curacy worth 120 florins in tithes, which does not please me.
For as Gregory bears witness in one of his homilies, it is hard
for a person who does not know how to control his own affairs
to be made judge of another's.[7] Therefore I shall the more
quickly take off this garment which weighs me down. I have
often written to you that this was my one ambition: by the hard
work of a few years to achieve leisure for the rest of my life. If
what Pier writes is true, I guess that his is the surest way to reach
my goal. And so if he has gone away, write to him as seems best
to you and have someone copy my letters so that you can send
two copies, on account of the distance and the risks, and urge him
to answer.[8]

I see what the Cardinal of Pisa writes about the post of Secretary. Certainly if I thought as much of that office as some people,
I should have come home long ago; but if everything goes
to pieces, this job that I have now will not fail me. I think
less of the Papacy and of its offshoots than they would believe.[9] I desire to be a free man, not to be a public servant.
Only accomplish what Pier promises and you will see me leave
here with more dispatch than other people give me credit for.
I shall leave with the expectation that things will turn out as you
say, for they please me as they please you, and the month of
June shall not see me here. I should come sooner, if I were not
waiting for something from the Roman Curia around the time
of Easter. Will you write to the Cardinal of Pisa not the reason
but simply that I am coming? For what I have written to you in
another letter, that I would leave here after the month of February, could not be accomplished because the man who was
supposed to come changed his plans. But now that it cannot
be done in any other way, I shall come at the expense of the
Crucified.

We shall discuss the rest upon my arrival, but I especially
ask you this one thing: not to discuss my plans with anyone. I
am uncertain about the future; man proposes but God disposes,[10]
and we are all inclined to slander. And so these things must be

carried out in secret; I mean the Hungarian matters.[11] Greet our friend Nicolaus and brother Ambrose.[12] Farewell and love me. London, the twenty-second day of February [1422].

LETTER

XVIII

I wrote you two letters, one in Latin and one in our mother tongue,[1] about my opinion of the post that Pier de Lamberteschis was offering. I said that I was pleased with what he planned to do for me, provided the terms were made so clear that I should not be starting out on the basis of a mere supposition but for something definite and well worked out.[2] Then I received a letter from you written quite lately and along with it the copy of a letter from Pier with a sort of postscript, all of which pleased me.[3] But I stand firmly on my first statement, provided the field is fertile enough for a crop, as Pier fancies. But I shall come home to you, and then when the conditions have been compared and the reasons discussed from every angle, we shall, I hope, choose the wiser course.

I want you to know this from the beginning: that I put freedom and time for study ahead[4] of all the other things that many people particularly value and desire. And if I see that I am going to get them, as our friend Pier hopes, I shall go not only to the Sarmatians but to the Scythians,[5] especially if I get a chance to study Greek.[6] I want to drink in the Greek greedily so as to escape those horrid translations, which so torment me that I find more irritation in the style than pleasure in the matter. Pier tells me that he will write again with a definite offer as soon as possible and that he thinks his letter on the matter will be in Florence before Easter. This pleases me because we shall be able to decide earlier what to do, but I do not know whether I shall be able to leave as soon as I had hoped; not that I have changed my mind, but I ought to be guided by circumstances.

I had written to you that my master had given me a certain small living with a cure of souls which I considered of little

value because I did not wish to assume the burden of the priesthood. But two days ago he offered me another worth forty
pounds, clear of expenses; and having given up the former one,
I accepted this. If it were not a benefice with a cure of souls I
should not desire more; but the burden of the cure weighs upon
me too heavily. I think I shall find a benefice free instead of this
one and without the parish worth twenty pounds.[7] If I can do
this, it will be enough for me and I shall look no further. But I
do not know when I shall find it; and I do not know whether it
would be better to come home at this point, as things now stand
or to wait a little while and see if I can effect this change.

There is the additional difficulty that I do not know whether
my master will be angry with me if I ask leave of him so suddenly, though I grant you that this does not matter. For I shall
ask as if I intended to return in six months, and there is an old
proverb that baggage is packed on the way.[8] But so that you may
not feel doubtful of my return on account of this, I give you my
word that I shall not be here beyond the month of May, unless
perhaps I have to wait a little longer to find a traveling companion, which cannot detain me later than the feast of St. John.[9]
But because we are uncertain as to what the future will bring
please keep all this secret. For if I go to Hungary,[10] it will be a
secret to all except a few; I shall pretend to be coming here and
shall feed those fellows of yours on stories. But I do not care
much about the secretaryship. Let others make a fuss about it
as they wish it, for if all else fails I have something to live on
here and that in luxury. Farewell and remember me to Nicolaus.
London, the fifth day of March [1422].[11]

If you should have an answer from Pier soon, write it to me as
soon as possible; for, as I told you, I do not know whether I
shall be able to leave when I wish. I must get some money for
my traveling expenses[12] and I ought to get that out of my benefice; for that man of yours would not give me anything. I shall
find some friend who will lend me something against my crops:
venderò in erba [or else I shall sell them to him while they are
still green].[13]

LETTER
XIX

I wrote you in three letters[1] that I was pleased with the offer
that our friend Pier Lamberteschus had made, provided I was
going to a definite post. In his last letter to me, he assured me
that he was on the point of starting as soon as possible and that
what he now had in mind he would put into action as soon as he
got there and would write to me again to Florence. If he does
this, we shall arrange the matter soon. I shall be here until I
can scrape together some money from my benefice for my travel
expenses, for I have no means from any other source, but I shall
not stay here beyond the month of May unless perhaps for the
sake of finding company.[2] But with you and with Nicolaus[3] I
shall discuss both myself and my problems; and so I think we
shall reach a better decision. I ought also to go to Rome on business. But I shall obtain leave from my master for six months,
promising to return and then, as Terence says: "the hen has
cackled, the soothsayer has forbidden,"[4] and so forth. Therefore do not broadcast this business to anyone, for there will be
need of secrecy for many reasons which I shall discuss with you.
Farewell, London, the sixteenth day of March [1422]. Send the
letter which is tied to this one to my kinsman[5] so that it does not
come into anyone else's hands.

LETTER
XX

I wrote you in several letters that I was going home in May
or at the latest at the feast of John the Baptist with this in mind:
that I should follow your advice and Pier Lamberteschus' in
the offer he makes me in regard to Hungary.[1] He told me in a
later letter that he would write to you in Florence to tell you
about the definite arrangements he had made so that I should

not set out on a false hope. I asked you in my last letter, since he had said that his answer would be in Florence in March or before Easter, to let me know his verdict as soon as possible. I am surprised that you have not done so yet, if he has sent you any answer at all.

For I would not want to start out as the saying goes, like a fly without a head, especially since a friend of mine from the Curia advises me to wait here until the coming council[2] because the Curia is in the worst possible state. But I would have gone home long ago in hope of a word from Pier if my benefice were not holding me back. My master gave it to me and since it is a curacy I do not want to keep it any longer because of the burden of the parish, which I consider an extremely heavy one, but am seeking to exchange it for some benefice without a parish, the kind a mere clerk can get.[3] Now I am involved in an activity which I cannot conclude in a hurry as I would prefer but I hope to leave within two months, as I am very anxious to do so.

A certain canonry has been offered to me, which would pay me one hundred florins a year wherever I am or at least eighty.[4] If I get this, I want nothing more, and I shall put an end to any desire for riches or rank but be free to study literature as I have always wanted to do. For as I have often written to you, this was always my desire and I came here on account of it, to accumulate a little on which to live free for my studies;[5] and even if everything else fails, at least I seem to have accomplished that. But if Pier's good opinion and his petition have any influence, I shall take what he offers me. For this pleases me beyond all else; and if by honest toil as this is, I can procure a living for my future perhaps I might give up the benefice which, although it be without a parish, is still a worry and a burden. And so please, as soon as you can, let me know Pier's answer. Meantime I shall exchange this benefice and when that is done, I shall come directly to you;[6] because, even if my hope in Pier comes to nothing, I ought to go to the Curia at Rome. Goodbye and write to me again. At London, the twenty-fifth day of May [1422].

LETTER
XXI

Yesterday I received a letter from you which I read with the greatest pleasure[1] because of its contents. First of all, I am glad that you received the letter in which I answered you and Pier that I would follow your advice and I persist in that opinion; but as I wrote to you a little while ago, I cannot come home so soon as I should like to because I have to delay a short time. Ever since I acquired this benefice, I have been trying constantly to exchange it for another without a Cure; but I have not yet found one and I am exerting all my energies just to that purpose.[2]

As soon as I have accomplished it I shall set out for home, but if I cannot find what I want I shall wait until I have an answer from Pier about any definite assurance he can give me. And if he writes as I hope, I shall delay no longer, since I consider this cure as bad as a disease. But if he could not achieve what he had offered, I shall have to wait here until the next council[3] and meanwhile concentrate on making the exchange which I mentioned. For it does not seem to me to be a wise plan to give up this little thing which I have acquired through so much effort for some hope which might fail us. And so it seems better to wait until Pier replies, and I shall make my plans then according to what he says. This I assure you: that if he gives me a firm offer, I shall leave here as fast as I can and never mind my benefice if I have not been able to exchange it in the meanwhile.

Someone has kept me hung up for two months already by promising me that he would give me a certain prebend[4] in return for this church of mine but now when I press the matter and long to come to the point,[5] he has withdrawn from his promises. To believe their promises is like holding a wolf by the ears.[6] But be sure as soon as Pier answers to let me know about it for that is all I am waiting for. I do not want you to distrust me; if I have time and leisure to describe his achievements, I shall do something of which you will approve. My spirit is willing: I do not know whether I have the strength, but "labor omnia vincit improbus"[7] [persistent toil overcomes everything].

During my four years here I have paid no attention to the study of the Humanities and I have not read a single book that had anything to do with style.[8] You can guess this from my letters, for they are not what they used to be but in a short time I shall get back my former facility. When I consider earlier historians,[9] I am discouraged from writing; but when I consider contemporary ones,[10] I become more confident and hope that I shall be inferior to few if I make a big effort.[11] You make it your business to let me know Pier's answer as soon as possible.

I am glad to hear what you write about the Archbishop of Milan,[12] if it is true; for finding such unparalleled authors is a real cause for triumph but it does not seem convincing to me. For the Archbishop is a man who, if he had found any such thing, would have carried it off with him at least to be copied. I fear, moreover, that he is asserting rumors as established facts, as often happens. Would you imagine that a man of such high rank, supported by the power of the empire, and of such great influence would have experienced any difficulty in acquiring books when he was asking barbarian donkeys for them, if he really had found them, as you say? It would have been to their advantage to give the books to a man who could have interceded for them before the Emperor. Besides our friend has an ambitious nature,[13] he does not disdain praise or glory; if he had found the works of such historians he would have sounded forth his own trumpet,[14] concealing nothing. There would be no need of asking him, he would give it out spontaneously. I am a mere worm, and yet I took along a copyist into Germany. How much more easily could he have engaged not one but many copyists? I shall believe it when I see it.

As to the *Orator*,[15] which you say has been found at Lodi (and Franciscus Barbarus[16] bears witness to the fact), I believe what those men say, and it is a great treasure. I am pleased that my things which were in Pisa[17] have been rescued. I thank you for attending to it. Farewell and love me and greet Nicolaus for me. London, the tenth day of June [1422].

LETTER
XXII

As I wrote you elsewhere, nothing keeps me here except the trouble of exchanging my little benefice, which, because of present conditions, is much more meager[1] than I had been led to believe. I should not want to lose now by hurrying unwisely something that I have sought, after spending so much time and so much mental anguish on it.[2] If in these next two months something arises that I want, I shall straightway finish off the business and come to you. But even if I achieve nothing, I shall still come to you. But if Pier writes anything definite which we can follow up or try out, I shall not wait for either change or immutability, but I shall leave everything behind and not merely come but fly.

You should not think that I like it better here than at home, but, as you know, I have been rolling this stone longer than should have been necessary for the sake of a quiet future. However, it seems to me ridiculous to hope for anything quiet in this life, in which there is nothing stable but rather constant agitation. And indeed I very often laugh at myself for seeking a little quiet in a place from which many intellectuals, thinking it the greatest caldron of disturbance, flee in droves.

The easier way would be to abandon all these worldly concerns, all the empty cares, annoyances, and daily plans, and to flee into the haven of poverty, which is freedom and true quiet and safety.[3] But this is granted only to the few; only for those whom the Father has chosen, as Truth says. But I agree with the general opinion, that just as men say that they have many friends although they have and have had very few, so I would call a life peaceful in which there is a minimum of annoyance. I have desired this for a long time but, through the fault of circumstance or of the times, I have been misled and do not know whether I am on the right track. For as I wrote you in another letter, I realize what a grave step it is to undertake the office of a clergyman and how much those who live on a benefice ought to be tormented by responsibility if they have any conscience. For since the rewards are not given to one who does not labor, he that will not work, as the Apostle says, neither shall he eat.[4] But these things are easier said than done and, as the saying goes, "Let us fall into the hand of the Lord . . . and let me not fall into the hand of man."[5]

But yet if this attempt of Pier's were to come off, this promise I should say, I should leave these sacred occupations which I took up only unwillingly; not that I in any way despise the religious life, but because I do not think I shall ever be the sort of man they say I ought to be. Therefore I hope all the more that Pier will accomplish what we want. I am grateful for the remarks of the Cardinal of Pisa[6] about the secretaryship for the sake of the honor; but the office itself is not a beginning of freedom but a treadmill of servitude. Understand what I mean: I am not looking for the kind of liberty which is free of every care and annoyance, for that existed long ago and in a former age, but I am looking for the kind of freedom in which I am subject to fewer people,[7] if, as Tullius says, I am to live as I wish.

The first state would be holier but the Spirit bloweth where It listeth,[8] and the characteristic of God is not wishing or hurrying but pitying, for He has the power to act whenever He wishes not from the merits of the man who calls but because he calls.[9] Our friend Ambrose lives the religious life, and I consider him particularly happy; for he counts everything as dung provided he makes his profit from Christ.[10] And we who do not have strength of mind wish to keep pursuing this middle way, where, while serving God, we yet are not slaves to the world. But when I come home we shall thoroughly discuss my collected musings on this subject and we shall figure out what I most need to do. Every now and then when I think critically of the fact that I have so meticulous a care of my future leisure and future quiet and so much concern for my future life, although I have no need of anything to preserve it except food and clothing, which are easily acquired, especially by a man who is not lazy, I find myself ridiculous.

But we shall discuss this when we meet. I am extremely glad that Tullius' *De oratore* was found in perfect condition and the

Orator and the *Brutus* complete. Nothing annoys me more than the fact that I cannot be on the spot to enjoy them with you.[11] But I hope I soon shall be. There is no need to answer the rest of your letter. May God answer my prayer to be back with you as soon as possible. But I am waiting especially for Pier or rather for his letter, so that I shall not always have to fasten my plans to the wind. Farewell and love me as you are used to. London, the twenty-fifth day of June [1422]. Thank you very much for having my cloth delivered to my home. Greet Nicolaus for me.[12]

LETTER
XXIII

I have received a short letter[1] from you which there is no need to answer for there is nothing in it that requires an answer except one thing: you ask me to let you know my exact position and I can do that in a few words. I have been made Secretary to the Pope with no appeals or very few.[2] It pleases me because I have regained the rank[3] I used to have, but I do not know what I am to do until the Bishop of Winchester arrives.[4] The Pope was glad to see me. I shall guess soon whether it pays me to stay in the Curia or to go back to Britain. It is always considered the part of a wise man to obey circumstances. If I see that by this method I shall obtain what I desire, that is, a little livelihood, which I can keep a hold on as I work away quietly at my studies, I shall stay here. But if not, I shall try everything to achieve what I have so long been panting for. Do not forget what I once told you about the farm that I was going to buy to live on, provided it was free of taxes.[5] For I want to be free, if I can, of the annoyance of taxes, inasmuch as it is right for me to say it.

Cinthius Romanus[6] has complained to me that you have insulted him by refusing him that book so many times. I have made excuses for you and myself at the same time by saying that you do everything with the best intentions. I have said that the book ought to be copied soon;[7] every day he asks me *purtiella bene*. Please copy the book[8] and let me know whether you have begun. Please send me my separate notebooks, that is, the excerpts from various books that I have read. There are many of them and they are scattered; please collect them all together and send them to me as soon as you can. Farewell. At Rome, the fifteenth day of May 1423.

I should like to have the *De oratore*, the *Brutus*, and the *Orator.*[9] Please send them to me, if you have them, as soon as possible; but if not, borrow them from Nicolaus[10] or from someone else as you need them and be sure at the same time that I have all the parchment I need to copy them, because I have my heart set on writing them out or having them written. I have written to ask Franciscus Barbarus[11] to send us my orations of Tullius which he has. Open the letter if you wish, and when you have read it, seal it up and see that he gets it. Please send me as soon as possible the letter I wrote to you about Baden[12] when I was in Germany.

LETTER

XXIV

I gather from your letter that you are being conscientious about what I asked you to do. As for your asking me how much I want to spend,[1] I do not know what I should put down as a limit, first of all because I do not have much money and secondly because a fixed price often either tempts the buyer to go beyond what he meant to spend or else discourages him. My idea was to spend up to four hundred gold pieces, not because I have that much but because I was in hopes of borrowing some small share of it from you and another share from someone else and repaying you out of my first earnings.[2] But I do not know what to do: the war, which seems threatening, as I see it, upsets me; I see that its beginning is easy but its end and outcome hard.

He is young and powerful and he cannot be injured without spending a lot of our money. Once upon a time he could have been resisted with little effort but now that is all changed; and yet very little or rather no attention is paid to Forlì, where he has taken over the government and runs it in the name of the heir.³ I can say nothing with regard to your comment on the Pope. I say only this: that if he has any feeling against our Republic, it should not surprise us, if you think of how much offense was given him at one time by a number of people.⁴ It is not up to me to judge such important questions: I should wish only this, that either we might know how or be willing to make peace; now we shall just go on pouring out money. "The wild land of Africa trembles at the dreadful tumult."⁵ But enough of this. It will turn out according to God's will. I should like to make sure that the burden of my taxes does not send me to the bottom.⁶ See what you can find that is for sale and what sort of place it is and what the profits and burdens are. If there is a tax to be paid, I won't touch it. I have given this same commission to one of my friends who is a citizen of Siena.⁷ I think that I shall find something better there and cheaper than at Florence. I have set my heart on peace and quiet. If I could secure it by this purchase, please do what I wish; but if not, I do not want to be mixed up in more trouble. Write me what you find and your own advice in this matter. If I cannot be in Florence I shall be elsewhere. Places make no difference to me; where I am at peace and comfortable, there will be my country.⁸

The Pope looks upon me quite kindly;⁹ I hope he will not lose sight of me. I shall not be insistent or troublesome at the beginning, which is important to everyone but has always been especially important to me in everything. But as you know: "Persistent toil overcomes everything."¹⁰ I have the things you sent me. My worn-out clothes¹¹ which you have I should like to have sold. Will you find out what price they will bring and what each one is worth and let me know about it, for if they are not worthless I want them sold. Send me as soon as you can the book of precedents¹² that have to do with the Curia, for I need them. And see that the other things that I asked you for are brought to me. I have received from Cologne the fifteenth book of Petronius Arbiter,¹³ which I arranged to have transcribed when I went there lately. Please send me the Eclogue of Calpurnius¹⁴ and the fragment of Petronius which I sent you from Britain, and do not forget my notebooks; there is a great deal to add to them. Take care of yourself. At Rome, the twenty-eighth of May 1423.

LETTER

XXV

I laughed when I read the last letter I received from you, both because of your comments and because I saw that you were a little upset by my letters to you. And so it is right, just as lazy and slow horses need a spur, that you should sometimes be goaded; otherwise you would not have replied at all unless the moon had risen in Capricorn.[1] But there is one thing, joking aside, about which I want to warn you for the sake of our friendship. Although everything in your letter delighted me, I was annoyed to read this one thing, that as far as I could see you were in a temper when you wrote about Nicolaus.[2] I quite believe that he did not answer you so courteously as your own dignity and your friendship with each other demanded. You ought to have borne it calmly; for things that are done in a rash moment of anger and not thought over and considered should be taken lightly. We must put up with human nature and our habits, which are difficult to change, especially the ingrained ones. We have many vices in us and, if they cannot be corrected, they must be borne with an even temper, just as we would bear the faults of our friends to preserve our friendships rather than throw away the pleasure of intimacy and their affection for us, in order to avoid their faults too.[3]

You know what the laws of friendship are; you know how common it is in the nature of men to slip; you know how rare virtue is; you know that disagreements and quarrels often develop between the best of friends; this is the fault of passions which appear unexpectedly of their own accord and force us suddenly to say many things for which we are instantly sorry. Reason ought to teach us moderation and not allow things to go so far; therefore, Nicolaus, please if he offended you in any way by his words, do not think it was Nicolaus but a certain swifter impulse that immediately vanished. Perhaps it ought to have seemed strange to someone else but it is wrong for you, who know his nature, to be annoyed by his words, especially when this heat cools off so soon. Please take care of our Nicolaus not only for yourself but also for me and use your discretion as you have learned to do from reading and from experience. To tell the truth, it was very distressing to me to feel that you were so upset both because I saw that I had been the cause of this trouble and because I want you to be calm. And so if you want to do me a favor, give us back the man you used to be.

I am glad that you will use your energy on the matters about which I have quite often written, which do not require further discussion. Do what can be done; let the rest wait for a convenient time or be forgotten. If we come to Siena,[4] as I hope, we shall talk face to face and together discuss things one by one. I have written again to Franciscus Barbarus about my Orations and I have asked Nicolaus to show you my letter. He does not answer or send the book. I do not know whether he received the letters, I want to find out about this; for if it is established that he received them, I shall then write to Guarinus and complain[5] that I have been offended, and I shall take no more account of another man than he himself wishes.

✿   ✿   ✿   ✿   ✿

After I had written this I received from you a very short letter but one full of affection. I am delighted with your arrangement for me to have a cover for my bed, and whatever you arrange will seem pretty to me. When it is finished, see that it is brought to me in Rome and get the money from Nicolaus. If the breviary[6] and the other things I want cannot be found, do not bother about it; and some day we shall find something up to our standard. I have not sent you the Petronius hoping that I could bring you the book myself. But if that hope fails, I will see that it is brought to you. This is a small point: that I put it off not out of carelessness but on purpose. You really put on an exhibition of rhetoric when you accused me of being slow and added that our friend

Petrus de Canino's[7] parchments had been hidden from you. This too I think in the same way is nothing.

You can be as rhetorical as you like; I am a little deaf. Farewell and be sure to give this letter to my mother. In haste at Rome, the eleventh day of September 1423.

LETTER

XXVI

It was not business that kept me from writing to you but a scarcity both of material and of words. Besides there are various little occupations in which I am involved which do not bother me so much in themselves as does the expectation of them. For I ought to be ready at the mere nod[1] of the princes of the church so as not to offend their sanctity, for their indignation is easier to arouse if I forget to do anything than is their mercy.[2]

In some things too the beginnings are arduous and wearisome so that what is amusing, quick, and easy to those who have long held the position is to me troublesome, slow, and burdensome.[3] "But persistent toil conquers everything."[4] I try also to produce something worthy of myself and I creep into the good graces of the Prince,[5] whom I seem to see fairly well disposed toward me; and we have very little to do. All the same I am distracted by worries and afraid of everything and constantly nervous.

The books have come back which you consigned to our friend Nicolaus and also your loose quires which through the carelessness of the carrier (and it is true of the Quintilian as well)[6] have been a little spoiled by rain. I am writing a letter to Ser Angelus Pieri,[7] a fellow citizen of mine, to which another has been attached. Please take care that it is delivered to him as soon as possible and see that the other is delivered too. I think that at last we are on our way to Siena if the fates are with us. Farewell, in haste. At Rome, the night of the eighth of October 1423.[8]

I am waiting for your letter and the mattress and news of our Republic as to whether you expect there will be war or peace.[9]

You might ask Ser Martinus[10] what he thinks ought to be done in my case, that is, how I can avoid the taxes or rather those extortions of yours;[11] and please send me his answer and tell me also whether this letter reaches you. I am anxious to know this because of the other letter that is fastened to it. It is essential that this letter should be delivered so answer me as soon as you can.

LETTER

XXVII

I did not answer your last letter because I thought you had fled from the plague[1] as you said you would, but from the letter I received today I gathered that you are still in Florence. I am glad that you have finished Marcellinus and should be gladder still if you would send me the book for I shall give it to the Pope[2] myself. I am astonished that he has been so impatient in asking for it. I have received the mattress and it pleases me immensely for it is most beautifully made and big enough and, what is more important, not very expensive. I had written to Nicolaus to tell you if you had not left to have another one made a little thicker. This one is a little bit thin, especially in such cold weather, and I am extremely grateful to you for it. When I have received the Marcellinus, I shall let you know.

As for my taxes, for I must use a trite and homely word, say nothing more about them. That remarkable man Laurentius de Ridolfis[3] tells me that I can very easily be defended, since I have received a benefice,[4] and that that is the best way and no danger is connected with it. But I shall have to come to attend to those matters myself for I see no other way for it to be done, but I do not know when that will be. So far we have not been able to elicit anything for certain as to whether or not we are to come to the Council; some say no and some say yes and so far "the case is before the court."[5] If we go in your direction I shall betake myself to you at once. And now you shall have the

Petronius for you may know this was the cause of the delay: I
had decided to bring it with me but we are always hung "uncertain of what the fates will bring or where they will let us
settle."[6] If I had thought we should be here so long I should
have sent Petronius to you long ago, and I am not even sending
him now because I am still hoping to bring him with me but in a
few days we shall know for certain.

I am sorry that our Nicolaus has suffered so over the deaths of
those men; one must not muse too long over what can in no way
be foreseen, like death. If Laurentius' books come up for sale,
I think they will bring high prices. But please, if there is anything good to be had at a reasonable price, be sure that your
Poggius gets something.[7] For I want to prepare a sort of furnish-
ing of books so that some day I may live in peace on it, as I wish.
I should like any sheet from Ptolemy's *Geography* if that can be
done; remember in case it should by chance come up; and also
Suetonius and the other historians, and particularly do not let
slip Plutarch's *Illustrious Men*.[8] But if you cannot find any
breviaries or Bibles forget about them.

You write that you are going to Bibiena;[9] whatever plan you
make, may God show you favor. But I wonder why you do not
rather come to Rome;[10] the air is pure here and there is abundance of everything except wine. You have been saying for thirty
years now that you want to see Rome. There never was a better
time: everything is completely peaceful and quiet; the journey
is safe, the inns are not bad, and the road is easy; besides, what I
think more important, your Poggius is here and, I think, you will
not object to being with him. We shall talk together; day and
night we shall live together; we shall root out every trace of
ancient times; we shall talk about everything under the sun;
Jupiter himself will not be happier than we. Besides I have a
little apartment where you can lodge; you will not have to bring
a lot of things with you. Even if you come naked there is enough
to outfit you; you will not have to bother about anything; I shall
look after everything so that you can be completely free of care.
So decide to come to us and you will not need to seek much
advice. I shall send my mule to meet you at Siena and a horse

too with a servant, who will lead you if you decide upon it. Please, please do come, out of friendship for me. Nothing, Nicolaus, could possibly give me greater pleasure. Oh, what complete flawless delight it would be if Nicolaus and Poggius could be in Rome together. By Heaven, I would rather have one of our gossips than the Papacy.

So change your project and come here, and do not let the distance or the fierceness of the winter frighten you off. You shall have the best horse or mule in the world and it will carry you gently and you shall have a servant to wait on you; what more could you want? I shall come for you myself and bring you here on my back. Send me the answer that you know will please me or rather come yourself. Goodbye and love me.

Please send me Tullius' *Orations* on paper and likewise those that I brought from the monastery at Cluny;[11] for Franciscus Barbarus is treating me badly. Write to him, please, since you sent him the little book. You have a long letter, written with great speed and at night. At Rome, the sixth of November 1423. Tell Nicolaus or the others[12] who pay out money to give those nineteen florins that I sent to be paid to my mother to my brother because my mother cannot come to collect them.

LETTER
XXVIII

I was wondering why it was that after you left I had received no letter from you to tell me what you were doing and where you were; for I never heard anything more about you although I often asked and, furthermore, I could not write to you because I was not sure where to send the letter. I have been on the move too. For when the Curia had betaken itself to Tivoli[1] and many people died there of the plague, and the Pope moreover had hidden himself in a mill somewhere, I decided that life was more important to me than money and retired to Reate.[2] There I spent nearly two months with the utmost peace of mind, with leisure for our books, free from the bustle of civilization. There

I drew up two letters, one to the Archbishop of Crete[3] and the other to the Bishop of Dax.[4] There was also a third letter from Tivoli I had already written to Antonius Luscus.[5] I shall have them all copied and send them to you; not that they are worthy of you but so that while you are reading them (they are really rather long) you will escape a bit from your worries, which indeed oppress you more than they should. For I know that you love not only me myself but also my writings and that you make so much of them that, as often happens with fools whom we encourage in a race by praising them, you may encourage me to write by your praises. It was Caecilius,[6] I believe, who thought he would be satisfied if the good people of Cosenza approved of him; and in the same way, as long as you are satisfied I do not care greatly for anyone else.[7]

But this is too much about the trivial stuff I write. I am so glad you got back safely to Florence.[8] For these are threatening times when whatever loss is avoided should be reckoned as gain.[9] What you write about being troubled by many annoyances makes me sad for your sake, since I should like you to be quiet and free from every anxiety. But believe me: you are not the only one. We are all worried and the whole of life is a burden. The greatest troubles occur precisely where we would least expect them.[10] Yet the fault lies altogether in ourselves; we search them out and hunt for them when they have been hidden. They do not bother us unless we want them to. I measure other people by myself: if I were satisfied with what is my lot, I could live more freely and more honestly and without effort. But now I toil away, concentrating on unnecessary things and looking into a future which will perhaps never occur. As happened to me about my brother:[11] I had thought of getting him a wife and taking care of everything that would be needful to support a family and I was imagining hundreds of other things. God snatched him away from us and cut short all my plans and may He be blessed forever; for He knows perfectly what is right for us and this consoles me. But my mother's[12] loneliness and bereavement torment me, for she is old and wasting away with the wretchedness of a sick woman. This too is hard. I had sent instructions

that my home was to be a refuge for my friends, and many of
them were already thanking me for the hospitality they received; now my home will be abandoned, filthy, and silent. God
be praised; believe me, I am quite upset at being left so alone.
Perhaps it will force me to change my way of living. I am writing
to our Ser Pier to talk with Master Laurentius de Ridolfis about
defending me from paying those taxes of yours in the way he
gave me hope of doing when he was here. I beg you to force him
into answering my questions and also to discuss with him the
matter in this letter, for if there were any hope of my being
defended I should come home to you immediately. I was highly
delighted with your letter but one thing offended me: you
addressed me in the plural.[13] Why have I changed? Or do you
follow a silly impersonal policy? I am just the same as I was;
away with this form of address. At Rome, the fourteenth of
October [1424].

LETTER
XXIX

I have not received any letter from you since I left except
those few little verses which you wrote to me for my cousin
Nicolaus de Uzano.[1] And so I was a little surprised and, to be
truthful, quite cross with you because you wrote me nothing
even about the letters of Cicero which I had begged for Antonius
Luscus.[2] I have never been able to tell him anything definite and
just now I am more uncertain than ever, so please answer. For
I am ashamed when I see Antonius every day and he asks me if
there is news of those volumes of Cicero. But I blame it on your
laziness and shift the blame from myself. I want to ask you
particularly about the Lactantius;[3] complete the job, if you can,
for twelve new florins. Add Nicolaus to the project too and urge
him on, although I am a fool to retain you as a promoter when you
need one yourself. Please write to me as soon as possible
whether you have any works of Petrarch for sale from the library
either of Coluccius[4] or of someone else, and how much they are.

For one of my friends is looking for them and urging me to get them for him. You must help me. Goodbye. In haste. Rome on Easter Eve at night [1425].

LETTER

XXX

I give you leave to discharge a vow for my kinsman Nicolaus de Uzano. At the end it states that as soon as he conveniently can he is to send as a gift to the church of St. James[1] as much as he spends in going back and forth. If he is poor, as you write, he is not obliged to send anything. For it says "as soon as he conveniently can"; and so if there is some inconvenience about it he is not held to it. I tell you this so that you may notify him and the Archbishop[2] also, in whose charge the matter rests, so that they do not attach great importance to those words or think there is an obligation to send the money. Let him commute the vow and set aside the weight of money to be given when the opportune moment arrives. I have drawn from Nicolaus'[3] bank the sum of one ducat and thirty-three coins of Bologna, for that was the total amount. Give my letter to Nicolaus de Uzano and commend me to him, and see that the money is given back to Nicolaus.

Please send me the Lucretius,[4] which will be copied in two weeks and then I shall send it back to you. And this I want especially: send also the little book of Nonius Marcellus,[5] which I sent you along with some other things from Paris, written in ancient script; you will be doing me the greatest kindness. I am copying the *De oratore*,[6] filching free time for myself though with difficulty; but still I have begun and shall finish. Then it is my intention to copy the *Orator* and the *Brutus*. And so send me as soon as possible either your volume, if you have it, or tell our Nicolaus to send me the same book which I once had and not to go back on me in this matter. The bug has bitten me and while the fever is on it helps me and pushes me. If the book comes it will be completed; otherwise it will cool off. Besides I need Cicero's *Letters to Atticus*,[7] which I copied and which our friend Cosmus now has; for the scribe is writing them pretty inaccurately because of the model. I shall quickly correct them if I have this book of Cosmus' and so send it to me. Ask Cosmus for me to let me have the book for a little while; I shall send it safely back to him. Do the same about the Lactantius and the ten books of Livy;[8] do not fall asleep, and answer me, please. Goodbye from Rome, the fourteenth of April [1425]. Do not forget to answer and send the books. Let me know too if there are any books of Petrarch's for sale in Coluccius' library[9] or elsewhere and what they are and how much they are, for a friend of mine has asked me this many times and he must be humored.

LETTER
XXXI

I have now almost finished the *De oratore*. But the *Orator* and the *Brutus*, which I had asked you for, have not yet come. You must want to be looked down on if in such a big city and in such a mass of books you cannot dig up this volume for us. I beg you to see that we have a copy from Nicolaus[1] or someone else; you put the blame on Nicolaus' laziness but I do not know which of you is lazier. However, I shall smart for these things.[2] If you delay I fear that this enthusiasm for copying which I now have will evaporate in the overwhelming heat;[3] believe me it will run off in sweat unless you help me as soon as possible.

Please also see that Cicero's *Letters to Atticus*, which Cosmus[4] has, are sent here; the book has been copied but too incorrectly. I wanted the Lucretius for two weeks and no more but you want to copy that and Silius Italicus, Nonius Marcellus, and Cicero's *Orations* all in one breath; because you talk of everything you will accomplish nothing.[5] I need as soon as possible twenty quaternions of folio measurement, for I hope to have a copyist whom I can tolerate. And so I earnestly beg[6] you to make sure that I have the parchment as quickly as possible and not to waste time over this. Hurry as much as you can; get money from Nicolaus in my name. Give the parchment either to Cosmus or to

Nicolaus,[7] whichever one of them is more ready to send it. Farewell. In haste. Rome, the twelfth of May [1425]. I should like to know what you are doing.

LETTER

XXXII

I am sending you a letter for your Benvenuta[1] which states that the Prior of San Lorenzo[2] can change that womanly vow of hers into some other pious work. I have furthermore had this matter entrusted to the Prior because he is your neighbor; therefore free her from her anxiety. The letter costs little, and I make her a present of it, for I also want to provide a step for her feet so that she may go to heaven. If there is anything she wants, write and it shall be done with the utmost care.

I am sorry that we have been beaten by the stupidest of enemies,[3] but the damage is not to be reckoned so great as the disgrace and shame. If we were falling before the blow of a strong man it would be extremely bad, but to fall to the attack of a weak enemy is the worst of calamities; I would bear our defeat calmly if this were the result of another's valor, not of our own negligence and stupidity. And indeed that proverb is very true that God takes away wisdom from him whom He wishes to destroy.[4] I never would have believed that there was such folly[5] in our rulers whom I see without plan or sense, so that they let everything go to ruin; they care for nothing except graft and profit, which they do not give up even when placed in the greatest danger. I believe that this is arranged by some fate to punish our sins.[6] But if only they alone were suffering who caused this trouble and who now, after giving us the plague,[7] give us no cure. For I take it very hard that we are so subject to the defects of a few wrong-headed men who seek not what is theirs but what belongs to other people that we are a laughing-stock and an object of contempt to all the nations, to such a degree that we are even pointed out. To fall bravely is admirable but to fall with disgrace and dishonor is extreme shame. But the fates will find a way.[8] Take care of yourself and write me what you think about our common affairs. Rome, the last day of May [1425].

XXXIII

You know that Bartholomeus de Bardis,[1] a man very devoted to you and, what I consider important, interested in our work but hemmed in by a host of business responsibilities, can satisfy his desire for study all too little. Sometimes though, he steals a little time for himself which he spends on reading. He is anxious to have some books which may encourage him to study. For you know that those who devote their attention to other men's books generally return their recollection of what they have read along with the books. And so at my persuasion he wants you to buy him a few volumes[2] which will be pleasant and useful. I shall list them. First of all Suetonius and also Terence and Quintus Curtius,[3] all of which I left for sale with your stationer Peter.[4] Add anything that seems good to you; for Bartholomeus is rich and wants books. So do our errand and do not put it off; let the price be what seems best to you. Goodbye and write soon. Rome, the twelfth of June [1425].

XXXIV

I think you know my character well enough to bear it patiently if I ask you for something in haste or if I answer something even while the moon is in eclipse. You know that sometimes I burn so with the desire for something that even haste seems to cause a delay. I asked you first for parchment of folio size; then when I decided to have Cicero's *Orations*[1] copied by my scribe it seemed to me that the volume ought to be bigger on account of the quantity of orations. Therefore I asked for another somewhat

larger size of which I sent you a sheet later which I had forgotten
to enclose in my letter. Besides I looked here for the parchment
and bought fourteen quaternions. And so I can wait for two months
if I have to. The sheets which I bought are as white as can be
found; see that yours as as nice. I still want you to send me
twenty other quaternions. You can send me my Cluny *Orations*[2]
without paper, and please do it. But if our Nicolaus is busy give
the volume to Cosmus[3] to see that it is sent as soon as possible.
If I have the parchment through the whole month of July I shall
think you have done well by me, but if it comes sooner I shall
praise your efficiency.

I have copied the *De oratore.* For a long time now, I should
have liked to copy the *Orator* and the *Brutus* in the same way
both for the public good and for my own; and I wanted to do this
so that I should not spend this noontide asleep but in doing some
more honorable work. Since it cannot be done we shall sleep. I
have gone without that volume for a long time and shall go without it in the future without complaining; say no more about this
matter; I do not want to be a nuisance to anyone or to seem demanding. This I know: if I had anything it would be my friends'
as much as my own for it is shameful for them to want to be thus
solicited for a thing for an honorable use. Write me what orations
are in that volume besides the *Pro Cluentio, Pro Roscio,* and
Pro Murena. Two days ago I discussed the Julius Fronto pretty
carefully with the administrator of the monastery of Monte
Cassino.[4] He promised to send me the book as soon as he went
back if only he could find it; for he says that many disappeared
a few years ago. He asked me for the name of the book and I
shall give it to him before he leaves, and I am sure we shall
have the book. And so understand that I am not sleeping or feed-
ing you with words and an empty promise as others do. If you
send me the Lucretius you will be doing a favor to many people.
I promise you not to keep the book more than one month and
then it will come back to you. Goodbye and love me. I shall train
you in patience as you deserve. Rome, the fourteenth of June
[1425].

LETTER
XXXV

When I read your letter, I see and appreciate your great efforts to carry out my requests.[1] But when I consider the matter itself, I see great negligence for which I do not however blame you except that since you know how slow Nicolaus is you ought to have given the sheets of parchment and the books to Cosmus. For I know that they will take forever to come. I have asked both you and Nicolaus so often for the *Brutus* and the *Orator*, which I should have already copied, and so far nothing has been done about them. If there ever is a time when the situation is reversed I shall give you as good as you give, as a taste of your own medicine. If the Julius Fronto comes, and I do not doubt that it will come unless it is lost, these things shall be brought to Poggius by his own carriers. The parchment which I ordered in folio size I want for transcribing the *Verrine Orations*[2] in one volume and likewise in another volume the *Tusculans* and the *De finibus bonorum et malorum;*[3] I want another set for the *Letters to Atticus.*[4] Now reflect on it and see whether this measure will do for these volumes and make sure that it seems to suit their elegance. If I can keep this secretary from getting away from me it will help me a great deal. For he writes very well and in a script which recalls antiquity and to which I pushed him with the greatest difficulty. But he is from Naples and he is so frivolous that to hold him down I need a millstone. Now please if you come across any books which you think are worthy of me, either buy them or take an option on them until you let me know. Now that I have begun I want to collect myself this property that will be worth more in every age than monetary savings.

Rinucius left us intending to go back to Florence.[5] I know he will go to see you right away. Examine him in your own way. I see Antonius[6] very rarely, for he lives in the Vatican palace in charge of the church and shrines which our gods and goddesses have left to travel to other places. He has a wonderful garden with a flowing fountain[7] and so like Numa[8] he takes counsel with Egeria to give us laws. The place is secluded and suitable for a philosopher or a poet. For orators, as you know, like to be in a crowd, but Antonius, it seems, wants to be a philosopher and so he separates himself from the mob. There is a great deal of talk by our people about the Ligurians,[9] to the effect that it has turned out well, but the majority of our enemies say this is untrue; anyway it seems hard to finish what has been begun. May God favor us but still I am frightened of everything. I devote myself to literature and every day I read something or correct it or improve it, far from the thought of these things which always hurt my ears. Goodbye and do what I ask you, not by letters but by action itself. Rome, the twenty-third of June [1425].

LETTER

XXXVI

You write me about Nicolaus' slowness and negligence; they are nothing new. I should rather be surprised if he changed his habits; they have not only hardened but become like rock. He is a little more diligent in exactly those things where it is the greatest kindness to be very negligent; as for his friends, not only does he not put them in second place but they do not even come last. But as the man is, we must put up with him. That is why I have asked you again and again to give my orations to Cosmus,[1] who is generally more careful in looking after his friends. For his kindness is such that he would long ago have sent us the book although he himself also seemed to be doubtful about the letters of Cicero which I wanted. I do not know what to blame, unless me myself since perhaps I ask more of my friends than is right. But I measure other men's spirits by my own. I ought to have been a king, then most certainly I would scorn those stupidities of yours, for they must not be called by a name more serious, and throw them aside and crush them. And I do not blame you in any way, but your slow deliberation, your immense delays to speak freely, your scornful or perhaps rather lazy disregard. What is the point of this, what good can it do among friends except to destroy whatever good will there is? I have asked, I have begged, I have pleaded so urgently for the book from Nicolaus[2] for more than two months; and I would already have copied it if he had been at all considerate about it but perhaps it is a terrific effort to send it.

But enough of this; for granted that I write fasting, yet these things move me to speak to you as I am used to doing. The other day several mule drivers came, and your little package lies at the door. I think it fears summer and will wait for the autumn. If it comes some day, I shall meet it on the road with fasces and with a litter; but take care that meantime it sleeps in feathers, so that it does not desert on the way. I said Rinucius[3] was on his way to you, not that he was coming back, and so whether he went of his own accord or because he was sent, he did not come back. It was not right for me to write more fully. Please give his letter to Ser Loisio.[4] Farewell, Rome, the seventh of July [1425].

LETTER
XXXVII

The letter I received from you the other day needs a short reply. That I have paid the dues of the city some twenty-three years now, the books of the Camera bear witness. After the first census was made in 1400 I was enrolled in them and have always paid my taxes since then, although generally one third. If you need a witness for this, see that our friend, Ser Pier, informs you so that you can satisfy Cosmus and the rest.[1] As for the Pliny[2] of the Bishop of Winchester which you ask for, it is indeed in old script but with a French flavor, for you know what we mean by the French form. And yet in some ways it seems better. But it is far from being written in what we usually call *lettera antica*. I cannot vouch for the quality of its corrections; for granted that in a certain part which I have read it has been corrected, it is still possible that the rest is corrupt. And so I neither persuade you nor dissuade you; because of the merchant-men[3] which are said to go there every year it is easy to get the book without any expense. There will be no loss in this affair.

About the Monte Cassino, that is the Julius Fronto, I go on fretting, but it is remarkable how few go there or come from there to us. Still I shall be as diligent as the circumstances allow.

About Antonius,[4] who has died, I wrote you nothing because we both began to be sick as the same time; when I had recovered I went to visit him in Matthaeus de Bardis'[5] house where he had been taken from the Apostolic Palace.[6] As soon as I saw him I began to wonder what would be the outcome of his illness and, contrary to the doctors' opinions, I was always doubtful of his recovery.[7] I did not write about this to you so that if it were true, I would not be the author of sad news; or if it were false, I would not seem frivolous and silly. And so I kept silent, awaiting the outcome,[8] which I always suspected would be unhappy. However I am speaking of his body, for as to his soul, it left this life like those which go of their own free will, not those which are pushed. The last day on which he talked a little I did not see him, so that I would not distress him by my tears, which I could not have held back. These doctors had so weakened him that in a little while he went out gradually like a candle.

I want to have parchment for the *Verrines*[9] and the *Philippics*. Please send it as soon as possible. This secretary of mine,[10] to whom I have taught the old style of writing with great effort, is a Neapolitan. When I write this consider him the filthiest sort of man with the worst possible habits, for you know that nothing so shameful can be thought of but that it matches the life of those men. He is the very dregs of the earth, and the whole tribe is like a sink of all forms of iniquity. And so I stand his wicked-ness unwillingly, but I have decided to endure everything until he has finished this job of speeches for private persons. But I even doubt if he finishes it, he is so careless, frivolous, and quarrelsome. But I have another one, an untrained Frenchman; I shall use him. Farewell, in haste, at night. Rome, the eighteenth of August [1425].

LETTER
XXXVIII

I am glad if you are well; I hope to get well myself. This whole week I have had something wrong with my right eye, which had long since begun to water, I think because I caught a cold in it. On the advice of a physician who seemed to know about this ailment and who said that he had already cured many people, I put some kind of water into my eye, and this so affected it that the fluid seemed not to trickle out of it but to flow back into it. And so for several days I have been leading an epicurean life, living on bread and water and likewise barley.[1] Epicurus would gladly have received me at a banquet in his gardens, where he used to promise his guests water and barley, claiming that they would do very well with him on that kind of food.[2] Besides this I have had my back rubbed continually and have used what they call a cupping glass to draw liquid out of my head. And today I have taken a mild laxative, not to clear out my body but to clear out the material that is already liquid. Therefore tonight there seems to be a slight improvement in my eye, for before dinner I had a slight fever, either because my body was upset by the novelty of my diet or by the rubbing or by the cramps which have tormented me all day long since I took the laxative. Still I hope to throw it off very easily. I have been dictating this to my secretary after dinner in the third hour of the evening to avoid sleeping. For I could not only not write myself but not even see air.[3]

But enough of this. Please attend to the parchment and the *Philippics* as soon as you can; I have asked you for them too often already. I wish you would tell our friend Nicolaus for me that I have received his letter but that as far as I know the servant has not come and that if he had come, I could not have done what he asks. However I expect to be well again very soon and then I hope to finish the business. I have written Ser Loisio[4] to get me a little fennel. When he took the money from Nicolaus' bank I do not doubt that he bought it. Please be sure to have it sent to me as soon as possible; I shall be very much pleased. Goodbye and love me as you always do. At Rome, the first of September [1425].

XXXIX

I know that you were quite worried by my last letter, which was written by my secretary. On the strength of this letter I want you to abandon all your concern,[1] if you felt any, for I have recovered from a very nasty illness, and both my eyes and the rest of my body are perfectly well again, except for my mouth where I have lost a molar. As a matter of fact, it had to be pulled out, such was the violence of my cold. I do not know what to ask you for except to take care of the parchment as soon as possible and also of the book which I have asked for so many times and likewise of the fennel which I asked for most recently.

I think Antonius' books[2] ought to be sold unless he decided otherwise. If there are any, and I think there ought to be many which would suit me, please put them aside insofar as seems proper and do not put anyone ahead of me. Granted that you know many people who are much richer than I am, I do not admit that there is anyone fonder of you than your Poggius, and so you ought to satisfy me in this very honorable wish. Tully asks Atticus[3] to buy him certain books and, as the most learned of all men, says that he wants to prepare a fortress for his old age. If a man so learned and of such great wisdom sought this protection most avidly amid so great a supply of books and asked for them so often that he seemed to want nothing more, what ought I to do who am a poor man with no wit, in this famine and lack of books, especially of my own? Therefore arise while there is still an opportunity and fetch me something from this treasury, even if there should be "five score bronze gates, five score of massy steel."[4] There is nothing now that I want more, and so if you want to do something to please me very much do this and you have blessed me indeed. For I feel age creeping on,[5] "sickness comes creeping on, and dolorous eld,"[6] for which I need the solace of the kind of belongings which are better than any doctor's remedies. For sometimes doctors do not cure the body, whereas this always cures the soul. Farewell and love me, in haste at Rome, the eighth of September [1425]. — Since the mail carrier had not departed on his usual day my letters remained at home through his negligence, for I am a long way from the merchants, but whenever they are delivered I hope that you will be glad of them. Farewell, give this letter to Ser Angelus for my mother[7] and ask him to see that it is so carried that it is delivered to my mother for it is important that she should get it.

LETTER
XL

I have found out from your two letters to me about Antonius' books. What a stupid thing to do, to thrust that treasure into a place where it will do no good. I cannot think what his purpose was to establish Greek books among those two-legged donkeys who do not even know a word of Latin.[1] He did not dedicate them to the Muses but to dust and worms; I believe he was afraid that someone might enjoy them. Yet unless he forbade the sale of them in his will, they will I think have an auction soon for reasons of avarice or ignorance. You write that you have found the tragedies for sale, you think for seven gold pieces, and the *De officiis*. Indeed I have long wanted the tragedies myself, and so if it seems to you that the money would be well spent on them, please buy them for me. But try to get the *De officiis* for Bartholomeus, who wrote some time ago to Cosmus or rather to his bankers to give you the money which you were asking for; ask Nicolaus for the money for the tragedies. See about the Lactantius too[2] and what can be done about it; and if anything else comes to hand which you think would be nice for us, attend to it yourself and do not wait for another order.

Some time we shall dig Julius Frontinus from that field at

Cassino, but it is hard to rouse our barbarians to take an interest in anything except money. If I had been alert when the man who brought us the Severus[3] was going there, he would have brought us both authors, for he was that brother who was with the Cardinal of Piacenza[4] and he did not tell me he was going before he went. This kind of man is rarely seen, unless he needs something or is begging. But I am stirring Angelottus[5] and I do not give up the hope that we shall get the book shortly. A man from the Monastery of Cluny will leave the Curia very shortly; he has become a friend of mine through my own efforts and promised to take care to have the Tertullian[6] copied and undertook to do it. I have hopes that he will do something because he needs my help; still he is a monk but he does not seem in the least bad; he has some education and knows the book. When I discussed the payment and promised that it would be at hand wherever he wished he said that he did not want money at all; for he has undertaken the whole job and indeed apparently willingly. Time will show what he is like. I am waiting for the parchment; see that I get it even if it is bad, provided that it is soon. I am writing to my mother to see to the Trebiano which you ask for. See that she gets the letters quickly before she leaves, for she is coming to visit me after the vintage, and so send her the letters and at the same time see to the wine. Farewell, at Rome, the twenty-eighth of September [1425].

LETTER
XLI

Yesterday I received the little bag containing the parchment, the *Philippics* and the tragedies, along with the fennel, most of which I have already given to my friends. The parchment suits me perfectly, but please be sure that I get the rest for the *Verrines* for I am going to begin them next week. Also finish the quinternions which I wrote some time ago and do not be so nasty to the artisans that they get angry with you. Let them be a little better than the ordinary quality, and that is enough for me since it cannot be made any differently. The tragedies are beautiful but seem to me a little too expensive. Any cost above six florins is burdensome. I believe I shall turn them over to our friend Bartholomeus,[1] who indeed has more money than Poggius and is greedier. I have been trying hard to get the book from Monte Cassino; if my messenger were efficient we would perhaps root it out. Goodbye, and love me as usual. Rome, October the nineteenth [1425].

LETTER

XLII

Nicolai mio gentile tu se' un sodo,[1] *et un marochiuto pedante;* and this is the theme of my letter. The one which I received from you yesterday full of surprise that I should think that you paid too much for the tragedies I read with amusement and pleasure. Why, kindest of men, should you think that I should indeed have so lost my taste because I said that those tragedies[2] seemed expensive to me? I did not say that they were expensive but that they seemed so *for me,* considering them not for their own value but for my resources; but if what I said displeases you I shall recant, although you are altogether too tyrannical in wishing me to agree so completely with your opinions that you not only leave me no judgment but not even free power of appraisal. Are you not fierce,[3] as our friend Terence said, because you have authority among the instructors of youth who bow to you and do not dare to utter a word unless prescribed. Please see whether the moon was in Capricorn[4] when you got my letter, for every letter contained nothing but appreciation and proper complaint. I like the book and have no desire to send it back. I said that perhaps I would turn it over to Bartholomeus. I approve of your judgment in details and praise it but in such a way that I may also have some opinion of my own,[5] even some feelings. You know that our judgment agrees on most things, though, and in this mine will not be far from yours.

I have answered the first section of your letter; but before I go

on to the rest please, dear Nicolaus, address me like a well-
educated person and do not insist on being foolish on this one
subject, insulting both me and your own training. Keep this
nonsense for those fancy names and address me in the singular
as you used to, for I am just the same as I was and I hope no
worse. I am awfully pleased that you bought the parchment that
you mention. Truly nothing would have pleased me more than if
you had sent it and the Spartianus[6] as soon as possible for I had
asked you to. For since my copyist had finished Justin[7] the other
day, today he began the *De finibus*,[8] but after this we shall go
back to the histories and then to Seneca. I am glad that you have
got the money from Nicolaus and praise your careful thrift, for I
am now beginning to swim in a drought. There is no water and
my thirst for books is increasing. Julius Frontinus is not to be
found at the monastery at Monte Cassino. For the man to whom
we entrusted the errand wrote us that he had looked for the book
for a long time but could not find it at all; this is of little importance; we shall fish elsewhere. I have written often for the
books which I left in England, but I am not sure whether I shall
have them through the services of one of our merchant ships.
For Alexander, with whom they were left, has tricked me badly
in more important things; may the gods destroy him utterly.
Martial's *Epigrams*[9] are also very incorrect and in a hand that is
not at all old; you will make no money out of that.

My copyist about whom I wrote you will be with me until he
finishes the *Verrines*,[10] which he will begin in three weeks. For
now I am making him rewrite the first four quaternions of the
Orations, and I am putting the *Verrines* last because the lettering
does not please me. You have almost all the news, but I am keeping the honey for the last. A friend of mine, who is a monk[11] from
a monastery in Germany and who left us lately, sent me a letter
which I received three days ago. He writes that he has found
several volumes of the kind you and I like which he wants to
exchange for the *Novella* of Joannes Andreae[12] or for both the
Speculum and its supplements, and he sends the names of the
books enclosed in the letter. The *Speculum* and the supplements[13] are volumes of great value; so see if you think the exchange should be made. Among these volumes are Julius

Frontinus and several works of Cornelius Tacitus still unknown to us. You will see the inventory and find out whether these law books can be bought for a decent price. The books will be deposited in Nuremberg where the *Speculum* and supplements ought also to be taken; it is easy to bring books from there as you will see from the inventory. This is a selection; there are many other books. For he writes in this vein. As you asked me to mark the poets for you to choose those you would like from the list I have found many from which I chose some which you will find on the enclosed inventory.[14] Dear Nicolaus, write to me as soon as you can what to answer him so that everything may be done according to your judgment; I care for only a few things, which you will see for yourself. Goodbye, I have written this in great haste. Rome, the third day of November [1425]. — Tell Nicolaus[15] as soon as possible not to send his copy of the *De finibus* because I have found one, and the one which I am getting ready will be finished before his comes. So your affairs go stumbling on.

LETTER

XLIII

Even if there is nothing in your letter which I think particularly requires an answer I shall answer you briefly for the pleasure of talking to you. I see a lot of Rinucius so as to learn something from him about the things which I learned long ago and which now have entirely escaped me. I go to see him whenever I am through with my work to read the *Gorgias* and to hear him read. But there is one difficulty: the distance between places. He himself lives near St. Peter's and I near the Anthium,[1] and so it is seldom that I meet him except when I go home, which is difficult, for the Pope lives on the Esquiline Hill, where the Church of Santa Maria Maggiore is. And so I get something done with great effort, but I do not stop pestering him. Not long ago I did not know him, but he seems very kind; I admire his learning but it is greater in Greek[2] than in Latin. Whatever others may say stick to your own way. When I get there we shall talk more about him; I want you to remember this about me, that I do not always say what I feel; but I try to please the hearers sometimes and to think it kind to be more apt to praise than to blame where one will not hurt anybody.

The books which I used to have in England I have arranged to have sent to me, and those and any others I may have I want here with me. But books from Monte Cassino cannot be got without trouble, for we ought to find a learned man to go there. But where is there one? However I shall be on the watch if any opportunity presents itself.

Nicolaus Bildeston,[3] doctor of laws, ambassador of the King of England, is a very pleasant man and a very great friend of mine, for we both served the same master and were inevitably together. He is anxious to have some of Petrarch's books;[4] please try to dig something up for us that he can take with him. He will buy them no matter what the price; but please take care that he is not cheated; at the same time perhaps he will buy a *History of the Emperors*.[5] Whatever he asks of you, please do your best for him; that will give me the greatest pleasure. Treat him as if he were your Poggius, in his desires.

Next month I think I shall go to you so as to pay my debts; if I cannot do it otherwise, I shall have an auction or some other bold measure, for I see that this difficulty will go on too long and will not come to an end unless the fates decree it. But there is much to be feared, if you make your forecast on the basis of many points which I think about and which fill me with dread. But here I stop. If possible my sins shall be purged elsewhere than in Florence in paying my debts. Goodbye and write me what you feel and what you yourself think of public affairs. Rome, the twentieth of November 1425.

LETTER

XLIV

I wrote you long ago a dispatch full of fury and with perfect justice, that you are such a slowcoach where my business is concerned. For if my copyist had waited for your parchment he would have had a long holiday, but at last it came and I am pleased. I could wish that there were more leaves of folio size, for no book can be completed in only nine quaternions. I would like another nine or ten but you need not hurry much about them; if you are not only slow but skip this errand completely, I do not care much. The rest of the sheets are somewhat larger (I mean the second lot) than those you first sent for the *Verrines* and so I shall keep those sheets and add the rest to the *Verrines* and the parchment from this city too. I know you went to a lot of trouble to get this parchment; and you have such beautiful manners and the other men with whom the matter must be handled are so ill mannered. If you come upon any sheets for a larger volume, buy them for me but do not hurry too much. I shall not ask you for anything more except to do my errands little by little, step by step. Many people hate to hurry but I hate delay and waiting.

But that is enough. I approve highly of the treaty made between us[1] and the Venetians; but many say that our dignity is inadequately protected in it, especially since the decision to make peace depends on them, so that we have to accept the terms which they decide to give and at their time. But if that were so, I should prefer to fall honorably than to stand disgracefully. I want to know the conditions of the peace;[2] please write them to me when you can and when they are published.

I like your description of your Sicilian friend;[3] those people are very observant and versatile and clever. If he writes me something I shall gladly answer him: you know my practice. I wish I could be as generous with money as with letters into which I put little effort and less expenditure; then the burdens of the war would not be so heavy on you.

I have sent our friend two letters about the books even by different couriers, and besides I ordered that when the letters got to Nuremberg they be taken to the monastery by someone who should bring back an answer. I have arranged to pay for this and so I hope that we shall know something more certain very soon. That prior at Cluny gave me his name, which I have lost; it was written on a scrap of paper. I cannot find anyone who knows it; this prevents my writing to him.

Now pay attention to what I write from here on. Please when you write to me stop telling me about the Princes,[4] and do not say anything which, in case your letter should somehow get into strange hands, could offend someone, I mean my superiors. For you can talk to me as to yourself, but I fear other people. As Demosthenes,[5] I think, used to say, he heard nothing more willingly than voices which praised him; by the same token some men bear nothing worse than criticism of themselves, which must be avoided, especially among those who can take reprisals. Goodbye, in haste, the fifteenth of December [1425].[6]

After I had written this and also several verses to Nicolaus, the desire came over me to write something to your Sicilian, whom you recommend to me in your letter; and so on the same impulse I seized my pen and scratched out a few lines, which I am sending to you. Copy the letter and send it to him; it will be enclosed in this one, for it is late now and I have other things to do. I have written as the spirit moved me; if anything seems to you too foolish, hold it back.

LETTER

XLV

I wrote you in my last letter that I was going to England,[1] but shortly afterwards the project broke up and indeed by my efforts. So I am free of this burden or at least I hope so. I do not wonder that you have done nothing about my affairs and have not written to me since you expected me. As for Nicolaus,[2] since he is not only slow by nature but also has to attend to his own affairs, I do not blame him but I do not commend him much either. I asked him many months ago now to buy my property so that it would be free from future extortion but I have never been able to find out his intentions, and he always answers me like a Sibyl.

Write me please what you think I should do. If you think anything worthwhile could be done in my absence, I should be delighted, since then I should escape both the bother of a trip on horseback and also the expense. If the future tax did not exceed the severity of the past one I would come to the assistance of my country to the extent of my estate and I would not refuse the burden, since I hear that this levy will last only a year; but if it is more, I shall not pay a cent.[3] For I am a clergyman and have a benefice but no inheritance whatever.[4] So look around and see how this burden can be avoided. Take counsel as it seems best; then advise me as to what you think should be done as soon as possible and pay no attention to Nicolaus; see that you do what is right for you to do for Poggius. I do not know whom to get to plead for me if you fail me. Consider whether it seems a good idea for you to talk to the officials[5] charged with this business, but if you are in any doubt take Master Rinaldus de Albizis[6] with you to speak on my behalf, for he knows that I cannot possibly do any harm; ask him for me if you need him; I do not think he will refuse this task. Consider the time and the whole affair and write me so that I may follow your advice.

I have had an answer from Germany; that letter was delivered, so I hope to have a letter from the monk in a few days and then I shall write you everything. I have sent you your *Verrines;* I have kept only the *Orations,* so as to avoid the repeated inconvenience of fetching and carrying back the books. Everything will be bound here. The copying of the history of Spartianus has already begun. I asked you once before for the works of Seneca; please take care that I get a copy. I remember that there was a volume of the works of Seneca among Coluccius' books.[7] I do not know whether Leonardus Aretinus has it; write me where it is and what is in it. At least be sure you answer this letter as quickly as possible. Take care of yourself, Rome, the eighth of February [1426].

LETTER

XLVI

I have received your letter which I have been awaiting eagerly for a long time and which gave me the greatest pleasure. I shall send you this short answer although you wrote me a long letter because I am waiting to see you and to talk to you directly. O what fun it will be to have you here! What talks we shall have! What discussions of all sorts of things![1] I feel as though I were talking to you already and hearing and answering your well-known voice.[2] Cosmus has been with us here, and he is a good advance guard for you.[3] He gave me convincing hope that you would be here shortly[4] for he assured me that if you had not been hindered by the severity of the winter[5] which, as you are a beginner, discouraged you, you would have come with him. But he does not doubt that it is your intention to come as soon as you can.

I have taken a little lodging next to yours, to which you may go so that you can be alone with her.[6] You will have a good room either alone or with her and she will rub your feet if you are tired. You cannot help but come belatedly, even if you come immediately, for all things are ready.[7] If I know of your approach ahead of time I shall meet you on the road. Cosmus promises you horses and a servant if you need them and your Poggius will be on the spot. You shall have a mule[8] or a horse which will carry you gently and not shake you, so that even on horseback you will be free of all care.[9]

There is no plague for you to fear; the air is perfectly pure. In that flood of barbarians, when a little while ago everything was weighed down by their disgusting smell, a few people died and no wonder for they filled the city with impurity, ordure, filth, and lice. But now that the Jubilee[10] is over, everyone is in very good health, and there is not only no plague but not even the faintest suspicion of any.[11] For if there were any danger, I am not such a fool as to invite you to a place of sickness and so make us see that you are not only on your way but flying to us. Leave off your delays and reconsiderations and shake yourself free not only of sluggishness but of softness. It is like a weak woman not to be able to bear cold or heat either. Make a trial[12] *di cotesto tuo guidalesco e vedi come regge a martello* [of your guide and see how he reacts to the hammer]. Lent is upon us; the time is of the best for the city and so see to it that you come and do not look for company for that is a source of delay. We are waiting for you with the greatest impatience. See that you do not disappoint us for I should declare perpetual war on you without truce. Goodbye and expect an answer to your letter when you get here. Rome, the twelfth day of February [1426].[13]

LETTER

XLVII

I shall at least answer briefly the letter which I received from you after a long silence when I was outside the city in Castellum Pontificis.[1] And first as to what I think has been put in place of an introduction: you criticize me for giving dinner parties and spending money on them. My, how I laughed at your foolishness, for I would rather call it that than ignorance, for measuring me by your own interests and for believing rumors. There came into my mind this remark of Terence's: "There is nothing more unjust than an ignorant man; he thinks nothing is right unless he does it too."[2] You cannot criticize me if I invite my friends and guests to dinner; truly that is an old and well-worn custom and I have never heard or read of its being held a vice. If perhaps the expense bothers you or the provisioning of the feasts, do not limit another's style of entertaining to suit your own stinginess.[3] Be content with your little pound of sausage; receive your friends with whatever economy pleases you; keep your money for taxes and sweat over them because you cannot escape them; I shall stop when I want to. I consider the merits of those whom I entertain, and I do not satisfy merely myself but their reputation which is more important. I could not however entertain you[4] both because my house was inadequate and I myself was like a stranger and new in the city, poor and lacking in everything. But what you pretend about my procuring fennel to excite thirst, I think you said as a joke.

I shall say no more about the books from Germany except that unlike you I am not asleep but awake. But hopefully if the man I count on keeps his promise, the book will come to us either by force or willingly.[5] Even so I have made an effort to have an inventory of one of the very old monasteries in Germany where there is a large collection of books, but I shall not tell you any more so that you will not annoy me with your sarcasm. If you want to have the Spartianus, see that I have the Aulus Gellius[6] and twenty quinternions of parchment, folio size, and if they are not white, it does not matter. Send me the Lucretius too,[7] which I should like to see for a little while. I shall send it back to you. See that I have the parchment as soon as possible or else write that you either will not or cannot get it, for I shall get it elsewhere. Please tell Nicolaus to send me the copy of the *Gallic* and *Civil Wars*,[8] which he has in my handwriting; I want to have it copied again. I shall take great care of the book, but let him not postpone it forever. There is need of some dispatch, so please answer this too. Please send me also the Cato and Varro *On Agriculture*.[9] Answer if the moon be not in Capricorn. Goodbye, at Rome in haste, September the twelfth [1426].

LETTER

XLVIII

Bartholomeus de Bardis[1] has told me, for I have not had a word from you, that you have patched up your friendship with Leonardus Aretinus;[2] and although I would have preferred to have heard it from you, still I was terribly glad to hear even from someone else what you knew I had been longing for. For you know how often, how carefully, and at what length I discussed this reconciliation with you; nothing could please me more than it does. I discussed it with Leonardus, too, when I saw him, and when he was away I urged him by letter[3] to forget the past and to show you his former good will. I am properly delighted that this has been accomplished through your willingness and through the efforts and eagerness of Franciscus Barbarus,[4] both for your sakes and indeed for my own, since I was a friend to each of you and since I was quite worried lest I should offend one or the other when I had wanted to keep the friendship of both. Please, dear Nicolaus, and it is not in accordance with your wisdom that I should advise you, do everything you can to make this reconciliation last and, while it can be done, to renew your former friendship with Leonardus, so that this disagreement of yours may seem a restoring of affection.[5] You know what your age demands, as well as literature and learning. We must endeavor to make our reading about learned men and the precepts of the wise do us some good in life, so that, as the Apostle says, we shall not be revealed as mere hearers of the word but doers of it.[6]

But I am teaching my grandmother.[7] Good will drives me to write this, and I would have written more if I were not afraid either to wish to teach a great scholar or to distrust your good sense.[8] I am quite surprised that Bartholomeus says you are offended by the last letter I wrote to you and are annoyed at something I wrote too freely, but if the error was mine, you ought to have borne it calmly as is suitable for a friend and to have mentioned it to me or if I made no mistake it is unworthy of you to get angry. If however there is something which is biting you, see whether the fault is yours for I take my cue from you. When you read my letter, please remember also what you wrote yourself, and if you joke realize that I may be joking too. But if you make a charge, I demand that you allow me to defend my case before you as judge and prosecutor; pay a little attention to your own language and see if I have answered you crossly in any way. For you have said, objecting that I did not write to you, that I was busy giving parties like the English,[9] and then you add that this was what came of my studying. If I were another Zucharus,[10] fastening my mind and brain upon food and cookshops, or one who practiced cookery, neglecting all other occupations,[11] or if, like that fellow Gnato,[12] I were followed by poulterers, fishmongers, fowlers, and all sorts of pastry cooks, what more could you throw at a man who for a long time has shown no aversion to the study of literature, except that this is the result of his studies?[13] If you speak your mind freely to me (and you are welcome to) do not entirely deny me the right of free speech, but let us write these things to each other for amusement or the exercise of our wit.[14]

This is not the first letter in which I stirred you up, nor do I think it will be the last. However, if you wish to establish a law for me as to how far I may go in my letters, you may do so as far as I am concerned; I shall obey you and shall compose my letters according to your regulations,[15] unless perhaps you want me to become a sycophant. Here I shall disagree with you and not stick to any rule,[16] and I would rather keep silence than lie. I used to think your ears burned when you heard certain subjects, but they are more delicate than glass. Have you not known me to my very fingertips,[17] as they say? Do you not know that I may do what I please in your company and you in mine? And what would our friendship be if you could not stand me or I you? What if we had to weigh every word between us as if we were strangers? Go ahead and write, swear, rage, thunder, and shout all you want; I shall laugh when I see you wrought up. Do you believe that I lay a great deal of importance on how you behave? You are entirely wrong.[18] Why, you ask, do you reply so sharply? To talk to you, to excite you, to shake you up so as not to be silent myself, for I prefer to send you a rather harsh letter than none at all; besides, to show you that you have in me a pupil in your own kind of snappishness so that you will not think that you alone are skillful in this line.

But this is too much on a trifling subject. See that I have the books which I asked you for and the paper too and especially the Aulus Gellius. I shall truly be very pleased if you send the Cornelius Tacitus;[19] if you do so, I shall return your Spartianus; I ask you for this very insistently. Tell Leonardus Aretinus[20] not to forget to send me the works of Seneca as soon as possible, for the Epistles have already been copied; the rest are waiting, which I have in an uncorrected edition. Please ask Nicolaus too to send the *Gallic* and *Civil Wars,* which he has in my handwriting; I have written to ask him for them but I get no answer. Goodbye and answer me even if you are angry, for then your letters bring me the greatest pleasure. Rome, the twenty-first of October [1426].

LETTERS
XLIX

I had told our friend Cosmus, just as you write, that that monk from Hersfeld[1] had told someone that he had brought an inventory of more books according to my list. Afterward when I questioned the man thoroughly he came to me bringing the inventory, full of words and empty of matter. He is a good man but ignorant of our studies, and he thought that whatever he found that was unknown to him would be unknown to us too and so he crammed it with books which we have, the same books as you have known elsewhere. However I am sending you the part of his inventory which describes the volume of Cornelius Tacitus[2] and of other authors whom we lack; since these are short little texts, they must not be considered of great importance. I have given up the great hope which I had built on his promises; that is the reason why I did not make a particular effort to write you this, for if there had been anything unusual or worthy of our wisdom, I should not only have written to you but have flown to you to tell you about it in person. This monk is in need of money; I have discussed helping him, provided only that he gives me for this money the Ammianus Marcellinus,[3] the first Decade of Livy, and one volume of the *Orations* of Cicero, to mention works we both have, and quite a few others, which although we have them, are not to be disdained. I asked furthermore that they be carried at his risk as far as Nuremberg.[4] This I am handling. I do not know how it will turn out; however you will find it all out from me in due course.

I am surprised at what you write, that you suspect that I am hiding works which were in the inventory so that they may not be known. How did this get into your mind, when you have known me to my very fingertips?[5] Would I ever wish to hide anything from you? Have you not always had a share not only in all my actions but even in all my thoughts? Do you not know that nothing good is fun to own without a friend to share it? Get rid of the idea that I should want anything not to be public property that was written for public enjoyment. Bartholomeus de Montepolitiano is exerting himself to get us the Lucretius;[6] if he succeeds, we shall start on other things later. For now we must not try to handle other books for fear that in seeking many, we may give them the opportunity of refusing us this one. We must go little by little, for they are barbarians and full of suspicion. Since I asked this Nicolaus of Trier[7] many questions about Pliny's *History,* he has added to the volumes which he told me he possessed a fairly big one of Pliny's *Histories.* Then when I told him to make sure it was not the *Natural History,* he said that he had seen that book too and had read it but that it was not the one about which he had talked, for it contained the German wars. How much he is to be believed I shall judge when what he mentioned about Cicero's *De republica* and the other volumes comes to light. So far I neither despair nor do I trust in his words for he is learned and, it seems to me, neither overtalkative nor overmendacious. I hear that he will return to his country soon and then will come back to the Curia. Then we shall know everything more accurately. There is a letter from a friend of his to whom he gave the responsibility of sending the books, saying that he had sent them to Frankfurt, so that from there they might be taken to Venice.[8] And so indeed our expectations will quickly produce either something to be used or to laugh at.

I would have sent you the Propertius,[9] but after I came home somebody or other came here and was leafing through my books; when he came upon it, he asked me to lend it to him for a few days to read. But he has not brought the book back, and I completely forget who he was. At least when I ask all my friends: "I say, have you my Propertius?" they deny it one by one. I fear therefore that the good poet has emigrated, and since the man is a rascal he did not want to live in a chaste household.[10] But if he comes back, I shall see to it that he is not ashamed to live with me and that he shall have no reason to go away.

I am waiting for the Valerius Flaccus,[11] the Pedianus, and the Varro,[12] which perhaps I shall copy unless you put it off until the winter. When Cosmus and I went to see the gate we found no inscriptions; for that temple which they are tearing down[13] to get the lime is without inscription but there is an inscription on the

Via Ostia[14] near the river bank which I sent you another time; it is on a certain tomb made entirely of marble on which the fasces are carved too. For you received all the inscriptions from Tivoli from me some time ago. Our Cosmus belongs to the Board of Ten; he has a big job and no leisure.[15] I would prefer that it were at another time when he might have put up some opposition to these robbers; now I do not see what good he can do except to watch the accounts, since other men have charge of running the war. Give him my greetings. Goodbye, Rome, the fifteenth of May [1427].[16] Then give my regards too to Brother Ambrosius and to Laurentius and Carolus.[17] I am waiting for the parchment and the books, though you are a little on the slow side. One of my two copyists is idle because of you; please hurry, for time is slipping by which is particularly good for writing, and this bothers me.

LETTER
L

You were quite right in suspecting that when I sealed the letter I forgot the inventory which I had mentioned in it. Now I am sending it to you. But you misunderstand when you think that while I am attending to getting us the Decade of Livy[1] and the rest of the volumes about which I wrote you, I left out the one book which we especially need and which indeed I want most of all. Indeed I have sent word to that same monk either to bring it with him, for he thinks he is coming back soon, or to have it brought by another monk; I ordered the others taken to Nuremberg[2] but this one to come directly to Rome, and he undertook to do it.

Nicolaus of Trier is being so badly treated that he is ashamed and sorry that he came to the Curia; for he has obtained nothing from the Pope, so that he is furious and leaving both us and our books. So the times go; still he will be asked to give at least the *De republica*[3] back to Italy. I alone wanted to send someone to Germany to have the books brought here but those people say no who are in a position to say no and ought to say yes.

Propertius[4] has come back to me; I shall send him to you as soon as somebody appears who will carry him. Your paper is asleep and my scribe has been on his vacation for a long time now through your diligence. I believed you and contrary to custom I put this new burden on you; if I had ever believed you, the paper would have been here long ago and still you write so often that it will be sent tomorrow. I shall deal with our book and paper when it pleases you, for this man would be idle for a year if I waited upon your carelessness. Goodbye, at Rome, the thirty-first of May [1427].

LETTER
LI

I laughed heartily at the last bit of your letter in which you apologize for what you had written about gluttony[1] and about some other more obscure thing which cannot be expressed in Latin unless we are willing to call it "coitus." You do not seem to me to recall the words you used about me when Laurentius de Medicis[2] had told you that I had been suffering from a cold. For he wrote to me that when he told you that according to my letter I had not been feeling well, you had answered him in these vulgar words: "He would not suffer so much if he took less pleasure in the she-ass,"[3] as if that had been the cause of the ailment of all the people who are struck down with this illness, as nearly everybody was. And so when I had heard that you also were suffering from the same kind of disease, I thought your illness had the same cause as you had attributed to mine; therefore I wanted you to be deprived of the cause so that you might recover more quickly and now that you have done so I rejoice that you are well.

Now to more important matters. When the Cornelius Tacitus[4] comes I shall keep it hidden with me for I know that whole song: "Where did it come from and who brought it here? Who claims it for his own?" But do not worry, not a word shall escape me. I am waiting for my parchment; when it is convenient,[5] please see that it is brought to me. Paulus de Marganis[6] has likewise asked me for parchment for one Decade. If you can, take this job on after me and attend to it for me so that with your help I may please my friends. For he will transcribe the Decade of the Punic Wars,[7] which my scribe will use afterwards. Please send me my book by Marinus[8] when he comes. I have not yet finished your Varro[9] for I have become less industrious in my writing. The Decade of Livy which you sent has reached me; I shall take great care of it. I have heard nothing about the Cornelius Tacitus, which is in Germany. I am waiting for an answer from that monk. Nicolaus of Trier has not yet gone back. I have not heard anything lately about the books.[10] Yesterday when I asked him about the matter he said he had no definite information. I have stopped worrying about books we do not have and have turned my attention to those we do have for I hear nothing but rumors. Goodbye and remember me. Give my respects to Brother Ambrosius and Carolus as soon as you see them. Rome, the twenty-fifth of September 1427.

LETTER
LII

You have sent me the Seneca[1] and the Cornelius Tacitus[2] which I am glad to have. But the latter is in the Lombard script and for the most part illegible; if I had known that I would not have given you the trouble. Once when I was staying with you I read another copy written in ancient script; I do not know whether it belonged to Coluccius or to somebody else. I should like to have that or some other book which can be read, for it will be difficult to find a copyist who can read this volume correctly; so try to let me have another one if it can be done. You can surely do this if you are willing to exert yourself.[3] But you have sent me the book without any paper; I do not know in what state of mind you acted, unless you would put the moon in the Ram.[4] For what book can be copied if there is no parchment; so please attend to this and likewise to the other book but first attend to the paper. Also get me some for the Decades of Livy[5] as I wrote long ago.

I have heard that you went to Siena.[6] I cannot imagine why unless perhaps to learn from them a serious way of life and a doctrine of good hope; but I thought that you were annoyed enough at public salaries without looking for another source of annoyance.[7] I should like to know whether you went there on pleasure or business, for this would be of great importance. Tell me the reason and that honestly, which you can defend against my criticism, especially since I have become somewhat "headstrong."

You want to know what this means: I have a room full of marble heads; among them there is one that is elegant and complete; the others have broken noses but would be rewarding for a good workman.[8] With these statues and some which I am getting I want to decorate my "Academy"[9] in the Vald'Arno, where I mean to rest if any rest can be had in this tempestuous sea; but still something must be prepared even for sleep if not for quiet. Our hope drags us on to continuous exertions, and when we die only death brings us release from them for our bodies and I hope also for our souls. Farewell, I am glad I have no more paper or else we should philosophize longer by candlelight. In haste, at Rome, the twenty-first day of October [1427].

LETTER
LIII

I praise the diligence which you applied to obtaining the parchment; I praise the parchment too, for it is beautiful. I have not complained about the price but I have said that the volume seems to me somewhat too large. I do not like putting two Decades together. For the greater the period of time covered, the bigger the book.[1] I want the Decades to be separate and that is that. If indeed they were united the weight would be absurd and the size awkward and unmanageable.

I shall send you Caesar's *Commentaries*[2] as soon as I have found someone to carry them carefully so that you may have them rubricated and bound. I have a copyist of uneducated intelligence[3] and peasant habits. For four months now I have done nothing but teach him in the hope that he may learn to write, but I fear that I am ploughing the seashore.[4] He is now copying Valerius,[5] on whom he proves his ignorance, but day by day he becomes stupider. And so I yell, I thunder, I scold, I upbraid; but he has ears full of pitch. He is leaden, a blockhead, wooden, a donkey, and whatever can be mentioned that is duller and clumsier. Damn him. He is bound to me for two years; perhaps he will improve.

You write that the Chancellor[6] has been dismissed from his position. It would have done him more credit to have resigned when he found there was opposition to him. Indeed there is a sort of proper generosity in giving away what one cannot keep. I have quite enough in the way of both honors and money. I do not desire to become rich, that is, actually opulent, for truly I am rich. I have put a limit to my desire and that so close that I shall swiftly reach it. I want to rest some time. But if I were in that position I should, like the swells of the ocean, be tossed up and down. And so I leave this effort to you and the rest of my friends. There is no kingdom of such value that I would be willing to change my state for its sake. I am in the most famous place on earth;[7] I enjoy the greatest freedom; I earn enough to lead a simple life with little effort; I do not care who rises or sinks; I am not afflicted with any desire to get ahead.[8] My situation suits me. What can be added to such a life? I surpass Croesus in wealth, which is at its greatest when you have put an end to greed. Since I have suppressed greed and put a brake on it,[9] who is richer than I am? Goodbye, and if you love me please be mute on this subject. Rome, the sixth day of December 1427.

LETTER
LIV

A scholarly man has come here from North Germany; he has traveled over a large part of the world; he is a man of keen

intelligence but unreliable. He claims that he has seen ten
Decades of Livy[1] in two large, rectangular volumes written in
Lombard script and that the title of one of the volumes says that
it contains ten Decades of Livy and that he has read quite a bit
of both volumes. He is so firm in his assurances that he is easy to
believe. He has reported this to the Cardinal de Ursinis[2] and to
many others besides, all in the same words, so I think that he
did not make it all up. What do you think? His assertions and his
honest expression make me feel there is something in it. For it
is better to take a risk in a direction from which a great reward
can be won than to be suspicious of everything. Consequently I
wanted to write you this so that you might talk it over with
Cosmus[3] and make a careful effort to get these volumes; for it
will be easy for you. The books are in the Monastery of Sora,[4] of
the Cistercian order, two German miles from Roschild, that is, a
little more than one day's journey[5] from Lubich.

Prick up your ears, Pamphilus.[6] There are two volumes, large
and oblong, in a Lombard hand; they are in the Cistercian
Monastery of Sora, two miles from Roschild, which you can
reach in two days at the most from Lubich. So see to it that
Cosmus writes in detail as soon as possible to Gherardus de
Bueris[7] to go there himself if need be; yes, by all means let him
go to the monastery. For if this is true we shall triumph over the
Dacians. The Cardinal[8] is going to send someone or other there
or he will entrust it to someone who is leaving very shortly after
this. I would not want such a morsel to drop from our jaws,[9] so
hurry up; and be careful not to go to sleep. The man has spoken
so emphatically of these books that, although he seemed too
garrulous, there is no reason why he would lie so brazenly,
especially since he has been offered no reward for his lies. And
so I, who hardly believe what I see, am inclined to think this
story is not altogether false and that in this one thing it is re-
spectable to make a mistake. Now you run and urge Cosmus to
spend some money to send a letter there safely as soon as
possible. Goodbye. Rome, the eighth of January [1428].[10] Whatever you do, be sure to let me know. In haste. Tell our friend

Leonardus the Chancellor[11] all about this. Almost all the Danish kings are buried in that monastery.

LETTER
LV

You know that there is a famous statement in one of Marcus Tullius' letters: that the more virtuous a man is, the less he believes others to be evil.[1] You are truly a good man, you judge others according to your own moral standard, and you do not turn your attention to crimes which are foreign to your nature. But still, since I think you are also wise and clear-sighted, I am surprised that some subjects escape you alone that are very well known to others. You had a very close friendship with Joannes Aurispa,[2] a man who, they say, is infamous, leading an evil life with filthy habits. I told you in Florence, when I saw him by chance, that I was not at all attracted by his appearance. Later I learned many things about him here that were unworthy[3] not only of a scholar but even of a private citizen, and I was exceedingly surprised that the Florentines[4] had given him as teacher to their sons, who could not learn anything honorable from him. For learning should be rejected if it is unaccompanied by a life of virtue, of which this man is totally devoid. But the mistake of others is forgivable because of the authority of those who seemed to know best. But how is your mistake to be forgiven when you seem to add your influence to their errors? Granted that long ago because of some affliction in your mind you had not recognized the habits of this man John and had exalted him with praise; granted that you winked at many things or protected his spite; take care lest it be too contrary to your dignity and virtue.

The man who offers support to a criminal is more at fault than the criminal himself. The reason I write you all this is that there is a certain young man here with a senator of the city whom Aurispa accuses of theft, and theft of what? Good God! of Greek books![5] Here I could shout, as did Cicero in his oration *Pro*

Sestio, "Oh herdsmen longing for learning!"[6] This young man who was unacquainted not only with the Greek but with the Latin tongue, drawn by a zeal for Greek literature, plundered a bundle of Greek books,[7] among which there was by chance a *Metamorphoses* of Ovid. But how contrived and falsified this is can be seen from the letters of that same Aurispa, who although he is the contriver of the pretence is nevertheless caught in the contrivance. Who . . . is consistent; he writes the senator three letters, the first in the vernacular, in which he says, if I know how to translate it correctly into Latin, that someone who had formerly served him, by the name of Lambert, has stolen from him a silver belt, a black bonnet, and likewise a pair of boots. Antonius Panormita[8] had discovered these things at his house in Rome. Therefore he is afraid that this man may have perhaps made off with some books which he had left in Florence with one of his friends, by the use of some false subterfuge. He asks the senator to take care to have his things restored to him and to guard the man until he can find out from Florence about the books. This fellow did not know how to make up a good story. For the senator was informed that he had stolen the belt from Rome before he stole the books from Florence. If this is so, it was extremely negligent of that Florentine not to report that the books were missing. The amount of Aurispa's household goods was so large and varied that he did not know that he had been robbed of three things but had to be notified of this by others, and yet he had never before complained of having lost anything of this kind. And so here is to be detected either Aurispa's malice in accusing another out of his imagination or else negligence that is not at all Sicilian. And there is an old proverb: that it is difficult to commit a theft in the home of a thief.[9]

In the second letter, which he sent in Latin after he had been asked to produce the name of the man in whose home he had left the books so that through that man's evidence the matter could be cleared up, he now says that he no longer believes, as earlier, nor fears that the books were carried off by deception. But he openly says, to use his own words, that some corrupt man who used to serve him in Florence, after he deposited his books with a particular friend in Florence, had stolen some volumes of great value,[10] among which was Ovid, the book of letters, and the aforementioned other things besides. In the first letter he wrote that he feared that the books might have been removed under some countersign; in the second he says that they were stolen while they were on deposit. You see how these stories disagree. This guileless Sicilian did not know before he left Florence whether the books he had sent had been delivered to his friend. He did not see him afterward; he did not question him; he acted in good faith. Why? Does not the third letter accord well with the others, so that nothing is in dispute? For he says that there was a bundle of seven Greek volumes and of Ovid's *Epistles.*[11] His servant, while he himself was wrapping the rest of his books together in a waxed cloth, had carried off the bundle all wrapped and tied, by stealth, and he himself had made a guess as to the event because Ovid's *Epistles* were found here. This is surely ridiculous. First, what an incongruity it was that Ovid's *Epistles*,[12] which, if you were to carry them around through all the libraries, would not be worth a ha'penny, should be mixed in with Greek books and those very precious, as he writes. Besides, since the *Epistles* belonged to the young man, for he had copied them in his own hand for study, why did he need to introduce someone else's book among his own, especially a book belonging to someone who would not be with him much longer? Then how could he mix these *Epistles* with his Greek books[13] and tie them together on his departure when they were not at home but with a man called Antonius of Urbino, who at that time was copying them, and after Aurispa's departure gave them back to Lambertus? You might interrogate Antonius on this subject, both as to whether he had the *Epistles* and when he returned them; and if you find that this is true, you well may think that this whole story of the books is a fabrication and a lie. For granted that he, Aurispa, might not have told a lie when he wrote to the senator that the *Epistles* of Ovid were known to be his and also the books of the *Metamorphoses*,[14] I believe he wrote thus to you and yet I do not think that you will again maintain what you say, namely, that this young man confesses that he had the Ovid and the bonnet; for he says that he received from him the belt at about the time of his departure from Florence.

I led this man to Antonius Panormita,[15] inquiring very carefully into these matters. He cleared himself so thoroughly that no blame seems to be attached to him and he testifies that he will come to Florence,[16] if necessary, and also to Bologna to clear himself. On the subject of the bonnet, he answered laughing in Panormita's presence that Aurispa had had only two coverings for his head, a hood and the bonnet, given him as a gift, not bought for three sovereigns as he writes to the senator. Panormita did not deny this. He says that the hood was afterwards given to one Theotonicus[17] in payment for the writing of I know not what. And so it is a wonder, unless Aurispa goes completely bareheaded,[18] that his only covering should be stolen from him, unless perhaps it was removed from him while he slept and after he awoke it did not enter his mind to cover his head because of the extreme heat. Aurispa writes furthermore that Antonius Panormita had known about the book and other things. I know from Antonius himself that this is totally false, because I went to see him for this precise reason. For he never saw the volume of Ovid nor the bonnet that belonged to Aurispa, but only the belt, which the young man wears openly. This same young man is truly amazed that Aurispa[19] dares to write that the Greek books were stolen since he himself delivered them secretly, tied up and divided into a number of bundles, with the help of porters to the home of the ambassador of the marquis[20] so that they might be shipped in his name with no duty attached. He did not employ this young man for this enterprise so that he might not know where the books were. But why do I argue these matters? I send you a copy of Aurispa's letters, from which you can readily see that he clearly lies. But you will say: what is it to you that you should defend him with so many words? First I am moved by outrage over the matter and then by sympathy to protect a man who seems to me innocent against a very wicked man, in connection with whom I have heard of so many different evil deeds, both Greek, so to speak, and Latin, that I shudder at his name. Then too for the sake of the senator, who asked me to answer you on this subject, especially indeed for your own sake, for I would not want you to be made the tool or assistant of another man's wickedness when you are a man of the greatest respectability.[21] And although you glow with such grace and virtue that no one's crime could defile your name, an association with men of that sort is likely to cast quite a shadow over the honor of those with whom they are involved. And so do not unstitch but tear off whatever connection of any kind may exist between you and him and leave this man who is unworthy of your company to his own baseness. For sometime he will of necessity fall into the pit which he has dug, and his "violent dealing shall come down upon his own pate."[22] You relax as usual in good humor and love me as your own. Rome [1428].

LETTER

LVI

I wrote you a letter which I afterward hesitated to send you fearing your annoyance.[1] For it was written in some agitation of mind and, as they say, all in one breath, and you have a habit of sometimes being cross if I write you anything too freely. And there is nothing that I desire less than to make you angry with me in any way. But later I preferred to have whatever I had written reach you and undergo your judgment and correction, if that were necessary, rather than seem to mistrust your kindness and affection, which you have always had in special measure for me. For I am convinced that you will bear calmly whatever I write to you and will not become upset, as you used to do over trifling matters, but will accept what I say with an even temper and in the same spirit as it is said. Therefore read this letter and if there is anything by which it offends you, throw it into the fire,[2] so that it may be purified by its punishment. Consider that I have written nothing, being an irritable and inexperienced man who deserves any sort of penalty you like, which I shall gladly undergo, although if there is any fault in me it is the fault of love and good will. For you know that lovers also often make mistakes while they strive to please. But regardless of its merits or lack of them, throw the letter into the fire so that it may not be spread abroad, not on account of Aurispa, for what could be more profitable than to speak in favor of me and against Antonius,[3] but on account of the want of eloquence in the letter. For it is written in haste and in a rude and disorderly style, so that I should not like to have it fall into the hands of others.

Judge Aurispa's letter in the light of what I have written, if you trust me. Even Antonius Panormita did not take a contrary view when I discussed these matters with him. Answer Aurispa[4] as you please, as long as you write that he is convicted by his own letter and that the case presented by him against the young man is far from true. Goodbye and since you love me love my letter too, although it is not worthy of being loved. Rome [1428].

LETTER
LVII

I have been correcting Cicero's *Philippics*[1] with an ancient codex which is so childishly written and so faulty that in the parts which I copied I needed not guesswork but absolute divination. There is no woman so stupid and uncultivated that she could not have written it better, but you know that I am pretty clever about such things. Still I could not correct everything because the last two pages are missing and there are many blanks in the rest; and yet we are well repaid. For besides what I copied before there are also many blanks in two of the orations. Therefore when I come to you I shall bring my *Philippics* with me so that you can use them while I am with you. Goodbye, the fifth day of June, 1428. I gave Bartholomeus de Bardis[2] the Decade of Livy[3] and the Cornelius Tacitus to send you. In your Cornelius there are several pages missing in various places and in the Decade a whole column, as you will be able to see. 1428.

LETTER
LVIII

Buy me a bed, either a new one or an old one, whichever is easier and quicker, provided it is low and does not exceed the measurements I sent you, for my room is small and I am a small man. There is no other requirement connected with you and Laurentius[1] except to get a bed ready for you, which is indeed necessary as I live in my house as if I were a traveler. You however will feel not that Lucullus is receiving Pompey[2] to dinner but that Epicurus is receiving one of the Stoics in his own garden, where there was this inscription: "Here well mayst thou abide, my gentle guest";[3] and then it added: "with water and mush." And so you are mistaken if you think that I will receive you with great splash, for you will be friends coming to visit a sober and frugal friend, who thinks of nothing less than to stuff his stomach, especially when his guest is Nicolaus the master of moderation. My little lodging will be filled not with wealth but with affection and good will and gaiety, which is the foundation of all feasts when the better part of the whole day is spent[4] in both sipping and nibbling. Bartholomeus de Bardis I think will join your company; I can think of nothing more festive. Goodbye and I shall bring the booklets which you ask for with me or see that they are sent. Rome, the seventeenth of June 1428.

LETTER
LIX

Yesterday when I was in Genezano[1] I received a letter from you which I read with the greatest pleasure. Today I came to Rome after leaving the Pope, who I hope will come to Rome next week, and so I will make this short both because it is night and because I am a little tired from the trip and cannot keep awake any longer. I gave your letter to Panormita. Minias of Lucca[2] has recovered from a long illness[3] and tomorrow he will be brought back here in a litter for he is not strong enough to ride horseback. Nicolaus of Trier writes that he has sent another letter with a fuller description of those books, but the letter has not come and so we are as uncertain as ever. I do not know whether he says this to explain the matter or to extricate himself. I have found out that he will be with us this winter and I think with the books, for he has been told in writing to come back early[4] and bring the books; if he does so we shall be free of this worry. Cornelius Tacitus is silent in Germany and I have heard nothing new from there about his activities. You shall have the pamphlets that you ask for when you are through with the ones you have. I do not want you to be burdened with more material lest you be overwhelmed by your various undertakings.[5]

You have an answer to your letter; now hear about me. I bring you a tiny profit from our little trip; although you will consider it trifling still it should please you somewhat. We were at Ferentino,[6] Bartholomeus de Montepolitiano and I, he to amuse himself and I to look for ancient remains with one of our friends. He received us sumptously but we were there only one day, in which I was never still, although the heat was terrific. I wandered over the whole city first of all and searched in it for a citadel of ancient workmanship. The city is situated on a mountain, and the top of the mountain is surrounded by a stone wall. All of the wall that still stands is up only to ground level on the inside but outside it shows in many places and is steep so that the size of the construction is astonishing. There is besides a huge square tower, on two sides of which there is lettering which you will see. Outside the city near the wall on a steep slope of the mountain there is a carved stone in this shape next to the road, to which it is very difficult to climb. On the inner side is an inscription which I am sending you because I think it will please even your sick stomach. But see that you understand the abbreviations correctly, for there are many of them, and let me know what you make of it.[7] It was a most difficult task for me to read those letters, first the ones that are on the tower of the fort for they are far from the eye and largely eaten away by age, and then those which are on that rock. I sweated for several hours, and sweat indeed

I did in the midday sun, but hard work conquers all.[8] I was not able to explore the surroundings any farther although I wanted to, because my companions were in a hurry. I have no more paper and sleep is overcoming me. Goodbye, in haste, the eleventh day of September 1428.

LETTER
LX

Three days before the Ides of September, when I had come back from Genezano at night half dead and sleepy, I hurriedly scribbled a letter to you. The next day when I had slept rather late I forgot to give it to the banker to send. In this letter I am first answering your letter, then I shall tell you about our walking trip, which was not altogether frivolous. I wrote you that I had found an inscription in a tower of the very old fort at Ferentino and another in another place which was not to be despised. The one in the gate[1] was very hard to read, partly because of its height and partly because of the manifold creepers which covered the letters; and the letters themselves in many places are obliterated because of age. The inhabitants were amazed at my reading[2] what they did not remember anybody's having read, since they said the letters were Greek. But two young girls lessened the effort of reading and understanding. They were more or less grown up and stood at their house near by, favoring me with their prayers; and when my eyes were tired I often glanced at them so that I might use them as a mirror to restore my vision. Do not think that I am making this up or saying it for fun. Their good looks and applause did me a lot of good, and lest you suspect that there was anything wrong about it, they were the sisters of a man who was my copyist for a long time. Afterwards he entertained me at home and his sisters received me not as somebody who is fierce and inhuman but as an amusing gossip, so that they did not run away from me as a stranger or fear me. Then I copied another inscription with greater effort, for its position was also inaccessible and the sun seemed to burn in the open

rocky place, while there was no relaxation for the eyes as there
had been before. There are said to be quite a few other inscriptions but in various places which I did not have time to see.
Moreover, on that day I had no rest, for after I copied these inscriptions, I went to Alatri[3] to see a most magnificent castle there
with an old wall which is still standing for the greater part. It
is really a wonderful thing; but there is no inscription which I
could see. From there after sunset I went back to Ferentino and
next day to Genezano. There you have my walking trip.

Please send me the paper and the Josephus[4] which I mentioned and get me the parchment for the Aulus Gellius, which
I should like you to borrow from our friend Leonardus and send
it to me with the paper. Give my regards to Cosmus and Laurentius. Goodbye, Rome, the fifteenth day of September [1428].
I am writing to Leonardus Aretinus about the Aulus Gellius;[5]
give him the letter and ask for the book and at the same time a
particular letter of his which I should like you to send me.

LETTER
LXI

You are certainly a fool and thoroughly unkind always to
interpret my letters in the worse way. I wrote you about the
young girls not to make up a story but to tell you the truth. Perhaps you are a Stoic,[1] who in the same circumstances would
have looked the other way. I did not go to that place because
they were there, but after I came they arrived on the scene to
make my acquaintance because of all they had heard from their
brother about me. What sort of howl would you have put up if
I had written you what happened afterwards? For I went home
with them, I greeted them and shook hands with them and
talked with them for an hour or more and had a meal and a drink
with them, and when I left they gave me an embroidered hand-
kerchief. Are you not ridiculous? Do you not see that I did
nothing but what was full of culture and good will? If you are
rude and gruff, please yourself; I am a man more inclined toward

gentleness and friendliness[2] and I shall not deny it. I would prefer wherever I am copying inscriptions to have young girls with nice figures standing near me rather than to have a buffalo with wide horns or a wild bull. You order whichever you prefer.

The other day after cleaning the wall I copied another inscription with great difficulty which I had never been able to read before because of the ivy and the creepers. Several women were passing by for the inscription is on a gate[3] on the way to Tivoli; and the women were very good looking. Do you think I considered that bad luck? Some of them stood near by and laughed at my work as if it were ridiculous, and I laughed merrily with them. Do you think, you severe judge, that this should be considered wrong? What chance brings us is not wrong because it is full of pleasure. But I shall punish you; you shall not have the inscription which is outstanding unless you apologize. For as to what you write that you have formerly had the greatest difficulty in understanding, because of the abbreviations, I read it all straight through very easily and understand it except for the four letters placed in order, that is: H. A. I. R.[4] Let me know if there is anything you are not sure of. I shall offer myself to you as an Oedipus.[5] Take care of the Aulus Gellius and the Josephus and the parchment. Goodbye and give my regards to Laurentius and Cosmus. Rome, the second day of October [1428]. Nicolaus of Trier will be with us soon.

LETTER
LXII

I have the parchment and the books with which you gave me great pleasure. My copyist is at the end of the ninth book of the first Decade.[1] After that he will begin the Aulus Gellius[2] and finish it shortly. If possible, see that I have Josephus' books *Contra Appionem grammaticum*,[3] which I want to add to the histories of the Jewish wars. I am sending you the inscription about which I wrote you in another letter; it will please you. I do not know what more to write you; you will soon see Antonius Luscus,[4] who is a very learned and delightful man. I know that you with your usual kindness and good will toward him will see much of him and that he will be to you a source of great pleasure; please give him my greetings.

There is one solace, if there can be any, which will help you: apply yourself to literature and busy yourself in it. But I shall provide myself with another way while there is time. Believe me, except for my home, my vineyard, and my garden,[5] there is nothing else to be found in my property for which I would assume any burden. It is better to live well anywhere than to live badly in a fixed place. I do not cling to the name of my homeland; I shall acknowledge as my homeland[6] the place where I can live free from all the cares that I see oppressing you and many other people. The country shall be my homeland if I can live there according to my taste, but if I cannot, like the swallows, I shall change climate and seek a land where it is milder. Laugh if you want, as you always do at my intentions, I shall stick to my own opinion. Goodbye, at Rome, the twenty-ninth of October [1428].

LETTER
LXIII

Day before yesterday when I was with Bartholomeus de Bardis[1] (for perhaps you know that he has been sick) he received your letter, which he gave me to read and asked me to answer. But when I had read it to myself, I did not see anything which needed an answer. You asked him to give your letter to Garsia,[2] and at the same time you described your daily life and your talks with Antonius Luscus[3] which amuse you so much. If I were with you perhaps I could have added quite a bit of wit to your conversation. But here we are just plain freezing so that even the south winds which have prevailed here for some time do not warm us.

I wrote you in an earlier letter that the parchment which you sent me was useless and inadequate for the Aulus Gellius, and I wrote to Ser Angelus to get me some more as soon as possible so that my secretary would not be idle. Please hurry it along and goodbye; give Antonius Luscus my greetings. The thirteenth day of November [1428].

Your ears are too delicate[1] and avoid whatever they are unwilling to hear or you were mortified when you wrote a letter a little more vehement than usual or else you were angry about my letter because it was in the vulgar tongue.[2] For why should you make such a scene or go to so much trouble about some parchment which I would rather have burned up than turn into bother for you. You apologize and claim to have done the right thing, repeating some ancient remarks which I do not remember having made and which I am sure were meant to be funny.[3] What need was there of all this talk? When I write to you from now on I shall use a ruler to measure my words or a scale to test the weight of each word and I shall say nothing that is not kind, polite, polished, and humble, so that if it were tested on the square it could not be criticized. Accept my apology as befits a friend and stop this nonsense. Is it right for you to send me a black mark because I wrote that some of the parchments were a little too large while others were a little too small? But the moon thwarts me and the sun is no help to you.

But the beginning of your letter is of such a kind and on such a mournful topic that I wonder that you were not too exhausted to have written so much. We have lost a friend[4] whose successor will not be easy to find. It is a difficult and arduous thing, dear Nicolaus, to find a man who can be called a friend. And so we must grieve for this loss about which I have written you nothing, for I was floored for several days by sorrow and also by fear. While he was sick with the fever, I seldom left him; and when he was dead I began to be quite afraid myself, and so I went walking around the city and seldom came home. There was nothing I hated more than the night when I had to go home and leave the company of my friends, for loneliness is bad for sorrow and for fear.

But let us forget all this. It is easier to feel sorry than to change things. I am delighted with your diligence in connection with the fourth Decade; it is now being written and I do not much care whether it is corrected before or after it has been copied, although I have two volumes which are pretty correct among the bad ones. There seem to be many lacunae in this fourth Decade.[5] Your Josephus is being copied outside my house and will soon be finished. I do not know what will come of the Aulus Gellius; these secretaries of mine give me so much trouble that often I would prefer to be without books than to have them made in such an atmosphere of hostility. I am waiting for the books *Contra Appionem grammaticum,*[6] which I shall add to the history. Make sure that I have them before Christmas. The first and second books of the fourth Decade are so small that they hardly cover seven leaves. Write me whether yours are like that. I know that at present you do not need Cicero's *Orations;* I need them very much however, for they are the only ones I have. I know that you do not do any copying in the winter; but if you want them for any reason, I shall send you first whichever volume you prefer and when you have finished that I shall send the rest. In this way I shall satisfy both you and myself. Goodbye. Greet Antonius Luscus for me. The air here has become healthier on account of the cold, and I have not heard of any other deaths. Rome, the twenty-sixth of November [1428].

LETTER
LXV

I have been waiting a long time for Josephus' *Contra Appionem grammaticum* but it has not yet come.[1] I do not know whether this is due to other people's indifference or your own; still whatever you do I accept in good faith and think that you mean well. I am pestering you because my secretary has already finished the rest of the work and I cannot keep him in idleness.

Therefore send the book as soon as possible. You will not only be doing me a kindness but you will also be doing a public service and helping that man's reputation. For I make books[2] not only for myself but for other people also and even for posterity, which the wise always keep in mind. But if perhaps you have developed a grouch as you sometimes do, work it out on me alone; I am quite willing to be not only criticized but also punished.

The paper which I have just received is very dirty and furthermore expensive. Petrus[3] treated Ser Angelus too much as an ignoramus. I could have better parchment than this here for less money. And in fact I shall not use this. Give my thanks to Petrus for treating me so as to deserve my confidence. Goodbye and send the book or let me know that you are not going to send it. Rome, the seventh of January [1429].

LETTER
LXVI

I do not know whether it was the weather or your diet that made you nauseated so that you were cross, but I wanted to fix you a feast which would stimulate and improve your appetite so that it would not only make your stomach active but would also make you gape.

Nicolaus of Trier[1] has written a letter with an inventory of the books he has; among them are many volumes which it would take too long to mention. He says that he has many of the works of Cicero, among which are the orations *On the Agrarian Law* and *Against Piso,*[2] and the *De legibus* and *De fato,* and many others in fragments which if they were whole would be worth a lot of money. Besides there is another volume which contains twenty works of Cyprian of Carthage;[3] and besides that something I greatly value, a complete Aulus Gellius, he thinks, and what will please you even more, a Quintus Curtius, containing the first book. He says nothing about the end, but I think since the beginning is there, the rest of it must not be missing. But all this is unimportant; he has another volume in which there are twenty comedies of Plautus.[4] This is a great prize and must not be underestimated. These are the names of the comedies with their opening lines, if he made no mistake, for I have copied from his letter: Plautus' *Amphitruo;* another whose name is missing; the *Aulularia;* the *Euclio;* the *Captivi;* the *Bacchides;* the *Mustellaria;* the *Menaechmi;* the *Miles;* the *Mercator;* the *Pseudolus;* the *Poenulus;* the *Persa;* the *Rudens;* the *Stichus;* the *Truculentus;* and the *Trinummus*. It begins "Dum bellum gereret, amanti argento filio," etc. He puts down the beginnings of these comedies, which I leave out on account of an inflammation in my eyes which is keeping me from writing for any length of time. He says he was wrong about the *De republica*[5] and that it was Macrobius' book on the *Dream of Scipio,* but he has not given up hope of finding it. He says that some scholar told him where it was and he will go there as soon as possible.

I shall send you an inventory of the rest of the books when I have time for there are some of considerable value. But what bothers me is that he is not coming to Italy for quite a while and that meantime a lot of accidents could happen. I told the Cardinal[6] that he should send someone equipped to bring us these books since we ought not to wait for Nicolaus' arrival; if he does not do it, we are lost. Therefore warm up Cardinal de Ursinis to the idea with a letter, and I shall stir him up too. The only difficulty will be financial for people here cool off when expense is great; therefore discuss it with whoever seems best to you. But if the money were available, the best plan would be to send someone with brains who would know how to meet the man and bring us the books. Do as you please. The monk from Hersfeld[7] came without a single book; for that reason he was thoroughly berated by me. He assured me that he was going back very soon for he was engaged in a suit in the name of the monastery and that he would bring us the book. He asked me for a lot of favors. I said I would do nothing unless we had the book; so I hope that we shall have it because he needs our favor. You have enough for dinner. Goodbye, in haste, Rome, the twenty-sixth of February [1429].

I forgot one thing; I have heard that that excellent man and

lover of his country, Joannes de Medicis,[8] is dead. I was much
distressed and still am, not only that our country should lose
such a citizen but also that his sons should lose such a father and
that we should lose such a good and delightful friend, although
I ought to say patron. I am sure that both Cosmus and Laurentius[9]
are overcome with the greatest grief, as is to be expected from
their own nobility of character and their father's. But they must
use wisdom, since there is need for it, just as much in adversity
as in prosperity. Tell Cosmus not to forget what I once told him,
for there is not the same pattern for everything at all times and
for all men. Goodbye, for I have written too much.

LETTER

LXVII

I shall answer your letter at greater length another time for
my eyes are still bothering me so that I cannot write by lamp-
light, and writing tires me. You urged me in your letter to console
our friend Cosmus.[1] I meditated for a considerable time on
whether to write to him and since I thought, if I wrote, I would
have to express myself more elegantly than most but there was
not time for it, I kept quiet instead of saying something silly.
Now I have decided to obey you. And so, a little while ago, when
I came home, I took up my pen[2] and hastily scribbled a letter
into which I threw whatever came into my head. If I had thought
it over beforehand I would have done it more perfectly.[3] Read
the letter, and if it does not seem to you altogether ridiculous
and witless, give it to Cosmus with this understanding: namely,
that I wrote it on the spur of the moment. If it does not seem to
you to be worthy of me, tear it up instead of letting it go out of
your hand covered with corrections. For I wanted to please you,
but I fear that I have pleased neither myself nor you. But read
the letter and decide whether to give it to him. If I do my duty,
even though the words are simple, I do not greatly care. But
write and tell me what you have done in this case.

I am stirring up the Cardinal[4] to send for the books; he has
promised to send for them after Easter.[5] If by chance my letter

pleases you, take care to let me have a copy of it, because I do not have time to copy it. Goodbye. "Che gli occhi mi. . . ."

I have just finished a short essay[6] about which I shall write to you in another letter, and I shall send it at the same time for you to read to get your opinion of it.[7]

LETTER
LXVIII

Perhaps you think that I have neglected to write you a list of the books which Nicolaus of Trier mentioned; not at all, but I am angry sometimes that the very people to whom I make myself very easily available in their difficulties make themselves difficult to me over trifles. And so I am often peevish and pretend to neglect things in which I am very much interested. When I was shown Nicolaus' letter, as soon as I came to the title of Plautus' comedies, I shouted that we had got a great prize; and straightway I seized my pen and in haste made up a list[1] which I am sending you folded in this letter. The others thought nothing of what they had not understood, but when they had been alerted by me they began as is customary with the ignorant to think it of great importance. I asked him for the letter[2] so that I might tell you about it in more detail; he refused to give it to me. I read his letter again and, except for what I have mentioned to you, there is nothing of great importance. I have often sought to have a copy of his letter made for me, although I have sought it more for your satisfaction than my own. So far I have not been able to have it; he held it up by procrastinating and by bringing up one excuse after another. Nicolaus, however, names few of the books but says that he will send the inventory; when it comes you shall know all about it. I am with that delightful man Laurentius[3] every day; and I cannot be separated from him for I find his character so attractive. I am trying to draw him out of his sadness over his father's death and to recall him to the pleasures of life. For although the event is very sad, nothing is more foolish than to dwell too long upon something which can neither be avoided nor cured.

Rinucius has left the Cardinal;[4] the reason is their own business, and it is not my affair to unravel the answer of the Sibyl. I want you to know one thing: that these Satraps of ours are chosen vessels, as it were, of ingratitude. It is a vice common to all those who have more power than they ought. But our priests so comply with the commandments of God that they escape not only this vice but also any suspicion of it. A man who trusts in such a rudder will certainly sink. But that is their problem; nevertheless Rinucius was a Greek[5] for long enough.

I am sending you by Laurentius the little book which I have finished, the one against avarice. I ought to keep it hidden so that no one may think that it is directed against him,[6] until the time comes for publishing it. You will examine it and carefully too. I believe unless I deceive myself, if you consider our native efforts it will please you, provided of course that you do not compare it with the eloquence of the Ancients. I have none of the orations of Cicero,[7] except the ones you ask for; they are like food with which I keep up my health. I have sent nearly all my books home;[8] therefore let these stay with me now, and another time what you ask will be done. I shall send you the Aulus Gellius also, I think, by Laurentius. Goodbye, greet Cosmus and Carolus for me, Rome, the third day of April [1429].

A certain Joannes de Toscanella[9] has written me a letter which I received yesterday when I was at dinner with our friend, Laurentius. So that he would not think himself despised, I scribbled him a few lines; for although I have time I do not feel much like writing, and yet I do not know what answer to make to that kind of man. Please send him the letter; read it first and then seal it.

LETTER

LXIX

Laurentius de Medicis will give you the dialogue which I have finished, *Against Avarice;* please read it with the same care and diligence that you use on other things. Examine not only the sense and sentences but also the words and syllables one by one.

First see if you like the order and then the speakers. I had given Cincius[1] the leading part in the attack on avarice. But Antonius Luscus did not at all like the case against avarice put in the mouth of a man who is considered stingy. So I changed the character and gave it to Bartholomeus. In the second place it is attacked by Andreas of Constantinople,[2] who, since he is in holy orders, seemed a proper person to answer Antonius and to use quotations from the Holy Bible to censure the offense of avarice.[3] Antonius, who is something of a spendthrift, defends avarice, for it is less invidious if a vice is defended by someone with whom it has no connection so that he seems to have taken this stand not because of his nature but for the sake of argument. When I read what we produce, I mean the men of our own day, I do not altogether disapprove of this work of mine; but when I call to mind our predecessors, I seem to stammer and I am ashamed and irritated at what I have written. Sometimes I like the end of the dialogue and sometimes I dislike it, but I am waiting for your judgment on the whole thing.

Believe me I shall abide by your decision as to whether it is to be published or hidden. Do not let your affection for me mislead you or your desire to commend me. This is my first little work which is about to come into the field of competition or into the wrestling ring, as it were, and so it ought to be fit to bring home not disgrace but glory. Look at the preface too and see whether it is pertinent and suits the subject, and finally study the whole work carefully. Please lend it, if you wish, to our friend, Ambrosius,[4] so that you may find out what he thinks about it; then give it also to Leonardus Aretinus[5] to read but in such a way that you may inform me of your own opinion first, for I shall write to him that I also want his opinion, so that he may not feel himself neglected. And yet I fear that he may think himself insulted by this essay on account of the suspicion of avarice. But all my strictures are meant to be general; if anyone thinks that they are said about him, simply let him think so. I have not put any title on it, so that it may not be known to be mine before you have approved it. If, as I hope, it pleases you, then it will be your job to send the little book to our friend,

Barbarus,[6] and I shall also send you a letter to him to be sent with it. Please answer as soon as possible, for I shall be very wrought up until you write.

I received your very short letter full of irritation and fury.[7] I see that you now share in the difficulties which Horace said surround old men,[8] for you are too crotchety and bad tempered.[9] I do not know if you have ever seen me so frivolous in writing that you could imagine that I had written to you about the Plautus just to make fun of you. I have never done this even over trifles; why do you think that I would do it in an important matter? When I wrote to you the last time I thought that I had included the list in my letter; it was through forgetfulness that it was not enclosed and I did not notice it until very lately when I was going through some of my papers. If you think it was done through carelessness or scorn, go ahead and think as you please. But I have received only two letters from you and you say you have written to me a hundred times; you have never written to me without my answering you. But I shall behave more cautiously with you from now on, since you are so edgy. You will hear things first from other people and later from me, so that you will have no reason not to believe them whether I write gospels or epistles. For you are too fussy[10] and too rigid in dealing with your friends. But I shall leave this for another time. Please attend to what I mentioned above and I shall be very grateful; these are small matters and do not require an answer. But I have written this so that you may not delude yourself. Goodbye, Rome, the sixth day of May 1429.

LETTER
LXX

I have given a letter for you to our friend, Laurentius, and along with it I sent you my book for your opinion, which will either protect and defend my work or else condemn it. Therefore read my nonsense; meanwhile I shall hang with my soul in mid-air, waiting for your opinion. So free me as soon as possible from

this worry and write me what you think about its being published or hidden. But in my letter I forgot to write one thing,
that you should put down the name of the man who praised
Dionysius, the tyrant, and who wrote a little book against Plato;[1]
for I have forgotten it and I do not have my books to look it up.
Therefore add the name in the space where it is missing. Let this
prove to you that I am forgetful, so that you may not be surprised
when my memory fails me in other things, since it fails me in
those which I try hardest to remember. Goodbye and love me;
Rome, the fourteenth day of May [1429].

LETTER
LXXI

Twice the postman has come to us now without any letter for
me from you since Laurentius went back to Florence. This
convinces me that you do not like my dialogue at all,[1] for you
used always to congratulate me as soon as possible when you
received from me anything literary which you liked. Now since
you have kept quiet so long after Laurentius' arrival, I guess
from this silence of yours that the matter was unworthy of your
ears. Perhaps you do not dare to object to my work for fear of
deterring me from writing, but perhaps you do not want to lie,
since it is contrary to your habits, by praising me beyond what
you really feel. Therefore, write me, please, as soon as possible,
unless it is inconvenient, and rescue me from dangling in uncertainty of mind. If it really seems unworthy of publication,
send me back the little book so that it will not fall into somebody
else's hands, for I do not want to end up in disgrace instead of
glory. Goodbye, Rome, the first of June [1429].

LETTER
LXXII

I cannot tell you how delighted I was to hear from you your
opinion of the dialogue.[1] Do not worry about my being the kind

of person who cannot bear to hear the truth or to whom a friend's opinion is unwelcome, especially yours when you speak to me from your very soul. See how much I think of you and how highly I value your judgment. I had shown the dialogue to Antonius Luscus[2] and also to another man who is a very good scholar; both of them approved of it either to be pleasant, for I do not mean to flatter me, or because they really thought so. But since I know that your judgment is keen[3] and acute[4] in such things and since I am convinced that you are fond of me, I decided to publish nothing without your advice, from which you can see that I count more upon you alone than upon all the others.

But to return to the things which you say you do not like, not to defend them or to refute your opinion but just to have a pleasant conversation, first of all know that I will not publish this little book during the life of the present Pope. Since many people accuse him of the very thing[5] which is the subject of the book, I would not want anyone to think that it was written against him while he could ban it. For although he is by nature easy and kind,[6] I do not want to find out what my detractors can do with him by intriguing against me,[7] since it is safer to keep silent than to say things which someone else might think were aimed too pointedly at himself. For it is not the others that I fear. No one will think I was writing about him unless he has condemned his own character in advance; but there is no one who does not think himself good and want to be considered so. And so even if the book seemed to you worthy of publication, I should keep it at home until a moment came free from any suspicion of danger.[8]

Now as to the fact that the names of the interlocutors displease you because of their barbarian sound and that it does not befit those whom you consider stingy to reprove avarice: first we must use names by which men are called,[9] and if the names are unattractive, it is not my fault but the fault of our times and our religion which introduced them. But you will say many people are so named that the names of the characters selected for the dialogue would be tolerable. Granted but I had to take people who were here and who could meet and who were not altogether ignorant in order to make it plausible that they could have held this discussion. For I want you to understand this about their characters: Antonius Luscus and Bartholomeus[10] [de Montepolitiano] are in my opinion very generous. I had given the chief part for attacking avarice to Cincius,[11] who is considered stingy; I gave the defense to Antonius, who is almost extravagant; I had done this intentionally so that the stingy man might attack avarice and the extravagant man might defend it. But Antonius could not bear it at all; he said, "Do what you like about me but it is really ridiculous for Cincius to speak against avarice and I cannot stand it." Since there was a shortage of characters who could be introduced into the discussion, I turned the whole thing over to Bartholomeus for lack of speakers.[12]

Now you say you do not like the mention of Friar Bernardinus[13] and also the introduction to the dialogue; I did not do this to praise him but to criticize a little these infuriating brawlers and wranglers[14] from France.[15] At the same time, through their nonsense, it seemed opportune to add the way they offend since they do not restrain themselves from those vices which especially hurt the public. You know it is the practice of dialogues to deal with things which are either true or probable and to make one thing come up for discussion as it arises out of another. But let us take another approach. You must know that I mentioned Isidore[16] not for lack of authority but because in attacking the avarice of priests those men seemed most suitable of whom they think highly and whom they study daily in their canon law. But he can easily be removed without any damage, for I do not think that you would despise statements of Paul the Apostle or Augustine or Chrysostom,[17] and I use those three as authorities. I used Burgundio so that it might not be thought that I was using my own translation although his version is quite inadequate and devoid of style, especially since the quotations are taken from a Greek and a great scholar. But this name can be suppressed without loss. I hesitated a long time as to whether I ought to cite the saints as authorities or to use their statements without referring to their names.[18] But the words will seem to have greater weight if they are said by the voices of such great men, and I see that it was a habit of our beloved Cicero to use the language and opinions of other people.[19]

That you consider this essay inferior to my letters I feel is just, and I grant that it is so. But I did this on purpose for I not only did not seek elaborate diction but in many places actually avoided it. Read the works of Cicero, that is, all his dialogues (excepting the *De oratore*): they are of a certain quiet and peaceful sort of eloquence if you compare them with his orations or his letters.[20] I did not want to seem too fancy or as if I had been fishing out all the flowers and ornaments of rhetoric. But some people seem to you to be too much praised in the preface. I, dear Nicolaus, do not think that all the praise of all those men either is or was true, but there are many elements in it which add scope and dignity to the subject matter. And yet if you study my words carefully you will see that there is not so much praise in them as it seems; for I do not attribute immortal glory to those men but great praise and a name that will last for many centuries.[21] When I said that they were outstanding in every kind of learning, I was thinking in particular of Leonardus; there seemed to be some point in paying him a small tribute that actually went beyond what I really think of him. But these things can be modified. I have written in order that you may see what moved me.

As Laurentius told you, if the Pope leaves here I shall go to you instantly; but if he stays in the city, I shall see you and talk with you and discuss the whole thing with you in detail and follow your advice. For I sent the book to you to get your advice, and I have no burning desire to publish it since I should wait for a more suitable time. But I want the thing ready so that when there is a good opportunity it can be brought out and in such a way that I will not be ashamed of having published it. For, as you write, I know that not only the opinions expressed but also every word and syllable will be pondered. But I care less for the words; it is the opinions that move me. For when I read other people's writings, there seem to be good grounds for not being afraid of many men's criticism; there are others who are eloquent and good in style but in such a way that I am not inferior to them. But of this when we meet.

Everything shall be polished up to suit you. You keep the book until I talk it over with you and do not discuss it further with

anyone except Nicolaus[22] [de Medicis]; Friar Albertus de Sarteano[23] is a very good friend of mine because of his many good
qualities for he is a scholar and very kind and I think a man of
great integrity.[24] He is in the city and has discussed with me the
interdict and its iniquity. Your General[25] cannot bear the virtue
of any honest man, for the glory of good men[26] makes his eyes
water.[27] I shall make every effort to have the interdict removed.
If you see that sycophant, criticize him as much as you want. I
like very few of that order. You must know one thing: that the
charges brought against him by the General are false and arise
rather from the malice of others than from his own fault. Goodbye, and love me as you always do. Rome, the eleventh of June
[1429].

LETTER
LXXIII

If you are well, good; I am too. My departure, not to say flight,
from the City was sudden; therefore I wrote nothing to you or
to any of my friends. I was upset and terrified by the death of
Bartholomeus de Montepolitiano,[1] a very distinguished man and
one of my best friends. Then occurred the sudden and unexpected departure of the Pope,[2] from whom I could not get permission to come to you, since he said that Cincius alone could
not satisfy him and so he did not want me to leave him. Therefore
I betook myself to Agro Cassinati, the pleasantest place of all
I have seen, and I was there six days with the Cardinal of
Piacenza.[3] I saw the library of the Monastery,[4] and I found a book
containing Julius Frontinus' *De aquaeductu urbis;* it also contains Firmicus' *Matheseos Libri VIII,*[5] but at the beginning the
first book is missing and also part of the second. I do not know
whether you have read this book elsewhere, so I should like you
to write me about it. I carried the volume away with me to copy
the work of Frontinus, although it is so full of mistakes and so
badly written that I can hardly read it. While I was there I fished
out a marble bust of a woman, wholly undamaged, which I like

very much. It was found one day when the foundations of some house were being dug. I took care to have it brought to me here and then to my little garden at Terra Nova, which I shall decorate with antiquities.[6]

You will see all this when I come to you, which will be as soon as we go back. Antonius Luscus was very wise in this matter as in all the rest, for, foreseeing this storm, he took himself into port with a favorable wind.[7] And so he is not affected by this troublesome Campagna, to use a new word, by this rough hilly country in which, as he says, people eat raw meat and drink cooked wine. The houses are more than rustic; I wish he could share in their conveniences. Give him my greetings. I came today to Anagni;[8] I shall go back at once to Ferentino, where I have rented a little house. The Pope will be there, so they say, since he still so loves solitude and small inns. Goodbye, and give my regards to Laurentius and Cosmus. Anagni, the ninth day of July 1429.

LETTER
LXXIV

Today I received a letter from you saying that you had sent me another and had asked something about some Bull or other. I never received the letter and so do not know what you asked. If you want anything, you had better write again; I promise you my careful attention.

I ask you, since I cannot come to you, to answer the letters which I wrote you from the City in reply to your letter on the structure of my dialogue.[1] I also wrote you recently from Anagni about my trip to Santo Germano, and about the Frontinus. I am so glad you received my Decades[2] and the Aulus Gellius;[3] I want them to be ruled in red and bound. I could not write you this from the City on account of my grief over the death of my dearest friend and on account of my confusion of spirit, deriving partly from fear and partly from the sudden departure of the Pope. I had to leave my house and settle all my things; a great deal had to be done at once so that there was no opportunity for writing or even for drawing breath. There was besides the greatest grief, which made everything else much harder. But to go back to the books. The first and fourth Decades were written by the same man; I want them to be bound separately and, since the quantity of pages is great, I want it to be cut down around the edges where I made the space wide on purpose, so that it could be cut down to a moderate volume. This must be attended to, especially in the fourth Decade, which contains fewer quaternions. So keep this in mind. I shall now give up the work of writing books;[4] but there is one book which, if I can find a copyist, will be in my collection. That is Pliny's *Natural History*.[5] Therefore please prepare for me sheets for a slightly larger volume than those of the first and fourth Decades. Tell me whether the handwriting of the man who copied the Aulus Gellius pleases you, for he is still with me. But I may decide on a new man on our return for this book; therefore make sure that there is no shortage of parchment. If you liked the volume of the Decades, take it as a sample.

The Pope is at Ferentino, where I am too. I am trying to keep well. I have had little opportunity for literature these days during which we thought more of flight than of studying; but I shall devote some time to it while the sun is blazing, during which time I stay indoors. Give my regards to Antonius Luscus, Cosmus, and Laurentius. Goodbye, at Ferentino, the fifteenth day of July 1429.

LETTER
LXXV

Yesterday I received from you an answer to the letter I wrote you from Anagni,[1] and at the same time you answer about Master Franciscus.[2] I talked some time ago with the Pope concerning permission to visit the Holy Sepulcher and the other places you mention in your letter. The Pope said he would give him permission if he were willing to go somewhat further and take a letter from the Pope to the Sultan;[3] I answered that I thought he would be willing to undertake this errand. Therefore, if he were willing to undertake this job, it would be an honor to him, and the mission on which he would be going is quite easy and not much trouble. He could go first to Alexandria and to Cairo and then go back to the Sepulcher[4] and then to Rome; and if he carries along what the Pope wants, it would be no slight opportunity to get the Pope's good will. Advise him to undertake this errand and, if he is willing, let him come here for information about his duties and for his letter, and he will be quickly sent off. But let him not think that he will get any money;[5] we shall repay his merits in other ways. I believe that he will lose nothing by this effort; at least he will not fear either the General or anybody else in the Order. Answer me as soon as possible or let him come himself all ready for the journey, for I shall send him off as soon as possible. If he does not want to go, I shall not say a word more. You have point one. Tell him not to be afraid of the General or the Procurator[6] for I shall satisfy both of them; the Procurator is entirely under my thumb. Still it will be proper for him, if he wants to seek permission from his Superior if he is accustomed to do so. But let him fear nothing; let him come with merely two or three friars.

I shall send you the Julius Firmicus[7] when we get to Rome. I have the greatest friendship with the Abbot of Monte Cassino[8] so that I need no one to intercede. Still I shall write to the Cardinal,[9] to keep my good reputation. The book is corrected and has hardly any errors, it seems, except for the absence of the first book. About the Plautus and the other authors which are away off among the Germans, this is no time to do anything about them or to discuss them for we are all scattered in various places. There are very few of us with the Pope and the others are forbidden to come here, and so we live like hermits.[10] Still I hope, as I understood from the letters of Nicolaus of Trier,[11] that he will come to the City with the books around the first of November, and that was why the Cardinal[12] did not send one of his men there as he had determined to do. But I was very anxious and actually urged him to send someone for the books. But you know "our habits"; "we" are completely indifferent to everything except ambition and greed. I wrote you what to do about my books in another letter in which I answered yours, which was short but sensible. You advise me in it to take a holiday sometimes and give myself up to reading; this is good advice and comes from your great affection for me. I follow it as much as my business allows, and I cling to the intention that some time I shall live for myself alone, rid of this kind of care.

Many people wanted to persuade me that after the death of my friend, Bartholomeus, I ought to undertake the responsibility for the many things which he managed[13] and so insinuate myself into the Pope's intimacy and take over whatever was to be done of my own accord. But I am thoroughly against this point of view and have no wish to thrust myself forward but rather to withdraw a step. For this would not be the beginning of peace but rather of tremendous labor, and instead of the liberty which I desire it would be to submit to complete servitude. Let anyone climb who wants to. I am content with my position and my property[14] and want nothing more than to be able to enjoy these properly. I see people die who hold the highest positions, "no pile of brass or gold keeps fever from the sick body of its owner."[15] Your Poggius is content with very little and you shall see this for yourself; sometimes I am free for reading, free from all care about public affairs which I leave to my superiors. I live free as much as I can; it gives me the greatest pleasure. I am troubled by no ambition[16] or desire for wealth; if anything is given me, I accept it gladly. When it is not available, I am not worried in the least, and yet to this day nothing has prevented me from having an honorable and generous life. No one is richer than I if this spirit remains in me. But enough about me; these things must be proved by actions not words.

I wish I had been with you when Friar Albertus[17] and Nicolaus and Carolus visited you. But if, as I hope, we live long enough, when we come back to the City I shall rush ahead and fly to you. Goodbye. Greet Laurentius and Nicolaus and our friend, Brother Ambrosius. In haste, at Ferentino, the twenty-third day of July

1429. If I have a chance, I shall go to see Arpino,[18] Cicero's native place, for it is only sixteen miles from here. Please tell Ser Angelus[19] from my village that I am well and that he should tell my relatives so.

LETTER
LXXVI

You think, as I seem to see from your letter, that I am making fun of you in the matter of Friar Franciscus;[1] I was not joking with you at all but speaking seriously. And so what I wrote in my letter is true. It will be acceptable to the Pope if he undertakes this job. For he wants I know not what from the Sultan. He can, as I wrote, go to Alexandria first and then to Cairo and then go back to Jerusalem[2] and then, if he does not want to come back or wants to stay on the Island of Chios,[3] he can notify the Pope through one of his associates of the results of his interview with the Sultan. I should not say another word about this matter to the Pope, for he would think himself spurned if I said that he had refused this work.[4] Therefore answer immediately. If Master Franciscus should agree with my advice, he would undertake this work, provided it were not too contrary to his advantage. I am not joking with you but speaking with great seriousness. Still, if he should not want to go on this journey, I shall take the matter up again with the General if he wants me to and I am sure that I shall get whatever I want. For the Procurator[5] will return in a few days; he was sent by the Curia to a safe, remote place and I shall get whatever I want from him, for he is a great friend of mine. I assure you and confirm the decision of which I wrote you lately that I will not spread my sails on the deep[6] but will reduce them, for the sea is big and rough and if one trusts oneself too much to it one is in danger of the loss, not only of one's body but of one's spirit. I shall avoid this and keep myself in harbor as much as I can, for even if there is no place for rest, as there cannot be during this pilgrimage of ours, at least there will be little opportunity for a storm. All the effort I have undertaken to this day has brought me no result except food and clothing. This is all I have got from my labors for my very own; all the rest has gone to other people. What madness it is to undertake tremendous efforts for things which can be obtained with little effort and to live in a constant state of agony.

Your Poggius will look out for himself; let other people say what they want. I consider it the part of a stronger mind to give up what other people so greatly desire rather than to pursue it; death seizes them more quickly than the people who keep their leisure. So I shall not step into anyone's shoes. For I cannot say that I shall not be involved in greater efforts, but I shall not seek them; I shall bear a burden when it is imposed but in such a way that I seem to refuse it. You may confirm this openly if anyone should ask you more about me. Farewell. Give my regards to our Luscus,[7] Cosmus, and Laurentius. Ferentino, the thirteenth day of August [1429].

LETTER

LXXVII

Today I received a letter from you which I shall answer briefly because I expect to come to you very soon. For I have asked permission from the Pope[1] which he has neither refused nor granted, but from my guesses I am sure I shall obtain it. If anyone is eager for rank and honor, let him stick to the Pope's side;[2] but I, being far from ambitious, go well away from him. I write this so that you may see that I persist in the course I have laid down. Many people are surprised at it, but I make up excuses to suit each occasion.

But we shall talk of this and many other things together if we are given a chance. I have not yet seen Arpino for I have not yet found the time to go there; but perhaps day after tomorrow, when the Pope is said to be going away,[3] I shall go there to find out whether there are any remains of ancient buildings.[4] But I do not promise you this. We shall discuss the girl and the books when we meet. Goodbye in haste, Ferentino,[5] the eighth day of September 1429.

LETTER
LXXVIII

I have followed your advice to stay here for some time and not set out for Rome so fast; now I am sent for and in such language that I cannot delay any longer.[1] For the Pope not only is surprised at my delay in returning but also reproves me for it; and although my reasons are honorable, still the tongues of my ill-wishers and detractors are quick to criticize me. Therefore, God willing, I shall start tomorrow, which will be the twenty-second day of this month; and I shall take care to keep well as long as it can be done.

Please look after the parchment for the Pliny[2] as well as for the other volumes which I had ordered from the man who binds the books; see that they are prepared quickly and brought to Rome as soon as possible. At the same time ask Leonardus for the first part of the Pliny and the *History of Illustrious Men,* which he translated from Plutarch, and ask Cosmus for his volume, which contains their lives.[3] Do all this carefully. I do not have the orations which you ask for. See whether you will have time to write there since I seem to see that there are many signs and indications of an incipient plague, so that I think that you, if you are wise, will come to Rome; but more of this some other time. Get me the parchment and the books and do not forget Cosmus; for I have two secretaries and no work for them unless you help me. Goodbye, and give my greetings to our Carolus.[4] In Terranuova in haste, 1429.

LETTER
LXXIX

In order to satisfy you[1] I am sending you through our Candidus[2] the old volume of the *Orations* of Cicero[3] and likewise Nonius Marcellus, which you ask for so constantly that it seems that all your work and study depend on them. But when you receive them I know that you will put them away somewhere for many months, not to say years, where you will not see them; and you will deprive me of reading them. You have now kept the Lucretius for twelve years and the Asconius Pedianus[4] too and the Petronius Arbiter[5] for seven or more; it seems to me that your tomb will be finished sooner than your books will be copied. Now you ardently desire the *Orations* and the Nonius as if the rest were already finished and you had the greatest leisure. Begin by sending one of them back to me for I am not so busy that I do not sometimes have time to read. See that I have the Lucretius[6] if you can, for I have not yet been able to read the whole book since it was always abroad; and now I should like to make it a proper resident. And see that I get back the Nonius Marcellus as soon as possible, for you live amid a copious supply[7] of books, and I in such want that they cannot be had anywhere around here.

I am not begging you for the paper the way I do for the books I want for I have no scribe, since the one who was here alone has gone away and the two who were to come have not come yet. I have been asked to send back the book to Monte Cassino and I shall send it back for I have copied, as you know, the book on aqueducts which was my special interest; the rest does not greatly please me and therefore I shall give it up easily.

I am quite well now; take care that you stay well too. So far we are not free of a suspicion of the plague which occasionally runs through the city, bobbing up here and there. It has afflicted some people; granted that they were few and far between, still we are not safe. Commend me to Cosmus and Laurentius and Carolus.[8] Rome, the thirteenth day of December 1429.

LETTER
LXXX

You have in your letter alerted me at length to the hindrance which has come up to prevent building on the site belonging to the Observantia,[1] and you say that I am frequently found guilty of creating this obstacle. But you write that you do not wish to decide casually about me or to judge me unless you have heard

from me. You are acting justly in this and like a friend, to trust
yourself alone more than all others, since you have known me
well, as they say, to my fingertips.[2] I wish you would always
affirm this when something is said to you against me, that surely
I have done nothing, I mean in matters of importance, unworthy
of a good man. I could with one sentence refute all rumors of
this kind, by saying that I do not fear the judgment of good men,
since it will be just and in my defense and I despise the judgment of bad men. But I do not want to say, as many other people
do, that my conscience is enough for me; I want my case to be
proved even to those who are outside it. To do this, the matter
must be reviewed a little more deeply. Many scandals in many
places arose long ago from these monks of the Observantia,[3] not
from the good brothers, for they are few, but from those who,
with a pretense of virtue, were sowing a multitude of errors and
were involved in all sorts of disgraceful schemes. You know
Augustine's famous remark in a certain letter: that no one does
more harm in the Church than a man who behaves badly while
he bears the name or the badge of holiness;[4] for he says no one
will dare to refute such a man, and his wickedness will be extended enormously through his example, since the sinner is
honored by people's reverence for his order. Brother Bernardinus,[5] who is learned and wise, brings to his sermons the
greatest moderation and the greatest care in speaking; he abandoned with fairness of mind the one practice in him which
seemed to deserve some blame and he has behaved in many
places in such a way that he has offered cause for no error or
disturbance among the people.[6] But many of the others who
want to imitate him climb into the pulpit without any learning
or virtue, with nothing to offer except impudence and stupidity.
Some, when they could not bear the association with their fellows through obstinacy and through pride, used to leave the
others and in the hope of glorifying their religion would build
new places and seek permission to wander and an opportunity
to rule other men.[7] For many of these people think so much of
themselves that they believe it right for them to obey no one and
to rule other people. I mention facts that are well known; I

leave out what is hidden and concealed, for if you knew, you would consider these places not congregations of the faithful or places of religious men but the workshops of criminals. But I leave out things which are so dishonorable that they cannot be honorably discussed. Since all this was the subject of many rumors (for they were partly before our eyes and partly reported by God-fearing men), it was decided to summon a number of friars of this kind from each province to correct it.

And so last summer there was a meeting of some eighty of the better educated of them, among whom was Albertus de Sarteano, a man who is not only learned but saintly. Among other things it was decided that there should be a general Chapter at the Feast of Pentecost[8] but that no one from the Order should preach except six; among those thanks to me was Albertus himself. Certain constitutions were made besides and also edicts of which I was not the originator but the framer, which then seemed necessary to repress widespread insolence. And among them there was this special decree[9] that no new place should be built for these monks until the Chapter was held; that if any had been begun, it should be torn down and that cloisters in which there were fewer than six brothers should be closed and the brothers dispersed to other places, but in no place should there be fewer than eight brothers. Many other things were accomplished too which it would take too long to describe, but they all seemed to be useful and Albertus himself is my witness to them.[10] I know that you will disapprove of these decrees unless you hear more; but, dear Nicolaus, please believe your Poggius when he tells you from the bottom of his heart that these things were all necessary. I could prove this before you as judge if the argument would not be too long. But I assure you of one thing, that not all these mountebanks are honest just because they are dirty with their heads bowed. There are many people in that order with whom I have strong ties since they have learning and lead a saintly life, but mixed with them is a huge crowd of reprobates who go about swollen and inflated and despise whatever is contrary to their views.

But let them see to themselves. Therefore, when these decrees

had been passed and they were well known to me, for I had
issued them, and when I was in my own country and heard that
woods were being cut down and a site marked out and buildings
built, I said at once that this could not be done on account of
the new laws. Afterwards when I came to the Curia, the dignity
and rank which I hold demanded, since I knew the Pope's mind
in this matter, that I inform him of the things which I had seen
done contrary to his decree.[11] From this it followed that he wrote
to the Bishop of Fiesole to prohibit it;[12] this was done not in the
name or by the authority of Poggius but by the Pope's authority.
The task of writing was entrusted to me; the work was mine, the
judgment someone else's. For those who say that I did this
under the influence of Master Antonius of Arezzo[13] are telling
lies. During the dinner of which you write, we discussed this
matter as happens when one thing leads to another. What I said
then, I do not rightly remember, and the words which are said
at night in drinking and eating are not of such importance that
they must be committed to memory. One thing I know, he did
not ask me for anything dishonorable and I did not promise him
anything. I am not so lightweight as to be moved by his words
when there was no honorable reason for it; I have a sort of
friendship with him but it is not so great that for his sake I would
exceed the bounds of honesty or wish to displease others in
some matter in order to please him. I do not think I have done
anything in my whole life, especially since I first came to the
City, which was intended to injure anyone; I have never harmed
anyone; I have never knowingly hurt anyone; I have never
treated anyone with contempt, and if any now think that they
have been harmed or that their desires are not being satisfied,
let them think whatever they want; reason means more to me
than popularity or fancy.

One thing I had left out which bears upon the matter: it was
decreed that no new place should be built until the next Chapter
meeting.[14] It goes no further; let them have patience for a little
while, if they will. If they won't, let them write to the Pope; I
shall not prevent their getting what they want. But I beg you
not to believe everything you hear; for I see in your letter that

you are quite upset, as if this prohibition had been unjustly
decreed. If I could talk to you I could set your mind at ease. I
want you to believe that I would have opposed their writing to
the Pope if I had thought that my opposition would strengthen
my stand or that of my associates; and granted that I am bad,
for Seneca says[15] that we are all bad, still you know that I am
fond of good men. You have never seen me joined in good will
or friendship with evil-doers but always associated with those
who were better than I. I do not despise religion or those dedicated to it but give them the greatest honor if they offer any
appearance of virtue. But I have been deceived so often and let
down so often that now I do not know what to believe or whom
to believe. So many are dishonest, so many cover the sin in their
souls with the face, expression, clothes, and semblance of virtue.
Here in the Curia many things come to light which are unknown
to others. For this is a sink of men's vices so that it becomes a
mirror in which the doings and the character of thousands are
reflected. You have here a long apology: if it has convinced you,
I shall be acquitted; if not, I shall seek someone to put my case.
But if you want me to do anything in this matter so far as I am
able, write to me. Goodbye and love me.

P.S. If any of those brethren complain that they have been
deprived of their very pleasant home,[16] they do this not without
justification in my judgment; for that nectar of ours, Jove's
drink, attracts many, not only foreigners but also citizens. Plato,
who was no Christian, chose for the Academy an unhealthy
spot[17] so that when the body was uncomfortable the mind would
be stronger and have time for improvement. But these men who
pretend to follow Christ, choose pleasant places, full of luxury
and every amusement, not in solitude but in very crowded districts, not to have time for their minds but for their bodies. Are
you taken in by their words? Do you endure their folly without
being horrified by their ambition? Do you not reject them, as
you used to, when these tales reach your ears? But I do not want
to be too rude for I am outraged and therefore I shall stop, although I have plenty to say. Goodbye, and show this letter to
Brother Ambrosius[18] so that I may know his opinion. Rome, in
haste and all in one breath, the sixteenth day of December 1429.

LETTER
LXXXI

You know very well that the entire blame for the silence which you complain has existed between us (I should say it existed in you alone) has nothing to do with me. For after the letter in which I answered your last letter, in which you discussed with me the building arrangements of the monks, I wrote to you through Candidus[1] when I sent you some of the books you asked for. Then I sent you three letters, granted they were short, which you never answered. Therefore I was afraid that my letters had offended you, for I was forced to suspect that from your silence, and so I too began to keep silent so as not to irritate you. Now I guess from your letter that you are annoyed with me on account of the one you received from me through Candidus; if you have changed your habits and do not want to hear the truth, I shall keep mine and shall write and speak according to my true opinion. There was nothing in that letter, I think, which ought to have offended you, unless, as I have often written to you, you are made of glass. I am amazed that, although you have so often heard me talk to you according to my true feelings, both in letters and in conversation as if to my other self, you, nonetheless, like a stranger and totally ignorant of my habits, are astonished if I express anything too freely. What indeed did I say in that letter which should have been taken the least amiss by a true friend? If I lied in any way, I am willing not only to be corrected but to be punished; but if indeed I remarked in some trifling matters on your delays, you ought rather to concentrate on correcting them than on getting angry with me. All your books are always ready for me[2] so that they ought to be considered no more yours than mine, if it is correct to say that we call the things we use our own. But I send them back to you when they have satisfied me, and I have never kept any of your volumes more than a year.[3] I am not rich in books but very poor, so that I ought rather to be supported with other people's wealth than with my own. Still such as it is, you may use it.

But consider whether you are doing right in this matter for

you seem to me to be making a mistake. You have now kept the
Lucretius for fourteen years and the Asconius Pedianus too.[4]
You have also kept the Petronius Arbiter and the *Silvae* of Statius
and the *Orations* which you got from me. Does it seem just to
you that, if I sometimes want to read one of these authors, I
cannot on account of your carelessness? You ought first to finish
one thing and then another; in that way you would have freed
yourself of annoyance and given me a chance to read what I
want. And do not think for a moment that I do not desire to
satisfy you ahead of others. But since you cannot copy more
than one book at a time[5] I do not see why you ask me so thick
and fast for books, especially since so many of them are still
waiting to be copied. I want to read Lucretius but I am deprived
of his presence; do you intend to keep him another ten years?
See that you do not indulge your habits too much, dear Nicolaus.
But you even complain about the Julius Firmicus. If the book
had been mine, I would have presented it to you; but since it
belonged to the Monastery of Monte Cassino, do you believe the
Abbot would have waited for it for ten years? As for the Frontinus
and the fragment of Aratus which you mentioned, they are here
with me[6] and I shall send them to you when I know that you
have copied the earlier ones I mentioned. For I shall not roll
up so many brief works into one volume, out of which none can
be untangled. I urge you to send me either the Lucretius or the
Asconius, which I shall have copied as soon as possible and then
I shall send them back to you to keep as long as you like; if you
do the same about the Petronius, I shall be very grateful.[7] The
reason for my not having written you anything about the comedies of Plautus was the same as I mentioned to you before; I
had decided to wait for your letter and to tell the truth, although
it is not profitable, still to speak in my own fashion, nothing so
serious had happened to me that I needed to write to you earlier.

Now indeed, I shall write to you more often and gladly. Nicolaus of Trier has come here, bringing with him sixteen comedies
of Plautus in one volume, among which are four which we have,
that is, the *Amphitruo,* the *Asinaria,* the *Aulularia,* and the
Captivi; twelve, though, are a prize; they are the *Bacchides,*

the *Mustellaria,* the *Menaechmi,* the *Miles Gloriosus,* the *Mercator,* the *Pseudolus,* the *Poenulus,* the *Persa,* the *Rudens,* the *Stichus,* the *Trinummus,* and the *Truculentus.*[8] Nobody has yet transcribed them, for the Cardinal is not making a copy of them for us; so far nobody except me has asked to. The book is in an ancient and corrupt hand like the Quintilian[9] and there are many imperfections in it. I shall not have it copied before I have read it and corrected it for, unless it is copied by a learned man, all the work will be in vain.[10] But I have decided to wait a little before I talk more about it to the Cardinal, for when he is pestered he gets angry but if I keep silent he will think nothing of it. He reported certain ridiculous things about the Aulus Gellius and the Curtius; that the Aulus Gellius is in truth cut short and imperfect and that its end ought to be its beginning and one leaf which he thought was the beginning of the Curtius is ridiculous and silly; the rest has fallen on its sponge. In the matter of the place to be built in our territory, I shall see that they get what they want.[11] Dear Nicolaus, I beg you and entreat you again and again for the sake of our friendship not to get so excited about my letter and not to weigh each word in the balance and reduce it all to your own bad humor. For I am just as I was, though perhaps a little freer in talking to you, especially since I have persuaded myself that I am talking to someone to whom I can say what I want; but if you want to have me stroke your head[12] and bow and scrape, I shall do that, even unwillingly,[13] rather than have you get angry with me so often. Goodbye and love me as you used to. I am ending because there is no more paper. Rome, the twenty-fifth of December 1429.[14]

LETTER

LXXXII

Today, dear Nicolaus, I celebrated my birthday[1] among scholars. I have never celebrated it before; not that it was of great importance that a man of such small account as I had been born into the world but really in imitation of the ancients whose cus-

tom this was[2] and because we saw it done by our friend, Coluccius,[3] who was a man full of virtue and eloquence. I celebrated
especially because today has brought me the beginning of my
fiftieth year,[4] so that the day was particularly worthy of remem-
brance, of being celebrated and noticed, for it brings the beginning of a new jubilee, which we read was a time considered very
solemn among the Hebrews.[5] For you know that in their language Jobel means the number fifty, at the beginning of which
we understand that the Hebrews were accustomed according to
an ancient law to free their slaves and forgive debts and remit
taxes. I believe that those men who established the custom were
wise men who intended by this symbolic act to give us, before
whom they set it up as an example, a reason for freeing our souls
from the slavery of vice. For if they assumed that the liberation
of the body should be undertaken with so much care, if they
thought that their debtors should be relieved and their debts
removed at this time, we ought to work that much harder to
free our souls which are oppressed with vices from the most
miserable and sordid slavery of all and give them their independence. This matter, although the whole extent of our life
requires it as necessary, the fiftieth year seems to demand especially, at which age we have a lot of strength left and we ought
to look forward as our years decline to the end already coming
into sight and to keep it, as it were, set before our eyes. And so
I think that this freedom of spirit alone standing out far beyond
anything else is designated by this Jubilee, and this is what we
ought above all to seek for and to pursue.

This rite of ancient observance has now added for me the concern, and no small one at that, that I should also seek to claim
my freedom, the freedom of which the philosophers tell, who
think that bad men are slaves and good men are free. I truly
consider them fortunate who have the gift of enjoying in their
early years this freedom of spirit which is given to very few
people; and I suspect that, as a rule, it is most conspicuously
lacking where it is considered to be most abundant. But those
people, too, are not to be despised whom a more advanced age
leads to the cultivation of virtue, a pretty difficult matter and one

in which few people succeed. For it is difficult, according to the old Greek proverb,[6] to be good, and it is not the lot of everyone, of every mind and intelligence, but of those "whom righteous Jupiter loved or burning virtue raised to the heavens."[7] As far as concerns me, dear Nicolaus, since my years demand another life, as old Terence says, other customs,[8] I shall take care, care of no everyday kind, that the arrival of the new Jubilee may also give me an approach to the liberty which we desire.

Now I do not want you to think that all of a sudden, like some mean and clownish hypocrite of whom there are a great many, I am going to retire from society so that I may prefer to seem free sooner than to be so; but I shall go step by step into the right way of living, avoiding the pitfalls, first of all which age by its very nature now rejects. Our years bring many benefits, but in one thing they are especially kind when they take away with them the strength of the senses which are in revolt against the soul. It is said that recognition of disease is a sign of future health; but since what is wrong with me is familiar and constantly before my eyes there is reason to hope that your friend Poggius will soon have himself under control. Surely ambition and greed are two very sinister rocks on which the greater part of humanity is shattered, and they have already left me, to my relief. Something else, about which you used often to follow me up and sometimes make fun of me, time itself in which things daily grow colder has removed, thanks to my advancing years, so that I now could not do what it would have been my duty not to do; I now must live at peace with a kind of human being — and a specially unwarlike kind — in a field where victory is the idlest kind of success one can win.

This is what I had especially wished today, that you had been here for my birthday party, which your dignity[9] would have made far more distinguished, established here among my greatest friends; for you would have had as companions at the banquet Antonius Luscus, Andreas of Constantinople, Cincius, Ludovicus Orcanus,[10] and Rinucius. But since you could not be with us, my letter will represent my birthday to you. Goodbye and love me, Rome, the eleventh day of February 1430.

LETTER
LXXXIII

I am glad that you are safe, especially at this time when everything is dangerous. For although life is always uncertain, these
plagues make it more uncertain still; and they are so frequent[1]
and they seize upon so many places that we must fear that we
shall all be killed just by them alone. My country has not yet
recovered from the plague which troubled it five years ago.[2] Now
again it seems that it will succumb to a massacre equally violent
which came upon it very suddenly. I do not know why this is;
if we look to our sins, there is always a far greater abundance
of evil than of good, and I think that those who preceded us
were even worse than we are. Also for the most part it is the
wicked who escape these sicknesses. Here the air has not yet
become pure again, for quite a few people have died but there
is this about it: they are believed to have died more from contagion than from the impurity of the air since many people
escape.

But let us get back to our own affairs. I see what you write
about the library[3] and what you mean about the city; you do not
know what harm there is, for you have not been in what we call
our Campagna. Tomorrow I shall go to the Pope; for he wants
me with him, and as long as he stays in the country, I will stay
in a certain cottage which does not have the plagues of Egypt
but has all the sufferings of Job. Indeed it would not be suitable
for our donkeys. The Pope is at Grottaferrata;[4] I do not know how
long he will stay there, but meanwhile I shall wander around
through the whole area of Tusculum, which is very near us, if
the rain permits. I wish you could be here with me during the
night; you would hear the donkeys singing so loudly that they
would wake[5] even a drunkard.

I have done nothing that I wanted to do about the Plautus.[6]
Before the Cardinal went away I asked him to send me the book;
he refused to. I do not understand the man; he thinks he did
something splendid, when actually he had nothing to do with
finding the book but has behaved in such a way that a book

found by somebody else is hidden by him. I have told both him and his attendants that I shall never again ask him for the book and that is the truth. I should rather forget what I have learned than learn anything new from books of his. I am having the letters of St. Jerome copied by one of my secretaries, and I have reached number one hundred. I have searched through several volumes and collected from them about one hundred and forty letters. I have heard that in the Monastery of Monte Cassino there is a volume in Lombard letters in which there are two hundred and twenty-five epistles.[7] I wrote at once to the Cardinal of Piacenza, who has fled thither from the plague which began at home, to send me the volume. If he does so I shall be delighted; for I have not heard so far of so many of the letters of St. Jerome being found. Will you write me how many you have seen, for, after I begin, I shall seek out all that can be found; and when those have been copied, I shall have a holiday from secretaries. I was not able to get the Pliny from Leonardus Aretinus.[8] I do not know why; that is the only book which I still want, and if it were not for the inaccuracy of the available texts, I should not bother Leonardus.

The war with Lucca has been begun very stupidly,[9] and I do not know how it will end; I never liked it and it was not a time, when the former scars had not yet healed,[10] to expose the body to dangerous wounds. Cicero wrote[11] that if the cause was good, one should not blame the beaten side though it lost; I say that if the cause is bad, one should not praise the winning side though it won, for it is not right to praise policies for their outcome.[12] To finish briefly what could take a lot of words, I have never seen or read about a more stupid government or one in which good counsel had less power. Aristotle justly said that democracy was worst of all, for in it no virtue has any standing.[13] Let the people who govern our state attend to this; my only wish is that the rashness of a few may not harm the whole population. The tyrant of Lucca, who has so long oppressed his city and accumulated such a fortune, has been dislodged from his glory and is in prison[14] and is even being tortured, I hear, to make him reveal his treasure. God, the Lord of vengeance, has acted generously;

for every man waits his destined hour;[15] even the cities are
doomed to their fate. Let us spend our leisure with our books,
which will take our minds off these troubles, and will teach us
to despise what many people desire. Give my respects to Cosmus and Laurentius and Carolus;[16] and to these add our Sibyl.
Write me her name so that we can make a ladder for her to climb
to heaven. Goodbye, at Rome, the third day of September
[1430].[17]

LETTER

LXXXIV

I gave some specific errands to Master Franciscus of Pistoia[1]
when he left us. Among them the most important was to look
for any marble statue, even if it were broken, or any unusual
head which he could bring back to me with him. I said that there
was a great supply of them in the places through which he was
going. He has indeed been quite careful in carrying out my com-
missions; for yesterday I received letters from him written from
Chios[2] in which he informed me that he was holding in my name
three marble heads by Polycleitus and Praxiteles. They are
heads of Juno, Minerva, and Bacchus,[3] which he praises highly
and says that he will carry with him as far as Cajeta. I do not
know what to say about the names of the sculptors; as you know,
the Greeks are very wordy and perhaps they have made up the
names in order to sell the heads more dearly. I hope that I am
wrong to suspect this. He also writes that he had got these heads
from a man named Caloiros, who had recently found nearly a
hundred undamaged marble statues[4] of marvelously beautiful
workmanship in some cave. He does not write further, using
his health as an excuse, for he had caught the tertian fever. He
adds besides that a man called Andreolus Justinianus will send
you something.

I know that when you read this you will be on fire with a
desire to go there and you will want wings to fly; for the wind
would not keep up with your haste, not even in flight. Now I

shall stay here to dream. I immediately wrote back to Master Franciscus and I wrote to Andreolus, too[5] (for he is, as I hear from our friend Rinucius, a pretty knowledgeable man), asking them to find out whether any of these statues could be had either for a price or a prayer, and to use great care and diligence in this matter, and to let me know the result as soon as possible. I wanted you to have a share in this discovery. I think that these statues are of gods because of their heads and that they were hidden in some shrine. He writes that the head of Minerva has a laurel crown and that of Bacchus two horns. When they arrive, I shall place them in my little gymnasium. The Minerva will not feel out of place with us; I shall put her among my books. The Bacchus ought to feel grand, for if he deserves a lodging anywhere it is certainly in my country where he is particularly worshiped. We shall also have a place for Juno, for since at one time she was the wife of an adulterer, she will now be a concubine. I also have something here which I shall bring home with me. Donatellus saw it[6] and praised it highly. I do not want this letter to have anything else in it except the gossip about the statues; so goodbye and love me. Rome, the twenty-third day of September [1430].[7] When I had written this, I received your letter; since it needs a long answer, I shall leave it for another time.

LETTER

LXXXV

I can tell from several of your letters that you are quite worried about both public and private affairs[1] and to such a degree that I see that your cleanliness is irritated in this filthiest of cities. Therefore, in order to call your attention away from troubles of this kind, I wrote you three days ago[2] about those marble heads and statues too, lately found, in which you will surely take some pleasure.

Now to carry you back again to antiquities which especially please you, I shall tell you of my walks in the country when the

Pope transferred himself to Grottaferrata. For although we were
not away more than fifteen days, I spent the whole time in exam-
ining the country with the greatest pleasure. For I did not seem
to be outside the city, but in the city itself, there is such a quantity of buildings and magnificent villas; there are many swimming pools and many reservoirs for collecting water; there are
aqueducts, partly arched, partly built underground, and so dis-
tributed everywhere that almost every villa could use its own;
there are broken columns and various kinds of marble scattered
through the fields; also stones visible in huge piles leave inti-
mations of great things in our minds.[3] There still exist very large
remains of quite a few villas filled with various bits of ornaments
and fragments of statues; there are arches and vaults and sub-
terranean passages and cellars[4] so large that some of them stretch
for more than a stadium; I think that these must have been the
habitations of the slaves, for when they came home from the
fields at night, they were thrown into these cellars like dungeons
from which they could not escape.[5] There are also some prom-
enades, beautifully built and still whole, of the same shape as
those in the city which are popularly called *capociae*[6] but of
more elegant construction.

I have wandered through the whole district of Tusculum. I
have also been to Tusculum itself, where there is a magnificent
villa in a high place and practically whole; almost the whole of
the plain of Tusculum overlooks the sea and the City. There are
huge remains of another villa, the walls reaching far into the
distance, patterned in stone and brick, with arches all of one
design turned in every direction so wide and reaching so far
and so built one above the other that today a fortress of considerable magnitude has been built on top of them. I think this
must have been the villa of Clodius, who, Cicero said, built
the most ridiculous structures in his Tusculan villa, or else the
villa of Lucullus. At Grottaferrata there was a villa which must
have been Cicero's or have belonged to someone like him. It
was certainly a private dwelling, as shown by the walls which
still remain all the way around it, and especially by the cellars,
which go the full length of the villa, and by the swimming pool

of ancient design, from which, since it is in the higher part of the ground, one can see the City.[7] To it comes an ancient aqueduct, which is led down from the mountain nearby.

We were also in Albano, where besides the remains of the baths and the stadium and a wall built of squared stones, I saw nothing unusual; there are scattered remains of villas which from the size of their ruins appear to have been remarkable. I did see a most astounding achievement, a channel cut deep into the hill to drain the water from the lake which is a little more than a mile away from Alba.[8] I do not know its name and it is not the Alban Lake which Livy mentioned;[9] for that is on the other side in the plain toward the sea, whereas this one is three miles around, surrounded by the highest mountains. The shore is full of buildings and quite a number of statues, and there are many places with a very pleasant outlook in which it would appear from the various heaps of ruins that there were magnificent dwellings. You would say that not only the city but even the whole region was supported on arches. To these delights, in which I spent the day as I walked around, I added some at night, so that nothing seems to have been missing from my pleasure.

I was settled in a castle or rather a most disgusting hovel which is called Borghetto,[10] a mile from Grottaferrata; the place was full of a variety of animals, especially donkeys and dogs, and the night was divided between their braying and barking. The dogs have the first watches of the night until cockcrow as if they were placed there to guard the camp, filling everything with the loudest and most confused barking. The donkeys followed them as if each had a share of the watch in his own position but with a milder sound, and when one began the rest answered in order, so that they produced a certain sweet harmony with their rude braying, a harmony that encouraged sleep; and not only once but often through the night they sang a similar song with mixed voices. I think that they believed that they were complimenting and flattering me in this way because I was a stranger. Although too much of this sometimes made it annoying to me, still because they encouraged me to sleep and because their skill in singing made the camp safer from danger, I soon turned my annoyance into amusement.

I wish you had been with me; for I know what your patience is like and that you would have got the greatest amusement from this chorus and would have forgotten the troubles of Rimini.[11] But I do not wish this letter to exceed its bounds and I want this one to contain only my trip in the country, just as the earlier one contained the description of the statues. Goodbye and give my good wishes to Cosmus, Laurentius, and Carolus. Rome, the twenty-seventh of September[12] [1430].

LETTER
LXXXVI

Your letters upset me a good deal, dear Nicolaus, because I gather from them that you are much troubled, first by our internal dissensions which have caused us much inconvenience[1] and also by the very heavy oppression of the war[2] which has been weighing on our country for some time.[3] Such conditions are truly disturbing; such tumults are being prepared that everyone, as I see it, must be weary of his fate. For we are all in suspense about the future which is so uncertain and so difficult to interpret that if anyone wanted to comment on the things which in the last few years have gone contrary to his hope and his expectation and on what seems to hang over us, he would say that no man, no matter how wise, could possibly figure out how all this will turn out. He could only forecast that this storm, this tempest, which we see shaking and destroying Italy was preparing some even greater shipwreck;[4] but he would say that the end will be what the fates decree. Something stronger than we are certainly rules us, dear Nicolaus, which our strength cannot oppose, and it is our duty to endure calmly the common conditions which God may send us. It is hard indeed to go against Fate, and it is too large a matter to fall to the decision of the common people. You see what a conflagration the war with Lucca has started in Italy,[5] but you know yourself how suddenly and how needlessly, with no mature deliberation, this war was undertaken and how all good men detested it. I always disapproved of it, if you remember my letters, for I was afraid that it would be the cause, in which I hope I am mistaken, of some even greater calamity. Nevertheless the majority has prevailed over merit and greed has overcome reason, so that fate is displaying its power; as a result from a small spark we see the whole of Italy aflame with war on land and sea. And so you are quite right to deplore the state of the country and to regret that it is ruled more by caprice than by good counsel and that it is agitated (which is generally the most pernicious thing of all) by the quarrels of parties out of all proportion to the needs of the Republic. But it is paying a suitable penalty, since, although the scars of an earlier war were not yet healed and although it had not yet recovered its strength, weak and defenseless, with no equipment and with no settled plan, it jumped hastily and boldly into another war, as if it had not yet found out how undependable its citizens' counsels are in time of war. And even this would not have done so much harm if, once the war was started, they had directed it with some wisdom and by common agreement.[6] But while some were raging with envy, some with greed, and some with bitter hatred of their fellow citizens, all together they led the state to the brink of destruction,[7] and so bad policy has been seconded by still worse actions; while some, putting their private fortune ahead of the advantage of the state, preferred something else to the defeat of our enemy. The outcome of this admirable behavior is plain to see. Many villages were lost, some were destroyed by fire; and our country has been damaged and devastated in many places. Meanwhile we are worn out by constant expense and forced to serve the lust and insolence of the soldiers, which is the greatest torture of all.

I shall leave out worse things which seem to threaten us. Two kings who are not to be disregarded are on our necks, relying not so much on their own strength[8] as on the discords of the Italians, and whoever does not fear them seems to me imprudent

rather than brave. And yet these kings[9] would not be very fright-
ening if our own people had not lost all reason and prudence
both for conducting our affairs in peace and for managing a war.
I have often wondered not only privately but also in conversation with other people how it happens that, although there are
many wise, learned, and far-seeing men in our city whose individual intelligence and wisdom you would praise, the government is badly run and foolish decisions are preferred to wise
ones,[10] so that the wisdom of many men, added together, is
turned into the greatest nonsense. And certainly, either our
citizens do not have the prudence for which they are given credit
or else they keep it for their private affairs and discard it in public
matters where they are led astray by their private interests.
Whichever of these you may accept as true, it would be better,
in my opinion, if those people who are intent on their own business and on money would take counsel for the peace and quiet
of the people, instead of mixing in things of which they can
discern neither the beginning nor the end. Now surely our citizens ought to be persuaded by experience, the real teacher, that
they have no gift for the art of war, since they have never seen
a line of battle drawn up or a fort. For what is more ridiculous
than for people to be in charge of a major war who have never
performed the tiniest bit of warlike duty?[11] But in reality men
who have never so much as seen the blade of a sword give orders
from their safe retreat to the actual commanders in the war as
to how the forces should be deployed and attacks made, towns
stormed, and the enemy driven back. You well know how, as
a result, affairs have prospered in this season, so that we can
truly say that we deserved all that has befallen us. And yet I wish
I could attribute these things to fate as I had begun by doing
rather than to the incompetence[12] of our leaders; granted that
we prove the predictions of the stars by our own stupidity.

But since these things cannot be changed, there is still hope
that we may not be more tortured by public disaster than is our
portion, since nothing can be added or subtracted from our
destiny even if we spend our days and nights in deliberation

and worry of this kind. For there never was or will be any lack
of reasons for complaining if anyone wants to respond to either
private or public misfortune with tears. Both in peace and in
war very few are found who bear their destiny well, for both
prosperous and adverse fortunes are difficult; the one kind makes
a man lose his sense of proportion, and the other kind makes
him very depressed. Therefore there is nothing free of complaint even for those whose good fortune is publicly admired.
And there never was any state so well established that there was
not a lot wrong in it. But we turn our minds to the present evils
which are distressing us, and we cannot keep from being upset
when we are tormented by the stupidity and wickedness of
others.[13] But since these things can neither be changed nor
corrected by our efforts, it is better to laugh like Democritus[14]
at the common folly than to weep at it. It is the business of a wise
man to try to do what he can and to leave the rest to the gods,[15]
to hope for the best, and if things turn out badly to bear them
patiently. I think, therefore, that we should abandon futile
worry over the things that oppress us and turn our minds to our
studies. When the things of the moment displease you, take time
for the past which will distract you from these troubles. I, in
the manner of our Terence, have convinced myself that many
unpleasant things are going to happen, and I have prepared
myself for them without fear "and count as gain good that comes
unforeseen."[16] I want you to believe me that I disapprove of
many of our public affairs but no particularly bitter worry distresses me, no special care burns me, and no great anxiety tor-
tures me. Like a stranger passing by I hear and see all this without alarm, though it turns many pale. Let those who are charged
with the common welfare attend to these matters. I have already
decided what I shall do even if things turn out as many people
fear: namely, that I shall devote myself to Greek literature,[17]
which I now touch as if feeling my way in the dark. But I have
already been lengthy enough; the pleasure of talking to you
draws me on. Goodbye and love me, Rome, the twenty-seventh
of November [1430].

LETTER
LXXXVII

I am glad that you reached Verona in spite of all the difficulties of the journey.[1] We must set these travels of yours beside the labors of Hercules.[2] And so, see that our friend, Carolus, puts them in writing. I believe that it was less difficult for Hercules to cross Libya than for Nicolaus to cross the mud of the Via Flaminia and bear the dangers of the Po, but these things you especially should bear with a brave spirit, since you are accustomed to bearing other things quietly when they seem to suit your habits. The cold which bothers you I think can be prevented by warm clothes and fire, or else you can hide in some inner chamber where the force of the wind will not reach you.

I have sent for the letters of St. Jerome, but the Abbot[3] has given the excuse that the volume is very large and cannot be sent in the care of just one man. One of the monks wrote me that it contains one hundred and forty-five letters, but I already have one hundred and seventy which I shall send you when you go back to Florence to have illuminated[4] and bound. If I had found any more I would have added them to these volumes for I have already made them into two. What you write about Petrus de Verona[5] is an empty dream. He hardly knows what we have; I asked him about this after receiving your letter and he laughed at my question. But another man, a Florentine, who has just come from France, reported to me that a man he knows well told him that he had seen the missing ones in some monastery. This story is very like earlier ones; still I wanted him to write to his friend and inquire carefully about the facts and ask for the beginning of every book. He has done it and sent the letter here; it is no loss, even if nothing comes of it as I expect. The Plautus I have so far not been able to get; now if I could, I would not, and I promise you that I shall not beg the Cardinal for it any more nor shall I read it these next three years even if he grants it to me of his own accord. It is being copied and will be sent as a gift to the Duke of Milan,[6] who asked for it in a letter. The Marquis of Ferrara has also asked for it; it will be given to them but so corrupt that it will truly seem to have returned from exile among the barbarians. Our man wants what you might call the honor of a triumph from this book as if he had found it by his own effort and expense. He asked Antonius Luscus to add something at the beginning to establish the tradition of so important a matter. And so he made certain iambics which he added to the work as a kind of prologue;[7] but if ever I have the book transcribed I shall throw away these new verses and stick to the old Plautus. No one, believe me, will copy the Plautus well unless he is well educated; for it is in the same writing as many old books, which I think must have been written by women with no separation between the words, so that one often has to guess. Let others ask for it as they please. I shall not read Plautus for the next three years, even if I have to forget what I know.

You have written to me lately about the Pliny,[8] that you want to copy it. I was most amused by your statement. I want to find out from you how the book is getting on; but I think it has fallen on its sponge;[9] in summer the heat, in winter the cold hinders you and you *col ghiribizare*.[10] If I had the Pliny, it would be convenient for me, since my copyist will stop writing in a few days for lack of material. The one who writes better I have sent away; this year he wrote the Decade of the Second Punic War, so that everything would be in the same hand, and the *Letters to Atticus*.[11] I have nothing to write because you are away from Florence; perhaps I shall send the other one away too.

The war with Lucca,[12] you can be my witness, I have always disapproved, both on account of the injustice of its origin and the knavery of many of the citizens; no good end can be expected from a bad beginning. Still I should prefer anything to going into another war with the Duke, for it is difficult to guess its outcome; and believe me, his ruin will drag us with him. It would be better to give up what has been badly begun and to come to our senses for a while. But let those who are in charge of the matter see to it. My voyage is in harbor.[13] But remember this: in less than four years you will see Italy full of barbarians and many people made their prey unless we keep out of war. Goodbye and love me. Greet Carolus for me, Rome, the sixth day of January 1431.[14]

LETTER
LXXXVIII

Although I know, dear Nicolaus, that you do not admire what goes on in our generation because, I think, you concentrate on deeds of earlier men, which were indeed magnificent and worthy of the highest praise;[1] still I think that you should not despise some of the more recent happenings, especially those which occur very rarely, and with some thought given to the fame and the splendor of the circumstances. The things that we read must certainly be considered of the highest value, and they can be more easily admired than imitated by men of our time. But nevertheless the genius of historians has conferred no little dignity and greatness on our forefathers for they describe even small events so brilliantly that they are accepted as important.[2] We, however, despise our own history and attack it in the telling and with a certain intellectual disdain. If anything is done that is worth remembering, it is forgotten for lack of writers,[3] so that our deeds seem small and ridiculous, not so much by any defect in them as by our own fault. But let other people feel as they wish, I enjoy such occasions as are vouchsafed to us and of which at long intervals we are spectators. And if it occasionally happens that some image of former glory[4] is manifested to us in them, I enjoy a double happiness,[5] on the one hand seeing things which delight the eye, since they are far from usual with us, and on the other hand, enjoying with my mind[6] those historical events which we admire when we read about them.

I shall therefore describe[7] to you the arrival of our Caesar[8] at Rome and his coronation, and you in reading this, with your mind relieved of the private worries which sometimes inevitably torment you, will enjoy some of the pleasure with me, hearing things which very few men of our age[9] remember having seen. But I want you to abandon the bitter critical attitude[10] which you generally use toward contemporary matters, and if everything else displeases you at least listen patiently to me while I tell you what happened. On the day that Caesar entered the City (for he entered on Ascension Day and by the gate which is behind the tomb of Hadrian,[11] in accordance with the ancient form of the ceremony) a whole multitude of the population, both men and women, poured out to see him[12] as he was making the journey. The City of Rome is now divided into thirteen districts[13] and contains a slightly smaller number of people than it did when it was divided into fourteen. From some one district each year are chosen eight boys of the equestrian order[14] to celebrate the public games and they lead the various ceremonies of the games, and both they and their horses are dressed up in particolored clothes and marked. These boys and the other performers in the games which form part of the regular celebrations, who are there in accordance with tradition, were instructed to precede the King and to make the day a festive one. There preceded the King first of all equipment of various kinds in a long procession, partly for personal adornment and partly for military use. Then followed a tremendous number of men on horseback, some of them citizens, some of them strangers who had met and joined outside the City. Then came various embassies of kings, princes, and peoples, among whom were the orators of the Greek Emperor,[15] who attracted to themselves the talk and the eyes of everyone with considerable wonder, partly because of the novelty of their clothes and their remarkable headgear and partly because of the thickness of their hair and beards. There were many noblemen mingled with this procession who had come from various places to this celebration; besides this there were a crowd of trumpet players and flutists and many other people who filled the ears[16] of the onlookers with the sound of various instruments. After these came the men I mentioned as chosen from various regions for the games, holding silken flags in their hands and themselves remarkable for their costume. Then followed all the magistrates of the City and those who hold any public office, each one in his robes, and some in suits of gold, with which their horses were also covered and which they said was the antique garb.[17] After that came a long line of people on foot, some of them carrying olive branches, some of them carrying things they call torches. I could not learn the ancient name but the thing is an ancient custom, since ancient sculptures show, in the triumphal arches, that they were carried before the emperors,[18] and in other places that they were carried in front of the consuls among the fasces. When they move these things with their hands all at once in rhythm, they produce a festive, happy, and lively effect from the sound of the bells. In front of these people, as was the custom with earlier emperors, went a noble youth in a purple doublet and gold wig, scattering silver money among the people,[19] an unusual sight, but quite in keeping with the imperial position. Finally the priests came just before the King, singing hymns. Then at last Caesar himself came, riding on a white horse, under a gold canopy which noblemen carried on gilded poles, and he was the finest sight of all. For his expression is very kind and benevolent and his face is humorous and generous; his beard is nearly white and thick; there is such affability and majesty in his expression[20] that people who do not know him can tell by his appearance and distinguished expression that he is king over others. After him followed armed knights from our country, chosen from those whom the Pope pays. In this company he reached the Church of St. Peter in the traditional style and was received out of doors by the Pope who was sitting in front of the steps of the church,[21] before the door of the outer portion, amidst the loud cheers[22] and plaudits of many excited people. Then after they had advanced to the high altar together and a solemn Mass had been performed, one went to his destined palace and the other to the one he always uses. Here you have the entrance.

Now listen to the coronation which followed on the Feast of Pentecost, on the last day of May.[23] I know that this custom of crowning the emperor as we now do it is not the ancient one but was started long ago by Charlemagne,[24] king of the Franks. When Constantine and his son Leo were ruling the Greeks[25] and when he and all the other emperors had long since left Italy, which was torn on all sides by wars and at that time oppressed on the one hand by the fierce and barbarous nation of the Lombards and on the other by the Moors, without any resource and practically without life, when Rome also was in the worst possible difficulties, Charlemagne[26] was called to help the city by Stephen, the Pope at Rome. After he had conquered Desiderius, the king of the Lombards, and overcome the barbarians, he was called Emperor for his merits by the Roman people and was crowned by Pope Adrian. This coronation custom was observed by his successors and has been preserved to our day.

As you know, it was the custom among the ancient emperors to wear a laurel crown in their triumphs;[27] when the authority to have a triumph had been awarded by the Senate and the right to wear a laurel crown, it was the special glory of the winners of triumphs. The right to wear a laurel crown in perpetuity was first given to the dictator, Caesar, by the Senate, and the later emperors used this right at their own pleasure, despising any higher authority of their superiors. But since that custom has fallen completely into disuse and has disappeared, not only from use but from the memory of men, let us think that this more recent custom, which has been kept up for nearly seven hundred years, is an ancient one[28] and, abandoning what custom has already disposed of, let us follow the usage which our ancestors piously established and which has been passed down to us and approved by the agreement of Christians. When our emperors are elected,[29] before the consecration and coronation, they are called Kings of Rome through a confusion of vocabulary, as if the name of Emperor were to be valued more highly than the name of King. But the ancient Romans, after the expulsion of Tarquinius Superbus, on account of their hatred of kings, obliterated the name and established by a vote in the Senate that never should a king be allowed in the City thenceforth; although every year many people, on account of their skillful and fortunate action against the enemy, were called *Imperatores* as an honor by the soldiers.[30] Hence among the other leaders of the state of his day even Marcus Tullius Cicero[31] was called *Imperator* by the soldiers in Asia. Julius Caesar, however, when after frequent victories he had often been called *Imperator* by the army, seized the name not of Emperor or of King but of Dictator,[32] because the name King had incurred so much hatred for itself in the City. Since he desired the name of King but feared the indignation of the people, he arranged an expedition against the Parthians and asserting that it said in the Sibylline books that the Parthians could not be overcome except by a king, he managed to have himself named King, which provided a reason for the conspirators to hasten his death.[33] None of the later emperors dared to call himself King of the Romans. Actually the title Emperor did not belong perpetually to Caesar, any more than the title Consul or Praetor or Tribune of the People.[34] For the early Augusti, although they kept the surname of Caesar and Augustus, were called sometimes as often as seven times,[35] sometimes less often, Emperor, Consul, and Tribune of the People. For the title signified not an office but an honor. For when things went well against the enemy, it was the custom as an honor for a consul, pro-consul, or praetor to be applauded and greeted as Emperor[36] by the soldiers. I do not know where this new custom of naming a man first King and then Emperor came from.[37] I think it must have arisen among the barbarians who, since they did not know the early history or understand the force of words[38] and since the name of King was more usual among them, living as they did under kings and since they saw an emperor as unique and rare, thought that far nobler which they observed to be rarer and more unusual. However this grew up, the title obviously was not introduced with clear understanding by these later people.

But what a fool I am to dare to batter at the ears of a scholar with these tales.[39] When the day of the coronation had come, Caesar entered the inner porch of the church and gave his oath[40] to the Pope[41] before what is called the silver door,[42] according to the custom of his forerunners. Then he went further into the church behind the high altar and stood at the right, dressed like a deacon, and was anointed by the Bishop of Ostia[43] with the sacred oil; I think that the name of Augustus must have come down from this. For you know that the ancients called places that were consecrated to augury[44] "augusta"; and this name, considered as holy, was given by the Senate to Octavian.[45] In observance of this even our emperors are called Augustus after consecration. After this, he came to the Pope, who was celebrating mass at the altar, and who received him with a kiss; and during the ceremony the Pope first put a white miter on his head, so that the horns rose above his temples, and then on top of this he placed a golden crown. Then the Pope gave him a golden orb and scepter and a naked sword, as if he were a soldier of Christ, who would take up arms if necessary to defend the Church of Rome and the faith of Christ. After these ceremonies were finished, according to custom, he put on a cope; and then the Pope and the Emperor mounted their horses and started together toward the Bridge of Hadrian. Emperors used at one time to travel on foot as far as this place, holding the Pope's bridle; this Emperor was prevented by his gout from keeping the custom.[46] When they reached the Tomb of Hadrian, the Pope went home, and the Emperor continued with his miter and crown and priestly vestments as far as the Basilica of the Lateran, amid the applause of the rejoicing population. On the bridge, while he was crossing it, he got down from his horse and gave military decorations to several brave men and boys.[47]

These things filled the whole City with the greatest rejoicing, for the festive day was beautiful and the most solemn of all that I ever saw in the City; and I pray that, as it brought the greatest rejoicing, so it will also bring with it peace and concord. Farewell, dear Nicolaus, and if I have been long-winded, do not be surprised for I have nothing to do and I thoroughly enjoy a talk with you. Answer me when you want to. Rome, the sixth of June [1433].

LETTER

LXXXIX

I am glad that you liked my letter, for I take no pleasure in my remarks, although I know they are unpolished, unless you approve of them, since I know that you are rarely susceptible to flattery. But when you write that I told you that the election of the Emperor began with Charlemagne, your observation is incorrect. For I wrote you that it was not the election but the coronation[1] which began then.[2] I did not say a word about the election which, I think, was established a little more than three hundred years ago by Pope Gregory the Seventh, who was ·a native of Germany.³ I said nothing about that for want of history books which I sent some time ago to Florence,⁴ for I did not want to state anything of which I was not sure and for which I could not give a definite reason. But the Emperor left here wanting to see Florence. If this works out, he will be received with great pomp and ceremony. If any of you keeps a record of this he will be doing the right thing.⁵

I read to the Pope that part of your letter, that is practically the whole of your letter, which had to do with monks.⁶ He laughed and regretted the wickedness of things in general; he asked me what I thought should be done. I said that the responsibility should be given⁷ to some good man; but he asked where such a man is to be found. Finally I left it at this: that if you suggest someone whom you approve, it seems he will do what you want; that is, the place will be reformed. So let me know to what man or men⁸ this task should be given, one who will not fall down on the job in any way. The General of the Order is expected any day; he is a great friend of mine. When he comes, I shall discuss the matter with him and I shall urge him to clean up that thorny field by pulling out the brambles. The Emperor did not suggest to us or persuade us to dig out the Pincian Hill⁹ to look for treasure. But some of his men did make a vain attempt to do so while the Emperor not only laughed at them but also ridiculed them. The Pope is wiser, for he would rather use visible treasures than hidden ones.

A collector in Greece has died,¹⁰ and the man of whom you spoke left a month ago to get his property.¹¹ I have not found out as yet what his field is, but he says that he knows a great deal about Greek literature and owns the works of many Greek authors; we have not yet found out how much he knows about the Latin ones. But when he comes back we shall find out for he has been made a secretary; there is so much to do that six people are not enough for the work which an old man and weak at that could easily accomplish. Goodbye and love me and stay at home in this heat; that is, I have found, the best method of escaping the extremes of this climate.[12] Rome, the sixteenth of August [1433].

LETTER

XC

I heard of the fall of our Cosmus with misery and with the deepest regret;[1] but such is the state of our times that keeping quiet is safer though less honorable. This is the result of factions in the state[2] and of popular agitation.[3] If complaints did any good, I could bewail his private misfortune; but since things once done cannot be altered or reformed, we must be calm in bearing this sudden change[4] of fortune and console ourselves with what the mercy of God has left us.

But enough of this. As to what you write of my interceding for that church which you hope will be free, I shall gladly do what I know will please you. But I believe that the church at Arezzo will not be given to the man you hope[5] but that the opportunity will go to another; I do not know who it will be, for many people are suggested and it would not be proper to write who I hope will get it. Send me the name of the man you mentioned and whether he is in orders, so that if at any time there should be a chance, I could speak for him, provided he is the kind of person for whom I could or would dare to intercede with a free conscience.[6] For when I ask the Pope[7] something he generally questions me on what my conscientious opinion is. If, with a frank expression, I sponsor somebody about whom I have found out, he answers my requests; and he also takes my word in many matters, because he understands clearly that I speak the truth sincerely and do not intervene for anything which he could honorably refuse. And so I have changed his former dislike into the greatest favor,[8] so that he has great confidence in me. I am writing this so that when you tell me of something you want from the Pope you will not speak against your own conscience because I match mine to yours without any exception, knowing that you are a good man and truthful.

I see the affairs of our Italy so confused that I have more fear than hope; here everything is in upheaval, and I do not see that things are more secure elsewhere. I have very little leisure and that I devote, when I can, to Greek literature, calling my mind away from the thought of present and imminent trouble. But this especially bothers me, that in matters about which I am doubtful, and there are many of them, I have no one to consult.[9] Goodbye and love me. Rome, the seventeenth day of October [1433]. Greet Carolus Aretinus for me if he is with you.

LETTER

XCI

I wrote you some time ago and sent you the letter which I wrote to Cosmus to comfort him in his misfortune.[1] I asked you to read it and to let me know whether you thought it should be delivered to him. In a new and unaccustomed way and with a curious, silent laziness you have not answered me at all. At least you ought to have sent me word that you received the letter, if you did not want to give me your opinion. You are completely changed, by old age or by circumstances or by private worries.[2] Your behavior will make me keep silence with you also and not write to you as I used to about public or private matters. Please write me whether you received my letter;[3] for if it went astray, I shall send another. I was already too late in sending the letter for it to be delivered to him. For this reason I shall wait for your answer; but if you neglect me I shall make up my own mind. Goodbye, the ninth day of January [1434].

LETTER

XCII

I am delighted that you and Carolus,[1] who are both eloquent scholars, should approve of my letter; after you have sent it to Cosmus I shall publish it freely. For I kept it concealed at home

until you answered me and you did that more slowly than I
wished, so since I was rather angry with you, I wrote you a few
lines the day before I received your letter, scolding you for your
delay in this matter. I am sending them to you anyway so as not
to hide any of my thoughts from you. You must read everything
calmly as usual and not take it amiss that I talk to you somewhat
confidently as is the custom among friends. See what I expect
of you. Although I could have held back the letter, still I prefer
to have you know my fault, if it was one, than to hide it. But
since I feel that you approve of my Cosmian letter, so to speak,
of that type, I shall bother you with another letter of a different
type which I wrote some time ago against a certain impudent
fellow[2] who had provoked me. Since I later made up with him,
I hid the letter and even took out his name; still I want you to
read it and show it to Carolus and write me what you think
about it.

I know that you already know how things are going with us
here; but they could not be worse than they are. Unless you
anticipate it, this storm will shortly burst upon you or rather will
destroy you; that is the plan of the man behind it, for he has
always hated peace.[3] It is fitting that the Scriptures be fulfilled[4]
and his deeds produce their results. I fear that our Italy will be
cut to pieces, first by ourselves and then by the barbarians who
will grow strong from our weakness. But let those consider this
to whom it matters most. I shall concentrate on literature, as
much as public affairs allow. Goodbye and love me, Rome, the
twenty-first day of January[5] [1434].

LETTER
XCIII

I have collected in a small volume a number of letters which
I once wrote to you. I have decided to dedicate it to one Franciscus of Ferrara,[1] and I have added a letter at the beginning,
of which I send you a copy. But I miss many of the letters which
I had sent you from France and from Germany and also letters

sent from Rome before I set out for France.[2] These were truly
more graceful, it seems to me, and would bring me considerable
reputation, because they dealt with the discovery of a variety of
literary works which I brought to light by my concentrated
efforts,[3] after they had previously been hidden in darkness and
unknown even to the Latins. So I beg you and beseech you to
search for them carefully, since I am sure that they are at your
home. When some time ago you sent me some letters and I
asked you for the ones I speak of now, you said that an unidenti-
fied man had borrowed quite a few from you and that when he
returned them, you would send them to me. So make a special
effort to find them for me. Examine your whole library and go
through all your written material; and if you find any letters
written outside Italy, except those written in Britain which I
have, please send them to me. For I shall add them to the ones
I already have before they are bound. This is something that
neither you nor I should regard as unimportant. For since many
people[4] consider my letters of greater worth than they are and
ask me for them daily, I want to satisfy them as much as I can,
since this can increase our glory and reputation somewhat without the least damage. And so now get to work, while you are
staying at home because of this exceptional heat, and search for
those letters. We are really well here and you stay well too.
Bologna, the eleventh day of July 1436.

APPENDIX

The letters in the Appendix all relate to the discoveries of lost or incompletely known classical texts made by Poggius and his two friends, Cincius de Rusticis and Bartholomeus de Montepolitiano, while they were serving in the Curia at the Council of Constance. The letters—four from Poggius describing the discoveries, one from each of his friends, and two letters to Poggius congratulating him—convey the elation felt by the Humanists over these additions to their knowledge of ancient literature. The letters incidentally give a veiled but rather clear picture of conditions at the Council that motivated Poggius' employment in England, a major subject in the letters to Nicolaus in this book.

Cincius Romanus to his most learned teacher Franciscus de Fiana

LETTER
I

Published in *Diatriba Praeliminaris in duas partes divisa ad Francisci Barbari et aliorum ad ipsum epistolas* (Brescia: Joannes-Maria Rizzardi, 1741), I, viii–xi, and edited by Ludwig Bertalot, "Cincius Romanus und seine Briefe" (*Quellen und Forschungen aus italienischen Archiven und Bibliotheken*, XXI [1929–1930], 222–225).

Let us break our silence occasionally, for it seems outrageous and contrary to the ties of friendship and against nature that those who are separated by a considerable distance, though they are bound by the strongest affection, should not take to writing letters back and forth, for simply thinking of an absent friend will not suffice when one is given the opportunity of writing to him.

Since the chief pleasure in friendship derives from familiarity, people who receive letters, as symbols of their friends, find no small satisfaction in them. Therefore I urge you vigorously to be kind enough while you have the physical ability (for you have the mental ability all the time) to write me something. I promise to give my letters to be delivered to you to all the couriers leaving Constance for Rome. Take this letter as my assurance in the matter, like a hostage. But let us come to the point, which ought to make you very happy.

In Germany there are many monasteries with libraries full of Latin books. This aroused the hope in me that some of the works of Cicero, Varro, Livy, and other great men of learning, which seem to have completely vanished, might come to light, if a careful search were instituted. A few days ago, Poggius and Bartholomeus Montepolitianus and I, attracted by the fame of the library, went by agreement to the town of St. Gall. As soon as we went into the library, we found *Jason's Argonauticon*, written by C. Valerius Flaccus in verse that is both splendid and dignified and not far removed from poetic majesty. Then we found some discussions in prose of a number of Cicero's orations which make clearly comprehensible many legal practices and many modern equivalents of ancient institutions. We also found one book, a small volume but remarkable in the greatness of its eloquence and wisdom: Lactantius *On Men of Both Sorts*, which plainly contradicts the statements of those who claim that the state of mankind is lower than that of beasts and more hopeless. Among other books we found Vitruvius *On Architecture* and Priscian the grammarian's comments on some of the poems of Vergil. There was also in that library one book made of the bark of trees; some barks in the Latin language are called "libri," and from that, according to Jerome, books got their name. Although this book was filled to overflowing with writings which were not exactly literature, still, because of its pure and holy antiquity I greeted it with the utmost devotion. In fact we have copies of all these books. But when we carefully inspected the nearby tower of the church of St. Gall in which countless books were kept like captives and the library neglected and infested with dust, worms, soot, and all the things associated with the destruction of books, we all burst into tears, thinking that this was the way in which the Latin language had lost its greatest glory and distinction. Truly, if this library could speak for itself, it would cry loudly: "You men who love the Latin tongue, let me not be utterly destroyed by this woeful neglect. Snatch me from this prison in whose gloom even the bright light of the books within cannot be seen." There were in that monastery an abbot and monks totally devoid of any knowledge of literature. What barbarous hostility to the Latin tongue! What damned dregs of humanity!

But why do I hate a tribe of barbarians for this kind of indifference to literature when the Romans, the parents of the Latin tongue, have inflicted a greater wound and heaped greater abuse on our native language, the prince over all the others? I call to mind innumerable libraries of Latin and Greek books in ruins in Rome which were carefully built by our ancestors, according to an inscription in Greek letters which was removed from the Porta Capena through one man's concern. These libraries were destroyed partly through ignorance, partly through neglect, and partly so that the divine face of Veronica might be painted. Anyway, I think that the perpetrators of this loathsome crime and those who did not stop them ought to suffer the severest punishment. Indeed if the laws say that he who has killed a man deserves capital punishment, what penalty and what suffering shall we require for those who deprive the public of culture, of the liberal arts and actually of all nourishment of the human mind, without which men can hardly live at all or live like beasts? Two things used to stand out in Rome: the libraries and the monumental buildings which (and I shall omit the libraries) easily surpassed, in size and beauty, the pyramids of Egypt, the Basilica of Cyrus, and other wonders of the world which Herodotus mentions. Every day you see citizens (if indeed a man should be called a citizen who is so degraded by abominable deeds) demolishing the Amphitheater or the Hippodrome or the Colosseum or statues or walls made with marvelous skill and marvelous stone and showing that old and almost divine power and dignity. Truly I would prefer and would pay more for a small marble figure by Phidias or Praxiteles than for a living and breathing image of the man who turns the statues of those glorious men into dust or gravel. But if anyone asks these men why they are led to destroy marble statues, they answer that they abominate the images of false gods. Oh voice of savages, who flee from one error to another! For it is not contrary to our religion if we contemplate a statue of Venus or of Hercules made with the greatest of skill and admire the almost divine art of the ancient sculptors. But mistakes of this kind are to be blamed not only on those we have just mentioned but on the former governors of the city and on the popes, who have continually consented to this destructive behavior which lowers the dignity of mankind.

It happens too that many books of Holy Scripture and many sacred structures have been lost through the carelessness of those who represented Christ on earth. We consider them the more despicable because the cure for all evil is expected from them. But I believe they follow the dictum of some wretch who, when he doubted that he could acquire for himself the name of virtue, burned the temple of Diana at Ephesus. So these priests of our religion, since they could not appreciate the excellence and beauty of the City and could accomplish nothing, strove for this kind of ruin and destruction. Let us pursue such inhuman, such savage stupidity with curses. And you, my teacher, gifted as you are in both poetry and prose, write something against these destroyers of our illustrious monuments. If you do so, you will assure yourself henceforth immortal glory and them perpetual shame. Farewell.

Bertalot dates this letter "summer 1416."
On Cincius, see Letter XXIII, note 6, and Letter LXIX, note 1.
As Voigt says (*Wiederbelebung*, II, 22), Franciscus de Fiana is "hardly known." He was a member of the Curia in the first decade or two of the fifteenth century. He was a pupil of Petrarch and a friend of Coluccius Salutatus (see *Epistolario*, Vol. III, p. 59; Vol. IV, pp. 110, 171, 196, 233, 236). He wrote a treatise defending ancient Latin poetry: *Contra ridiculos oblocutores et fellitos detractores poetarum*, preserved in Cod. Vat. Ottob. 1438, ff. 132r–147v.

In recent years, Giuseppe Billanovich has made a number of important discoveries about Franciscus de Fiana, his friendships, and the contents of his library. See "Giovanni del Virgilio, Pietro da Moglio, Francesco da Fiano," *Italia medioevale e umanistica*, VI (1963), 203–234.

I found this very useful reference in Miss A. C. de la Mare's splendid book, *The Handwriting of Italian Humanists*, Vol. I, fasc. I, The Association Internationale de Bibliophilie (Oxford: Oxford University Press, 1973), p. 37. This book unfortunately appeared too late for me to make thorough use of it in my own work but it will henceforth be an indispensable tool for all students of Poggius and his circle.

Leonardus Brunus Aretinus to Poggius

LETTER
II

Published in *Leonardi Bruni Aretini Epistolarum Libri VIII*, Laurentius Mehus, ed., 2 vols. (Florence: Bernardus Paperinius, 1741), Pt. I, pp. 111–113 (Bk. IV, ltr. 5).

If you are well, good; so am I. At our friend Nicolaus' house I read the letter which you wrote about your last trip and your discovery of some books. I think there is cause for rejoicing not only about them but also about your apparent confident expectation of finding others. Surely this will be your glory, that by your efforts and diligence you are restoring to our age the writings of great men that were already lost and gone. And this will be a joy not only to us but to our descendants, that is, to our successors in our studies. For your deeds will not be passed over in silence or be wiped from memory, but the story will persist that what was regarded as gone beyond recall was recovered through your industry and restored to us. Just as Camillus was called a second founder of Rome after Romulus, who established the city, while Camillus restored it after it was lost, so you will deservedly be called the second author of all the works which were once lost and now returned to us by your integrity and diligence. And so I would urge you and beg you insistently not to give up this glorious endeavor but to rise up and persevere. It will be our

concern here that lack of money does not interfere with you, and
you must realize that there is a great deal more profit in this
discovery of yours than you seem to think. For Quintilian, who
used to be mangled and in pieces, will recover all his parts
through you. I have seen the headings of the chapters; he is
whole, while we used to have only the middle section and that
incomplete. Oh wondrous treasure! Oh unexpected joy! Shall I
see you, Marcus Fabius, whole and undamaged, and how much
will you mean to me now? For I loved you even when you were
cruelly deprived of your mouth, of your mouth and both your
hands, when you were "spoil'd of your nose and shorten'd of
your ears"; still I loved you for your grace. Please, Poggius,
satisfy this deep desire of mine as quickly as possible, so that if
kindness means anything I may see him before I die.

As for Asconius and Flaccus, granted that they both are pleas-
ing, still I do not think they are worth as much trouble, since if
neither of them had ever existed, Latin would have scarcely
been the worse for it. But Quintilian is the father of rhetoric and
the master of oratory to such a degree that when you have sent
him here freed from a lengthy and cruel prison sentence among
the barbarians, all the peoples of Etruria ought to rush out to
congratulate you. I am amazed that you and those who were with
you have not immediately set your eager hands to work on him
but have put him off to copy more trivial things while I would
dare to say that he, after Cicero's books on the Republic, was the
most missed of the Latin writers and mourned beyond all others.
It is important to me to advise you not to waste time on the
authors whom we have here but to hunt for those we lack, and of
these the works of Varro and Cicero should come first. Farewell
and love me and commend me to the protectors of Milan and
Arezzo. Once more farewell. In Florence, September fifteenth
1416.

On Leonardus Brunus Aretinus, see note 22 of Poggius' Letter II,
to Nicolaus.

In an earlier letter to Poggius, Bk. IV, ltr. 4 (*Leonardi Bruni Aretini
Epistolarum Libri VIII*, Pt. I, pp. 109–111), Leonardus congratulated
him on his discovery of two of Cicero's orations. The letter is dated the
second of January 1415.

Poggius to Guarinus Veronensis

LETTER
III

Published in *Poggii Epistolae,* Thomas de Tonellis, ed., Bk. I, ltr. 5; Vol. I, pp. 25–29. Reprinted in *Poggii Opera Omnia,* Vol. III.

Although I know well that no matter how busy you are each day, your kindness to all and your affection for me in particular always make the arrival of my letters a pleasure to you, I ask you especially to pay most particular attention to this one; not that there is anything in me which would have any claim even on a person who was completely at leisure, but because of the interest of the subject of which I am about to tell you. I know it will bring the utmost pleasure to you, who have long been an expert, and to other learned men. For what, for Heaven's sake, is there that could be more delightful, more pleasant, and more agreeable to you and the rest of the learned world than the knowledge of those things whose acquaintance makes us more learned and, what seems even more important, stylistically more polished. When Mother Nature gave the human race mind and reason, two wonderful guides to a righteous and happy life, she could think of nothing finer to give. Then she gave us one thing that perhaps may be the greatest gift of all, the use and understanding of speech, without which mind and reason would not have been of any use to us. For it is speech alone which we use to express the power of our mind and which separates us from the other beings. And so we must be deeply grateful to the pioneers in the other liberal arts and especially to those who by their concern and efforts have given us rules for speaking and a pattern of perfection. They have made it possible for us to excel other men in the ability in which all men excel beasts.

You know that while there were many writers in the Latin tongue who were renowned for elaborating and forming the language, there was one outstanding and extraordinary man, M. Fabius Quintilian, who so cleverly, thoroughly, and attentively worked out everything which had to do with training even the very best orator that he seems in my judgment to be perfect in both the highest theory and the most distinguished practice of oratory. From this man alone we could learn the perfect method of public speaking, even if we did not have Cicero, the father of Roman oratory. But among us Italians, he so far has been so fragmentary, so cut down, by the action of time I think, that the shape and style of the man has become unrecognizable. So far you have seen the man only thus:

> "Whose face and limbs were one continued wound,
> Dishonest, with lopp'd arms, the youth appears,
> Spoil'd of his nose, and shorten'd of his ears."

Surely we ought to feel sorrow and anger that we have done so much damage to the practice of oratory by our careless destruction of a man so eloquent. But the more we regret and blame ourselves for the damage that was formerly done to him, the more we should congratulate ourselves that by our energetic search he has now been restored to us in his original appearance and grandeur, whole and in perfect condition. For if Marcus Tullius rejoiced so fervently when Marcus Marcellus was returned from exile, and that at a time when Rome had a great many able and outstanding men like Marcellus both at home and abroad, what should men do now in learned circles, and especially men who devote themselves to oratory, when the one and only light of the Roman name, except for whom there was no one but Cicero and he likewise cut to pieces and scattered, has through our efforts been called back not only from exile but from almost complete destruction? By Heaven, if we had not brought help, he would surely have perished the very next day. There is no question that this glorious man, so elegant, so pure, so full of morals and of wit, could not much longer have endured the filth of that prison, the squalor of the place, and the savage cruelty of his keepers. He was sad and dressed in mourning, as people are when doomed to death; his beard was dirty and his hair caked with mud, so that by his expression and appearance it was clear that he had been summoned to an undeserved punishment. He seemed to stretch out his hands and beg for the loyalty of the Roman people, to demand that he be saved from an unjust sentence, and to feel it a disgrace that he who had once preserved the safety of the whole population by his influence and his eloquence could now not find one single advocate who would pity his misfortunes and take some trouble over his welfare and prevent his being dragged off to an undeserved punishment. But how often things turn out spontaneously which you dare not hope, as Terence says.

For by good luck, as much ours as his, while we were doing nothing in Constance, an urge came upon us to see the place where he was being kept prisoner. This is the monastery of St. Gall, about twenty miles from Constance. And so several of us went there, to amuse ourselves and also to collect books of which we heard that they had a great many. There amid a tremendous quantity of books which it would take too long to describe, we found Quintilian still safe and sound, though filthy with mold and dust. For these books were not in the Library, as befitted their worth, but in a sort of foul and gloomy dungeon at the bottom of one of the towers, where not even men convicted of a capital offense would have been stuck away. As I know for certain, if there ever had been any other men who explored these prison houses of the barbarians where they confine such men as Quintilian and if they had recognized them after the custom of our ancestors, they would have found a treasure like ours in many cases where we are now left lamenting. Beside Quintilian we found the first three books and half of the fourth of C. Valerius Flaccus' *Argonauticon,* and commentaries or analyses on eight of Cicero's orations by Q. Asconius Pedianus, a very clever man whom Quintilian himself mentions. These I copied with my own hand and very quickly, so that I might send them to Leonardus Aretinus and to Nicolaus of Florence; and when they had heard from me of my discovery of this treasure they urged me at great length in their letters to send them Quintilian as soon as possible. You have, my dearest Guarinus, all that a man who is devoted to you can send you just now. I wish I could send you the book itself but I had to satisfy Leonardus; but you know where it is, so that if you want it and I expect that you will want it as soon

as possible, you can get it easily. Farewell and love me as I
do you. At Constance, 15 December, A.D. 1416.

The date in Latin is "eighteen days before the Kalends of January
1417," which puts it back to 1416.
On Guarinus, see Letter VII, note 12.

Franciscus Barbarus to Poggius

LETTER
IV

Published in *Francisci Barbari et aliorum ad ipsum Epistolae* (Brescia:
Joannes-Maria Rizzardi, 1743), pp. 1–8.

Even if you may well be satisfied with your awareness of your
own outstanding accomplishment and with the very great goodwill which the world of learning feels toward you and which you
deserve, I have thought it proper, on account of the bond of
literature which ties us particularly together, to thank you and
not to pass over in silence the tremendous service you did for
mankind, by sending us a list of those books which by your effort
and diligence you have recovered for us and for posterity, so
that we enjoy the greatest satisfaction and jubilation, both at
home and in public. For no news could have been brought us
that was more joyful and welcome than that which relates both
to your glory, dear to us as that properly is, and to the expansion
of culture in the highest degree. I do not believe that anyone,
unless he wanted actually to be ungrateful and to be recognized
as such, could think in silence of so much concern for the general
welfare, of so much effort for the good of all mankind, of so many
benefits that will last forever. You made out that what you were
about to do was easy, since it was for the common cause, whereas
in fact the storms of winter did not slow you down, or snow, or
the length of the journey, or the roughness of the road, from re-
leasing the monuments of literature from darkness into light.
You and your helpful companion Bartholomeus have endowed
Tertullian with life, and M. Fabius Quintilian, Q. Asconius

Pedianus, Lucretius, Silius Italicus, Marcellinus, Manilius the astronomer, Lucius Septimus, Valerius Flaccus; you have revived the grammarians Caprus, Eutychius, and Probus, and many others who had suffered a like fate, or you have brought them back to Latium from a long absence. The result is that even while I missed you when you were far away from me, I rejoiced mightily that you were there. Why not? Since you could have accomplished almost nothing more glorious or more welcome to scholars than to have brought back more than you expected, more than you sought, more than you hoped for of those monuments of antiquity, hidden in the dust, to put before the eyes of learned men. It is reported as the glory of that great man Lycurgus that he was the first to bring back whole to Greece from Asia the work of Homer scattered in bits in various places, which he had found preserved entire among the descendants of Creophilus. If the world of learning, wherever it is, knows anything, ought it not to give you a civic crown in witness of the life and salvation which you have restored to it? Since it was brought about by your talent that learned men can henceforth easily expect immortality; especially since not only famous men but even any trifling citizen would consider his rescuers worthy of this honor. We accept Aesculapius as belonging among the gods because he called back Hippolytus, as well as others from the underworld, when he had reached the day fixed as the last of his life, and thus allowed him to die only some years later. If peoples, nations, and provinces have dedicated shrines to him, what might I think ought to be done for you, if that custom had not already been forgotten? You have revived so many illustrious men and such wise men, who were dead for eternity, through whose minds and teachings not only we but our descendants will be able to live well and honorably. If our ancestors decided that a triumph should be awarded to those who had captured forts and cities and provinces and if I had as much dignity, power, and gratitude as they who were the most important in the literary Senate and in the house of the Muses, I should decree a triumph for you, since surely their learning and their reasoning power could bring the human race more benefit by far than the deeds of a few illustrious generals ever brought. For as these deeds have sometimes freed a few soldiers or a single city or occasionally one province from impending dangers with great slaughter of men and have turned men from frugality to every and all kinds of lust, so there must be no doubt that culture and mental training, which are adapted to a good and blessed life and fair speech, can bring no trifling advantages not only to private concerns but to cities, nations, and finally to all mankind.

The Athenians, when they consulted Apollo, in their opinion the wisest of their gods, received the answer that the outstanding citizens would be those who told their children of whatever was best and most beautiful. Although that meant learning, which makes children worthy of being free men, they, in the manner of the Lydians, took it to mean gems and gold although that did not make them more prone to honesty, temperance, and loyalty but to greed, stinginess, lust, and frivolity. Cato, in Cicero's judgment the perfect Stoic, when he had brought the most distinguished philosopher Athenodorus from Asia, believed that he was more deserving of glory than Gn. Pompeius or L. Lucullus, since he, unarmed, had brought more honorable spoils from Asia than they had achieved with all their forces and battles. Of these Pompey, the winner of the Mithridatic war, when he had come to his home to see and greet the very learned Possidonius, forbade the lictor's striking the door as was the custom and he bowed the fasces to the home of Letters, though he was the man whom the east and the west had learned to obey. What more? Did not Caesar the dictator admit that his enemy Marcus Tullius had achieved a greater crown than all his triumphs, because it was more important to enlarge the boundaries of the Roman mind than of the empire? Why, because our ancestors regarded poets and military victors as worthy of the same crown. There are innumerable examples, which I, so as not to be interminable, shall omit. No one should be averse to an honor for your colleague or for you because M. Marcellus and P. Scipio were not drawn in a triumphal chariot when they, without being in public office, brought the Syracusans and the

Spaniards under the dominion of Rome; because the highest and most honorable Princes of the Church of Rome sent you and Bartholomeus, publicly chosen to perform this duty. But if a triumph was not decreed for Q. Fulvius when Capua was taken or for L. Opimius when the Fregellani were forced to surrender, because it was right to decree a laurel crown for the enlargement of the empire but not merely for the recapture of something that had once belonged to the Republic, who will have such a poor grasp of such matters that he would not have considered you worthy of a statue, since he agrees that statues should be dedicated to the Olympic champions who derived their nobility not from themselves but from their flanks and shoulders? Let him realize that you have accomplished by your intellect and hard work things that could not have been done except by men of learning and dedication. Besides, when Sextus Pacuvius Taurus, aedile of the plebs, had restored one statue of the Sibyls and M. Messalla two statues of them which had been set up near the rostra and when many others had restored sacred temples or private dwellings, they received no mean praise. What have you not accomplished in restoring to us the Orators, Poets, Historians, Astronomers, and Grammarians who would undoubtedly now be lost forever? Forthwith no debased or worn-out honor ought to be paid you but something special and new. Indeed those Germans ought to be branded with shame for leaving celebrated men buried alive for so long, men whose lives should be established in the memory of all mankind to the greatest possible degree. If their burial occurred through thoughtlessness, what could be more careless? If it was through intent, what could be more cruel? Will there be anyone so jealous as to think that I do you too much honor? Whom moreover do I honor? Those truly who have brought more assistance than ever and finer ornaments to this Republic of letters. Our ancestors wanted to dedicate an altar, build temples, and make sacrifices to Liber because he was the discoverer of the use of the vine, which for the most part is the cause of lust, rage, and madness. Shall we now deny even a moderate level of honor to the discoverers of the greatest books? If our ancestors had been jealous of innovation, they would not have honored virtue and hard work with so many famous monuments and we should have been deprived of many well-worded precepts and many examples of right living. It is known that a statue of C. Terentia or Suffecia, the Vestal Virgin, was decreed, to be placed where she chose, because she presented some part of the Tiber shore to the Roman people; if a woman could be so honored for a gift of her fortune, who will not consider it unjust if I do not decree a statue to you and your companion, not decked with laurel, not on horseback, not gilded, but in a toga and of bronze in the valley of the Muses? I should like, dearest Poggius, to have all men by my example consider your care and industry and diligence worthy of imitation, not of envy. Verily, if this most excellent custom of preserving the memory of men were not already established and rooted in antiquity, I myself would compose in writing in the loftiest of language the reasons for this monument.

But since the condition of our time and our Republic does not permit us this favor, you will have to be satisfied with my reminding you of Cato the Elder, who entrusted his achievements not to marble or to silver images, which are destroyed by storm, by violence, and by time, but to the perpetual memory of his fellow citizens, forever. If you will think about this, you will bear the injustice of our time with equanimity and greater comfort. For what can you achieve that is more magnificent and glorious than that these immortal merits of yours should not be kept in darkness or hidden but should be placed in the light not only of Europe but also before the eyes of the German province and in the ears of all peoples and all nations? How great an achievement is it that in this common joy all men congratulate you, all thank you, because you have devoted your concern to the dignity and advantage of the Republic? By this means it will turn out, I hope, just as cherries were called Lucullan and jujubes Papinian, after Lucullus had brought the one from Pontus after his victory over Mithridates, and Papinius had brought the other from Syria to Italy, and just as apples are called Appian after Appius of the Claudian tribe and pears Manlian after Manlius, so these seeds of literature which by your ability and effort you brought from Germany into Italy will someday be called Poggian and Montepolitian. Why should I hope for such a thing? Because if certain kinds of fruit from distant lands, by keeping their names, have extended the lasting fame of the instigators of their migration, why should I not desire the same for you who have delivered to us these most valuable and extraordinary fruits of culture and learning? It will add to our joy, when you receive the rich reward of your efforts, if sometime, as I dearly wish, a man will hold the highest power in the government of the universe who from an early age has devoted most of his effort and time to learning, to virtue, and to deserving respect. For it will be the duty of a wise Pope to keep your good deeds in his memory and to hold you in high esteem, since he received no small distinction from you in this matter and in my judgment your accomplishments should be considered all the greater for being unexpected. I think I have expressed an opinion of you and your colleague which is serious and worthy of the Republic. If any of those who delight in your praise says anything more complimentary, I could easily agree to go along with it. Still I think you will be pleased with this effort of mine, since I think that a triumph seems your due for your extraordinary intelligence and since it is awarded as a testimonial of virtue to those who deserve well of the Republic by the agreement of its most distinguished men. Enough of this.

All that remains is for me to advise you and urge you to put your whole heart and soul into the matter and the rest of that journey for which, as you have written to our fine and learned friend Guarinus of Verona, you had carefully prepared yourself, so that you may not put off or lose any opportunity of enhancing the public good or your own reputation. For what more can Roman literature expect from you than you have already produced since it has been led to hope (for you seem to have been born for this purpose) that through you the books of Cicero's *De republica* and of Varro's treatises on the divine and the human, and Crispus' and Livy's books, and Cato's *Origins*, to say nothing of others, will be returned to us. Therefore, dearest Poggius, keep on as you have begun; let nothing be too old for

you to judge that it may lead to these studies and to the liberal
arts. May your labors bring you peace, your outlays glory, and
your good fortune the most abundant reward. You have had to
work all the harder on this because the ill health of our dear
Bartholomeus has put the whole responsibility on you. Since I
had hoped that his work and his sharp eye would contribute no
little to literature, I do not know whether by his collapse and
our fate we have fallen below our high hopes. Therefore we have
turned all our hopes on you just as steersmen tossed in a violent
storm and stripped of every bit of the ship's equipment are apt
to fix their eyes upon the blessed anchor. You therefore, all by
yourself, will accomplish so much by your efficiency that we
shall suffer correspondingly less from Bartholomeus' illness
through your devotion and concern for this job, an illness which
is a great worry to all literary men. Truly if you do not accomplish this, I have no idea who else will answer our hopes; and
you will seem to have done well by both the common good and
your own reputation. For this reason, so that you may sail along
more comfortably, I urge you and beg you to be sure to have
anything copied that you find and consider worthwhile. For
what good would finding it do, if once found it cannot be used?
For as the former is commonly attributed to good luck, the latter,
for good reasons, is attributed to good sense. And it will not be
unsuitable for you to protect your own advantage, whose foundation you have established not on mere gossip but increased and
supported with fact. You will recall the ancient example of
Andronicus of Rhodes. For when Sylla sent the library of
Apellicon from Athens to Rome and put the grammarian Tyrranio
in charge of it, Andronicus brought in copyists and copied the
books of Aristotle and Theophrastus, which were practically unknown, and sent them to the greatest scholars; and nearly all the
surviving texts are derived from his and he himself, for his
diligence, is highly respected by posterity. This I judge that you
must do too; for I seem to see all men who care for poets, orators,
historians, philosophers, mathematicians, who finally are devoted to letters, competing in praise of you, for I think the
practice of literary rhetoric is no trifling matter. A statue was set

up by Asinius Pollio to M. Varro for taking care of the books which formed the first public collection in Rome and that, in my opinion, brought him no less honor, since it was set up by a leading orator and very distinguished citizen, than when Pompey the Great rewarded the prefect of his fleet with a naval crown for the defeat of the pirates. But if the cost is too high for your pocket, divide part of this expense between me and others who cherish traces of ancient virtue, according to your judgment. For not only have I decided to obey you as a censor but I have also set this extraordinary responsibility upon you without your suggesting it. Therefore, it is not by excuses but by deeds that you will satisfy your glory, my desire, and the honest expectation of the learned world.

What you write of Cincius' special affection for me gives me great pleasure. You will cherish him too, and I will do all I can to increase it. Farewell. The sixth of July in the year of Jesus Christ 1417.

Poggius to Franciscus Piccolpassus, I

LETTER
V

Published by A. Wilmanns in "Die Briefsammlungen des Poggio Bracciolini," *Zentralblatt für Bibliothekswesen*, XXX (1913), 289–331, 443–463, especially pp. 459–460. Reprinted in *Poggii Opera Omnia*, IV, 320–321.

I do not want you to think, dear Franciscus, that in all this time I have written you only one letter because of negligence or disregard of you, which could be nothing but wickedness, but the state of our affairs has decreed it thus. For since it is my habit to speak my mind honestly, especially with friends, and since I saw that I could not do this with you, I decided that I must keep quiet, so as not to write something wholly contrary to my real opinion, which would be lying, or else pay the penalty of speaking the truth. Our affairs are in such a state of flux and have changed so much from day to day and are so at variance with each other that one should not despair at the adverse happenings or feel too much confidence in what is favorable. For so far I have seen nothing and felt nothing on the basis of which I could take my stand on either side, as I think you knew. For these matters are by no means hidden. The factions here are such as to make you think of Caesar and Pompey: the senate and all the nobility on the one hand, as they call those who seek the public good and support its cause, and on the other side, I do not know what to call those who seek private power, pretending it is for the public good. But now it has come about, I fear, that the defeated side would please Cato. For, as Cicero said, what is settled by force is seldom hailed into court. Often it is accomplished through agreement among princes but when bad mediators destroy principles by attacking Caesar, then ambition does all the more harm. For it seems fine to rule everyone, as he says, by sitting in two saddles. I do not know what to conjecture from these matters. You know that it happened in the case of Cicero, when the subject of preeminence in the state came up, that there was often such great rivalry that it was difficult to preserve the fabric of the state. Nor do I believe that it is the responsibility of man's judgment to see the end result. But still, since wise men claim that we can guess the future from the past, there is no hope left to us except Terence's comment that we will do well enough. "For if safety herself should want to save that family, she can scarcely do it." There is no reason for us not to achieve what we hope either by good counsel or by our own merits but we must pray for divine mercy. For without that I doubt that we can say: stop; the proclamation is made. But your friend Michael will explain all this in detail.

I urge you therefore not to come to us until you know that a pope has been chosen by the common agreement of all. For perhaps matters could turn out in such a way that it might happen somewhere else than here. For if the decision is reached through dissension, what do you think will happen and how great do you think not only the confusion but the revolution will be? Since you are wise, think about all this and keep the future firmly before you. Believe me, you will hold back if you are sensible and you will await the outcome and if, as I hope, it is good, you will not only keep your former rank on account of your integrity but you will also achieve higher rank. But if, God forbid, something bad should happen, you will be safer at home among your friends than in this barbarous and savage place. I had this news to write to you, the rest you will learn from Michael. I am glad that you have become a doctor in canon law and I praise your achievement for the honor of the rank, but it is enough for a good man to be learned. But since you have begun, take care, please, to seem to have acquired the trappings not only of a scholar but also of a truly good man. Farewell, dear Franciscus, and love me as always.

I want you to know that by my diligent efforts I have found many remains of the great men of the past. For twice now I have traveled through Germany alone. Very recently I have had a triumph: I have found seven orations of M. Tullius which had been lost before. Three of them are *Against the agrarian law;* the fourth is the *In Pisonem in Senatu;* the fifth the *Pro A. Cecina;* the sixth *Pro Rabirio postumo;* the seventh *Pro Rabirio per-duellonis reo.* There is also an eighth: *Pro Roscio Comedo,* which is without its beginning and end. You will learn the rest later.

Wilmanns dates this letter in the late summer or early fall of 1417, since Franciscus Piccolpassus received his doctorate on 12 July 1417 ("Briefsammlungen," p. 461 [*Poggii Opera Omnia,* IV, 322]). Martin V was elected Pope on St. Martin's day, 11 November 1417.

Franciscus Piccolpassus was born in Bologna and became an arch-priest there on 21 June 1419. He became bishop of Dax in Gascony in March 1423, bishop of Pavia on 26 February 1427, and archbishop of Milan in 1435, until his death in 1443 (Eubel, *Hierarchia,* I, 98, 409; II, 207). Twelve letters written to him by Poggius besides the two in-cluded here are known; one group dates from 1423–1426; the other 1439–1443. He was a friend and correspondent of Antonius Beccadellius Panormita, Petrus Candidus Decembrius, Guarinus, Franciscus Philelphus, Nicolaus Cusanus, and Aeneas Silvius Piccolomini. He mediated in a controversy between Leonardus Brunus Aretinus and Alphonsus de Sancta Maria de Cartagena. (See Sabbadini, *Scoperte,* I, 121; II, 18–19, 24–31.) Piccolpassus attended the Councils of both Constance and Basel. He left Constance in 1415 and returned late in

1417 or early in 1418, returning to Italy with Martin V. He owned a notable library, which he collected largely while at Basel. It was very strong in sacred literature. Sixty-five of his volumes are now in the Ambrosiana, many containing notes in his hand. He also made several discoveries of lost texts. Sabbadini dates this letter 18 September 1417. See Remigio Sabbadini, "Poggio scopritore di codici latini in Germania," *R. Istituto Lombardo di Scienze e Lettere. Rendiconti,* XLVI (1913), 905–908, and Angelo Paredi, *La Biblioteca del Pizolpasso* (Milan: Hoepli, 1961).

Poggius to Franciscus Piccolpassus, II

LETTER
VI

Published by A. Wilmanns in "Die Briefsammlungen des Poggio Bracciolini," *Zentralblatt für Bibliothekswesen,* XXX (1913) 289–331, 443–463, especially p. 460. Reprinted in *Poggii Opera Omnia,* IV, 321.

Four days ago when your dear Michael left, I gave him a letter for you describing our affairs, in what state they might be or were, and at the same time I gave him some rather secret messages for you. Meanwhile everything has changed for the better. For yesterday peace was made between the Emperor and the College and a firm and honorable agreement achieved through the efforts of the English, who have worked on this very hard for us. As a result, there is great joy among us all, and we hope that our business will turn out well. But since there are twelve hours in the day, I shall inform you daily, so that you will not miss anything. But still I advise you not to move until you hear more. If everything stays in place, as we all trust, we shall finish the job, I think, within a month. Farewell, in haste.

Bartholomeus de Montepolitiano to Ambrosius Traversarius

LETTER
VII

Published in *Ambrosii Traversarii Generalis Camaldulensium Epistolae et Orationes,* Laurentius Mehus, ed., 2 vols. (Bologna: Forni, 1968), a photomechanic reprint of the Florence, 1759 edition, Vol. II, cols. 981–985.

When that eminent man Emmanuel Chrysoloras joined the company around Pope John, he often used to talk to me with pleasure about your outstanding virtues, and he had no doubt that you were exceptional among the men of our times not only in character and in the holiness of your life but also in ability, concentration, and knowledge of both Latin and Greek literature. He used to say that he thought that only men endowed with such qualities were wise, because they do not become arrogant in prosperity and they endure changes of fortune for the worse in the midst of a virtuous life with equanimity. I was so fond of that man that as long as I could, and he permitted it, I did not stray far from the company of so great a teacher and I tried to become more intelligent through his wisdom; a day never passed, when I was in his delightful company, that I did not realize that I was the better for it. When he had died, I turned often to C. Romanus [*note:* Cincius?], who is an excellent person and one whom I dare to call splendid in character and habits as well as in training and in knowledge of the Humanities and expert in both languages. I learned much from Cincius which I had heard from Emmanuel; what I used to know, I have not lost; I have copied many short works of Plato, Protagoras "On Friendship," and Chrysoloras "On Fortitude" and his praise of the two Romes, with his urging and encouragement. For Cincius was Emmanuel's pupil for a long time and took up the same themes in praise of you that he used, with great seriousness. So it happens that confirmed by the established judgment and authority of so great a man I feel free to call you wise and blessed; not in the popular sense but as learned men and scholars use the term wise, though I think that I shall scarcely find such a man in Italy.

In this alone we follow the views of Epicurus, for granted that he believed that the greatest good resided in the body and we in the mind, that he took his stand on pleasure and we on virtue, still he said that there was never a day when a wise man was not blessed. I therefore have embraced all the disciples of

that great philosopher with special affection and the deepest
devotion; although I have never seen some of them, still I feel
that I know them from the letters they have written me and hold
them dear. It would take me a long time to unfold the tale of all
the kindness and courtesy Guarinus Veronensis, Franciscus
Barbarus, and Andreas Iulianus have shown me. You alone were
missing and lately you have preferred to surpass me in the
services which I ought properly to have rendered to you. For
just as you surpass me in life, cleverness, concentration, and
courtesy, so now you have anticipated me in testifying to your
goodwill towards me by your two letters which came as har-
bingers. In them you praise my work with extraordinary good
feeling toward me, by which you have chosen to value my
efforts and make them precious. For this I give most hearty
thanks to our immortal God that He deemed me worth preserving
so far, so that I may contribute to the general use of scholars
whatever is approved by the positive witness of such great
churchmen as you. Therefore to you, dear Ambrosius, I offer
myself, such as nature made me, so I shall be in our friendship:
merry, humble, and gentle, and, better still, such as you may
want me to be. Let me never think that I could ever reject the
friendship and close association of a man whom I know to be
endowed with the truest virtues, devoted to my father, and a
true worshipper of Christ. There is the added bond, as you say,
that we both love study, for since friendship develops if any
sign of goodness shines out toward which the soul can steer
itself and to which it can be attached, when this happens love
must follow. You can recognize this from the fact that I began to
love you for the splendor of your character before I knew you.
And as I want you to know my character meantime and to be
able to form an idea of what manner of man you have chosen to
love (for I am not such a one as glories in empty show or honor
or praise or who swells with pride or physical vanity), I hate all
boastful conversation, all flattery, all exaggeration, and find
them more repulsive, more oppressive, and more damnable than
any plague. Alas that I who am born of the earth, when the
time comes for me to return to ashes and give an account of this

brief life and of my stewardship of it before the tribunal of Christ, may I be kept from taking pride in dreams of self-exaltation or vainglory. Whichever distinguished men have really cared about culture and have achieved virtue and knowledge or have wanted to achieve them, these men have what they have hoped to have. Therefore use me as your close friend like a member of your family, as often as you like. For according to Cicero, there is nothing more delightful than a response to goodwill and an exchange of concerns and services. But if we add this fact too, which can properly be added, that there is nothing which so attracts anything to itself and draws anyone to friendship as a similar outlook, surely it will be accepted as true that good men love the good; if I am considered good, yet am a sinner; men learn from themselves that great men are joined together by their characters and their virtue as if by physical proximity. Nothing furthermore is more eager to match like with like or hungrier to do it than nature, but enough of this.

I wrote to you a few days ago and to the Chancellor of Florence and to Antonius of Pistoia how far I had progressed. Later I entered into a prison of ancient codices among which I hit upon Flavius Vegetius Renatus, an author of high repute in ancient times on military science. I decided to copy his text because he was renowned for his style and wise counsel and because he provides basic information about the ancient Roman army, so he will do us good, if we ever use him sometimes in camp or more gloriously on a crusade. Besides, I found an ancient book containing a selection on the meaning of words from the text of Pompeius Festus, useful to students and of remarkable genius.

Finally, Noble Friend, when these books have been copied and made available, I shall be ready for my journey so that on the twenty-second of January I shall set out for another monastery of the Hermits deep in the Alps, God willing. I hear that there is there a vast quantity of this sort of ancient volume and when I come back from there, there will still be three monasteries for me to visit; for although they are very difficult to reach and the way is rough and broken (for there is no approach to them except through precipices of the Alps and through rivers and forests) I know that the path of virtue is very full of toil and peril. After that, as you request, I shall describe all the sites and conditions to you. I am sending you a brief list of many volumes but not all, for a day would hardly be sufficient to list them all and it is hard for me to start on it. I should prefer to have you send a little note of those which seem to have vanished or to be buried by some unaccountable fate in darkness. Then I shall try to urge this poor little body to undertake the effort of rescuing them and not to flinch at the difficulties of their location, at the discomforts and at the increasing cold of the Alps. Finally I send you my heartiest thanks for the list of Plutarch in Greek which you were so kind as to send me and for your generous offer. For it was a great satisfaction to me to learn what works of that author had been brought by me from Greece to Italy. Finally I ask you always to share what I write to you with our friend Nicolaus, who is easily the outstanding scholar in all subjects in our time; I shall put off writing to him until I happen to find something, God willing, truly precious and worthy of so great a man. Farewell in Jesus Christ. From the town of St. Gall, the nineteenth of January.

(Note. Laurentius Mehus dates the letter 1418.)
On Bartholomeus de Aragazzis de Montepolitiano, see Letter XLIX, note 6; Letter LIX (text); Letter LXIX (text); Letter LXXIII, note 1; Letter LXXIV (text); Letter LXXV, note 13.
On Ambrosius Traversarius, see Letter XVII, note 12.

Poggius to Franciscus Barbarus

LETTER
VIII

Published by Albert Curtis Clark, "The Literary Discoveries of Poggio," *Classical Review*, XIII (1899), 119–130, see especially p. 125. Reprinted in *Poggii Opera Omnia*, IV, 239.

If you are well, good; so am I. Our friend Matthaeus [Barucius] has brought me your letter which is so kind that it gives me the greatest pleasure, not only because it is full of the courtesy of a fine man but also because it is full of your real affection and goodwill. I will not linger over your congratulations on the election of the Pope which are at the beginning of the letter. I am happy about it from the public standpoint, but if I consider how it affects me privately, I should prefer that he live, as was once said to the emperor. What you tell me of Guarinus troubles me a bit. I hope you will believe me, Franciscus, I want him to be rewarded for his merits, just as both our friendship and his fine character demand. But what can I do for a poor little man in such a mess, when neither reason nor character protects his position but luck controls everything? The struggle used to be over money; now it is because of ambition, and there is such a variety of votes and supporters that neither Cato nor even Paul could win an election against it.

The man who was the refuge of all scholars has died. I do not know what to say about the rest; it is better to keep quiet than to say even a little; these matters will work themselves out in time. Much is not unchanged but changing. Our friend Gasparinus will discuss it with you since he has witnessed it; he has heard a great deal from us. So ask him about it. As for me, if it were easy for me to write against those who can outlaw me, I would explain to you myself what hope there is for scholars but perhaps, if I live, they will not go unavenged. Some day I shall set myself free of fearing the thunder and lightning even of Jove. Now everything must be whispered and endured. Oh with what slow jaws they are sharpened for the right time, and would that Thyestes had not made such a feast. See what you can hope from others; I who have lived so long in this delayed hope of a country of my own am not yet, unless I am mistaken, either at the end of my rope or in total disaster. "I leave the cruel earth and the greedy shore and seek my country, lying beneath another sun, Britain, cut off from all the rest of the world."

It is hard for me but this is much harder: that those who have thus far seemed unworthy are promoted and the worthy are set aside. Besides, when you are not the man you used to be, why not be the man you want to be? But more about me some other

time and, I think, face to face. I have written this so that you
may realize that from our point of view there is no use going to
great effort for our friend Guarinus at this time to find him something worthy of his talent. A man has as much credit as he has
money in the bank. I advise him to study and to concentrate on
self-improvement, and if everything else fails, his conscience
will be satisfied. And yet I hope that some time in the future he
will obtain his high position, for he will shine forth among the
wicked.

I have finished with Guarinus. You can say the same of Franciscus Bracchus, to whom I am devoted because of his integrity
and kindly disposition. I have been talking with our friend
Cincius about them both. He, because of his goodwill toward
men of learning, replied that he would do everything he could
to raise their status. But what good will that do? Those who
can't, want to benefit good men; those who can, won't. Many
sympathize but nobody helps. Oh how I wish that this whole
group were to be put right within my reach, so that I might spit
out all this fury at them, while the sickness is current. I am
writing nothing back to Franciscus at present, for I know of no
way to free myself of him; either I must promise him my attention and efforts although, since they cannot bring about the
desired result, it is unworthy of a man to promise what he cannot
perform or else I must blame the times and the manners; this is
far from safe and not credible to many people, and even you,
if you are wise, will not know what you in fact do know. Please
answer him for me as seems best to you. But enough of this. I
have been much wordier than I intended, but the vastness of the
subject drew me on; it cannot be treated briefly.

Thank you for the twenty florins which you gave to Matthaeus,
for I am now free of debt, and so that I may begin to make some
sort of return, I am sending you by the priest Brandinus Pisanus,
who belongs to Cardinal Pisanus' household, Silius Italicus,
five books of Statius' *Silvae* and M. Manilius, the astronomer.
The man who copied the books was the most ignorant of living
men; one needs to use divination, not reading itself, and so it is
very important that they be copied by a scholar. I have read as

far as the thirteenth book of Silius and I corrected a lot, so that
it might be easy for someone writing it correctly to avoid similar
mistakes and to correct those in the later books, so see that they
are copied and then send them to Nicolaus in Florence. I want
the volume of the orations to stay here, and later I shall bring it
to you myself or send it by someone else, and that promptly.
Lucretius has not yet come back to me although he has been
copied. The place is rather far away and not many people come
from there, and so I shall wait until some people turn up who
will bring him; but still, if no one comes, I shall not put public
duties ahead of private needs. For I find no one in connection
with Ammianus Marcellinus who can help in the decipherment.
The priests here recommend the work and sit around praising
the subject and every day they ask me for a copy of the orations.
But not another word about the dismissal (?). Oh Portents and
monstrous beasts of every kind!

Gothein dates this letter "autumn 1417" (*Barbaro*, p. 362, note 30)
while Clark (*Classical Review*, XIII, 125–126) dates the letter from its
historical allusions between January and May 1418.

On Franciscus Barbarus, see Letter XV, note 32.

NOTES

The notes are numbered consecutively in each separate letter. The numbers inside the parentheses following the note numbers refer to the volume, page, and line in the Latin edition of the letters of Poggius edited by Thomas de Tonellis and published in Florence in three volumes in 1832, 1859, and 1861. These three volumes were reprinted by an anastatic process as Volume III of *Poggius Bracciolini Opera Omnia,* edited by Riccardo Fubini in 1964.

The references to the Latin text following the note numbers in Letters IV, V, LIII, LV, LVI, and XCIII relate to A. Wilmanns, "Über die Briefsammlungen des Poggio Bracciolini," *Zentralblatt für Bibliothekswesen,* XXX (Leipzig: Otto Harrassowitz, 1913), 289–331, 443–463; reprinted in *Poggii Opera Omnia,* IV, 261–324.

LETTER I

1(I,x:1). Poggius dedicated the first collection of his letters, those written to Nicolaus de Niccolis, to Franciscus Marescalcus Ferrariensis, about whom very little is known. His dedicatory epistle appears in *Poggii Epistolae,* Thomas de Tonellis, ed. (Florence: L. Marchini, 1832), Praefatio, pp. x–xi, reprinted in *Poggii Opera Omnia,* Vol. III, Riccardo Fubini, ed. (Turin: Bottega d'Erasmo, 1964).

Franciscus Marescalcus Ferrariensis is confirmed as the recipient of Poggius' first collection of letters in a letter written by Poggius to Nicolaus dated Bologna, 11 July [1436], printed in Poggius, *Historiae de varietate fortunae,* Dominicus Georgius, ed. (Paris: A. U. Coustelier, 1723), p. 255, and reprinted in *Poggii Opera Omnia,* IV, 261–262. The letter, XCIII in this collection, is the last letter from Poggius to Nicolaus that has survived.

Nothing, not even a short article, has been written anywhere about Franciscus Marescalcus of Ferrara. All we know is that he seems to have been in holy orders and to have been a young man when Poggius, at the age of 56, sent him this collection of letters. We do not know Franciscus' dates. He first appears in Poggius' correspondence in 1434.

Poggius' first letter to him is two years earlier than the dedication of this collection of letters. (See Tonelli Bk. V, ltr. 20; II, 63–64.) In it Poggius welcomes Franciscus Marescalcus as a friend recommended and introduced by Scipio [de Mainentis] of Ferrara (the uncle of Poggius' wife), with whom Poggius spends much pleasant time. Scipio (who was bishop of Modena) was very learned and reported Franciscus Marescalcus Ferrariensis to be so, too. (Florence, June 30.) A study of Paul Oskar Kristeller's *Iter Italicum*, 2 vols. (Leiden: E. J. Brill, 1963 and 1967) indicates Franciscus Marescalcus' close connection with a wide circle of humanists:

I, 199. Florence: Biblioteca Riccardiana No. 717 contains ff. 57–76: L. B. Albertus' *Apologi*, dedicated to Franciscus Marescalcus.

I, 245. Genoa: Biblioteca Universitaria Fondo Gaslini 49. Now C VII 46 contains letters of Petrus Candidus Decembrius to many recipients, including Franciscus Marescalcus.

I, 256. Lucca: Biblioteca Capitolare No. 544 contains (f. 505v) a letter from Franciscus Aretinus to Franciscus Marescalcus, 1479, the latest date known in relation to Marescalcus.

I, 315. Milan: Biblioteca Ambrosiana. X 9 sup. contains L. B. Albertus' letters to Franciscus Marescalcus.

I, 327. Milan: Bibl. Ambros. Ms. J 235 inf. again contains letters of Petrus Candidus Decembrius to Franciscus Marescalcus, among many others.

I, 382. Modena: Biblioteca Estense. Ms. Est. lat. 772 (Alpha R 8, 13) ff. 1–28: Frater Albertus Sarthianensis, *Epistolae:* to Franciscus Marescalcus among many others.

II, 35. Parma: Biblioteca Palatina. Pal. 267: L. B. Albertus, *Apologi*, with a preface to Franciscus Marescalcus (f. 49v).

II, 103. Rome: Biblioteca Casanatense. Ms. 1732 (c. III 3) f. 81v: Guarinus, poem on Ludovicus Sardus, addressed to Franciscus Marescalcus.

II, 135. Rome: Collegio di San Isidoro. Ms. 2/105. pp. 298–309. Letters by Albertus Sarthianensis addressed to Franciscus Marescalcus and others, all dated 1434.

II, 196. Treviso: Biblioteca Comunale. Ms. 41: ff. 37–57: L. B. Albertus, *Apologi* centum, dedicated to Franciscus Marescalcus.

II, 254. Venice: Biblioteca Nazionale Marciana. Marc. lat. XI 80 (3057) ff. 381–389v. Albertus Sartianensis: letters to F. Marescalcus and others.

II, 258. Venice: Biblioteca Nazionale Marciana. Marc. lat. XII 135 (4100) ff. 25–26v. Guarinus, poem on Ludovicus Sardus addressed to Franciscus Marescalcus. This poem of 104 hexameters dated Ferrara 1440 is also preserved in Cod. Ferrarese 151 NA-5 f.31v.

See Remigio Sabbadini, *La scuola e gli studi de Guarino Veronese* (Catania: F. Galati, 1896), p. 231. The poem is published as No. 761, Vol. II, pp. 392–395, by Remigio Sabbadini in *Epistolario di Guarino Veronese,* 3 vols. (Venice: R. Deputazione Veneta di Storia Patria, 1915, 1916, 1919).

Professor Paul Oskar Kristeller has very kindly called my attention to additional references to Franciscus Marescalcus Ferrariensis. He was a pupil of Guarinus Veronensis' and is thus listed in Ludovicus Carbo's funeral oration for Guarinus, published by Karl Müllner, *Reden und Briefe italienischer Humanisten: Ein Beitrag zur Geschichte der Pädagogik des Humanismus* (Vienna: Alfred Holder, 1899), pp. 89–107. It is published also in Giulio Bertoni, *Guarino da Verona fra letterati e cortegiani a Ferrara (1429-1460)* (Geneva: L. S. Olschki, 1921), pp. 160–175. On Marescalcus, see pp. 115, 166. Marescalcus conveyed Guarinus' congratulations to Poggius on his marriage in 1436 (see Ernst Walser, *Poggius Florentinus: Leben und Werke,* Beiträge zur Kulturgeschichte des Mittelalters und der Renaissance, XIV [Leipzig: Teubner, 1914], 171, and Sabbadini, *Epist. di Guar. Ver.,* II, 289 [694]). Two letters written to Marescalcus by Albertus Sartheanensis are printed in Franciscus Haroldus, ed., *Beati Alberti a Sarthiano Ord. Min. Reg. Observ. Opera Omnia* (Rome: Joannes Baptista Bussottus, 1688), pp. 238–241. Girolamo Mancini published a letter written to Marescalcus by Laurentius Valla, sending a message to Joannes Aurispa ("Alcune lettere di Lorenzo Valla," [*Giornale storico della letteratura italiana,* XXI (1893), 40]).

Marsilius Ficinus wrote Marescalcus three letters (*Opera Omnia,* 2 vols. [Basel: Henricus Petrus, 1576], reproduced in *Monumenta Politica et Philosophica Rariora,* Luigi Firpo, ed., Series I, No. 7–8 [Turin: Bottega d'Erasmo, 1962], pp. 644–645, 738–739, 776), and wrote a translation of Mercurius Trismegistus' *Pimander* for him (see Paul Oskar Kristeller, *Supplementum Ficinianum: Marsilii Ficini Florentini Philosophi Florentini Opuscula inedita et dispersa,* 2 vols. [Florence: L. S. Olschki, 1937], I, vi). Leo Baptista de Albertis dedicated his *Apologi* to Marescalcus (see Girolamo Mancini, *Vita di Leon Battista Alberti* [Florence: Sansoni, 1882, p. 165]) in 1437, right after Poggius had presented Marescalcus with his first collection of letters.

Professor Kristeller also reports the existence of a catalogue issued by Hoepli in 1922 entitled *Cento libri preziosi,* in which, under item 1, an antiphonary, appears the date of death of Franciscus Marescalcus Ferrariensis as 15 September 1482.

2(I,x:3). Nicolaus de Niccolis (1363–1437) was the leading copyist and collector of books and antiquities of his day and most generous in allowing friends and scholars to use them. None of his letters to Poggius,

Ambrosius Traversarius, Guarinus, Franciscus Barbarus, *et al.* survive, although all of his correspondents comment on his letters continually. Poggius' letters to him cover the years 1406–1436. For Nicolaus' character and achievements see *Poggii Epistolae* Bk. VI, ltr 12 (Tonelli, Vol. II, pp. 108–112) and *Poggii Opera Omnia*, I, 270–277. See also:

Girolamo Tiraboschi, *Storia della letteratura italiana* (Florence, 1807), Vol. VI, pt. 1, pp. 128–132. Vespasiano da Bisticci, *Vite di uomini illustri del secolo XV* (Florence: Barbèra, Bianchi e Comp., 1859), pp. 473–482.

Ambrosii Traversarii Generalis Camaldulensium . . ., Latinae Epistolae, Laurentius Mehus, ed., 2 vols. (Bologna: Forni Editore, 1968), a photomechanic reprint of the Florence edition, 1759, Vol. I, "Praefatio" and "Vita"; Vol. II, Book VIII and *passim.*

Giuseppe Zippel, *Nicolò Niccoli* (Florence: Bocca, 1890).

Angelus Maria Bandinius, ed., *Catalogus Codicum Latinorum Bibliothecae Mediceae Laurentianae,* 5 vols. (Florence, n.p., 1774–1777), Vols. 1–III.

Angelus Maria Bandinius, ed., *Catalogus Codicum Graecorum,* 3 vols. (Florence: Typis Caesareis, 1764–1770), Vols. I, III.

Remigio Sabbadini, *Le scoperte dei codici latini e greci ne' secoli XIV e XV* (Florence: Sansoni, 1905 and 1914), I, 40–183; II, 192–264; revised by Eugenio Garin and reprinted in *Biblioteca storica del rinascimento* (Nuova Serie, IV, 1967).

3(I,x:7). Conicerem quicquid in buccam venerat. For the colloquial phrase *quod* or *quicquid in buccam venire,* see Cicero *Att.* 1.12.4; 7.10 fin; 14.7.2; Martial 12.24.5. Poggius had copied Cicero's *Epistolae ad Atticum* in 1408. See Berthold Louis Ullman, *The Origin and Development of Humanistic Script* (Rome: Edizioni di Storia e Letteratura, 1960), pp. 27–28. See also Walser, *Poggius,* pp. 105 and 418 (inventory no. 56). Poggius also owned a Martial at the time of his death; see Walser, *Poggius,* p. 421 (inventory no. 58).

4(I,x:8). Poggius very seldom lapsed into Italian in any of the letters which have been preserved. Three letters wholly in Italian are known; see Letter XVIII, note 1. For the few Italian phrases in this collection see Letter XVI (Tonelli Bk. I, ltr. 12; I, 56:24–26; 60:11); Letter XVIII (Tonelli Bk. I, ltr. 18; I, 75:28–29); Letter XLII (Tonelli Bk. II, ltr 34; I, 166:23); Letter XLVI (Tonelli Bk. II, ltr. 1; I, 86:28–29); Letter LI (Tonelli Bk. III, ltr. 14; I, 212:11–12); Letter LXVII (Tonelli Bk. III, ltr. 30; I, 270:9); Letter LXXX (Tonelli Bk. IV, ltr 3; I, 301:20–21); Letter LXXXIV (Tonelli Bk. IV, ltr. 12; I, 323:15–16).

5(I,x:21–26). Collections of Poggius' letters were made for Loisius, Archbishop of Florence (see *Poggii Epistolae,* Vol. I, pp. xi–xii) and for Carolus Borniolus (Brognolus) (see *Poggii Epist.* Bk. X, ltr. 8; Tonelli, III, 20–21). See also Bk. VII, ltrs. 8 and 13; II, 159–161, 172–174.

6(I,x:28–29). See Vespasiano, *Vite,* pp. 8–12. Eugenius IV fled from Rome to Florence via Pisa in 1433. He stayed "some time" and went to Bologna. Vespasiano mentions events of several years during the Pope's stay in Florence.

Eugenius IV presided over the consecration of Santa Maria del Fiore in Florence 25 March 1436. See Ferdinand Schevill, *History of Florence from the Founding of the City through the Renaissance* (New York: Harcourt, Brace and Co., 1936), p. 362.

7(I,xi:8). Franciscus Marescalcus also appears in the correspondence of Guarinus Veronensis and of Albertus Sartheanensis during 1434. See Sabbadini, *Epist. di Guar. Ver.,* III, 321–322, notes on No. 666.

Guarinus Veronensis had at first praised Antonius Beccadellius Panormita's *Hermaphroditus* in a letter to Johannes Lamola. His letter was circulated as an introduction to the text. Guarinus Veronensis' enthusiasm was reversed by Albertus de Sarteano during discussions in Ferrara. (Albertus de Sarteano preached in Ferrara during Lent 1434 and visited Guarinus, Franciscus Marescalcus, and Philippus Bendedeus.) Albertus de Sarteano demanded that Guarinus retract his praise, which Guarinus did, in No. 666 (II, 209–214) to Johannes Lamola. A letter to Franciscus Marescalcus and Philippus Bendedeus of Ferrara, from Albertus de Sarteano written from Rodigio, 20 April (no year) attacks style without content, especially in philosophy and theology. He attacks *Hermaphroditus* and its author, as often urged by Franciscus Marescalcus, because of its dangerous corruption of youth. Franciscus Marescalcus had urged Albertus Sarteanensis to take this responsibility for the salvation of all men. Albertus wanted the writings of Poggius and Antonius Beccadellius Panormita sent to him by Franciscus Marescalcus Ferrariensis immediately to be refuted. See Edmond Martène and Ursin Durand, *Veterum Scriptorum et Monumentorum Historicorum, Dogmaticorum, Moralium Amplissima Collectio,* 9 vols. (Paris: Montalant, 1724–1733), Vol. III, cols. 775–777.

8(I,xi:9). Poggius' letters to Franciscus Marescalcus continue with regularity from 1436 to the very end of his life and become frequent in his final years. There are thirteen of them, a large number to survive to any single friend other than Nicolaus de Niccolis. They are Bk. VI, ltr. 7 (II, 96–97), Bk. VI, ltr. 22 (II, 128–129), Bk. XI, ltr. 13 (III, 71–72), Bk. XI, ltr. 22 (III, 84–86), Bk. XI, ltr. 30 (III, 100–101), Bk. XII, ltr. 20 (III, 150–151), Bk. XII, ltr. 25 (III, 166–167), Bk. XIII, ltr. 16 (III, 213–214), Bk. XIV, ltrs. 1, 17, 18, 24, 29 (III, 254–255, 276–278, 285–286, 290–291). They deal with Poggius' domestic life and especially his children, with his current work and quarrels, with his old age and infirmities, with clerical reminiscences and his sadness at leaving the Curia, even for the chancellorship of Florence on which Franciscus had congratulated him.

Franciscus is also mentioned, in 1459, in three letters from Poggius to other correspondents (Bk. XIV, ltrs. 25, 28, 30; III, 286–287, 289–291). They all deal with the education of one of Poggius' young sons and the help Franciscus was giving in arranging it.

9(I,xi:11). Poggius defended his knowledge of classical literature and his skill in imitating the style of Cicero and other great Roman authors throughout his invectives against Laurentius Valla. See *Poggii Opera Omnia*, I, 188–251. See especially Invectiva I, pp. 192–193, and Invectiva V, p. 247.

LETTER II

1(I,xiii–xvi). Francesco Novati, who also published this letter in *Epistolario di Coluccio Salutati*, Francesco Novati, ed., 4 vols. (Fonti per la storia d'Italia, Rome: Istituto Storico Italiano, 1891–1905), has a most interesting note (Vol. IV, pp. 471–472, note 1) on Poggius' revision of the letter, shortening it and removing much interesting detail, and on the two divergent mss. and publication traditions which developed as a result.

2(I,xiii:3). On Nicolaus de Niccolis, see the introduction to this volume and also note 2 on Letter I. Being ten years older than Poggius and a Florentine by birth, Nicolaus had an even longer and closer association with Coluccius Salutatus than Poggius did. On their relationship in the Florentine world of learning around 1400 and on their influence over Poggius, see Walser, *Poggius,* pp. 12–16, and Berthold Louis Ullman, *The Humanism of Coluccio Salutati* (Padua: Antenore, 1963), pp. 117, note 1, 125, and Theodor Klette, *Beiträge zur Geschichte und Litteratur der italienischen Gelehrtenrenaissance,* 3 vols. (Greifswald: Julius Abel, 1888–1890). The "Dialogi ad Petrum Histrum" are an account of real or more probably fictionalized discussions between Coluccius and Nicolaus, written in 1401 by Leonardus Brunus Aretinus for yet another devoted pupil of Coluccius: Petrus Paulus Vergerius. They deal with the great figures of Florentine literature: Dante, Boccaccio, and Petrarch, with both of whom Coluccius corresponded (see *Epistolario,* Vol. I, pp. 48–49 (Boccaccio), pp. 61–62 (Petrarch), pp. 72–76 (Petrarch), pp. 80–84 (Petrarch), pp. 85–88 (Boccaccio), pp. 95–99 (Petrarch), pp. 156–157 (Boccaccio), and Vol. IV, pp. 276–277 (Petrarch). For a recent study of the authenticity and credibility of the opinions expressed by Coluccius and Nicolaus in the "Dialogi" see Hans Baron, *From Petrarch to Leonardo Bruni* (Chicago: Published for the Newberry Library by the University of Chicago Press, 1968), pp. 123–137.

3(I,xiii:4). There is a vast literature on Coluccius Salutatus (1331–1406), the chief official and leading citizen of Florence from 1375 until his death. See Ulysse Chevalier, *Répertoire des sources historiques du moyen age: Bio-bibliographie,* 2 vols. (Paris: Alphonse Picard, Nouvelle édition refondue, 1905–1907), Vol. II, cols. 4126–4127, and Mario Emilio Cosenza, *Biographical and Bibliographical Dictionary of the Italian Humanists and of the World of Classical Scholarship in Italy, 1300–1800,* 6 vols. (Boston: G. K. Hall & Co., 1962–1967), IV, 3149–3156. Ullman wrote extensively on him and edited a number of his works. See Coluccius Salutatus, *De laboribus Herculis,* Berthold Louis Ullman, ed., 2 vols. (Zurich: Thesaurus Mundi, 1951), and Coluccius Salutatus, *De seculo et religione,* Berthold Louis Ullman, ed. (Florence: L. S. Olschki, 1957). A most useful study of him both as statesman and as stylist is Eugenio Garin's "I cancellieri umanisti della republica fiorentina da Coluccio Salutati a Bartolomeo Scala," in *Rivista storica italiana* (LXXI, Fasc. 2 [1959], 185–208), republished in Eugenio Garin, *La cultura filosofica del Rinascimento italiano* (Florence: Sansoni, 1961). See also Garin's edition of Salutatus' *De nobilitate legum et medicinae,* a favorite subject of discussion among later humanists, and his edition of Salutatus' *De verecundia,* both published in Edizione nazionale dei classici del pensiero italiano, VIII (Florence: Vallechi, 1947).

4(I,xiv:2). Poggius was always able to express his grief over his friends' deaths eloquently and convincingly. See his letters about Antonius Corbinellus (Letter XXXVII; Tonelli Bk. II, ltr. 29), Bartholomeus de Montepolitiano (Letter LXXIII; Tonelli Bk. III, ltr. 37), and Nicolaus de Niccolis himself (Tonelli Bk. VI, ltr. 12) to Carolus Marsuppinus Aretinus. The letter written about Nicolaus in 1437 bears a marked resemblance to this one and contains many of the same phrases.

5(I,xiv:6–9). Coluccius conferred two major benefits on Poggius: he took him into his circle, with all its intellectual stimulation, because of Poggius' evident skill as a copyist (see Walser, *Poggius,* p. 12) and for the same reason he was able to arrange an opportunity for Poggius to become a "litterarum apostolicarum scriptor" in Rome late in 1403 or early in 1404 (Walser, *Poggius,* p. 20, and *Epistolario,* Vol. IV, pp. 3–8, *Epist.* Bk. XIV, ltrs. 1 and 2). He was responsible too for Leonardus Brunus Aretinus' position in the Curia. See Salutatus' magnificent letter recommending Leonardus to Pope Innocent VII (*Epistolario,* Vol. IV, pp. 105–109, *Epist.* Bk. XIV, ltr. 15).

6(I,xiv:15). Petrus Paulus Vergerius (Petrus Histrus), far from Florence in Padua in 1391, wrote Coluccius this same grateful praise and addressed him as "father" throughout the letter. See Leonard Smith, ed., *Epistolario di Pier Paolo Vergerio* (Rome: Tipografia del Senato, 1934), pp. 62–63. In a letter written to Franciscus Zabarella on 8 October 1406, Vergerius called Coluccius "urbis illius primum atque precipuum decus." Novati assembled the letters, epitaphs, and eulogies written by the humanists after Coluccius' death, Vergerius' among them, pp. 478–480, in *Epistolario di Coluccio Salutati,* Vol. IV, pp. 470–519. Leonardus Brunus' letter to Nicolaus, May 12 (p. 470), says much that Poggius said but less rhetorically.

7(I,xiv:15). "amisimus portum ac refugium." For *portus* and *refugium* in this context, see regum, populorum, nationum *portus* erat et *refugium* senatus, in Cicero *Off.* 2.8.27.

Sabbadini says that the philosophical works of Cicero, including the *De officiis,* were widely known in Europe by Petrarch's day. See Sabbadini, *Scoperte,* II, 212. In Poggius' inventory at the time of his death are listed three mss. of the *De officiis,* one in Poggius' own hand: see Walser, *Poggius,* p. 419, nos. 9–11.

8(I,xiv:17–18). Joannes Tinctus de Fabriano, in his letter to Antonius Luscus (*Epistolario,* Vol. IV, pp. 474–475), also speaks of "extincto lumine italice facundie."

9(I,xiv:26–27). These qualities of Coluccius' are mentioned by Vergerius also in his eulogy (*Epistolario,* Vol. IV, p. 479) and by Jannotius Manettus in his life of Coluccius, whose selflessness and self-control he emphasized (Vol. IV, pp. 509–513).

10(I,xiv:28–29). See Ullman's chapters VII and VIII, on Coluccius' scholarship and influence (*Humanism,* pp. 95–126).

11(I,xiv:30). Novati also published (*Epistolario,* Vol. IV, pp. 501–505) an encomium on Coluccius by Domenico di Bandino d'Arezzo, which contains the statement (p. 504) "de te igitur scriptum arbitror. XII. Proverbiorum: de fructu oris tui replebitur unusquisque."

12(I,xv:3–6). See Ullman's Chapter IX on Coluccius' library (*Humanism,* pp. 129–209), and the devotion his pupils displayed toward him by copying texts or dedicating work to him. See Berthold Louis Ullman, *The Origin and Development of Humanistic Script* (Rome: Storia e Letteratura, 1960), pp. 24–27, for Poggius' ms. of Cicero; and Hans Baron, *Leonardo Bruni Aretino: Humanistisch-philosophische Schriften* (Leipzig: Teubner, 1928), pp. 160–161, for Leonardus Brunus' translations.

13(I,xv:6). "Sus Minervam" was one of Poggius' favorite expressions, used repeatedly. *Sed sus Minervam:* this is a proverb, the full form of which is "sus docet Minervam."

See the comment of Festus: "sus Minervam in proverbio est, ubi quis id docet alterum, cuius ipse inscius est" ["'A pig teaches Minerva' is a proverb meaning that someone teaches another something of which he is himself ignorant"].

14(I,xv:11–12). Poggius did write a rather pedestrian epitaph for Coluccius, published by Novati (*Epistolario,* Vol. IV, p. 484). He did not, apparently, write an after-the-fact funeral oration as he did many years later for Nicolaus de Niccolis; see *Poggii Opera Omnia*, Vol. I, pp. 270–277. See also *Poggii Epist.* Vol. II, pp. 113–117 (Bk. VI, ltrs. 14–16) in which Poggius explained his writing of the eulogy for Nicolaus and expressed his surprise and disappointment that no one else had done so.

15(I,xv:15–16). Walser provides evidence that Poggius was back in Florence briefly in October 1406 (*Poggius*, pp. 22, 328–329, Doc. 10).

16(I,xv:19). Vergil *Aeneid* 1.409. Poggius liked this sentiment; he used it in another letter to Nicolaus, in connection with Nicolaus' projected visit to Rome in 1423. See Letter XLVI, note 2 (Tonelli Bk. II, ltr. 1; I, 85:7–8).

17(I,xv:23). Novati devotes several pages (*Epistolario*, Vol. IV, pp. 588–590) to Coluccius' presumed private residence in Florence as well as to his real estate holdings elsewhere (pp. 572–588), whereas Demetrio Marzi in *La cancelleria della repubblica fiorentina* (Rocca S. Casciano: Licinio Cappelli, 1910), pp. 148–150, believed that he had no residence but his official one.

This particular way of expressing grief was a habit with Poggius; he used it again in connection with the death of Nicolaus: *Epistolae*, Bk. VI, ltr. 12; *Poggii Opera Omnia*, Vol. III; Tonelli, Vol. II, p. 111.

18(I,xv:26–32). Ullman was convinced that Coluccius died suddenly, actively engaged in his literary and governmental pursuits (*Humanism*, pp. 15, 65, 69). Two accounts of Coluccius' funeral are given in Marzi, *Cancelleria*, pp. 148–150. A list of his seven sons is given on p. 148, note 4. Novati published Leonardus Brunus' very moving letter of sympathy to Coluccius' sons (*Epistolario*, Vol. IV, pp. 516–519), which had been long known in Mehus' edition, *Epistolae* II, 11, pt. 1, pp. 45–47 (Leonardus Brunus Aretinus, *Epistolarum Libri VIII*, 2 vols. [edited by Laurentius Mehus, Florence: Paperinius, 1741]).

19(I,xvi:2). Coluccius' books were sold, nearly all to his friends in Florence, and especially to Nicolaus de Niccolis. See Ullman, *Humanism*, pp. 137, 278–280. For a detailed study of the further history of Coluccius' books, see Berthold Louis Ullman and Philip A. Stadter, *The Public Library of Renaissance Florence*, Medioevo e Umanesimo 10 (Padua: Antenore, 1972), pp. 97–99, 133–248, 314–315. Nicolaus still owed a considerable sum for books to Coluccius' heirs at the time of his own death (pp. 98–99).

20(I,xvi:3–4). On this portrait, or possibly death mask, see Novati's comments in *Epistolario*, Vol. IV, p. 560. Pope-Hennessy also interprets the passage as perhaps indicating a death mask, which was not uncommon at this period. Brunelleschi's is still preserved; see John Pope-Hennessy, *Italian Renaissance Sculpture* (London: Phaidon Press, 1958), pp. 8 and 304. Loyisius cannot be identified with certainty but Novati (*Epistolario,* Vol. IV, p. 474, l.5) gives the reading "Magistro" instead of Tonelli's "Muigino."

21(I,xvi:7–8). Coluccius' successor was his former colleague and close contemporary, Benedetto di Ser Lando di Fortino degli Orlandini, generally called Benedetto Fortini. The exact date of his election is unknown but he died in office on 10 December 1406 (Marzi, *Cancelleria,* pp. 153–156) and was succeeded by Pietro di Ser Mino di Ser Domenico di Ser Mino da Montevarchi, who was a favorite pupil of Coluccius' (see *Epistolario,* Vol. III, pp. 422, 523, 528, 556) and a participant in Leonardus Brunus' *Dialogi ad Petrum Histrum,* pp. 40–54, 59. He was a completely studious, unworldly man, a mystic, who, after serving as chancellor from 28 December 1406, left the office exactly four years later and became a monk at Easter 1411. (Marzi, *Cancelleria,* pp. 156–158.)

22(I,xvi:8). The literature on Leonardus Brunus Aretinus (1369–1444) is even more voluminous than on Coluccius Salutatus. See Chevalier, *Bio-bibliographie,* Vol. I, col. 711, and Cosenza, *Dictionary,* I, 272–290. His works were highly respected by his contemporaries, as is shown by the vast numbers of manuscript copies of them and by the many entries in Ludwig Hain, *Repertorium Bibliographicum,* 2 vols., 4 pts. (Milan: Görlich Editore, 1948), Nos. 1557–1596. He and Poggius were good friends for almost fifty years, starting when they were both disciples of Salutatus and increasing in the first decade of the fifteenth century when they both worked at the Curia. Fifteen letters from Poggius to Leonardus have been preserved, running from 1416–1438. There are also twelve letters from Leonardus to Poggius, beginning in 1404 and ending in 1431. The most interesting exchange involves Poggius' surprisingly sympathetic letter about the imprisonment, trial, and execution of the Hussite heretic, Jerome of Prague (*Epistolae,* Bk. I, ltr. 2; *Poggii Opera Omnia,* III, 11–20) and Leonardus' reply (a rare survival in Poggius' correspondence), in which he says; "Nudius tertius exemplum habuimus litterarum tuarum . . . de Hieronymi supplicio, quarum elegantiam equidem valde probo . . . Ego cautius de hisce rebus scribendum puto" ["Three days ago I received a copy of your letter about the punishment of Jerome, which I admit is very well written. . . . I think you ought to write about such matters with more caution"]. (*Leonardi Bruni Aretini Epistolae,* pt. 1, pp. 119–120 [IV, 9].)

Leonardus Brunus Aretinus was elected Chancellor on 29 December 1410, the first man to hold the office who was not a notary. He held it only until 4 April 1411. His successor was Paolo Fortini, brother of Coluccius' successor Benedetto. Leonardus succeeded him in the Chancellorship in December 1427 and held it until his death on 8 March 1444. See Marzi, *Cancelleria,* pp. 159–161, 189–197. See Novati's note on this matter at the end of his publication of the letter (*Epistolario*, Vol. IV, pp. 471–474, especially p. 474, note 2). See also Poggius' letter of congratulations to Leonardus when in December 1427 he was elected Chancellor on satisfactory terms (Tonelli Bk. III, ltr. 16; I, 215–216).

In recent years Leonardus' writings, both literary and political, have been critically scrutinized by Hans Baron in *The Crisis of the Early Renaissance*, 2 vols. (Princeton: Princeton University Press, 1955), *Humanistic and Political Literature in Florence and Venice at the Beginning of the Quattrocento* (Cambridge, Mass.: Harvard University Press, 1955), and *From Petrarch to Leonardo Bruni* (Chicago and London: Published for the Newberry Library by the University of Chicago Press, 1968).

The relationship between Leonardus and Nicolaus was not always friendly. They quarreled some time around 1420 and remained on bad terms for six years. Zippel attributed the quarrel to Ambrosius Traversarius' adverse opinions of Leonardus' translations from the Greek. See *Nicolò Niccoli*, p. 32, and *Ambrosii Traversarii Generalis Camaldulensium. . . Latinae Epistolae*, Laurentius Mehus, ed., 2 vols. (Bologna: Forni Editore, 1968), a photomechanic reprint of the Florence edition, 1759), Vol. I, "Praefatio" and "Vita"; Vol. II, *Epistolae*, Bk. VIII, ltr. 8 (Vol. II, cols. 366–371). Traversarius' comment on Leonardus' translation of Plato's *Phaedrus* is indeed unfriendly (col. 370): "Habet haec sua extrema traductio magnos buccinatores, atque in primis se ipsum. Ego quid de illa sentiam, fateri non audeo" ["This latest translation of his has great boosters (literally trumpeters) and himself in the forefront. What I think about it I dare not say"].

According to Girolamo Mancini, the quarrel between Leonardus Aretinus and Nicolaus was precipitated by Nicolaus' preference for Ambrosius Traversarius. See *Vita di Leon Battista Alberti*, p. 152. Mancini found this theory about the quarrel in Vespasiano's *Vite*, p. 244 (of Traversarius). Leonardus Aretinus' account of the quarrel in his letter to Poggius, Bk. V, ltr. 4 (edited by Mehus, pt. 2, pp. 117–125), does not mention Traversarius but blames the trouble on Benvenuta. This letter is tentatively dated 31 January 1421. In 1424, Leonardus wrote two invectives against Nicolaus, one in prose, one in verse (see Baron, *Schriften*, p. 173).

Leonardus Aretinus and Nicolaus were finally reconciled by Franciscus Barbarus in 1426. (See Zippel, *Nicolò Niccoli*, p. 33.) Leonardus seems to refer to Poggius' letter I, 16 (Tonelli) in his letter V, 4 to Poggius.

See also the comments on Leonardus Brunus' writings and Baron's interpretations made by Ludwig Bertalot in his review: "Rezension von Leonardo Bruni Aretino: Humanistisch-philosophische Schriften," edited by H. Baron, *Historische Vierteljahrschrift*, XXIX (1934), 385–

400; and in his articles on Leonardus Brunus: "Forschungen über Leonardo Bruni Aretino," *Archivum Romanicum,* XV, 1931 (1932), 284–323; "Zur Bibliographie der Überzetzungen des Leonardus Brunus Aretinus," *Quellen und Forschungen,* XXVII (1937), 178–195; and "Zur Bibliographie des Leonardus Brunus Aretinus," *ibid.,* XXVIII (1938), 268–285.

LETTER III

1(I,1:8–9; 2:13). For the condition of the Jews in Italy, Southern Germany, and Rome during Poggius' early life, see Cecil Roth, "The Jews in the Middle Ages," in *CMH,* VII, 632–663, especially pp. 649 and 663. See also Cecil Roth, *The Jews in the Renaissance* (Philadelphia: The Jewish Publication Society of America, 1959), pp. 138–139 and 350–351.

2(I,2:4). Leonardus Brunus Aretinus. Tonelli (note 2) says he was extremely famous for his learning and good character and as much Poggius' good friend as Nicolaus'.

3(I,2:14–16; 4:1–8). See *Switzerland,* L. Russell Muirhead, ed., The Blue Guides, 3rd edition (Chicago: Rand McNally, 1952), pp. 282–283. "The warm saline and sulphur waters (116–124° F) . . . are used for gout and rheumatism."

4(I,2:20). On Puteoli, see *OCD,* p. 901. See also *Southern Italy with Sicily and Sardinia,* L. Russell Muirhead, ed., The Blue Guides, 3rd edition (London: Ernest Benn, Ltd., 1959), pp. 91–93.

5(I,3:6). On Heliogabalus, see Leonardus Brunus Aretinus, *Epistolae,* pt. 1, p. 53 (*Epist.,* II, 16).

6(I,3:8–11). See *Switzerland,* Muirhead, ed., pp. 296–301 and the map at the beginning of the book.

7(I,3:18–19). *Switzerland,* p. 281. There was a Roman fort nearby. The German-Swiss border still runs close by. For a description of the Rhine Falls, see pp. 296–297.

8(I,3:28). For Poggius' later description of the Nile, see *De varietate fortunae* (*Poggii Opera,* Vol. II), pp. 149–150.

9(I,4:8; 6:2). See Paul Negrier, *Les bains à travers les ages* (Paris: Librairie de la construction moderne, 1925), Chapter 4, pp. 113–146, with numerous appropriate illustrations. See also "The Topography of Rome" in *The Romane Historie written by T. Livius of Padua. Also, The Breviaries of L. Florus: with a Chronology to the whole Historie and the Topography of Rome in old time.* Translated out of Latine into English, by Philemon Holland, Doctor in Physick (London, Printed by W. Hunt, for Gabriel Bedell, at the Middle Temple Gate, 1659), "Chap. XXV. of baths and bains in general," p. 1104.

10(I,4:16). Vergil *Aeneid* 6.306–307.

11(I,4:24). ad florales ludos. For *Florales ludi,* see *Inscr. Orell.* 2545.

12(I,4:28–29). See Lynn Thorndike, "Sanitation, Baths, and Street-cleaning in the Middle Ages and Renaissance," *Speculum,* III (1928), 192–203.

13(I,5:26–30). From the evidence of the letter Poggius wrote soon after this one to Leonardus Brunus Aretinus (Tonelli Bk. I, ltr. 2), this letter can be dated 1416. Poggius reached Constance in October 1414. It seems odd that he was not fluent in German a year and a half later.

14(I,6:2). flabello ventulum faciebant. For the idiom *ventulum facere,* "to make a breeze (by fanning)," see Terence *Eun.* 595.

15(I,6:9). vivendi libertatem. For *libertas vivendi,* see Cicero *Verr.* 2.3.1, paragraph 3.

Leonardus Brunus had sent Nicolaus de Niccolis a ms. of the *Verrines,* which he found in Siena in 1407 (Sabbadini, *Scoperte,* I, 75; II, 211). Coluccius Salutatus had also had at least a partial text of the *Verrines* (Ullman, *Humanism,* pp. 222–223).

16(I,6:15). Plato *Republic* 5 (Steph. 464c).

17(I,6:18–24). On the simultaneous use of the baths of ancient Rome by both sexes, see Jerome Carcopino, *Daily Life in Ancient Rome,* Henry T. Rowell, ed., E. O. Lorimer, trans. (New Haven: Yale University Press, 1940), p. 258.

18(I,6:24). Vergil *Aeneid* 7.53.

19(I,7:15). Menedemus Senex is a character in Terence's comedy *Heauton Timoroumenos.*

20(I,7:17–18). commercium sermonis. For this phrase, see Livy 5.15.5. Poggius had ample opportunity to know the first Decade of Livy (Sabbadini, *Scoperte,* II, 231–233, and Ullman, *Humanism,* p. 235).

21(I,7:18–20). Terence *Phormio* 85–86.

22(I,7:27–8:2). Carcopino, *Daily Life,* pp. 259–260, describes the ball games, similar to this one, played by the Romans in their baths.

23(I,8:6). For a discussion of the view of Epicureanism of one of Poggius' contemporaries, see the chapter on Laurentius Valla (pp. 19–36) in Paul Oskar Kristeller's *Eight Philosophers of the Italian Renaissance* (Stanford: Stanford University Press, 1964). Valla (1406–1457) was almost a generation younger than Poggius, and by the time he wrote his *De vero bono (De voluptate),* in 1431–1432, he was probably giving the ideas of the "Epicurea factio" more sophisticated treatment than Poggius meant in this letter.

On Epicureanism in the fifteenth century see also Eugenio Garin, *La cultura filosofica del Rinascimento italiano,* La Civiltà Europea (Florence: Sansoni, 1961), pp. 72–92.

24(I,8:8). Genesis 2:8.

25(I,8:12–9:4). Spas were still credited with most of the same cures in the early twentieth century as in the early fifteenth. See "Balneo-therapeutics," *Encyclopaedia Britannica*, 11th edition, III, 284–285, and "Mineral Waters," XVIII, 517–522, though fertility was no longer mentioned.

26(I,9:4–7). Here Poggius is joking, because Vestal Virgins, like the clergy, were meant to suppress and forego earthly desire and enjoyment (*OCD*, p. 1116).

27(I,9:9–11). See Albrecht Dürer's famous woodcut "The Men's Bath" in Arthur M. Hind, *An Introduction to a History of Woodcut, with a Detailed Survey of Work Done in the Fifteenth Century*, II (New York: Dover Publications, 1963), 384–385.

28(I,10:16). Terence *Hecyra* 461.

29(I,10:23–27). Leonardus Brunus Aretinus.

30(I,10:24–25). cum amicorum inter se communia omnia sint. For the thought, see *Vetus verbum hoc quidem est:* "Communia esse amicorum inter se omnia," Terence *Adel.* 804.

31(I,10:24). Nicolaus de Medicis is mentioned thirty-one times in Poggius' correspondence with Nicolaus de Niccolis and once in a letter to Leonardus Brunus Aretinus. See Raymond de Roover, *The Rise and Decline of the Medici Bank, 1397–1494*, Harvard Studies in Business History, Vol. XXI (Cambridge, Mass.: Harvard University Press, 1963), p. 37. He was a son of Vieri di Cambio de' Medici, who retired in 1393, after having been a very distinguished citizen of Florence. See Niccolò Machiavelli, *History of Florence and of the Affairs of Italy from the Earliest Times to the Death of Lorenzo the Magnificent* (New York: Harper Torchbooks, 1960), pp. 150–151.

Nicolaus de Medicis (1385–1454) and Cambiozzo or Cambio (1390–1465) were partners and established a bank of their own with offices in Florence and Rome. They were unsuccessful. By 1433 they had sold most of their real estate to pay off the liabilities of the bank. See De Roover, *Rise and Decline*, note 20 (p. 417). Nicolaus de Medicis and Cambio were well treated by Bartholomeus de Bardis despite their faulty dealings with Johannes Bicci de Medicis' bank (p. 204). One letter from Poggius to Nicolaus de Medicis has survived: Tonelli Bk. IV, ltr. 19; I, 343–344. See also *Poggii Opera Omnia*, IV, 731. It refers to Poggius' long-established friendship with Nicolaus, to their common interest in humanistic studies, to the recent decline in Nicolaus' fortunes, and to his dedication of his son to the Church.

Nicolaus de Medicis appears in numerous literary works: see Kristeller, *Iter*, I, 89. Florence: Biblioteca Laurenziana cod. Ashb. 494 (426). ff. 1–99. L. B. Alberti, "Della tranquillità dell'animo," a dialogue between Nicola Medici, L. B. Alberti, and Agnolo Pandolfini.

I, 139. Florence: Biblioteca Nazionale Centrale cod. Mag. XXI 170.
ff.1–41v. Nicolai Lune Enchyridion . . . ad Nicolam Medicem.
I, 148. Florence: Biblioteca Nazionale Centrale cod. Pal. Capponi
92, f.90 "L. Bruni, preface of his versions of Demosthenes to Nicolas
Medices."
Kristeller, *Iter*, II, 127. Rome: Biblioteca Nazionale Centrale f.1–75
Vittorio Emanuele II 738 (945.230) L. B. Alberti, "Della tranquillità
dell' animo," in 3 books, inc. "Niccòla di messer Veri de Medici homo
ornatissimo . . . ," f. 77: Vita di Niccole de Medici scritta da Lion Batt.
Alberti in a late hand.
II, 399. Città del Vaticano: Biblioteca Apostolica Vaticana cod. Pal. Lat.
1745, ff.1–4v. "Leonardi (Bruni) Arretini praefatio in orationes
Demosthenis ad Nicolam Medicem."
II, 475. Città del Vaticano: Bibl. . . . Vat. Fondo Chigi J IV 120 bis.
Demosthenes, *Philippicae*, tr. Leon. Brunus to Nic. Medices.
II, 482. Città del Vaticano: Bibl. Apost. Vat., Fondo Chigi. Cod. Chis.
J IV 148 f. 7v. "Leonardus Dathus presbyter," poem on St. Jerome,
with a preface to Nicolas Medices. Same poem in Cod. Chis. J V 194
f. 26v. Kristeller, *Iter*, II, 483.
Kristeller, *Iter*, I, 161. Florence: Biblioteca Nazionale Centrale. Cod.
Conv. Soppr. J I 13 (S. Marco 285) f.1. Leon Bruni: "Preface of his
version of . . . orations by Demosthenes, to Nicolas Medices."
On the civic and financial status of Nicolaus de Medicis, see Lauro
Martines, *The Social World of the Florentine Humanists* (Princeton:
Princeton University Press, 1963), pp. 323–324. On Leonardus' dedica-
tion of his translation of Demosthenes' orations to Nicolaus de Medicis,
see also Ludwig Bertalot, "Forschungen über Leonardo Bruni Aretino,"
Archivum Romanicum, XV (1931), 20–21.
        32(I,10:27–28). Tonelli identified Laurentius as the brother of Cos-
mus de Medicis. Both were great friends of Poggius' and great sup-
porters of humanist endeavors. Laurentius is often mentioned in
Poggius' letters in connection with such friendly errands as delivering
Poggius' dialogue *De avaritia* to Nicolaus de Niccolis in 1429 (see
Letter LXIX; Tonelli Bk. III, ltr. 32). He was permitted to carry the
treasured ms. of Plautus' *Comedies* from Rome to Florence (Walser,
Poggius, p. 103, note 1). He traveled to Verona and Venice in 1431 with
his brother Cosmus and with Nicolaus de Niccolis (see Zippel, *Nicolò
Niccoli*, pp. 54–55). He went into exile with Cosmus, 1433–1434, and
died young in 1440, at which time Poggius wrote a funeral oration for
him (*Poggii Opera Omnia*, I, 278–286). He is also a speaker, along with
Nicolaus de Niccolis, in Poggius' dialogue *De nobilitate*, written in
the year of Laurentius' death.
        33(I,10:27). Cosmus de Medicis (1389–1464) was perhaps the most
important historically of Poggius' whole circle of friends. Their friend-

ship was close and lifelong. Poggius' surviving letters to Cosmus belong to the decades 1432–1452, but Cosmus is mentioned very frequently throughout the correspondence. He was not only of immense importance financially and politically in Florence and throughout Italy for over forty years, but he was the most powerful, wealthy, and generous supporter of humanist efforts. The literature on him is immense: see Chevalier, *Bio-bibliographie*, Vol. II, col. 3175, and Cosenza, *Dictionary*, III, 2265–2267. His support of the rescue and dissemination of classical texts is evident not only from the letters of his humanist friends but also from the survival of many of his own books (see Bandini, *Catal. cod. lat.*, Vols. II and III, *passim*) and particularly for the responsibility entrusted to him in establishing Nicolaus' books as the Public Library of Renaissance Florence (see Ullman-Stadter, *Public Library*, pp. 3–27 and 310–313).

A most interesting example of the high regard in which Cosmus was held by his contemporaries is the *Collectiones Cosmianae Bartholomaei Scalae*, Cod. Laur. LIV, 10 (Bandini, Vol. II, cols. 643–651), a collection of poems, speeches, and letters in praise of Cosmus put together after his death by Bartholomaeus Scala, Poggius' successor as chancellor of Florence, and presented to Cosmus' grandson, Laurentius de Medicis.

For a detailed discussion of this laudatory collection see Alison M. Brown, "The Humanist Portrait of Cosimo de' Medici, Pater Patriae," *Journal of the Warburg and Courtauld Institutes*, XXIV (1961), 186–221.

34(I,10:28). In the text of the letter Tonelli has the reading of the date as *January*, which he says in note 3 is the reading in Cod. Riccard. 759, the ms. on which he based his text. He goes on to say that from internal evidence that reading is clearly incorrect and should be read as *June*. He explains that it is not customary to go to the baths in winter, that one would not use a fan in winter, and he notes that at the beginning of this letter Poggius mentions having dispatched his previous letter from Constance in February.

LETTER IV

1(Wilmanns, 302:3). Poggius here refers to a letter which he wrote to Nicolaus de Niccolis somewhere along his way from Mantua to London. Walser (*Poggius*, p. 72) thought the present letter might have been written in Paris, where Poggius is known to have stopped on the way and to have found a ms. of Nonius Marcellus; see Letter XXX, note 5 (Tonelli Bk. II, ltr. 22; I, 148: 22). The earlier letter mentioned here has not been found.

2(302:9–11). A quotation from Seneca *Epistolae* II.9.7 (Lucius Annaeus Seneca: *Epistles* XXI, p. 199, *The Workes of Lucius Annaeus*

Seneca, both Morrall and Naturall [London: William Stansby, 1614]).
Seneca does not mention Demetrius but quotes from Epicurus.

3(302:19). Poggius was born 11 February 1380, which would make
this letter belong to 1419; Poggius may well have spent several months
of that year in France, since Henry Beaufort was at Meulan-sur-Seine
with Henry V in May and is known to have been in England in October.
See Lewis Bostock Radford, *Henry Beaufort: Bishop, Chancellor,
Cardinal* (London: Sir Isaac Pitman & Sons, 1908), pp. 91–93.

4(303:2–6). This was a favorite theme of Poggius' during his years in
England: see Letter V (Wilmanns, pp. 300–301), Letter VIII (Tonelli
Bk. I, ltr. 8), Letter X (Tonelli Bk. I, ltr. 10), Letter XI (Tonelli Bk. I,
ltr. 13), Letter XII (Tonelli Bk. I, ltr. 14), Letter XX (Tonelli Bk. I,
ltr. 20), Letter XXI (Tonelli Bk. I, ltr. 21).

Poggius mentioned his family in Tuscany frequently and usually
adversely in his letters from England; see Letters X–XI, XIII–XVI
(Tonelli Bk. I, ltrs. 10–13, 15–16).

5(303: 13). Hieronymus *Epist.* XIII.2. Nicolaus owned at least two
texts of St. Jerome's letters; see Ullman-Stadter, *Public Library*, pp.
147–148.

6(303:14). 2 Thessalonians 3:10, a favorite quotation of Poggius' at
this time. See Letter V (Wilmanns, 300:15) and Letter XXII (Tonelli
Bk. I, ltr. 22; I, 82:28–29).

7(303:19). ut non unde veniamus, sed quo tendamus. For a similar
thought, see *Unde venis: Et quo tendis?* Horace *Sat.* 1.9.63; *Ep.* 1.15.11.

8(303:21). In another letter, Letter XV (Tonelli Bk. I, ltr. 11; I, 46: 7),
Poggius describes himself as "olim tum indignatione motus" when he
left the Curia.

9(303: 24–26). This is a theme that runs through almost all Poggius'
letters from England. See Letters VI–XXII (*Poggii Epist.* Bk. I, ltrs.
6–22).

10(303:31). impedimento est. For *impedimento esse*, see Terence
Andria 707.

11(303:33–34). Not everyone praised Nicolaus for selling his possessions. Both Leonardus Brunus Aretinus and Guarinus accused him of
having merely a commercial interest in his books and antiquities. See
Laurentius Mehus, "Praefatio," p. lxii in *Ambr. Trav. Epist.*

12(303:39). Horace *Sermones* 2.6.60–62;65–68. Translated by Smith
Palmer Bovie, 5th edition (Chicago: University of Chicago Press, 1969),
p. 141.

13(303:46–47). Poggius' statement here, that Beaufort did not want
him to leave until spring, suggests that the summer of 1419 was past and
that they were in England. The letter must have been written before
February 1420, when Poggius entered his fortieth year.

14(304:2). See Remigio Sabbadini, *Storia e critica di testi latini,* Biblioteca di filologia classica, 10 (Catania: Battiato, 1914), pp. 4–7, for Nicolaus de Niccolis "Commentarium," a list of mss. to be sought in German libraries by members of Julianus Caesarinus' mission there in 1431. See pp. 27–29 and 43–49: Poggius' discoveries made before his journey to England.

15(304:3–4). On fifteenth century diagnosis and treatment of hemorrhoids, see Dean Putnam Lockwood, *Ugo Benzi: Medieval Philosopher and Physician 1376–1439* (Chicago: University of Chicago Press, 1951), pp. 31, 73, 75.

LETTER V

1(Wilmanns, 300:3). volui tamen pauculos versus exarare. *Exarare* in the sense "to write" is used by Cicero only in his letters. See *id ipsum his versibus exaravi,* Pliny *Ep.* 7.4.5. Poggius had every opportunity to know Pliny's letters well from the ms. which belonged to Coluccius Salutatus. See Ullman, *Origin and Development,* pp. 16–19.

2(300:5). See also Wilmanns, "Briefsammlungen," pp. 289–331, 443–463. The type of church literature that was available to Poggius can be seen in the Appendix, "An Early Book List of All Souls College," pp. 469–481, in Ernest F. Jacob, "Two Lives of Archbishop Chichele," *Bulletin of the John Rylands Library,* XVI (1932), 428–481. For examples of the texts which Poggius was reading hastily at this period, see the twelfth, thirteenth, and fourteenth century mss. of the works of St. Augustine and St. Jerome which were later bequeathed to Balliol College, Oxford, by Poggius' acquaintance in his old age, William Grey. These are mss. 3, 6, 9, 10, 147, 156, 175, 177, 229, described by Roger Aubrey Baskerville Mynors in his *Catalogue of the Manuscripts of Balliol College, Oxford* (Oxford: Clarendon Press, 1963).

On the *Contra Faustum Manicheum* see S. Aurelius Augustinus, *Contra Faustum Libri Triginta Tres,* Joseph Zycha, ed. (Vienna, 1891), pp. 251–797. On p. 250, Zycha cites six mss., eighth to tenth century, for his *apparatus criticus.* See also the twelfth century ms. in the Library of Hereford Cathedral and the late thirteenth century ms. in the Library of Emmanuel College, Cambridge. See also Gustav Krüger, "Augustine, Saint," *Encyclopaedia Britannica,* 11th edition, II, 907–910, especially p. 908.

St. Augustine was at first a believer in Manicheism. He separated himself from the sect after his arrival in Milan in 384 and wrote several works against it during a long controversy, including *Contra Faustum Manicheum* in 400.

3(300:10). St. Jerome: Vallars, ed., Vol. I, p. 421, *Epist.* 69.

4(300:14). 2 Thessalonians 3:10. *Si quis non vult operari, nec manducet.*

5(301:11). Poggius found the work of Nonius Marcellus, "lexicographer and grammarian" (*OCD*, 2nd edition, p. 737) in Paris on his way to England. See Sabbadini, *Scoperte*, I, 83, and *Poggii Epistolae* (Tonelli Bk. II, ltr. 22; I, 148:22). Nonius Marcellus of Thubursicum in Numidia (fl. A.D. 323) was the author of an encyclopedic work *De compendiosa doctrina*, divided into three parts: lexicographical, grammatical, antiquarian. He was very careless and ignorant, but the work was important for "numerous quotations from early Latin literature." See John E. Sandys, *A History of Classical Scholarship*, 3 vols., 3rd edition (Cambridge: Cambridge University Press, 1908–1921), I, 220–221. For activities concerning the text of Nonius Marcellus' work, see Sabbadini, *Storia e critica*, pp. 32–33, 37–38. Nicolaus de Niccolis lent Nonius Marcellus to Franciscus Barbarus. A ms. was found in the Visconti library in Pavia by Bartholomeus Capra and sent to Leonardus Brunus Aretinus between 1407 and 1409.

Franciscus Barbarus wrote to Nicolaus de Niccolis that his Nonius Marcellus was being copied and would be returned. Venice, the Ides of September [1415].

6(301:12). See Sandys, *Classical Scholarship*, I, 258–270, on Flavius Magnus Aurelius Cassiodorus (ca. A.D. 485–580), author, quaestor to Theodoric, Praetorian prefect, founder of two monasteries. He wrote the *Historia Tripartita*, "an ecclesiastical history (from 306 to 439) . . . combining . . . the translations of the Greek historians Socrates, Sozomen, and Theodoret . . . by Epiphanius."

7(301:18). Vespasiano, *Vite*, p. 473. Nicolaus de Niccolis was one of four brothers, the others all merchants. On Nicolaus and his friends, see Leonardus Brunus Aretinus, *Epist.* V, 4, pt. 2, pp. 17–25, and Zippel, *Nicolò Niccoli*, pp. 75–91, for the text of Leonardus Brunus Aretinus' "Oratio in Nebulonem maledicum." Leonardus Brunus wrote to Poggius about his quarrel with Nicolaus de Niccolis in *Epist.* IV, 21, pt. 1, p. 136. He wrote to explain the quarrel; then realized that his letter did not reach Poggius. *Epist.* IV, 23 (pt. 1, p. 142): "Deinde tibi notissimum est non mea culpa has inimicitias cum Nicolao esse susceptas."

See Ambrosius Traversarius, *Epistolae*, I, lxxvi–lxxviii: "Vita Nicolai" by Jannotius Manettus. Nicolaus had one female servant: p. lxxvii, "Sybilla." See also the attacks on Nicolaus de Niccolis listed on p. lxi. Percy Gothein, in *Francesco Barbaro, Früh-Humanismus und Staatskunst in Venedig* (Berlin: Verlag Die Runde, 1932), pp. 110–113, gives a detailed account of Nicolaus de Niccolis' quarrels with his brothers and with Leonardus Brunus Aretinus and of the part played in them by Benvenuta (Sybilla). Nicolaus and Leonardus were reconciled in 1426 by Franciscus Barbarus. See also *Ambr. Trav. Epist.*, Vol. II, XVII, 4 (Ambrosius Traversarius to Franciscus Barbarus).

8(301:27). Poggius would indeed have been happy to have his best friend and mentor associated with him in his work. Furthermore, Nicolaus' piety was well known. See Vespasiano, *Vite*, pp. 473–474: "Fu cristianissimo, e molto vôlto al culto della religione; fu amico di tutti i buoni, e massime de' religiosi. . . ."

9(301:29). Vergil *Aeneid* 12.435. (John Dryden, *Aeneis* 12.644–645.)

10(301:30–35). Juvenal *Satire* 10.33–37. (John Dryden, *The Tenth Satire of Juvenal*, 47–55.)

11(301:36). Juvenal *Satire* 2.39–40.

12(301:39). pagella. This rare word is found in Cicero *Fam.* 11.25 fin; and in Jeremiah 36:23.

LETTER VI

1(I,30:11). See Neil R. Ker, *Medieval Libraries of Great Britain: A List of Surviving Books* (Royal Historical Society Guides and Handbooks, No. 3. London: The Royal Historical Society, 1941), pp. vii–xxi, 3, 6, 7, 8, 9, 10, 11, etc., for the kinds of books that Poggius would have found listed in a monastic inventory.

2(I,30:17). St. John Chrysostom in Vol I, *Cod. Lat.* of Bandini, Plut. XVI, Cod. XLI, Col. 304 (LXXIV, p. 122), Col. 305 (LXXXII–LXXXV, pp. 140–149), Col. 310 (CXXVIII, pp. 240–242): eleventh century.

The library of San Marco owned at least two works of St. John Chrysostom in Latin which had belonged to Nicolaus de Niccolis, one of which he and Ambrosius Traversarius had copied (No. 155), and two in Greek, among the many texts by this author that had come to the library through Cosmus de Medicis and others. See Ullman-Stadter, *Public Library*, pp. 141–143, 250–252. Hain lists thirty printings of works of St. John Chrysostom in the fifteenth century, although this covers only fourteen titles. Almost all the printed texts were translated by Poggius' contemporaries or scholars younger than they and therefore are not the texts which were available to Poggius in England. Ludwig Hain, *Repertorium Bibliographicum*, 2 vols., 4 pts. (Milan: Görlich Editore, 1948), Vol. I, pt. 2, pp. 109–114. St. John Chrysostom, *Sermones*. See Bandini, Vol. I, cols. 70, 79, 80, 83, 85, 89, all in Plut. XIV, Cod. I. Homiliae ac Sermones qui legebantur . . . ab Adventu Domini usque ad sabbatum Maioris Hebdomadae, selecti ex Operibus SS. Ambrosii, Augustini, Fulgentii, Hieronymi, Joannis Chrysostomi, Isidori . . . Origenis . . . St. John Chrysostom. Col. 70 (XIII, p. 14), Col. 79 (CVI, p. 91, and CII, p. 86), Col. 80 (CXII, p. 96, and CXV, p. 98), Col. 83 (CXLII–CXLIII, pp. 121–122), Col. 85 (CLXV, p. 142), Col. 89 (CIC, CC, CCII, CCIII, CCIV, pp. 182–191): twelfth century.

3(I,30:22). See Hain No. 5029. *Homiliae in Epistolam S. Pauli ad Ebraeos....* Commentarium... translatum a Muciano Scholastico. n.p., n.d.

4(I,30:24). Anianus was a deacon in the Campania and a supporter of Pelagianism at the Synod of Diospolis in A.D. 415. He translated several works of St. John Chrysostom. See J. A. Fabricius, *Bibliotheca Latina Mediae et Infimae Aetatis,* I (Hamburg, 1734), 288–290.

Paul Oskar Kristeller, *Iter,* lists:

I, 48. Como: Seminario Maggiore. Ms. 7. John Chrysostomus, homilie super Mattheum, translated by Anianus.

II, 5. Padua: Biblioteca capitolare. Cod. D. 46: John Chrysostomus, Comm. in Matthaeum, translated by Anianus.

II, 53. Perugia: Badia di S. Pietro. Cod. CM 34. John Chrysostomus, de Laudibus S. Pauli.

II, 326. Rome: Bibliotheca Apostolica Vaticana. Cod. Vat. Lat. 4314. John Chrysostomus, Homilies on St. Paul.

II, 423. Rome: Bibliotheca Apostolica Vaticana. Cod. Ottob. Lat. 11. John Chrysostomus, translated by Anianus.

5(I,30:25). St. John Chrysostom, In Ioannis Evangelium Homiliae LXXXVIII, a D. Francisco D. Mariotti Arretino ex Graeco in Latinum traductae, cùm Epistola ad... Cosmum Medicem.... Bandini, Vol. IV, col. 442. (Pluteus XIV Dexter Codex II.) St. John Chrysostom's eighty-seven [*sic*] homilies on the gospel of St. John were translated anew by Poggius' contemporary Franciscus Aretinus, with a dedication to Cosmus de Medicis, and printed in Rome, by Georgius Lauer, in 1470. See Jacques-Charles Brunet, *Manuel du libraire,* III (Paris, 1862), 536–537, and *Catalogue of Books Printed in the XVth Century Now in the British Museum,* IV (The Hague: Martinus Nijhoff, 1916), 36.

6(I,31:1). See Tonelli's note, I, 31, which identifies the Pisan translator of St. John Chrysostom as Burgundio (fl. 1145–1153). See also Fabricius, *Bibl. Lat. Med.,* I, 833–837.

7(I,31:4–5). An adaptation of Phaedrus, *Fables,* Book II, Fabula 5, 1.3. et aliquid deputare in lucro. For the idiom *ponere* or *deputare in lucro,* "To count as gain," see Terence *Phorm.* 246; *omne id deputare esse in lucro.* Poggius quoted frequently from Terence. See, e.g., *Phorm.* 708–709 in Tonelli Bk. I, ltr. 19; I, 76:18–19. Poggius' volume of Terence is No. 25 in the inventory (Walser, *Poggius,* p. 420).

8(I,31:11). Tonelli's note: "Henry Beaufort, bishop of Winchester and cardinal with title St. Eusebius." He was Bishop of Lincoln 1398, Winchester 1404, Cardinal 1426, and died 11 April 1447. See Ernest F. Jacob, *The Fifteenth Century: 1399–1485* (The Oxford History of England, edited by Sir George Clark, Vol. VI), pp. 198–200, for an account of the difficulties between Henry V, on the one hand, and Henry Beaufort and Martin V on the other, during Poggius' sojourn in England.

9(I,31:15,21). King Henry V in 1420 was in Troyes to sign the Treaty on May 21 with Charles VI of France, who thereby adopted Henry as his son and disowned the Dauphin. Henry married Catherine of France 2 June 1420.

An alliance between Philip, Duke of Burgundy, and Henry V had been arranged by Christmas 1419. See *CMH*, VII, 390–392. See also Holinshed's *Chronicles, Richard II, Henry IV and Henry V* (Oxford: Clarendon Press, 1923), pp. 93–97.

10(I,31:18). De Roover, *Rise and Decline*, p. 194. Martin V resided at Santa Maria Novella in Florence February 1419 to September 1420. The Rome branch of the Medici bank followed the Curia wherever it went.

An agreement between Martin V and Braccius de Montone was signed in Florence on 26 February 1420; see Peter Partner, *The Papal State under Martin V* (London: The British School at Rome, 1958), pp. 62–63. The agreement gave Braccius a great deal of territory in Central Italy, large sums of money, and promises of protection against his enemies, notably Sforza, but it also enabled Martin V to proceed to Rome in some degree of safety, despite his very obvious military and political weakness.

For conditions during Martin V's sojourn in Florence with the Curia, see St. Antoninus, Archbishop of Florence, *Chronicon*, Vol. III (Nuremberg: Anton Koberger, 1484), f. 158r-v.

11(I,31:22–23). For Beaufort's unconfirmed activities in the spring of 1420, see Radford, *Beaufort*, pp. 93–98, and Harold F. Hutchison, *Henry V: A Biography* (London: Eyre and Spottiswoode, 1967), pp. 186–190.

12(I,31:24). Tonelli, I, 31, note 3, identifies the Cardinal of Pisa as the Florentine Alamannus Adimarius, who was one of the leaders of the cause of unity at the Council of Constance. He acted as a delegate from the Council to John XXIII when the Pope fled to Schaffhausen. He took the principal part in many important debates and in making the rules for the election of Martin V. See Louise Ropes Loomis, trans., *The Council of Constance: The Unification of the Church*, edited by John H. Mundy and Kennerly M. Woody, Records of Civilization: Sources and Studies, Vol. LXIII (New York: Columbia University Press, 1961), pp. 187, 225, 280–282, 334, 374–377, 394–399, 415, 427–428, 434.

Pisanus left the Curia as legate to Aragon 17 February 1418. See Alec Glasfurd, *The Antipope (Pedro de Luna, 1342–1423), A Study in Obstinacy* (London: Barrie and Rockliff, 1965), pp. 263–264, for Adimarius' conspiracy while legate to Aragon to poison Antipope Benedict XIII (Pedro de Luna).

Bartholomaeus Platina, *Vitae summorum pontificum* ([Venice] Johannes de Colonia and Johannes Manthen, 1479), f. aa 3v, gives an account of the mission of Alamannus Adimarius to Aragon to persuade Benedict XIII to give up his claim to the Papal throne. For further details see the coat of arms of "Dominus Almanus Cardinalis Pysanus

Dyaconus Tituli Sancte Lucie (Came with 30 people)" in Ulrich von Richenthal, *Das Concilium so Zu Constanz gehalten* (Augsburg: Heinrich Stainer, 1536), f. 71v, and Alphonsus Ciacconius, *Vitae et Gestae Pontificum Romanorum et S.R.E. Cardinalium*, Vol. II (Rome, 1677), cols. 799–800.

For Alamannus Adimarius' influence at the Papal court, see Partner, *Papal State*, p. 54. See notes on Alamannus Adimarius from Conrad Eubel, *Hierarchia Catholica Medii Aevi*, Vols. I and II (Munster: Regensberg, Vol. I, 1913, Vol. II, 1914; reprinted, Rome, 1960), I, 32. Alamannus Adimarius is also to be found in Kristeller, *Iter*, II, 491. Cod. G 51. Nic. Mich. Bonaiutus, *Carmina et epistolae poeticae.* "The collection includes verses to Alamannus de Adimaris" and others.

13(I,31:24). Nicolaus de Medicis.

LETTER VII

1(I,32:2,18–21). There are many references to Nicolaus' agreeable and welcome letters in the letters to him of his friend Ambrosius Traversarius: see *Epistolae* VIII, 1, 3, 5, 35, 36, 41, 47. See also Guarinus' reference to Nicolaus' letters "Melle dulcioribus": *Epist. di Guar. Ver.*, I, 149, 172.

2(I,32:15–17). On the quality of Poggius' friendship with Nicolaus, see Poggius' letter to Carolus Marsuppinus Aretinus written right after Nicolaus' death. *Poggii Epistolae* Bk. VI, ltr. 12; II, 108–112.

3(I,32:18–21). Only one letter from a regular correspondent of Poggius', Leonardus Brunus Aretinus (pt. 2, 17–25; V, 4) survives from this period of his life. Franciscus Barbarus, Leonardus Brunus Aretinus, and Guarinus are known to have been writing to him before and after his stay in England. See Franciscus Barbarus, *Diatriba Praeliminaris in duas partes divisa ad Francisci Barbari et aliorum ad ipsum Epistolas*, 2 vols. (Brescia: Joannes-Maria Rizzardi, 1741), I, 1; Remigio Sabbadini, *Centotrenta lettere inedite di Francesco Barbaro* (Salerno: Tipografia nazionale, 1884), No. 37, p. 84; Leonardus Brunus Aretinus, *Epistolae*, IV, 4, 15, 21, 23; V, 4, etc.; and Sabbadini, *Epist. di Guar. Ver.*, I, 116–121, 157–158, 160–161.

4(I,32:21–22). Oblivioni datus sum tanquam mortuus. For the idiom *dare aliquid oblivioni*, "to consign to oblivion," see Livy I.31.3. According to Ullman, *Humanism*, p. 235: "Coluccio had the twenty-nine books (decads I, III, and IV) generally known in his time." Poggius did not produce his own text of Livy (Vat. lat. 1843, 1849, 1852) until some years after his return to Rome, 1425–1428 (see Ullman, *Origin and Development*, pp. 46–47).

5(I,33:2). Tonelli wrongly identified the Cardinal as Julianus Caesarinus, who was not promoted until 24 May 1426. See Eubel, *Hierarchia*, I,

49. The Cardinal S. Angeli in 1420 was Petrus Fonseca, who was promoted (sixth promotion, 14 December 1412) by Benedict XIII and died
at Vicovaro 21 August 1422 (*Hierarchia*, I, 30 and note 9). He was commended on 5 June 1413 to Ecclesia Astoricensis (Astorga, Spain) and in
1419 to Ecclesia Seguntina (Siguenza, Spain).

See also Ciacconius, *Vitae*, Vol. II, cols. 731–732, under "Four
cardinals who after the Council of Constance abandoned Benedict XII,
called XIII, Schismatic and damned and followed Pope Martin V."
Petrus Fonseca Portugallensis, Hispanus, Diaconus Cardinalis Sancti
Angeli. For Petrus Fonseca's biography, see Ciacconius, *Vitae*, Vol. II,
col. 746. Popularly called "Cardinalis Sancti Angeli Senior."

After the Council of Constance, Petrus Fonseca was confirmed as
Cardinal by Martin V, then sent as legate to Spain 1420, to Naples to
King Alphonsus, to Constantinople to the Emperor Manuel for the
union of the churches. His epitaph is quoted by Ciacconius, who says
further on (*Vitae*, Vol. II, col. 831): "On the first day of August 1418 in
Geneva the four Anti-Cardinals listed below, in obedience to Petrus de
Luna, were approved in their state and honors and truly confirmed as
Cardinals by decree of this same Pope [Martin V] given in Geneva on
the aforesaid day ... IV: Petrus Fonseca Lusitanus, Diaconus Card. S.
Angeli."

Richenthal gives Petrus Fonseca's coat of arms: "Dominus Petrus
Cardinalis Sancti Angeli presbyter tituli Sancte Sabine" and says that he
"Came with fifty-two people" to Constance (*Das Concilium*, f. 72r.)
See also Jacques Lenfant, *Histoire de la guerre des Hussites*, 2 vols.
(Amsterdam: Pierre Humbert, 1731), I, 177. Martin sent Petrus de Fonseca to lead a crusade against Petrus de Luna, 1421.

In Platina, *Vitae*, f. aa (7), there is an account of Fonseca's mission to
Constantinople to seek a union of the Eastern and Western Churches.
This was assigned by Martin V to "Petrum Fontesiccum Sancti Angeli
cardinalem hominem hispanum in quavis facultate doctum." In September 1421, Martin V sent "the Spaniard Pietro Fonseca, the Cardinal
of Sant' Angelo, to ... Naples with the Aragonese ambassadors to renew
practices of peace." See Partner, *Papal State*, p. 71.

At the time this letter was written, the Curia was still in Florence with
Martin V. They left Florence on September 9 and reached Rome on 28
September 1420. In the Archivio Segreto Vaticano, in *Reg. Vat.* 353,
9v–11r and 22v–23r, there are instructions to "Dilecto filio Petro Sancti
Angeli diacono Sancte Romane ecclesie Cardinali" regarding his mission to Aragon, Valencia, Navarre, and Castille to deal with the adherents of "Petrus de Luna qui ausu sacrilego se Benedictum XIII
nominare damnabiliter praesumit." These are dated Florence "iiii Id.
Aprilis pontificatus nostri anno tercio" and "vii Kal. Septembris" of

the same year, 1420, and confirm the fact that Nicolaus had ample opportunity to know the Cardinal. See also *Reg. Lat.* 209, ff. 14r–15r,
31r–32r.

6(I,33:7). Juvenal *Satires* 6.165, W. V. Clausen, ed. (Oxford: Clarendon Press, 1968), p. 77.

7(I,33:12–22). Poggius, through Cincius, attacks the avarice of the
clergy in his *De avaritia*. See *Poggii Opera Omnia*, I, 11–12, 22–23.

8(I,33:30–34:2). Since, according to Ciacconius, *Vitae*, Vol. II, col.
799, and Eubel, *Hierarchia*, I, 250, Alamannus Adimarius was a Florentine nobleman and former (for the single year 1400) Bishop of Florence,
he probably had long been acquainted with Nicolaus, who was already
a leading citizen by 1400.

9(I,34:4–5). Scis fidem esse raram. For *fides esse rara*, see Horace
Odes. 1.35.21. Poggius' volume of Horace is No. 42 of the inventory
(Walser, *Poggius*, p. 421). He quoted *Epistles* 1.2.46 in line 130 of this
same letter. Sabbadini (*Scoperte*, I, 23) says that Horace was "alla
portata di tutti" in Petrarch's time.

10(I,34:3,9–12). See Gothein, *Francesco Barbaro*, pp. 107–108, 361,
and Curt S. Gutkind, *Cosimo de' Medici: Pater Patriae, 1389–1464*,
Oxford Studies in Modern Languages and Literature (Oxford: Clarendon Press, 1938), p. 225. The letters of Nicolaus' friends frequently
refer to trips which he planned but never took.

11(I,34:20). The Archbishop of Crete is identified by Tonelli as Petrus
Donatus. See Eubel, *Hierarchia*, I, 216 and note 15. Petrus Donatus became Archbishop of Crete 18 April 1415, designated by John XXIII. He
had been an apostolic notary. He became Bishop of Civitas Castelli 5
December 1425 (Eubel, *Hierarchia*, I, 171) and governor of Perugia
with powers of papal legate, 25 October 1425 (*Reg. Vat.* 350, f. 175).

12(I,34:22–29). See Letter VI, note 10. See Sabbadini, *Epist. di Guar.
Ver.*, III, 115–116, on the deliberations of the City Council of Verona,
20 May 1420, on the subjects to be taught in Verona by Guarinus
Veronensis and the salary to be paid him for the next five years. See also
P. J. McCormick, "Two Catholic Medieval Educators. II. Guarino da
Verona," *Catholic University Bulletin*, XIII (1907), 232–249. P. 234:
Guarinus stayed in Constantinople five years after traveling there with
Manuel Chrysoloras in 1403. He taught in Florence 1410–1414. Ac-
cording to Jean Pierre Niceron, *Mémoires pour servir à l'histoire des
hommes illustres*, XXIX (Paris: Briasson, 1734), 122, Guarinus taught in
Verona from 1420 at 150 ducats annual salary. See also Giambattista
Carlo Giuliari, "La letteratura veronese al cadere del secolo XV, e le
sue opere a stampa," *Il Propugnatore*, V, pt. II (1872), 105–128. For the
most careful and detailed account of Guarinus' activities in the decade
1414–1424, see Sabbadini, "Vita di Guarino," in *Guariniana*, pp. 21–65.

During these years, Guarinus was in Venice and in Verona, having come to know the Florentine humanists well during his visit there as a teacher from 1410 to 1414 (pp. 15–21).

For Guarinus' activities in 1420, see also Carlo de' Rosmini, *Vita e disciplina di Guarino Veronese*, I(Brescia: Nicolò Bettoni, 1805), 13–14, 39.

Guarinus Veronensis was born in Verona December 1370 and died in Ferrara December 1460. Poggius corresponded with him from 1416 until his own death in 1459. Guarinus went to Constantinople in 1390, and returned to Constantinople after some years in Italy with Manuel Chrysoloras in 1403. (Sabbadini, *Scoperte*, I, 44.) Guarinus taught Greek in Venice 1414–1419. See *Speculum*, XXXVIII (April 1963), 351–353: review by Robert Weiss of Deno J. Geanakoplos, *Greek Scholars in Venice* (Cambridge, Mass.: Harvard University Press, 1962). Evidently Guarinus was in communication with friends in Florence in the summer of 1420. See Sabbadini, *Epist. di Guar. Ver.*, Vol. I, p. 308, Ep. 193, and Vol. III, p. 125.

13(I,34:29). desiderio ardeo. For *desiderio ardere*, see Cicero *Pro Mil.* 15 and *Tusc.* 4.17.37. According to Ullman (*Humanism*, p. 222), "the *Tusculans* is by far the most quoted" by Coluccius of the books he owned. For his knowledge of the *Pro Milone*, one of Cicero's orations which Poggius had found at Cluny in 1415, see Albert C. Clark, *Anecdota Oxoniensia . . . Classical Series — Part X. The Vetus Cluniacensis of Poggio* (Oxford: Clarendon Press, 1905), pp. i–xv.

14(I,34:30;35:1). The Bishop of Bologna is identified by Tonelli as Nicolaus Albergatus. Poggius' funeral oration for him is in *Poggii Opera Omnia*, I, 261–269. See Eubel, *Hierarchia*, I, 141. He was born 1375, chosen Bishop of Bologna 4 January 1417, confirmed as Bishop of Bologna 13 April 1418. See Eubel, *Hierarchia*, I, 145, and II, 6, 122. He was created cardinal *tit. S. Crucis* by Martin V on 24 May 1426. See also Jacobus Zenus, *Romanorum Pontificum, regum atque illustrium virorum testimonia de beato Nicolao Albergato . . .* (Rome, 1744), pp. ix–xiv, for a detailed account of Nicolaus Albergatus' troubles with the citizens of Bologna who were in rebellion against him and the Papacy.

15(I,35:4–5). St. Augustine, Sermo CCCXL. "On the day of his ordination." Migne, *PL*, Vol. XXXVIII, col. 1484.

16(I,35:11–12). Psalms 27:4.

17(I,35:13–14). On Nicolaus, Bishop of Bologna, see St. Antoninus, *Chronicon*, Vol. III, f. 158v.

18(I,35:14–15). 2 Corinthians 12:9.

19(I,35:19–21). St. John Chrysostom, "Sermon before his exile," III (Paris: Ed. Bernard de Montfaucon, 1837), 494.

20(I,35:25). St. Jerome, *Epist.* LVIII. Migne, *PL*, Vol. XXII, col. 584, par. 325.

21(I,35:30–36:15). On Nicolaus' quarrels and troubles, see Zippel, *Nicolò Niccoli,* pp. 30–33, and Hans Baron, *The Crisis of the Early Italian Renaissance,* Vol. II: *Appendices* (Princeton: Princeton University Press, 1955), Appendix 5, pp. 409–416.

22(I,36:8). Hic opus, hic labor. See *Hoc opus, hic labor est . . .* Vergil *Aen.* 6.129 (the Sibyl speaking of the descent to the lower world).

23(I,36:14). Naevius, *Fabulae Palliatae (Incertarum Fabularum Fragmenta), Naevius Poeta,* E. V. Marmorale, ed. (Florence: "La Nuova Italia" Editrice, 1953), p. 225.

24(I,36:18). Luke 6:37.

25(I,36:23). 2 Corinthians 9:7.

26(I,37:7–8). Horace *Epistles* 1.2.46.

27(I,37:13–14). St. Jerome, Commentary "in Michaeam," Lib. II, cap. VI, par. 509. Migne, *PL,* Vol. XXV, col. 1213.

28(I,37:15–16). *Putnam's Complete Book of Quotations,* W. Gurney Benham, ed. (New York: G. P. Putnam's Sons, 1929), col. 517a, identifies it merely as a proverb.

29(I,37:19–20). Colossians 3:5.

30(I,37:20–24). St. Augustine, *De baptismo contra Donatistas,* IV, 5, in Migne, *PL,* Vol. XLIII (Paris, 1841), *Sancti Aurelii Augustini Opera,* Vol. IX, cols. 157–158.

31(I,38:3). See Ranulf Higden, *Polychronicon* (Westminster: William Caxton, 1482), f. 405v. King Henry's illness prevented his expedition to rescue Jerusalem, "in the viii yere of the regne" (1421?).

32(I,38:4–6). For early monasteries in England still flourishing during Poggius' visit, see William E. Lunt, *Financial Relations of the Papacy with England,* Vol. II: 1327–1534 (Studies in Anglo-Papal Relations during the Middle Ages, II. Cambridge, Mass.: The Mediaeval Academy of America, 1962), pp. 55–66. See also Ker, *Medieval Libraries, passim.*

33(I,38:7–8). For histories of England available to Poggius, see John Taylor, *The "Universal Chronicle" of Ranulf Higden* (Oxford: Clarendon Press, 1966), Chapters 2, 5, and 7.

34(I,38:9–13). Macrobius, *In somnium Scipionis . . . explanatio* (Venice: Aldus and Andreas Asulanus, 1528), Liber I, f. 8r. Poggius repeats Macrobius' exact words.

35(I,38:13–15). See J. Wight Duff, *A Literary History of Rome in the Silver Age,* 3rd edition (New York: Barnes and Noble, 1964), pp. 138–158.

36(I,38:17). Alamannus Adimarius, see Letter VI, note 12, and Tonelli, I, 31:24.

LETTER VIII

1(I,38:2–3). See Lenfant, *Histoire . . . des Hussites,* I, 177. Martin V left Florence 11 September 1420 and reached Rome September 22.

2(I,38:3-4). Henry Beaufort.

3(I,39:6-7). Poggius' later letters are full of complaints about his lack of opportunity to read because his books were borrowed by his friends and not returned for years. See, e.g., Letters LXXIX and LXXXI, Tonelli Bk. IV, ltrs. 2 and 4; I, 294-295, 303-304.

4(I,39:12-13). Pacuvius, "Teucer," Fragment 380, Loeb. Quoted by Cicero *Tusculan Disputations* 5.37.108.

5(I,39:16-18). Poggius may have used the translations of Robert Grosseteste, a thirteenth century English scholar, Franciscan, and Bishop of Lincoln; or those of William of Moerbeke, a thirteenth century Flemish Dominican. See Henry Osborn Taylor, *The Medieval Mind*, II, 4th edition (Cambridge, Mass.: Harvard University Press, 1959), 421.

6(I,39:21). Poggius' limited knowledge of Greek probably was obtained from Manuel Chrysoloras, who taught in Florence 1396-1399 and traveled with the Papal court to the Council of Constance, where he died, 15 April 1415. See Giuseppe Cammelli, *I dotti Bizantini e le origini dell' umanesimo, I: Manuele Crisolora* (Florence: Vallechi Editore, 1941), pp. 47-49, 165. For Poggius' epitaph for Manuel Chrysoloras, see p. 169.

7(I,39:20-23). The works of Aristotle which could have been available to Poggius through the translations of Boethius and others were the *Categories*, the *De interpretatione*, perhaps the *Analytica priora* and *Analytica posteriora, Rhetoric, Politics, De anima, Physics, Parva Naturalia, Ethics, Meteorologica, Organon*. See Sandys, *History*, I, 527, 530, 570-573, 586, 607-608.

8(I,39:24). St. Thomas Aquinas wrote commentaries on Aristotle's *De interpretatione, Ethics, Posterior Analytics, Metaphysics, Physics, De anima*, ("and [commentaries] on Aristotle's other psychological and physical writings").

9(I,40:8-9). See Letter VII, note 10 (Tonelli, I, 34:9-20).

10(I,40:11). See Patricia H. Labalme, *Bernardo Giustiniani: A Venetian of the Quattrocento*, Uomini e Dottrine, 13 (Rome: Edizioni di Storia e Letteratura, 1969), pp. 24-25, and Sabbadini, *Epist. di Guar. Ver.*, I, 292-297; III, 119-121.

11(I,40:14). Poggius' father had bought land in Terra Nova as early as 1366. The letter mentioned here must have been intended for Poggius' family. See Walser, *Poggius*, p. 326, Documents 3-4.

12(I,40:15). Alamannus Adimarius, Cardinalis Pisanus.

13(I,40:15). The coat of arms of "Dominus Pranda Cardinalis Placentinus Presbyter, tituli sancti Laurentii in Lucina" and the statement that he "Came to Constance with forty people" appear in Richenthal, *Das Concilium*, f. 72v. Tonelli, I, 40, note 1, identifies "Dominus Placentinus" as "Branda Castilioneus, Cardinalis Placentinus." See Vespasiano,

Vite, pp. 118–120, and Tiraboschi, *Storia della letteratura italiana,* VI, ii, 616–624. Branda Castilioneus served Boniface IX, Gregory XII, Alexander V, John XXIII, Martin V, and Eugenius IV. He was a great authority on canon law and a very important papal diplomat. Poggius knew him at the Council of Constance. Branda Castilioneus founded a public library and was very generous to scholars. There are many references to him in Kristeller's *Iter*:

I, 277. Milan: Archivio di Stato: Autograph letters of Branda Castiglioni among those of many humanists.

I, 294. Milan: Biblioteca Ambrosiana cod. J 20 inf. ff. 1–24v. Joh. de Olomons de Casteliono, palma choralis seu de cantu ecclesiastico, dedicated to Card. Branda Castilioneus (1405).

I, 306. Bibl. Ambros. cod. P 50 sup. Domenicus Florentinus (i.e., ps. Fenestella) de potestatibus Romanorum, ad Brandam Castillionem, in 2 books.

I, 325. Bibl. Ambros. cod. H 48 inf. letters to Branda Castilioneus and others (ff. 105v–114).

I, 327–328. Milan: Bibl. Ambros. cod. B 116 sup. f.52–52v Collatio ad B. Castilio(no) Placentinum card. and cod. B 124 sup. ff. 1–5 Guarnerius de Castiliono, oration on card. Branda de Castiliono.

I, 352. Milan: Biblioteca Nazionale Braidense (Brera) cod. A D XI 45: Vespasiano's lives of Eugenius IV, Nicholas V, Alphonsus Aragonensis and card. di Piacenza (Branda Castiglione).

II, 130. Rome: Biblioteca Vallicelliana cod. R. 26. Epitaph of Branda Castilio.

14(I,40:14–15). For Henry V's interest in medicine, see Jean Adrien Antoine Jules Jusserand, *English Wayfaring Life in the Middle Ages,* trans. Lucy T. Smith, 4th edition (London: Ernest Benn, 1950), p. 98 and p. 267, note 8, and "Rolls of Parliament," 9 Henry V, Vol. IV, p. 130: "L'ordinance encontre les entremettours de fisik. . . ."

LETTER IX

1(I,40:2). 1420 was not a year in which the plague was recorded as severe in England. See George G. Coulton, *Medieval Panorama* (New York: Macmillan, 1938), pp. 505–506.

2(I,40:9). On the plague, see Charles Creighton, *History of Epidemics in Britain,* Vol. I: A.D. 664–1666, 2nd edition (London: Frank Cass and Co., Ltd., 1965), pp. 221–222. In comparison with earlier and later periods, England was relatively free of plague during Poggius' sojourn there.

3(I,41:2–8). At this time, Nicolaus de Niccolis was being violently attacked in writing by two of his former friends, Laurentius Marci

Benvenutus and Leonardus Brunus Aretinus. See Zippel, *Nicolò Niccoli*, pp. 20–21, 30–33.

4(I,41:8). See Giuseppe Zippel, "L'invettiva di Lorenzo de Marco Benvenuti contro Niccolò Niccoli," *Giornale storico della letteratura italiana*, XXIV (1894), 166–186. Zippel found the invective in Cod. Riccardiano 1200, f. 159r–162v. See his pp. 170–171: this section gives an account of Nicolò's five (?) brothers, followed (pp. 173–174) by an attack on Benvenuta and an account of her. Laurentius Marci Benvenutus belonged to the Arte della Lana and to the gonfalone di Santo Spirito. He held government offices, 1415–1423, and served as ambassador to Genoa. He died of the plague in 1423, having written his invective ca. 1420.

Kristeller located several more mss. of the invective:

Iter, I, 146. Florence: Biblioteca Nazionale Centrale Fondo Palatino. Cod. 163 (122) (Laur. Benvenutus), invectiva in Nic. Niccolum.

II, 134. Rome: Collegio di S. Isidoro. cod. 1/45, ff. 28v–35, same text.

II, 267. Venice: Biblioteca Nazionale Marciana. cod. Marc. Lat. XIV 219 (4631) ff. 102–107v. Laur. Benvenutus: invective against Niccoli.

II, 305. Viterbo: Biblioteca Capitolare cod. 13 (formerly d 38) ff. 106v–111v same text.

II, 555. Pavia: Biblioteca Universitaria cod. 73 f. 40. Poggius (i.e. Laur. Benvenutus) in Nicolaum de Nicolis, as well as a book which belonged to Laurentius Benvenutus.

II, 394. Città del Vaticano. Bibl. Apost. Vat. cod. Pal. Lat. 1659. Horace, owned by Laur. Benvenutus.

For further discussion of Laurentius Benvenutus, see Martines, *Social World*, pp. 324–325, and Baron, *Crisis*, II, 409–415.

For additional contemporary comment on the quarrels, see Leonardus Brunus Aretinus, *Epist.* V, 4 (pt. 2, 17–25). Ambrosius Traversarius to Laurentius: *Epist.* VII, 17 (Vol. II, cols. 345–346) may also apply here. See also Vespasiano, *Vite*, p. 244 in "Frate Ambrogio," section 6.

5(I,41:11–13). Luke 6: 27–33.

6(I,41:13–14). St. John Chrysostom, Vol. IV, Bernard de Montfaucon, ed. (Paris, 1836), Homilia III, col. 896.

7(I,41:17–19). Poggius was quick to respond with invective to anyone who attacked his friends or himself: see *Poggii Opera Omnia*, I, 164–187, for invectives against Franciscus Philelphus, who wrote an attack on Nicolaus de Niccolis in 1434.

8(I,41:21–23). See *Poggii Epistolae* Bk. VI, ltrs. 12, 14, 15, 16: Bk. VI, ltr. 12: To Carolus Marsuppinus Aretinus. Bk. VI, ltr. 14: To Feltrinus Boiardus Ferrariensis. Bk. VI, ltr. 15: To Guarinus Veronensis. Bk. VI, ltr. 16: To Franciscus Barbarus.

For Poggius' defense of Nicolaus, to the end of his life and beyond, against for instance Franciscus Philelphus, see Walser, *Poggius*, pp.

176-180, and *Opera Omnia*, I, 164-174, "In Philelphum Invectivae pro Nicolao."

9(I, 41:24-25). Alamannus Adimarius. See Walser, *Poggius*, p. 76.

10(I,41:26-29). Beaufort's whereabouts in the fall of 1420 is a mystery (see Radford, *Beaufort*, pp. 93-95), but his activities in the fall of 1421 are well documented (p. 99). On Beaufort's promises and performances see pp. 97, 290-294.

11(I,42:2). See Sabbadini, *Centrotrenta lettere*, p. 14. He gives a synopsis of a letter (24 February 1420) from Ambrosius Traversarius to Franciscus Barbarus, asking for help in arranging Guarinus' transfer from Verona to Florence to teach, at a salary of his own choice. The letter was published by Martène and Durand, *Amplissima Collectio*, Vol. III, cols. 581-582, *Epist.* XIX, and by Mehus, *Ambr. Trav. Epist.*, VI, 20 (Vol. II, cols. 299-300).

12(I,42:3). Ferendum est equo animo. For the idiom *Ferre aliquid aequo animo*, see Nepos *Dion.* 6.7; and Aur. Vict. *Orig.* 6.3. According to Sabbadini (*Scoperte*, I, 95; II, 217) Ambrosius Traversarius reported seeing a text of Cornelius Nepos in the possession of Hermolaus Barbarus in 1433, before it was known in Florence. The text of Aurelius Victor's *Origo gentis Romanae* was also unknown in 1420. Bessarion found it and bequeathed it with his library to Venice (*Scoperte*, I, 186-187; II, 203).

13(I,42:4). See Letter III, note 31 on Nicolaus de Medicis.

14(I,42:8). For Venetian trade with England, see Frederic C. Lane, *Venice and History* (Baltimore: The Johns Hopkins Press, 1966), pp. 4-5, 460.

15(I,42:9). According to Platina, *Vite*, ff. (aa 6v) and (aa 7r), Cosmus de Medicis had at this time interceded successfully for Baldassare Cossa (John XXIII), held in prison in Heidelberg by the Count Palatine. After Baldassare Cossa had sworn loyalty and obedience to Martin V and been created Bishop of Tusculum, he died: "Ferre enim vitam privatam non poterat" ["for he could not endure life without public office"]. Cosmus de Medicis took care of his funeral and burial: "Ut et primarius apud Florentinos cives et ditissimus omnium apud Italos ac fortasse apud exteras quoque nationes deinceps sit habitus" ["With the result that he was considered the leader among the citizens of Florence and the richest of all men in Italy and perhaps of other nations too from that time forth"].

LETTER X

1(I,42:3-4). The only letter to Poggius which survives from his years in England is from Leonardus Brunus Aretinus, dated by Mehus 31 January 1421 (see *Leonardi Bruni Aretini Epistolae* V, 4; pt. 2, 17-25,

and *Poggii Opera Omnia,* IV, 727). Presumably Poggius' other correspondents, Franciscus Barbarus and Guarinus Veronensis, whose letters
to him at Constance have survived, did not abandon him during his
further absence from Italy. For Franciscus Barbarus' letter, see Appendix, Letter IV.

2(I,42:8). See Letter IX, note 10 (Tonelli Bk. I, ltr. 9; I, 41: 26–29) and
Partner, *Papal State,* pp. 64–72.

3(I,42:15). In Poggius' family tree, published by Ludovicus Antonius
Muratorius in his *Rerum Italicarum Scriptores,* 25 vols. (Milan: Ex
Typographia Societatis Palatinae in Regia Curia, 1723–1751), Vol. XX,
facing col. 164, Poggius' brother is recorded as "Masculus cuius
nomen ignoratur" ["a male whose name is unknown"]. When his
brother suddenly died a few years later, in 1424, Poggius felt a slight
twinge of regret. See Letter XXVIII (Tonelli Bk. II, ltr. 17; I, 138: 6–13).

4(I,43:3). Poggius matriculated as a notary in 1402 (see Walser,
Poggius, Doc. 7, p. 327) and went to Rome where he became a *scriptor
apostolicus* in 1403 (p. 20).

5(I,43:11–12). Martin Hürlimann, *English Cathedrals* (Boston:
Houghton Mifflin Co., 1950), pp. 29–30. Salisbury was built all in one
style, 1220–1260. On Salisbury, see Dom David Knowles, *The Religious
Orders in England,* 3 vols. (Cambridge: Cambridge University Press,
1955), II, 331–353, esp. p. 352. Chapter 26: "Monastic Libraries."

6(I,43:13). Manuel Chrysoloras seems to have been in England in
1409, though the dates of his trip and the reasons for it are both uncertain; see Cammelli, *Crisolora,* p. 146. Manuel Chrysoloras was the
source of most of the Greek known to Poggius and his circle. He came
to teach in Florence in 1396 (pp. 34–35) on the official invitation and
private urging of Coluccius Salutatus, with whom he developed a great
friendship. See Ullman, *Humanism,* pp. 121–125, and Salutatus,
Epistolario, Vol. III, pp. 119–125, 129–132, and Vol. IV, pp. 333–344.
Chrysoloras spent four years in Florence and seven in other parts of
Italy before setting out for France, England, and Spain in 1408 (Cammelli, *Crisolora,* p. 145). He seems to have joined the Curia in Rome
in 1411 (pp. 153–159), where he became a good friend of Poggius'
companions Cincius de Rusticis and Bartholomeus de Aragazzis de
Montepolitiano. He traveled with the Curia to the Council of Constance,
where he died 15 April 1415, mourned by Petrus Paulus Vergerius
(pp. 167–169), Guarinus (pp. 169–177), and by Poggius with a funeral
oration (Walser, *Poggius,* p. 70).

For further bibliography on Chrysoloras see Chevalier, *Bio-bibliographie,* Vol. II, col. 2994, and Cosenza, *Dictionary,* II, 994–999.

7(I,43:24–28). Olive Cook, *English Abbeys and Priories* (London:
Thames and Hudson, 1962), pp. 9–18.

8(I,43:28). On Corvey in Saxony, see *Voyage littéraire de deux religieux Bénédictins de la congrégation de S. Maur,* II (Paris: Montalant, 1724), 254–257. For the former riches of Corvey now in other libraries, see Ludwig Traube, *Vorlesungen und Abhandlungen,* Franz Boll, ed., I (Munich: C. H. Beck'sche, 1909), pp. 193, 214, 219–222, 225–226.

Nicolaus was apparently right in suspecting that there might be texts of Origen at Corbie.

9(I,43:28–32). A manuscript of Tacitus' *Annales* I–VI, now Cod. Laur. Plut. LXVIII, cod. 1, was brought to Rome from Corvey (founded 822) in Westphalia in 1508. See Sandys, *History,* I, 484, 662–663, and Sabbadini, *Scoperte,* II, 254. Poggius' gloomy view of the Germans was probably derived from his encounters in Constance.

10(I,44:4–5). For travel to Oxford, see Jusserand, *English Wayfaring,* pp. 61, 72, 134–135.

11(I,44:9–14). On Nicolaus' proposed trip to Greece, see *Ambr. Trav. Epist.,* Vol. I, p. L, and Letter VII, note 10 (Tonelli Bk. I, ltr. 7; I, 34: 16–18) and Letter VIII, note 9 (Tonelli Bk. I, ltr. 8; I, 40: 8–9). See Franciscus Barbarus, *Diatriba,* I, xix, and *Ambr. Trav. Epist.,* Vol. II, *Epist.* VI, 10, col. 287. Nicolaus de Niccolis was born 1363, therefore he was 57 years old at this time. For his habits, see Vespasiano, *Vite,* p. 480. Vespasiano mentions Nicolaus' emphasis on cleanliness.

12(I,44:15). See *Poggii Florentini Dialogus adversus hypocrisim* (Lyons, 1579), pp. 18–20 in *Poggii Opera Omnia,* Vol. II, for his attack on priests for their ambition and hypocrisy.

13(I,44:19). See Poggius' letter (Tonelli Bk. II, ltr. 11) to Leonardus Brunus Aretinus about Nicolaus' disposition.

14(I,44:24–27). See Michael E. Mallett, *The Florentine Galleys in the Fifteenth Century* (Oxford: Clarendon Press, 1967), pp. 18–34, 207.

15(I,44:28–30). See Jannotius Manettus, "Vita Nicolai," in *Ambr. Trav. Epist.,* I, lxxvi–lxxviii. Manettus does not mention Nicolaus' ill health but comments on the delicacy of his senses and his aversion to the braying of donkeys, the rasping of a saw, or the buzzing of a fly.

16(I,45:5–6). nimis diu hoc saxum volvo. For a very similar expression, see Terence *Eun.* 1085, "Satis diu hociam saxum vorso." See Letter IX, note 10 (Tonelli Bk. I, ltr. 9; I, 41: 26–29). The reference to the rolling stone is to the myth of Sisyphus, about whom Poggius could have known through the *Odyssey,* in some form. See *OCD,* p. 994.

17(I,45:9–10). There is now in the Plantin-Moretus Museum in Antwerp a fourteenth century English ms. containing St. John Chrysostom's "Opus imperfectum in Mathaeum." This ms., No. 131 (M 216), formerly belonged to the library of Balliol College, Oxford. See Mynors, *Mss. of Balliol,* p. 376.

It is impossible to tell from any current English ms. holdings or mss.

of English origin just what texts of St. John Chrysostom actually were available to Poggius in England in 1420.

18(I,45:11–12). The Praedicatores are Dominicans. See Charles du Fresne Du Cange, *Glossarium Mediae et Infimae Latinitatis,* VI (Paris: Librairie des Sciences et des Arts, 1938), 456. See also Ker, *Medieval Libraries,* p. 68.

LETTER XI

1(I,60:9–61:2). For Henry's return to England with his wife Katharine on Candlemas eve in 1421, see Holinshed, *Henry V,* p. 115. Katharine was crowned Queen of England on St. Matthew's Day, 24 February 1421. See Holinshed, *Henry V,* pp. 115–118. For a detailed account of the feast following her coronation, see *Fabyans Cronycle,* 2 vols. in 1 (London: Wyllyam Rastell, 1533), Vol. II, ff. CLXXVI–CLXXVII, which describes the seating of the guests and the duties of the attendants, as well as the courses of the banquet. On the feast celebrating Queen Katharine's coronation, see also Ethel Carleton Williams, *My Lord of Bedford* (London: Longmans, Green and Co., 1963), pp. 65–66, and Agnes Strickland, *Lives of the Queens of England,* I (London: George Bell & Sons, 1889), 514–515.

Easter, in 1421, was on March 23. See Sir Archibald Hamilton Dunbar, *Scottish Kings: A Revised Chronology of Scottish History, 1005–1625* (Edinburgh: D. Douglas, 1899), p. 355.

2(I,61:15–18). For an account of the founding of monasteries in England, 1128–1437, see *CMH,* V, 672–691. On the history of the colleges and monastic foundations at Oxford and Cambridge, see Hastings Rashdall, *The Universities of Europe in the Middle Ages,* F. M. Powicke and A. B. Emden, eds., III (Oxford: Clarendon Press, 1936), 169–221 and 293–312.

3(I,61:23–25). For the course of study for the B.A. degree at Oxford, see Rashdall, *Universities,* III, 153–158.

Beaulieu Abbey, *Bellus Locus* in the New Forest, for instance, was established by the Cistercians under a writ from King John, 5 July 1203. See Sir James K. Fowler, *A History of Beaulieu Abbey, A.D. 1204–1539* (London: The Car Illustrated [1911]), p. 8.

See William of Malmesbury, *Gesta Regum Anglorum, atque Historia Novella,* Thomas Duffus Hardy, ed., Vol. I (London: The English Historical Society, 1840), Books I–II. Also see *A School Atlas of English History,* S. R. Gardiner, ed. (London: Longmans, Green and Co., 1902), maps 3–5, 7, 9.

4(I,61:29–31). A few well-known English book collectors existed before Poggius' time, notably Richard de Bury (1281–1345). See Walter

F. Schirmer, *Der englische Frühhumanismus: Ein Beitrag zur englischen Literaturgeschichte des 15. Jahrhunderts,* 2nd edition (Tubingen; Max Niemeyer Verlag, 1963), pp. 1–9. See also Francis Wormald and C. E. Wright, eds., *The English Library before 1700. Studies in Its History* (London: University of London, The Athlone Press, 1958), especially the chapters on the various institutional and private collectors preceding Poggius' time or contemporary with him: pp. 15–31 and 66–147.

5(I,61:32). For an account of a very special banquet, the coronation feast of Queen Katharine, see Holinshed, *Henry V,* pp. 116–118.

6(I,62:5). Romans 13: 11.

7(I,62:19–20). Matthew 24: 42.

8(I,62:24–26). Matthew 19: 29. Mark 10: 21.

9(I,62:30). vivens parce ac sobrie. See the following: *Vivere parce, continenter, severe, sobrie;* Cicero *Off.* 1.30.106. At the time of his death, Poggius owned three copies of the *De officiis,* one in his own hand. See Walser, *Poggius,* p. 419 (inventory 9–11).

10(I,63:1). Terence *Andria* 305–306.

11(I,63:2–4). See Walser, *Poggius,* p. 81. Poggius in this passage imitates Coluccius Salutatus' last surviving letter to him, 26 March 1406, in which Coluccius urges him to prefer Christian to pagan authors. See *Epistolario,* IV, 163–165.

12(I,63:17–20). John W. Barker, in *Manuel II Paleologus (1391–1425): A Study in Late Byzantine Statesmanship,* Rutgers Byzantine Series (New Brunswick: Rutgers University Press, 1969), gives a detailed account of conditions in Constantinople and the Peloponnesus 1413–1425 in his Chapter 5, pp. 290–385. One reason for Nicolaus de Niccolis' plan to travel in Greece may have been the appointment of Nicolaus' friend Petrus Fonseca, Cardinal-Deacon of Sant' Angelo, as legate to a proposed synod in Constantinople on 27 March 1420 (see p. 326); "hostilities between the Turks and the Byzantines blocked his dispatch." It seems possible that Nicolaus de Niccolis may even have hoped to travel with Petrus de Fonseca on his embassy to Constantinople, which was arranged while Martin V was still in Florence. See Joseph Gill, *The Council of Florence* (Cambridge: Cambridge University Press, 1959), pp. 30–32, and Georgius Hofmann, *Epistolae Pontificiae ad Concilium Florentinum Spectantes,* Vol. I, Part I (Rome: Pontificium Institutum Orientalium Studiorum, 1940), pp. 6–11.

Conditions in the Peloponnesus and around Constantinople were very bad during the last years of Manuel II Paleologus (died 1425). See A. A. Vasiliev, *Histoire de l'empire Byzantin,* 2 vols. (Paris: A. Picard, 1932), II, 326–330.

13(I,63:25). Ambrosius Traversarius (Bk. VIII, ltr. 5) reports to

Nicolaus a letter received from Laurentius de Medicis mentioning Nicolaus' ill health. See *Ambr. Trav. Epist.*, Vol. II, col. 360.

14(I,63:30). Walser, *Poggius,* p. 336, gives one document relating to Poggius' brother in 1423, a receipt.

15(I,64:7). Philippians 3: 19.

16(I,64:12–13). Nicolaus de Medicis.

LETTER XII

1(I,64:8). For the financial condition of the clergy, see George Macaulay Trevelyan, O.M., *Illustrated English Social History,* I (London: Longmans, Green and Co., 1949), 40–41.

2(I,64:13). Beaufort could afford to keep his promises. In the same year, 1421, he lent Henry V eighteen thousand pounds. See Hutchison, *Henry V,* p. 199.

3(I,65:4–5). dicere autem nil mihi esse religio est. Cf. the following of Terence: "Nihil esse mihi religio'st dicere." Terence *Heaut.* 228.

4(I,65:13). parietem plusquam caducum. Cf. Aelius Spartianus, "Hadrianus," 23, in *Historia Augusta: in caducum parietem inclinare.*

5(I,65:15). For traffic between England and Venice, see George B. Parks, *The English Traveler to Italy,* I (Rome: Edizioni di Storia e Letteratura, 1954), 281–282; Lane, *Venice and History,* pp. 5–6; and Mallett, *Florentine Galleys,* pp. 10–11, 82, 278–280.

6(I,65:18). According to De Roover, *Rise and Decline:*

p. 92: Gherardo Canigiani was a factor in London, in 1446;

pp. 111, 113–114: Gherardo Canigiani was acting as factor and temporary manager of the Medici Bank in London in July, 1463;

p. 128: He was listed as an authorized agent of the Medici Bank in London, 1455. He also wrote cargo insurance (unauthorized) at a premium of 50% (pp. 151–152);

pp. 329–331: Canigiani, in London, lent a total of £ 8500 to Edward IV, 1464–1467, greatly endangering the stability of the Medici Bank. The loans to the king, however, were necessary to obtain licenses to export wool;

p. 334: in 1472 the Medici broke ties with Gherardo Canigiani. His later prosperity was based on Edward IV's favor;

p. 335: Tommaso Portinari made an attempt to recover the Medici losses by a trick on Canigiani. Canigiani brought suit against the Medici, 1475;

p. 364: De Roover reports Philippe de Commines' admiration for the loans made by Canigiani to Edward IV. See *The Historie of Philip de Commines* (London, 1596), Book VII, chap. 6.

7(I,65:22). Some knowledge of the cost of customs' duties, transportation charges, etc., for woolen goods and other imports between London, Venice, and Florence eighty to a hundred years before Poggius wrote this letter may be gained from a study of Francesco Balducci Pegolotti, *La pratica della mercatura,* Allan Evans, ed. (Cambridge, Mass.: The Mediaeval Academy of America, 1936), pp. 15, 139–143, 146–147, 151–152, 195.

8(I,65:22). David Herlihy, in *Medieval and Renaissance Pistoia: The Social History of an Italian Town, 1200–1430* (New Haven: Yale University Press, 1967), pp. 105 and 116, records plagues in 1416, 1418, and 1423. I can find no mention elsewhere of plague in Florence or Rome in 1420 or 1421.

9(I,65:16,20,25). The Nicolaus mentioned three times in this paragraph must be Nicolaus de Medicis.

LETTER XIII

1(I,66:3–8). Pegolotti, *Pratica,* p. 195, says that 75 days were required for a payment to be transmitted from London to Florence via Pisa.

2(I,66:22). Chellus ("Chellus olim Dini Chelli de Troiana") married Poggius' sister Caterina in 1410. See Walser, *Poggius,* pp. 38, 329 (Doc. 13). He was also known as Chello del Maestro.

3(I,66:25–26). Nicolaus took a very relaxed view of the debts he owed, as evidenced by his not paying Coluccius Salutatus' heirs for the books he had bought from their father's library. See Ullman-Stadter, *Public Library,* pp. 98–99. Nicolaus died heavily in debt to Cosmus de Medicis too (Zippel, *Nicoló Niccoli,* p. 68).

4(I,67:1). For reports on the poor financial condition and dangerous political condition of Rome and the Papacy at this time, see Ludwig Pastor, *The History of the Popes, from the Close of the Middle Ages. Drawn from the Secret Archives of the Vatican and Other Original Sources,* Frederick Ignatius Antrobus, ed. (London: Kegan Paul, 1938), I, 241; II, 4–5.

5(I,67:5). Poggius must have been aware from his first meeting with Beaufort at Constance in September 1417 of the Bishop of Winchester's power, influence, and wealth. See the account of Beaufort's arrival and activity at the Council in Fillastre's diary (Loomis, *Council,* pp. 406–407).

6(I,67:9). See Letter VI, note 12, on Alamannus Adimarius. For the problems of the Curia at the time, both financial and military, see Partner, *Papal State,* pp. 68–73.

7(I,67:15–16). See Letter XV, notes 15 and 22, and Lunt, *Financial Relations,* pp. 419–420. Simon de Teramo was at the Curia in Rome in October 1421.

8(I,67:20). See Letter IX, note 4. Laurentius Marci Benvenutus.

9(I,67:20-21). All of Poggius' surviving invectives date from much later in his life; the earliest, against Franciscus Philelphus, who also had attacked Nicolaus de Niccolis, was written about 1435. See Walser, *Poggius,* p. 177.

LETTER XIV

1(I,67:3). For the chief English pilgrimage sites, see Jusserand, *English Wayfaring,* pp. 346–347. Beaufort's pilgrimage may have taken him to Truro, a Dominican friary far west in Cornwall. See David Knowles and R. Neville Hadcock, *Medieval Religious Houses: England and Wales* (London: Longmans, Green and Co., 1953), pp. 187, 314. The monastery which Poggius saw, older and handsomer than all the others in England, must have been Glastonbury (p. 5).

2(I,68:2). Probably his brother-in-law, Chellus, whom he calls his *cognatus* in Letter XIII (Tonelli Bk. I, ltr. 15).

3(I,68:7). By the time of the *catasto* of 1427, Poggius had property worth 566 florins, in a house, two cottages, three lots, loans, and government securities. See Martines, *Social World,* p. 124. On the fluctuations of the income and expenses of the Florentine government in the 1420s, see Anthony Molho, *Florentine Public Finances in the Early Renaissance, 1400–1433* (Cambridge, Mass.: Harvard University Press, 1971), especially chapter 5: "Administrative and economic effects of heavy taxation," pp. 113–152.

4(I,68:15). For duty on imports of bronze and tin, see Pegolotti, *Pratica,* pp. 141, 205, and for the cost of shipping wool and cloth between Pisa and Florence, see pp. 210–211 of this title.

5(I,68:21). Poggius seems to have traveled to Cluny and to Langres in 1414. See Clark, *Vetus Cluniacensis,* pp. i–iii, and Leonardus Brunus Aretinus, *Epistolae,* IV, 4; pt. 2, pp. 109–111.

6(I,68:26-28). This must have been a summer of great activity in Florentine shipping and trade, since the city was able to purchase the port of Leghorn from Genoa on 27 June 1421. See Charles C. Bayley, *War and Society in Renaissance Florence: The De militia of Leonardo Bruni* (Toronto: University of Toronto Press, 1961), p. 84.

7(I,69:1-2). Nicolaus was already well practiced in acquiring books from other parts of Italy and from other countries, so that importing them or pretending to should have held no terrors for him. See Ullman-Stadter, *Public Library,* pp. 93–104.

8(I,69:11-12). video te amice facere. For the idiom *facere amice,* see Cicero *Am.* 2.9.

9(I,69:16-28). Simon de Lellis de Teramo, an advocate well trusted by Martin V, was appointed in September 1420 to plead for "provisions" for the Papal government in England. *Reg. Vat.* 349, ff. 84v–85v, contains the papal brief appointing Simon de Teramo collector in England, dated Florence, "viii Id. Septembris anno tercio." He had the advantage of being known by and friendly with Beaufort from their time together at Constance. He made his official plea for financial assistance from the English Church, which he regarded as their due debt to Rome, before the English clerics assembled at Canterbury on 15 May 1421. See Jacob, *Fifteenth Century,* p. 234, and *The Register of Henry Chichele, Archbishop of Canterbury 1414–1443,* Ernest F. Jacob, ed., 4 vols. (Oxford: Clarendon Press, 1945–1947), I, xlii, and III, 66.

Poggius refers in Letter XIII (Tonelli Bk. I, ltr. 15), dated 19 July [1421], to Simon's being on the way back to the Curia and says in Letter XV (Tonelli Bk. I, ltr. 11; I, 52:10) that Simon spent four months in England. See also Lunt, *Financial Relations,* pp. 125–126, who gives the impression that one of Simon's assignments was to facilitate the providing of benefices in England to foreigners.

10(I,70:12). There is no evidence that Poggius ever succeeded in going to Oxford. See Roberto Weiss, *Humanism in England during the Fifteenth Century,* Medium Aevum Monographs, 4, 3rd edition (Oxford: B. Blackwell, 1967), p. 16.

11(I,70:14–16). Nicolaus de Medicis.

12(I,70:20). This early extravagance is symptomatic of the later extravagant loans to Edward IV of England which caused the decline of the Medici branch there and the explusion of Gherardus de Canigianis from the firm in 1472. See De Roover, *Rise and Decline,* p. 334.

13(I,70:22). For Poggius' youthful poverty, see William Shepherd, *The Life of Poggio Bracciolini* (Liverpool and London: Longman, Rees, Orme, Brown, Green & Longman, 1837), pp. 3–4, and Mehus' "Vita Ambrosii" in *Ambr. Trav. Epist.,* Vol. I, p. ccclxxx.

14(I,70:26). Poggius' brother-in-law. See above, note 2.

LETTER XV

1(I,45:2–8). Letter VI, Tonelli Bk. I, ltr. 6. Letter VII, Tonelli Bk. I, ltr. 7. Letter VIII, Tonelli Bk. I, ltr. 8.

2(I,46:7,11–16). See Partner, *Papal State,* p. 46, and Coulton, *Medieval Panorama,* p. 140.

3(I,46:9–11). For Poggius' idea of a desirable life, see his "De miseria humanae conditionis," Lib. II (*Poggii Opera Omnia,* I, 130).

4(I,46:14–15). See Jacob, *Fifteenth Century,* p. 195, for Beaufort's loans to Henry V in 1421, and Ciacconius, *Vitae,* Vol. II, col. 846, on Beaufort's immense wealth. See also Radford, *Beaufort,* pp. 290–291, and Shepherd, *Life of Poggio*, pp. 111–118. On the myth of Sisyphus, see Letter X, note 16 (Tonelli Bk. I, ltr. 10; I, 45:4–6).

5(I,46:23). See Hutchison, *Henry V*, pp. 165–166.

6(I,46:24). Curiously, there is not a word about conditions at the Curia in the long letter written to Poggius by Leonardus Brunus Aretinus at this very period. It is entirely devoted to explaining his quarrel with Nicolaus (V, 4; pt. II, 17–25).

7(I,46:26–32). See Partner, *Papal State*, pp. 67–69.

8(I,47:1–3). It would be interesting to know what evidence Poggius had for this statement, since the names of his good friends appear regularly in the Papal registers during the third and fourth years of Martin V's reign.

See Bartholomeus de Montepolitiano in:

Reg. Lat. 209, ff. 124r, 288v.

Reg. Lat. 210, ff. 9r, 203v.

Leonardus Brunus Aretinus in:

Reg. Vat. 349, ff. 37v–39r.

Reg. Vat. 353, f. 59r.

and especially Cincius in:

Reg. Vat. 349, ff. 19r–v, 37v, 93r–v, 140v–151r, 157r–v, and *passim*, including (ff. 191v–192r), a letter from Martin V to Cincius rewarding him for faithful service, erudition, eloquence, good character, and good habits. Dated Rome "apud Sanctum Petrum X Kal. Aprilis anno quarto."

9(I,47:3–12). See Ciacconius, *Vitae*, Vol. II, cols. 816–817. The whole passage is repeated from Platina's *Vita Martini V*, in which there is no mention of riots in Rome, or of plague, but only of a terrible flood which was caused by Braccius de Montone's vengeful destruction of the "Marmora Pedis Luci."

10(I,47:15–22). In Muratorius, *R.I.S.*, Vol. III, ii, col. 858: "De Martino V. E codice MSto Vaticano," Poggius' news from Rome is confirmed: "Iterum pestis valida bis in tribus annis Romam afflixit. Papa et alii Cortesani iverunt per Terras vicinas: ex qua peste multi, et nobiles Cortesani extincti sunt" ["Once again a fierce plague attacked Rome twice in three years. The Pope and members of his court went out into the countryside; many people and even noblemen of the court died of this plague"].

11(I,47:19–22; 50:6–8). For conditions in Italy and in the Curia, see St. Antoninus, *Chronicon*, Vol. III, f. 158v.

12(I,47:24). novo aucupio. For *novum aucupium* in the sense of "a new way of catching things," see Terence *Eun.* 247: "hoc novum est aucupium."

13(I,47:32). This is probably another reference to Beaufort, whom

Poggius seems to mean in the same sense in Letter VIII (Tonelli Bk. I, ltr. 8; I, 38:3).

14(I,48:12–15). Terence *Eun.* 46–47.

15(I,48:25;49:15). The "Collector," identified by Tonelli as Simon de Taramo [*sic*]. Tonelli used the correct spelling in Vol. I, p. 105. See Lunt, *Financial Relations*, pp. 419–421. Kristeller (see *Iter*, II, 194: Treviso, Biblioteca Capitolare Cod. I 177 f. 52) found a letter by Simon de Teramo. For additional letters and information on Simon's defects of character and later career, see Angelo Mercati, *Una corrispondenza fra curiali della prima metà del Quattrocento*, Studi e testi 157 (Città del Vaticano: Biblioteca Apostolica Vaticana, 1951), pp. 16–18, 64–71.

16(I,49:2–6). See Coulton, *Medieval Panorama*, pp. 142–153.

17(I,49:14). The next council was to be in Pavia in 1423. See Mandell Creighton, *A History of the Papacy during the Period of the Reformation*, II (London: Longmans, Green and Co., 1899), 145.

18(I,50:5). Poggius never ceased to think about the fluctuations in men's lives. See his works, written many years after this letter: *De infelicitate principum* (1440), *De varietate fortunae* (1448), which Walser (*Poggius*, p. 234) says had been on Poggius' mind ever since his return from England, and *De miseria humanae conditionis* (1457). This is corroborated by his long letter to Antonius Luscus (Tonelli Bk. II, ltr. 13; I, 112–119), which reads like an early, miniature version of Book I of the *De varietate fortunae*.

19(I,50:25–51:9). Poggius could hardly have been casual about his career at the Curia after the serious and vigorous letters of praise and admonition written to him by his cherished mentor, Coluccius Salutatus (*Epistolario*, XIV, 2; Vol. IV, 5–8 and XIV, 19; Vol. IV, 126–145).

20(I,51:11–21; 52:11–14). Simon de Teramo was wrong about the monastic libraries. Most of the well-known ones were built after 1440. See Knowles, *Religious Orders*, II, 352, note 4. His report of the great number of ancient monasteries is confirmed by Knowles and Hadcock, *Medieval Religious Houses*. For Simon de Teramo's activities as consistorial advocate at the Council of Constance, see Loomis, *Council*, pp. 443–444, 465, 508–509.

21(I,51:24–52:2). Apelles (fourth century B.C.) Painter. *OCD*, p. 79.

22(I,52:9–11). Although Simon de Teramo testified, according to Lunt (*Financial Relations*, p. 419), at "The convocation of Canterbury on 15 May 1421," the convocation took place in London. See *The Register of Henry Chichele*, III, 63, 66. Henry, Bishop of Winchester, was present, perhaps Poggius too.

23(I,52:20–23). The description Poggius gives fits either Glastonbury or Canterbury rather than any other English monastery. See Knowles, *Religious Orders*, I, 37–40.

24(I,52:29). Simon de Teramo returned to England in March 1423. See Lunt, *Financial Relations,* p. 420, but he kept up an official correspondence with English officials and clergy while in Rome: pp. 419–421, 562.

25(I,53:2–17). See Mallett, *Florentine Galleys,* pp. 10–17.

26(I,53:17–54:11). Nicolaus de Medicis. See Poggius' letter to Nicolaus de Medicis, written 22 January 1431 (Tonelli Bk. IV, ltr. 19; I, 343–344), which speaks of their great devotion to each other.

27(I,53:20–21). Persuasum est mihi iamdudum illum esse alterum me. See the following quotation from Cicero: "vide quam mihi persuaserim te me esse alterum" (Cicero *Fam.* 7.5).

28(I,53:21–22). nostra omnia, ut amicitie ius postulat, esse communia. For the notion, see the following quotation from Terence: "vetus verbum hoc quidem est: communia esse amicorum inter se omnia" (Terence *Adel.* 804).

29(I,53:29). ultro se offert. For the idiom *ultro aliquid offerre,* see Cicero *Planc.* 10.26.

30(I,54:11–12). See Sabbadini, *Scoperte,* I, 43–55, and Remigio Sabbadini, ed., *Carteggio di Giovanni Aurispa,* Fonti per la Storia d'Italia (Rome: Tipografia del Senato, 1931), p. xiv, for some of the Greek works which Aurispa sold to Guarinus before setting out a second time for Greece in 1421.

31(I,54:12–15). Sabbadini, *Epist. di Guar. Ver.,* I, 213–215 (Epist. 125) and III, 88–89. Guarinus was married in Verona on 27 December 1419 to Taddea, daughter of Niccolò and Fiordimiglia Zendrata.

32(I,54:16–22). Gothein, *Francesco Barbaro,* Chapter IV, "De re uxoria," pp. 61–99.

See also Poggius' praise of the *De re uxoria* in Tonelli Bk. I, ltr. 3 to Guarinus, who had sent the book to him in Constance in 1416.

For Franciscus Barbarus' marriage, see Gothein, pp. 123, 166. Franciscus Barbarus' son, Zacharias (1422–1491) was an eminent Venetian statesman.

33(I,54:23). Vespasiano, *Vite,* p. 480, says that Nicolaus "never had a wife, so that she might never interfere with his studies."

34(I,54:23–25). See Walser, *Poggius,* p. 353, Doc. 43. Poggius married Vaggia de Bondelmontis on 19 January 1436. See also *Poggii Epistolae,* II, 72:12–25.

35(I,55:1–7,15). See J. Haller, *England und Rom,* in *Quellen und Forschungen aus italienischen Archiven und Bibliotheken,* Vol. VIII, ii (Rome, 1906), pp. 255, 289–304 (Documents, esp. pp. 291–292). Simon de Teramo was greatly disappointed not to return to England but to find that Nicolaus Bildeston was sent on a mission to Rome instead. His appointment is in *Reg. Vat.* 359, f. 19v. Haller assigns it to 1422, addressed to Henry V.

36(I,55:3–8). Alamannus Adimarius, Cardinal of Pisa.

37(I,55:18). See Letter VIII, notes 7 and 8; Tonelli Bk. I, ltr. 8 (I, 39:20–23).

38(I,55:21–25). Nicolaus de Medicis.

39(I,55:26). This letter shows from internal evidence that it was written in 1421 and not, as dated by Tonelli (I, 55), 1420. This date is also given by Fubini (*Poggii Opera Omnia*, IV, 736). The strongest evidence for the later date is that it is clear that Simon de Teramo had been to England and had returned to Rome. There is ample documentation of Simon's being in England in May 1421; Poggius says furthermore that he had been there four months. Poggius mentions the war with Naples, which was averted by the mission of Cardinal Petrus Fonseca, who died on his way home, in Vicovaro, in August 1422. Poggius also mentions the Curia's being driven out of Rome by the plague, which could not have occurred between the date of their return to Rome, 20 September 1420, and the date of this letter, November 29, if it had been written in 1420. The cumulative evidence points to 1421 and therefore to a different order from that chosen by Tonelli.

LETTER XVI

1(I,56:7–20). Ciacconius paints a grim picture of conditions in Rome at the beginning of Martin V's government there: "Urbem Romam adeo diruptam et vastatam invenit, ut nulla civitatis facies in ea videretur. Collabentes vidisses domos, collapsa Templa, desertos vicos, coenosam, et oblitam Urbem, laborantemque rerum omnium charitate, atque inopia . . . dixisses, omnes cives, aut inquilinos esse, aut extremam omnium faecem eo commigrasse." *Vitae* (Vol. II, cols. 816–817). ["He found the city of Rome so broken down and deserted that it had not even the semblance of a city. You would have seen the houses falling down, the churches in ruins, whole quarters deserted, and the city filthy and foul and suffering from high prices and scarcity in every form. . . . You would have said that all the citizens were either foreigners or the absolute dregs of the world who had come together in Rome."]

Infessura speaks of the vast number of thieves on the outskirts of Rome who preyed on pilgrims and travelers (Stefano Infessura, *Diario della Città di Roma*, Oreste Tommasini, ed. [Rome: Istituto Storico Italiano, 1890; reprinted, Turin: Bottega d'Erasmo, 1960], p. 23). Poggius' most trustworthy adviser, who had the longest record of service as apostolic secretary at this time, Antonius Luscus, seems to have been in and out of the Curia during this period. According to Sabbadini (*Epist. di Guar. Ver.*, III, 65–66) he rejoined the Curia on 12 December 1418, after having left it at Constance. According to Luigi Pastine, "Antonio Loschi umanista vicentino" (*Rivista d' Italia*,

Vol. XVIII [1915], pt. 1, pp. 867–868) Luscus had been living in Vicenza when he returned to the Curia in 1422. Antonius Luscus was absent from Rome during most of 1421, on an embassy from Martin V to Philippus Maria de Vicecomitibus, and so could not be consulted (Giovanni da Schio, *Sulla vita e sugli scritti di Antonio Loschi vicentino* [Padua: Tipi del Seminario, 1858], p. 108).

2(I,56:22). See Walser, *Poggius,* pp. 42, 328, Document 10, in which Poggius acted as a witness to Bartholomeus' appointment as a canon of San Lorenzo in Florence, 30 October 1406. As noted (Letter I, note 4; Tonelli Praef., I, x:8) Poggius rarely used the vernacular in his letters. That note lists the places where it appears. It is interesting that in this case he quotes it from a letter from another apostolic secretary, accustomed as he was to writing official letters in Latin. Perhaps this is a sign of the gap between those secretaries who were humanists and those who were not.

Bartholomeus de Vincio was, like Poggius, a *Scriptor* and *litterarum apostolicarum Abbreviator* (see Walser, *Poggius,* Doc. 14, pp. 329–330). Both their names appear in one of the registers of Innocent VII, as early as 1404: *Reg. Vat.* 333, ff. 73r–v, 115r, 117r, 144r–v, 170v–171r, 285v–286r, 292v.

Bartholomeus' name appears so regularly in the registers of Martin V on into the tenth year of his pontificate (*Reg. Vat.* 349, ff. 138v–140r; *Reg. Vat.* 350, ff. 148r, 286v; *Reg. Vat.* 355, ff. 117r, 178r, 192r) that it seems most unlikely that he left the Curia.

3(I,57:15–21). Sabbadini, *Epist. di Guar. Ver.,* I, 677–679, letter 485 from Guarinus to Fantinus Georgius (Fantino Zorzi), who was then at home, but Sabbadini dated the letter (1420–1423?). See also Vol. III, pp. 84–85. Fantinus is also mentioned in a letter from Guarinus to Fantinus' cousin Petrus Georgius, very favorably; Sabbadini dated this letter June 1418. Kristeller (*Iter,* II, 9) found in Padua, in the Biblioteca del Seminario, Cod. 126, which contains letters of Pius II, Franciscus Barbarus, Poggius, and letters from Christophorus de Scarpis to Nicolaus Georgius and to Fantinus Georgius.

4(I,57:26). No letters from Poggius to Franciscus Barbarus written from England are preserved. The letters now known begin at Constance and, after a long gap, resume in 1426. See *Poggii Opera Omnia,* IV, 711–712. Franciscus Barbarus is frequently mentioned in Poggius' letters to other friends earlier. (See Tonelli Bk. I, ltr. 3 and Bk. I, ltr 4 to Guarinus; Bk. I, ltrs, 11, 12, 21 to Nicolaus de Niccolis; Bk. II, ltrs. 6 and 21 to Guarinus; Bk. II, ltrs. 2 and 7 to Nicolaus de Niccolis.)

Poggius' friendship with Franciscus Barbarus (ca. 1398–1454) lasted throughout their lives. Much that is known of Poggius' literary discoveries at St. Gall is reported in a letter of praise written to him by Barbarus in July 1417 (*Francisci Barbari et aliorum ad ipsum Epistolae*

[Brescia: Joannes-Maria Rizzardi, 1743], Epist. I, pp. 1–8). See Appendix, Letter IV. Altogether, seventeen letters exchanged between them have survived: four from Barbarus and thirteen from Poggius, who also dedicated his first published work, the *De avaritia*, to Barbarus. Franciscus Barbarus was also a friend of all the other well-known humanists of the period and corresponded with Traversarius, Leonardus Brunus Aretinus, Aurispa, Antonius Beccadellius Panormita, Gasparinus Barzizza, and Franciscus Philelphus. It was Barbarus who finally reconciled Nicolaus de Niccolis and Leonardus Brunus Aretinus after their long quarrel in 1426. For a full-length study of Barbarus, see Gothein, *Francesco Barbaro;* for further information see Chevalier, *Bio-bibliographie*, Vol. I, col. 424, and Cosenza, *Dictionary*, I, 397–403.

Franciscus Barbarus was even more a Venetian statesman and military leader than he was a humanist; he left no writings except his letters, his translations of Plutarch's lives of Aristides and Cato, and his short tract: *De re uxoria*. On his literary taste and holdings see Aubrey Diller, "The Library of Francesco and Ermolao Barbaro," *Italia medioevale e umanistica*, VI, (1963), 253–262.

5(I,58:6–17). Poggius was aware of Simon de Teramo as a powerful and effective advocate at the Council of Constance and therefore worth listening to. See Loomis, *Council*, pp. 443–444, 465, note 322; 508–509. The Cardinal of Pisa had also been a very active and important figure at the Council (pp. 187, 223–225, 242, 280, 334, 374, 377, 394–399, 415, 427–428.

6(I,58:28–59:5). On the financial structure of Martin V's government and especially the Papal court and on Poggius' financial expectations, see François Baix, *La Chambre apostolique et les "Libri Annatarum" de Martin V (1417–1431)*. Première partie: Introduction et textes. Analecta Vaticano-Belgica, Vol. XIV (Brussels and Rome: L'Institut historique Belge de Rome, 1942), pp. cccxliv–cdiii.

7(I,59:3–11). For an account of the narrow limits of school teaching in the early fifteenth century, see Eugenio Garin, *L'educazione in Europa (1400–1600)* (Bari: Laterza, 1957), pp. 13–39.

8(I,59:18). Oportuit enim parere tempori. For the idiom *parere tempori*, see *parere et tempori et voluntati*; Cicero *Vatin.* 1.2. The oration *In Vatinium* was one of six found by Leonardus Brunus in Lucca in 1408 and sent to Nicolaus de Niccolis (Sabbadini, *Scoperte*, I, 75; II, 210).

9(I,59:22). Terence *Eunuchus* 553: "aegritudine aliqua." See also *Heauton Tim.* 506.

10(I,59:29–32). Cardinal Pisanus had considerable ecclesiastical power because of his vigorous support of the election of Martin V (Loomis, *Council*, pp. 427–428). He also wielded unusual economic power (De Roover, *Rise and Decline*, p. 204).

11(I,59:30–32). For secretarial duties, see the review by O. T. of E. von Ottenthal, *Die Bullenregister Martins V und Eugens IV* (Innsbruck, 1885), in R. *società romana di storia patria, Archivio,* VIII (1885), 285–289.

12(I,60:6). Identified by Tonelli (note 1) as Fantinus Georgius.

13(I,60:8–11). See Mallett, *Florentine Galleys,* pp. 10–13. Nicolaus was Nicolaus de Medicis. Poggius' cloth was mentioned in Letter XII (Tonelli Bk. I, ltr. 14; I, 65), Letter XIII (Tonelli Bk. I, ltr. 15; I, 66), and Letter XIV (Tonelli Bk. I, ltr. 16; I, 68).

14(I,60:16). See Letter XV. This one should also be dated 1421, since it clearly follows Letter XV.

15(I,60:16–17). See Letter II, note 22.

LETTER XVII

1(I,71:3). Pier (*sic* in Poggius' Latin text) Lamberteschus is mentioned in this and in the three succeeding letters but not in Poggius' other works or in his correspondents' letters. His family was one of the wealthiest in the S. Croce section of Florence according to the *catasto* of 1427. See Martines, *Social World,* p. 112. For further information on the financial status of the Lamberteschi family, though not on Pier specifically, see Molho, *Florentine Public Finances,* pp. 168 (note 31), 181, 216.

For a fictional interpretation of Pier de Lamberteschis' offer, see [John Wilson Ross], *Tacitus and Bracciolini. The Annals Forged in the XVth Century* (London: Diprose and Bateman, 1878), pp. 174–193.

2(I,71:7–9). For some sense of what this salary represented, see Molho, *Florentine Public Finances,* p. 17 and the table of "monetary equivalences" facing p. 1.

3(I,71:12–13, 25–26). Poggius frequently sent a letter, unsealed, for a particular friend to read and forward to the proposed recipient. See, for instance, *Poggii Epistolae* Bk. VII, ltrs. 1 and 2, 6 and 7, where Poggius wrote to the Marquis of Mantua and entrusted the letter to Victorinus Feltrensis, whom he later reproached for not delivering it. Poggius' letter to Pier Lamberteschus has not survived.

4(I,71:16–21). The contents of this letter suggest that it was written in February 1421 or 1422, after the Curia returned to Rome in September 1420 but before the Cardinal of Pisa died of plague in Tivoli in September 1422 (Eubel, *Hierarchia,* I, 32). Pier Lamberteschus did not receive his permit for a mercantile expedition to Hungary until 30 October 1423. (See note 1 on Letter XX; Tonelli Bk. I, ltr. 20; I, 77:3–6).

5(I,71:23–25). Despite his return to Rome in 1423 and immediate employment in the Curia, Poggius did not produce his first published work, *De avaritia,* until November 1428. (Walser, *Poggius,* p. 126.)

6(I,72:2-3). Horace *De arte poetica* 139. Henry Beaufort finally bestowed the "Rectory of Drokensford in the Diocese of Winchester" on Poggius. See Weiss, *Humanism,* p. 18, note 5. See also Walser, *Poggius,* Document 18, pp. 333-334. Poggius gives the value of his English benefice in Florentine currency. See Iris Origo, *The Merchant of Prato* (London: Jonathan Cape, 1957), p. 23.

7(I,72:7-9). St. Gregory the Great, *XL Homiliarum in Evangelia,* Lib. II, Homil. XXVI (Migne, *PL,* Vol. LXXVI, col. 1200).

8(I,72:18-19). The risks are well described by Partner, *Papal State,* pp. 69-73. The Pope and Curia newly arrived in Rome (28 September 1420) were surrounded by hostile forces and armies of mercenaries marching against each other.

9(I,72:24). It must be remembered that Poggius had already served six popes and anti-popes (during the existence of two other anti-popes) in nineteen years. See Shepherd, *Life of Poggio,* chapter I.

10(I,73:10-11). Thomas à Kempis *De imitatione Christi* 1.19.2.

11(I,73:13). It appears that the position offered to Poggius by Pier Lamberteschus involved diplomatic relations with Hungary, ruled by the Emperor Sigismund, whom Poggius had had a chance to observe at the Council of Constance. Poggius' first papal employer, Boniface IX, had had a struggle with Sigismund, who claimed the right to fill the bishoprics in his own realm, beginning in 1404. *CMH,* VIII, 604.

12(I,73:11-12). Nicolaus de Medicis (see Letter III, note 31) and Ambrosius Traversarius, who, according to Tonelli's note, Vol. I, p. 213, was general of the monastic order of the Camalduli. He was a great friend of all the Italian humanists of his period and corresponded with them as well as with churchmen of all ranks. See Chevalier, *Bio-bibliographie,* Vol. I, col. 185; Cosenza, *Dictionary,* IV, 3455-3464; and *Ambr. Trav. Epist.,* 2 vols.

LETTER XVIII

1(I,73:3). Three letters by Poggius in Italian appeared in *Poggii Opera Omnia,* IV, 213-215, 611-613, and 647. One is to Cosmus de Medicis and was first published by A. Medin in "Documenti per la biografia di Poggio Bracciolini," *Giornale storico della letteratura italiana,* XII (1888), 363-365. The second is also to Cosmus and was first published by A. Fabroni, *Magni Cosmi Medicei vita* (Pisa, 1789), II, 116. The third letter is to Johannes, son of Cosmus de Medicis, and according to Fubini (IV, 643) exists in its original autograph form and was published by Walser (*Poggius,* p. 318, note 2). Fubini dates it 1449 because of its relation to another letter, to Cosmus, on the same matter.

2(I,73:8). Poggius did not want another disappointment like his underpaid underemployment by Beaufort.

3(I,73:8–11). Ambrosius Traversarius in his letters frequently mentions the pleasure Nicolaus de Niccolis' letters gave him. For instance: "Accepi proxime literas tuas plenas humanitatis . . ." ["I recently received a very stimulating letter from you . . ."]. (VIII, 3, *Ambr. Trav. Epist.*)

4(I,74:4–7). Poggius' respect and admiration for a life of study is most clearly expressed in his letter to Carolus Marsuppinus Aretinus (Tonelli, Bk. VI, ltr. 12; II, 108–112) on the death of Nicolaus de Niccolis and also in his "Oratio in Funere Nicolai Nicoli." *Poggii Opera Omnia*, I, 270–277.

5(I,74:9). On the Sarmatae, a nomad tribe that settled along the Danube in the first century A.D., see *OCD*, p. 952. On the Scythians, *OCD*, p. 968.

6(I,74:11–13). On Poggius' study of Greek, see Louise Ropes Loomis, "The Greek Studies of Poggio Bracciolini," in *Medieval Studies in Memory of Gertrude Schoepperle Loomis*, Roger Sherman Loomis, ed. (New York: Columbia University Press, 1927), pp. 489–512.

For Poggius' later attitude toward his own very free translations from the Greek, see his letters to Petrus Thomasius Venetus (Bk. IX, ltrs. 14, 26) and Antonius Beccadellius Panormita (Bk. IX, ltr. 23).

7(I,74:22–25). On the low income of many benefices, see *Register of Henry Chichele*, I, cxxv and cxlviii.

It is clear from Walser, *Poggius*, Document 18 (pp. 333–334), that Drokensford must have been the second living bestowed by Beaufort on Poggius, because Martin V permits him to hold it an extra year. Poggius here gives his income in English currency. For comparative figures on a benefice without a parish in 1453 in England, see Kathleen L. Wood-Legh, ed., *A Small Household of the XVth Century, Being the Account Book of Munden's Chantry, Bridport* (Manchester: Manchester University Press, 1956), p. xviii. The annual household expenses listed here for the years 1453–1460 never run higher than £13/9/3 a year.

8(I,75:8–9). in itinere componuntur sarcine. This seems to be ascribed to Pacuvius by Nicolaus Perottus in his *Cornucopiae, sive linguae latinae commentarii* (Venice: Aldus, 1513), col. 712. It appears in his analysis of Martial's epigram XV: "De Carpophoro."

9(I,75:13). The feast of St. John is June 24.

10(I,75:16). For Poggius' plan to go to Hungary, see the note on Pier Lamberteschus in Letter XX (Tonelli Bk. I, ltr. 20; I, 77:5–6).

11(I,75:21). Tonelli dated the letter *March* 5 without explanation; Fubini dates it *May* 5 (*Poggii Opera Omnia*, IV, 735).

12(I,75:26). If Poggius' expenses ran between £10 and £14 a year (see note 7 above) he would have plenty left over for travel.

13(I,75:28–29). Venderò in erba. *Vocabulario degli accademici della Crusca,* 5th edition, Vol. V (Florence, 1886), p. 196, sec. XIV, XV. "To use up the profit before the harvest is in."

LETTER XIX

1(I,76:2). No letters are unaccounted for here. We have Letters XVII and XVIII (Tonelli Bk. I, ltrs. 17 and 18; I, 71–75). The Italian letter is lost.

2(I,76:9, 15). Poggius seems here to be planning his return to Florence rather than to Rome. He returned to Italy along the Rhine by way of Cologne, where he found a fragment of Petronius, which he took with him. See Sabbadini, *Scoperte,* I, 83–84, and Letter XXIV (Tonelli Bk. II, ltr. 3; I, 91:12).

3(I,76:12–14). For conditions in the late winter and spring of 1422, see Radford, *Beaufort,* p. 100. Nicolaus, with whom Poggius planned to consult, must have been Nicolaus de Medicis.

4(I,76:18–19). Terence *Phormio* 708–709.

5(I,76:22–23). Probably "cognatus" here means Poggius' brother-in-law Chellus again.

LETTER XX

1(I,77:3–6). The feast of St. John is June 24. At this time Pier and Nicolaus de Lamberteschis were planning a mercantile expedition to Hungary with Antonius Frontis, Philippus de Caponibus, Zenobius de Panzaciis as associates. They received a permit to do so on 30 October 1423. See Johann Friedrich Böhmer, *Regesta Imperii,* Vol. XI, *Die Urkunden Kaiser Sigmunds,* Vol. I (1410–1437) (Hildesheim: Georg Olms Verlagsbuchhandlung, 1968), p. 401, Doc. 5667.

2(I,77:15). Martin V, in accordance with the agreements made at the Council of Constance, summoned a Council to meet at Pavia in April 1423. See Creighton, *Hist. of the Papacy,* II, 145.

3(I,77:18–27). For rules on Benefices, see *CMH,* VII, 153, 645–648. See also Charles Oman, gen. ed., *A History of England,* Vol. III: *England in the Later Middle Ages,* by Kenneth H. Vickers (London: Methuen & Co., 1914), pp. 229, 284, 305, 395, 408.

4(I,77:27–78:3). See Walser, *Poggius,* p. 334, Doc. 19. Perhaps the canonicate of the cathedral in Bordeaux.

5(I,78:8–10). The benefice which Poggius was given was "Drokensford in South Hants, now called Droxford." *Calendar of the Register of John de Drokensford, Bishop of Bath and Wells (A.D. 1309–1329),* Right Rev. Bishop Hobhouse, ed., I (Somerset Record Society, 1887),

264   *Notes: Letter XX*

xvii. On Poggius' benefice, see also *Calendar of Inquisitions post mortem Edward III*, Vol. XIV (London: Her Majesty's Stationery Office, 1952), p. 264, No. 257. "Writ, 28 June, 50 Edward III Southampton. *Inq.*, taken at Winchester, 24 July, 50 Edward III. Middleton, A. Toft, 25 *a.* arable, 1*a* meadow, 3½*a.* wood and 19s. rent, held of the bishop of Winchester, as part of his manor of Drokensford, in right of his church." On Drokensford, Poggius' benefice, see *Hampshire, Extracted from Domes-Day Book*, Richard Warner, Jr., ed. and trans. (London: Faulder, 1789), p. xxxiii: under "Names of the Hundreds Drocheneford ⌠Droxford Hundred⌡ ⌊No such Hun. now⌋,"; p. xxxvii: "Drocheneforde Droxford"; pp. 68–69 Latin and English: "The bishop holds *Drocheneford*. It was always churchland. It was assessed, T.R.E. at 16 hides; it is, now, assessed at 14 hides. Here are 16 ploughlands; . . . and 32 villagers and 13 borderers occupy 14 ploughlands. Here are 6 servants; and a church worth 20 shillings." This description was made in 1086.

For a description of the church in Droxford, see John Charles Cox, *Hampshire*, revised by Philip M. Johnston, The Little Guides, 6th edition, revised (London: Methuen and Co., 1929), p. 108.

6(I,78:20–21). Nicolaus de Niccolis and his wealthy Florentine friend, the merchant Pier Lamberteschus, were offering Poggius an alternative to staying in England or returning to the Curia. For the financial status of the Lamberteschi, see Martines, *Social World*, pp. 365, 369, 372, 375. One of the Lamberteschi was the wealthiest man in his quarter in 1427, as Giovanni di Bicci de' Medici, Palla di Nofri Strozzi, and Niccolò di Giovanni da Uzzano were in theirs.

LETTER XXI

1(I,78:2–4). Nicolaus' letters were received with enthusiasm by other correspondents, such as Leonardus Brunus Aretinus (*Epistolae* III, 19; IV, 1; Vol. I, pp. 96, 100). See also Letter VII, note 1.

2(I,79:8–9). in hoc omnem adhibeo diligentiam. See *diligentiam adhibere* ad rem, Cicero *Fam.* 16, 9.3,

3(I,79:16). The Council of Pavia, in April 1423.

4(I,79:26–28). For the definition of a prebend, see *Encyclopaedia Britannica*, 11th edition, XXII, 266. It was clearly what Poggius desired, since it was "practically a sinecure, and the holder has no cure of souls as such."

5(I,79:29). Ad calcem cuperem pervenire. For the idiom *ad calcem pervenire*, see Cicero *Lael.* 27.101. Poggius copied the *De amicitia* a few years after the date of this letter. His ms. is now Cod. Ricc. 504 in Florence. See Ullman, *Origin and Development*, pp. 41–42.

6(I,79:31). ac si auribus lupum teneas. For the idiom *lupum auribus tenere*, "to be in a situation of doubt and uncertainty," see Terence *Phorm.* 506, and Suetonius *Tib.* 25. Poggius owned a Suetonius bound in one volume with Quintus Curtius and other texts. See Walser, *Poggius*, p. 421 (inventory no. 46).

7(I,80:5). Vergil *Georgics* 1.145. Poggius went to England from Mantua late in 1418. See Walser, *Poggius*, p. 71.

8(I,80:6–11). This is a sad confession from the man who had rescued Quintilian from a dark and dismal prison (*Poggii Epistolae* Bk. I, ltr. 5 to Guarinus; Tonelli, I, 25–29). Poggius' fame derived largely from his discovery of the complete text of Quintilian, for which he was highly praised by both Leonardus Brunus Aretinus (*Epistolae* IV, 5; pt. 1, pp. 111–113) and Franciscus Barbarus (*Epistolae* I, 1, pp. 1–8). See Appendix, Letters II and IV.

9(I,80:11). In 1408–1409, Poggius had copied Cod. Laur. 67, 15, which contains Eusebius *De temporibus* in St. Jerome's translation. See Ullman, *Origin and Development*, p. 30. He also knew Tacitus from the last six books of the *Annales* and the first five of the *Historiae*, discovered by Boccaccio. See Sabbadini, *Storia e critica*, pp. 249–250. Three decades of Livy (I, III, IV) were well known to Petrarch and his successors. See Sabbadini, *Scoperte*, II, 231–232. See also Giuseppe Billanovich's two valuable articles: "Petrarch and the textual tradition of Livy," *Journal of the Warburg and Courtauld Institutes*, XIV (1951), 137–208, and "Dal Livio di Raterio (Laur. 63, 19) al Livio del Petrarca (B.M., Harl. 2493)," *Italia medioevale e umanistica*, II (1959), 103–178.

10(I,80:12). For the sources, ancient and modern, used by Leonardus Brunus Aretinus for his *Historiae Florentini Populi* and presumably also available to Poggius, see Donald J. Wilcox, *The Development of Florentine Humanist Historiography in the Fifteenth Century*, Harvard Historical Studies, LXXXII (Cambridge, Mass.: Harvard University Press, 1969), p. 32, note 3.

11(I,80:14). Si omnino nervos intendero. See Digna res est ubi tu *nervos intendas* tuos, Terence *Eun.* 312.

12(I,80:16–30). Bartholomeus Francisci de la Capra became Archbishop of Milan 7 February 1414. He had previously been Bishop of Cremona, since 1405. See Eubel, *Hierarchia*, I, 333, and Tonelli, I, 80, note 1. For Capra's service to the Emperor Sigismund and his successful search for classical texts, see Sabbadini, *Scoperte*, I, 76–86.

13(I,80:31–81:1). Praeterea natura amici paulum est ambitiosa. See *amicitiae ambitiosae*, Cicero, *Att.* 1.18. Poggius had every opportunity to know and observe Bartholomeus Capra in Rome 1404–1414 and in Constance. See Francesco Novati, "Bartholommeo Capra ed i primi suoi passi in corte di Roma," *Archivio storico lombardo*, Ser. 3, Vol. IX (1903), pp. 374–387.

14(I,81:2–5). personasset ipsemet buccine. See *personare buccini,* Jos. 6.13. This is one of Poggius' rare references to the Old Testament. Capra was accustomed to announcing and parading his discoveries and acquisitions. See Sabbadini, *Storia e critica,* pp. 50, 76. See also Leonardus Brunus Aretinus, *Epistolae* II, 10; III, 13.

15(I,81:5). See Walser, *Poggius,* pp. 57–58, for an account of Poggius' methods in his successful searches for Cicero texts in 1417. See Sabbadini, *Scoperte,* I, 100. See also Giammaria Mazzuchelli, *Gli scrittori d'Italia cioe notizie storiche, e critiche intorno alle vite, e agli scritti dei letterati italiani,* 6 vols. (Brescia: Giambatista Bossini, 1753– 1763), pp. 498–503, on Gasparinus Barzizius.

16(I,81, note 1). Tonelli identifies the discoverer of Cicero's *Orator* as Gerardus Landrianus, Bishop of Lodi. Poggius wrote him several letters many years after this find and dedicated his essay, *De nobilitate,* to him. Poggius also gave an account, in 1433, to Antonius Cremona (Tonelli Bk. V, ltr. 15; II, 51–52) of a dinner party attended by the Bishop, Nicolaus de Niccolis, Leonardus Brunus Aretinus, Carolus Marsuppinus Aretinus, and himself. Pastor (*History of the Popes,* I, 307) says that Landrianus was a patron of the humanists and collected a valuable library. Mehus (*Ambr. Trav. Epist.,* p. xlvi) gives an account of Landrianus' generous handling of his discovery, which was sent immediately to Gasparinus Barzizza (Cosenza in his *Dictionary,* III, 1918, says it was so that the ms. could be deciphered) and, after he and Cosmus Cremonensis had copied it, the text was sent to Guarinus in Verona and to Leonardus Justinianus in Venice.

For further comment on Landrianus' great discovery, see *Diatriba Praeliminaris . . . ad Francisci Barbari . . . Epistolas,* p. xxxvi.

17(I,81:11–13). Poggius' belongings which were shipped to Pisa are also mentioned in Letter XIII (Tonelli Bk. I, ltr. 15), Letter XIV (Tonelli Bk. I, ltr. 16), and Letter XVI (Tonelli Bk. I, ltr. 12). On Pisan maritime commerce, see David Herlihy, *Pisa in the Early Renaissance,* Yale Historical Publications, miscellany no. 68 (New Haven: Yale University Press, 1958), pp. 162–175. As usual, there are greetings for Nicolaus de Medicis.

LETTER XXII

1(I,81:3). Knowles explains clearly why Poggius found his benefice meager (*Religious Orders,* II, 171–173, 288–292).

2(I,81:5–6). animi sollicitudine. For *sollicitudo animi,* see Cicero *Clu.* 18.51. Although the *Pro Cluentio* had been known in the 1390s, when Antonius Luscus wrote a commentary on it, Poggius found it again in a ms. at Cluny in the summer of 1415. He sent it to Florence, where Franciscus Barbarus saw it that same summer. See Sabbadini, *Scoperte*, I, 77, 84; II, 211.

3(I,82:11–15). For the freedom from care that Poggius believed to be found in true religious poverty, see the Rule of St. Benedict, section XXXIII: *Regula S. Benedicti*, Gregorio Penco, O.S.B. ed., Biblioteca di studi superiori XXXIX (Florence: La Nuova Italia, 1958), pp. 110–111.

4(I,82:24–27). See Letter V, notes 3–4 and 2 Thessalonians 3:10.

5(I,82:31–32). 2 Samuel 24:14 and Ecclesiasticus 2:18 (Apocrypha).

6(I,83:6–7). See Eubel, *Hierarchia*, I, 32. The cardinal died soon afterwards at Tivoli, on 17 September 1422.

7(I,83:13–14). Cicero *Paradoxa Stoicorum* 5.34.

8(I,83:14–15). John 3:8.

9(I,83:18). Romans 9:11. Tonelli says of Ambrosius Traversarius (p. 83, note 1) that he was "General of the Camaldolese Order, a man very learned in Greek and Latin literature. Paulus Cortesius says of him, 'There was an inexhaustible love of reading in this man; for he never allowed any time to be unused. Every day he wrote or put something down from Greek or Latin literature. But he began much more than he finished. Certainly no one put more enthusiasm than he into rescuing books from the secret places of our ancestors.' Laurentius Mehus published the letters of Ambrosius, together with a life of him, in Florence in 1759."

Poggius is indulging in a pun here, for he refers simultaneously to his friend Ambrosius Traversarius and to the Church Father, St. Ambrose, Bishop of Milan (340–397). See St. Ambrose, *Expositio evangelii Lucae*, Book VII (Commentary on Luke X.35), Carolus Schenkl, ed., Corpus Scriptorum Ecclesiasticorum Latinorum, Vol. XXXII, pt. 4 (Vienna: F. Tempsky, 1902), p. 315, 1.8. Poggius paraphrases St. Ambrose's text.

10(I,83:20). Philippians 3:8.

11(I,84:8–10). See Sabbadini, *Scoperte*, II, 209. "The *Brutus* was entirely new; the *De oratore* and the *Orator* were once more whole." For all those who enjoyed the codex found by Gerardus Landrianus, Bishop of Lodi, within a short time of its discovery, see *Scoperte*, I, 100–101. It was immediately sent to Gasparinus Barzizzius, who had it copied by Cosimo Raimondi of Cremona. Soon afterwards, the *Brutus* was copied by Flavius Blondus. Mehus, in *Ambr. Trav. Epist.*, Vol. I, p. xlvi, reports that the rhetorical works were copied and sent to Guarinus at Verona and to Leonardus Justinianus in Venice. Poggius himself had the opportunity to copy the newly found texts, and his autograph copy, signed, is Cod. Laurentianus Latinus Plut. L. cod. XXXI. It is described at length and with admiration by Bandini, *Catal. cod. lat.*, Vol. II, cols. 516–519.

12(I,84:21). Nicolaus de Medicis.

LETTER XXIII

1(I,87:2). epistolam . . . conscriptam. For *epistulam conscribere*, see Cicero *Att.* 13.50.1.

2(I,87:7). See Walser, *Poggius*, p. 85, note 2. There is no surviving document to confirm Poggius' appointment now in the Vatican Archives. Poggius' name appears on a document dated June 1423 for the first time after his return from Britain (*Reg. Vat.* 349, f. 272r. Dated "Rome apud Sanctam Mariam Maiorem iv Kal. Julii anno sexto"). He never returned to England; the Bishop of Winchester, Henry Beaufort, never came to Rome, despite his extensive travels (Radford, *Beaufort*, pp. 115, 183).

3(I,87:9). ob recuperatam dignitatem. For *recuperare dignitatem*, see Quint. 11.1.79. Probably Poggius' greatest triumph in the field of classical texts was his discovery at St. Gall in 1416 of the complete text of Quintilian's *Institutio oratoria*. For an account of this ms. and the second text discovered by Poggius in 1417 and the mss. derived from them, see Sabbadini, *Scoperte*, I, 78, 82; II, 247–248, and Poggius' letter to Guarinus describing his first discovery, written from Constance in December 1416 (Bk. I, ltr. 5; I, 25–29). For the letter to Guarinus, see Appendix, Letter III.

4(I,88:2). Henry Beaufort did not go to Rome as expected at this time. His chancellor, Nicholas Bildeston, came instead. See Weiss, *Humanism*, p. 19.

5(I,88:10–12). By the time of the *catasto* of 1427, Poggius owned four farms near Florence. See Walser, *Poggius*, pp. 339–340. Poggius' aim to be free of taxes succeeded at most until the Florentine *catasto* of 1427. See *Poggius*, Doc. 27, pp. 339–341, and numerous tax records thereafter. Molho gives a clear analysis of the fluctuations of Florentine expenditures and levies in the 1420s, depending on whether the city was at peace or forced to hire mercenaries to fight its wars. See *Florentine Public Finances*, pp. 4–6, 53–59, 61–62, 73, 76, 87–103, 112.

6(I,88:14). Cincius de Rusticis was also an apostolic secretary (1414–1443). He died in 1445. He was, like Poggius, a searcher for mss. and went with Poggius and Bartholomeus de Montepolitiano to St. Gall in June–July 1416. See Cosenza, *Dictionary*, IV, 3116. Most of what is known of Cincius and his private correspondence was published by Ludwig Bertalot in his "Cincius Romanus und seine Briefe," *Quellen und Forschungen aus italienischen Archiven und Bibliotheken,* herausgegeben vom preussischen historischen Institut in Rom, XXI (1929–1930), 209–255. It contains Cincius' account to his learned teacher Franciscus de Fiano of the great discoveries of classical texts made by the humanists, including Poggius and himself, in St. Gall in 1416 (pp. 222–225). See Appendix, Letter I. It also contains (pp. 241–244) a letter congratulating Poggius on the birth of his eldest legitimate son, in 1438.

7(I,88:19). Dixi librum cito conscribi debere. For *librum conscribere*, cf. Cicero *Brut.* 35.132. It is probably mere chance that Poggius here used a phrase from the recently (1421) discovered text of *Brutus*, which Nicolaus de Niccolis was in the process of copying. See Ullman, *Origin and Development*, pp. 61–63.

8(I,88:21). Perhaps the book Cincius wanted was the Ammianus Marcellinus, which Nicolaus had finished copying in November 1423. See *Poggii Epistolae*, Bk. II, ltr. 7 (I, 97). See also Ullman-Stadter, *Public Library*, p. 101, on Cod. naz. C.S. I, V, 43 in Nicolaus' hand. Nothing in the inventory of Poggius' books made at the time of his death fits the description here. He owned two volumes of assorted *opuscula:* nos. 83 and 86 in the inventory. See Walser, *Poggius*, pp. 422–423.

9(I,88:26–28). For Nicolaus' ownership and copying of the texts of the *De oratore, Brutus* and *Orator,* see Ullman, *Origin and Development*, pp. 61–63. For the volume containing Cicero's *Brutus* and *Orator,* copied by Nicolaus de Niccolis and bequeathed by him to San Marco, see Ullman-Stadter, *Public Library*, p. 226 (no. 867). Nicolaus also left San Marco two mss. of the *De oratore* (nos. 865 and 866), one perhaps copied by Poggius (Ullman-Stadter).

10(I,88:29). Poggius is probably referring to Nicolaus de Medicis, but there is no reason why he should have had Cicero's rhetorical works at this time. For the travels of these texts after their discovery by Gerardus Landrianus, see Sabbadini, *Scoperte*, I, 100–101. Poggius copied Cicero's *De oratore, Paradoxa, Brutus,* and *Orator* in the ms. that is now Cod. Laur. 50,31 (see Ullman, *Origin and Development*, pp. 35–36, and Bandini, *Catal. cod. lat.*, Vol. II, col. 517).

11(I,89:2–3). Poggius had written to Franciscus Barbarus to return his ms. of Cicero's orations. For a discussion of Poggius' loan of the book to Barbarus and the latter's letter of apology sent when he returned it, see Sabbadini, *Storia e critica*, pp. 46–47. Barbarus' letter of apology was published by Sabbadini in *Centotrenta lettere*, p. 84 (XXXVII), and is dated 1436. For a discussion of this ms. (now *Vat. Lat.* 11458) see Ullman, *Origin and Development*, pp. 37–38.

12(I,89:6–8). This letter, III, was published by Tonelli as Bk. I, ltr. 1 (I, 1–10) and is one of Poggius' best-known letters. It has been quoted at length in many publications, including Negrier, *Les bains*, pp. 143–146.

LETTER XXIV

1(I,89:2–3). Poggius had evidently commissioned Nicolaus to buy him a piece of real estate, perhaps one of the four which he owned at the time of the 1427 *catasto* (Walser, *Poggius*, Doc. 27, pp. 339–341) or perhaps the one he sold in April 1427 (Doc. 24, p. 338).

2(I,89:3–11). Poggius does not make clear here what he was trying to buy; perhaps it was the house in Terranuova near Florence, which he sold in April 1427 to his brother-in-law. See Walser, *Poggius*, p. 338. In his funeral oration for Nicolaus, Poggius says: "Aderat amicis consilio, opera, obsequio, diligentia, etiam irrequisitus, eorum negocia pro suis ducebat" ["He was at his friends' service with advice, effort, compliance and conscientiousness, even without their asking and he considered their problems his own"]. *Poggii Opera Omnia*, I, 275.

3(I,89:14). Tonelli, I, 89, note 1, identifies the subject as Philippus Maria, Duke of Milan. Tonelli, I, 90, note 1, identifies the "boy" as Thebaldus Ordelafius, son of Georgius [Ordelafius] tyrant of Forlì; he was then barely ten years old.

For a clear account of the warlike activities of Filippo Maria Visconti and his seizure of Forlì from his ward, Tibaldo Ordelaffi, see Niccolò Machiavelli, *History of Florence and of the Affairs of Italy* (New York: Harper Torchbooks, 1960), pp. 162–163. For an account of the life and early death, at the age of twelve, of Thebaldus Ordelafius, see Frater Hieronymus Foroliviense *Chronicon foroliviense* in Muratori, *R.I.S.*, Vol. XIX, cols. 890–895. According to the *Chronicon foroliviense*, col. 888, the Pope, Martin V, had visited Forlì in February 1419.

4(I,90:5–8). See Poggius, *Historia Florentina*, Johannes Baptista Recanatus, ed. (Venice: Apud J. Gabrielem Hertz, 1715), Book V, p. 203. See also Leonardus Brunus Aretinus, *Historia fiorentina* (Venice, 1560), p. 227. Not only was Florentine foreign policy friendly to Martin V's enemies, but the citizens were gratuitously rude to him.

5(I,90:12). Ennius, *Annales*. Quoted by Festus in *De verborum significatu*, Lucianus Muller, ed. (*Quintus Ennius. Eine Einleitung in der Studium der römischen Poesie*, 1885), p. 42; s.v. Metonymia.

6(I,90:15–17). Poggius gives a long account of the diplomatic and political maneuvers connected with the Florentine decision to go to war against Filippo Maria Visconti. See *Historia Florentina*, Book V, pp. 204–213 (Recanati edition). His letters show the effects of it on the private citizen.

7(I,90:18). Perhaps Marianus Sozinus Senensis to whom Poggius wrote (Bk. III, ltr. 8, Tonelli, I, 199–201). Tonelli calls him "Celeberrimus huius aetatis iurisconsultus" ["the best known lawyer of this age"], but in 1423 he was still a very young man (Chevalier, *Biobibliographie*, Vol. II, col. 4297).

8(I,90:26). Cicero *Tusculanarum Disputationum Liber* 5.37.108. Seneca *De remediis fortuitorum* 8.2.

9(I,90:26–28). Platina (*Vitae*, f. 66r) stresses the care and good judgment used by Martin V in making ecclesiastical appointments: "in dandis beneficiis mira prudentia usus est. Non enim unicuique petenti ea conferebat; sed statim mente agitabat quis potissimum esset idoneus: cui talis cura demandaretur" ["He used remarkable caution in conferring benefices. For he did not confer them on anyone who happened to ask for one, but immediately deliberated in his mind on who might be by far the most suitable candidate; such was the care he felt should be devoted to it"].

10(I,91:3–4). Vergil *Georgics* 1.145.

11(I,91:4–9). For the cost of new clothes at this time, information is available in Iris Origo, *The World of San Bernardino* (New York: Harcourt, Brace and World, 1962), pp. 43–75.

12(I,91:4–9). The "book of precedents" which Poggius wanted was probably the sort of material treated extensively by Johannes Mabillon, O.S.B., in his *De re diplomatica Libri VI* (Paris: Louis Billaine, 1681), especially in Book I, chap. 3, sec. 1, p. 10; Book II, chap. 2, pp. 60–68; Book VI, sec. 207, pp. 618–619. The last item (95 in Poggius' inventory of books) is his *formularium cancellarie* (Walser, *Poggius*, p. 423).

13(I,91:12–16). See Sabbadini, *Scoperte*, I, 83–84.

14(I,91:15). For an account of the text of Titus Calpurnius Siculus' *Eclogues*, see Sabbadini, *Scoperte*, I, 16, 22; II, 205–206.

LETTER XXV

1(I,91:9). This apparently has some astrological significance. See Lynn Thorndike, *A History of Magic and Experimental Science*, 3 vols. (New York: Macmillan and Columbia University Press, 1923–1964), I, 179, discussing "The influence of the moon in each sign of the Zodiac." Thorndike refers to Galen. See his *Opera Omnia*, 20 vols., Carolus Gottlob Kühn, ed. (Leipzig: Car. Cnobloch, 1830), XIX, 529–573: "Galeni Prognostica de Decubitu ex Mathematica Scientia." Galen deals with the course of illnesses which develop while the moon is in the different signs of the Zodiac and how the outcome of the illness is affected favorably or unfavorably in conjunction with certain planets. It is not clear that this has any bearing on Poggius' remark or is it known whether this text of Galen's was known to Poggius, although he and his contemporaries referred to Galen; see Walser, *Poggius*, pp. 249, 457, 460. A modern text on astrology is perhaps more relevant. Katherine Taylor Craig's *Stars of Destiny: The Ancient Science of Astrology and How to Make Use of It Today* (London: Kegan Paul, Trench, Trubner and Co., Ltd., 1916), pp. 185–186, contains under the heading, "The moon in the twelve signs," the statement: "Moon in Capricorn. – Love of fame, prudent, economical; mentality high." She gives no source, but this seems to fit Poggius and Nicolaus rather well.

2(I,92:3–93:5). Poggius' understanding of Nicolaus de Niccolis' irascible disposition is clear from his letter to Leonardus Brunus Aretinus, Bk. II, ltr. 11 (Tonelli, I, 108–110). The quarrel discussed here seems to have been between Nicolaus de Niccolis and Nicolaus de Medicis.

3(I,92:16). ut vitemus et vitia. For *vitia vitare*, see Cicero *Rep.* 2.5.10. Poggius could have known only fragments of the *De republica;* the full text was discovered in 1820 by Cardinal Angelo Mai. The "Somnium Scipionis" which was available to the humanists is from 6.9–29 of the *De republica* and does not contain this phrase.

4(I,93:12). Poggius expected to attend the projected Council of Siena, as becomes clearer in Letters XXVI and XXVII. Martin V had confirmed the Council on 25 July 1423 but never attended it himself throughout its duration: 21 July 1423–March 1424. See Noël Valois, *Le Pape et le concile (1418–1450),* 2 vols. (Paris: Librairie Alphonse Picard et Fils, 1909), I, 13–93.

5(I,93:13–19). For Poggius' letter of complaint to Guarinus, see *Poggii Epistolae,* Bk. II, ltr. 6 (I, 95–97). The whole story of Poggius' volume of Cicero's orations is given by Sabbadini in *Storia e critica,* pp. 44–49. Franciscus Barbarus kept the orations until 1436, when he returned them to Poggius with a letter of apology. See Sabbadini, *Centrotrenta lettere,* p. 84, *Epist.* 37.

6(I,93:27). There is no breviary listed in the inventory of Poggius' books at the time of his death. See Walser, *Poggius,* pp. 418–423.

7(I,94:3). See *A Catalogue of the Harleian Manuscripts in the British Museum,* Vol. III (London: Eyre and Strahan, 1808). Bibliothecae Harleianae Cod. 4868 (III, 213). "Ad finem, 'descripsit hoc opus Petrus Cenninus, idibus Maiis, anno salutis nostrae 1467. Indictione 15.'" This ms. contains a life of Pliny the Elder and works of Pliny the Younger.

See also Bandini, *Catal. cod. lat.,* Vol. II, cols. 105, 157, 280. See the inclusion of Petrus Cenninus in a group with Poggius and other literary men older than he, col. 213. See also Mehus, "Praefatio" in *Ambr. Trav. Epist.,* Vol. I, pp. iii, xxvi, lv. This is a doubtful identification because of the time span between Poggius' letter and Petrus Cenninus' known activities.

LETTER XXVI

1(I,94:5–6). Oportet enim paratum esse ad nutum. For *paratum esse ad nutum,* see Cicero *Phil.* 7.6.18.

2(I,94:5–8). It is clear from Valois' account of Martin V's vacillations in regard to the Council of Siena that Poggius must have been very busy during the autumn of 1423. See Valois, *Le Pape*, I, 27–41.

3(I,94:8–12). The Vatican Archives confirm this statement. *Reg. Vat.* 349, which contains the documents of the sixth year of Martin V's pontificate, credits Poggius with much less of the work than his friends Cincius de Rusticis and Bartholomaeus de Montepolitiano. In *Reg. Vat.* 350, the following year, Poggius and Cincius were responsible for approximately the same number of papal letters and proclamations, while Bartholomaeus wrote twice as many as either of them.

4(I,94:12). Poggius' favorite quotation at this time: Vergil *Georgics* 1.145.

5(I,94:14). Presumably Martin V.

6(I,94:20). Nicolaus de Medicis. The Quintilian may have been Cod. *Vat. Urb. Lat.* 327. See Sabbadini, *Storia e critica*, p. 384, and Ullman, *Origin and Development*, p. 52.

7(I,95:2). Ser Agnolo di Piero appears in the records of all Poggius' purchases of real estate near Florence in 1427–1429, according to documents preserved in the Florentine Archivio di Stato. He was a notary. See Walser, *Poggius*, pp. 338–343. He is mentioned in six subsequent letters from Poggius to Nicolaus.

8(I,95:5–6). According to Valois, *Le Pape*, I, 28, the very date of this letter had been set for the Pope's arrival in Siena.

9(I,95:9). For the deterioration of Florentine-Milanese relations in 1423, see Bayley, *War and Society*, pp. 84–85.

10(I,95:10). Perhaps Nellus Martinus Saminiatensis Jurisconsultus, one of the two Florentine ambassadors to the Duke of Milan in 1423. See Muratori, *R.I.S.*, Vol. XX, col. 326, note x. More probably: Ser Martino Martini, "Chief notary on legislation" (*notaio delle riformagioni*). See Lauro Martines, *Lawyers and Statecraft in Renaissance Florence* (Princeton: Princeton University Press, 1968), p. 156.

11(I,95:11–13). A clear account of Florentine taxes at this period is to be found in Gutkind, *Cosimo*, pp. 17–23.

LETTER XXVII

1(I,97:3). According to Poggius' *Historia Florentina*, Book V, Filippo Maria Visconti refused to admit the ambassadors sent by the Florentine government "Ducis iussu se adire prohibiti sunt: asserentis se, cum ex ea civitate, quae pestilentia laboraret, venirent nisi post quadragesimum diem eos non auditurum" ["He said that they came from a city which was suffering from the plague"].

2(I,97:6). Evidently Nicolaus de Niccolis kept his copy of the Ammianus Marcellinus and sent Poggius the original codex, found by Poggius in Fulda and now Cod. Vat. Lat. 1873 (see Sabbadini, *Scoperte*, II, 192). Nicolaus' copy is now in Florence: Cod. Nazionale Conv. Soppr. I. V.43 (San Marco 335); see Ullman, *Origin and Development*, p. 63, and Ullman-Stadter, *Public Library*, pp. 101, 221.

3(I,97:17–19). Laurentius de Ridolfis (1362–1443), a celebrated lawyer of the time (see Tonelli, I, 97, note 2). According to Vespasiano, *Vite*, pp. 379–382, Laurentius was "singularissimo dottore in iure civile e canonico"; therefore he was well qualified to solve Poggius' tax problem. See also Martines, *Lawyers and Statecraft*, p. 483 and *passim*.

4(I,98:2). The benefice was presumably Drokenesford in the diocese of Winchester, conferred on Poggius 16 February 1423 (see *Reg. Lat.* 231, f. 239v; also Walser, *Poggius*, pp. 77, 333–334).

5(I,98:8–9). Horace *De arte poetica* 78.

6(I,98:13). Vergil *Aeneid* 3.7.

7(I,98:21–25). It seems probable that Poggius is writing here of Laurentius Marci Benvenutus, who died of the plague in 1423. The invective Benvenutus wrote against Nicolaus de Niccolis in 1420 suggests that he also collected books and was interested in scholarship, perhaps even knew some Greek. See Zippel, "L'invettiva," pp. 166–186.

8(I,98:28). The text of Ptolemy's *Geography* was brought to Italy in 1397–1398 through the effort and generosity of Pallas de Strozzis. See Vespasiano, *Vite*, pp. 272, 540, and Georg Voigt, *Die Wiederbelebung des classischen Alterthums*, 2 vols., 4th edition (Berlin: De Gruyter, 1960), I, 225, note 2.

According to Sabbadini (*Scoperte*, I, 43–44), Jacobus Angelus de Scarperia accompanied Manuel Chrysoloras on his return to Constantinople in 1403. He had learned Greek from Chrysoloras and was directed by Coluccius Salutatus to bring home Plutarch's *De viris illustribus*. He translated a number of the lives as well as Ptolemy's *Cosmography* (Voigt, *Wiederbelebung*, II, 21). See also Cosenza, *Dictionary*, II, 1802–1803. Nicolaus de Niccolis is known to have owned a ms. of Ptolemy's *Geography* in Greek (Ullman-Stadter, *Public Library*, p. 74), but which of the two Greek mss. in San Marco it was, if either, is not certain (*Public Library*, p. 262, nos. 1188, 1189).

Cod. Naz. C.S.I,X,44 contains Plutarch's lives of Caesar and Alexander the Great in Latin in Nicolaus' hand, which came from his bequest to San Marco (*Public Library*, p. 223). The catalogue of San Marco also lists four mss. of Plutarch's *Lives* in Greek (nos. 1172–1175, p. 260), at least two of which belonged to Nicolaus.

Suetonius' *Lives of the Twelve Caesars* was known during the Middle

Ages. (See Sabbadini, *Scoperte*, II, 9, 34.) Petrarch owned a copy of Suetonius' *Caesars* and numerous other histories (see Sabbadini, *Scoperte*, I, 24).

9(I,99:1). Bibbiena, a hill town on the upper Arno in Tuscany, in the Casentino; in the early fifteenth century a dependency of the bishops of Arezzo. See *Toscana (non compresa Firenze)*, edited by L. V. Bertarelli (Milan: Guida d'Italia della Consociazione Turistica Italiana, 1935, 2nd edition), pp. 332–333. From a letter of Antonius Corbinellus to Guarinus Veronensis (*Epist. di Guar. Ver.*, Vol. I, p. 164, *Epist.* 88) it appears that Nicolaus had spent some time in Bibbiena during an earliér year, to avoid the plague. Sabbadini dated the letter 1417.

10(I,99:3–100:2). By this time Poggius must have realized that Martin V would not go to the Council of Siena; otherwise his invitation would have been less sincere than it sounds. His statements about the safe and peaceful conditions on the road and in Rome do not exactly match his account of 1423 in his *Historia Florentina:* pp. 204–213. It appears from Ambrosius Traversarius' letter to Nicolaus de Niccolis (Vol. II, *Epist.* VIII, 8, cols. 366–367) that Nicolaus did go to visit Poggius in Rome at this time.

See Poggius' account of the remains of ancient Rome in his *De varietate fortunae* I, begun, according to Walser (*Poggius*, p. 237), in 1429.

11(I,100:5–6). For Ciceronian orations which Poggius found at Cluny, see Letter XIV, note 5 (Tonelli Bk. I, ltr. 16; I, 68:21). The orations on paper mentioned here cannot be identified with any specific codex described by Bandini, Vol. II. The ms. of Cicero's orations on paper is not easy to identify. For the ms. of the orations which Poggius brought from Cluny in 1414, see Clark, *The Vetus Cluniacensis*. Sabbadini, in *Storia e critica*, pp. 45–46, gives an account of how the orations came into Franciscus Barbarus' hands.

12(I,100:11–14). The manager of the Medici Bank in Florence in 1423 was Folco d'Adoardo Portinari (ca. 1386–1431). See De Roover, *Rise and Decline*, pp. 49–50.

LETTER XXVIII

1(I,136:9–137:1). Tivoli was perhaps not so safe as it was believed to be or perhaps men who had contracted plague elsewhere developed it there and, like Cardinal Pisanus, in 1422, died there. See Letter VI, note 12, and Eubel, *Hierarchia*, I, 32. In connection with the plague in the time of Martin V, see Muratori, *R.I.S.*, Vol. III, pt. 2, col. 858, and Letter XV, note 10 (Tonelli Bk. I, ltr. 11; I, 47:15–22). Jordanus Columna, the Pope's brother, the Prince of Salerno, had recently died of the plague, as Poggius mentions in his letter to Antonius Luscus cited here

(Tonelli Bk. II, ltr. 13; I, 116:4). Martin V was highly praised by his biographer for his brotherly devotion and disregard of danger in hastening to his brother's bedside before his death (Muratori, Vol. III, pt. 2, cols. 867–868).

2(I,137:3). Modern: Rieti. See *Italia centrale: Guida breve*, II (Milan: Touring Club Italiano, 1952), 210–211. The town still contains a considerable number of monuments that Poggius would recognize. It is a long distance, fifty miles or more, through the Appenines from Tivoli. Poggius could not, during his two months there, do much to serve the Pope.

3(I,137:7–8). The letter to Petrus Donatus, Archbishop of Crete, is Tonelli Bk. II, ltr. 14 (I, 120–126), and the letter to Franciscus de Bolpanis (or Piccolpassus: see Eubel, *Hierarchia*, I, 97) is Tonelli Bk. II, ltr. 16 (I, 128–136). Petrus Donatus (1380–1447) had been an apostolic notary in the service, like Poggius, of John XXIII (Eubel, *Hierarchia*, I, 216). He had recently, at the time of Poggius' writing to him, been in charge of setting up a Church Council at Pavia (1423) which was moved to Siena (1424) because of the plague. See Giovanni degli Agostini, *Notizie istorico-critiche intorno la vita, e le opere degli scrittori viniziani*, 2 vols. (Venice: S. Occhi, 1752–1754), II, 140. Petrus Donatus was a friend of many humanists: Franciscus Barbarus, Guarinus Veronensis, *et al.* See Sabbadini, *Epist. di Guar. Ver.*, I, 52, 54, 180, 222, and *Centotrenta lettere*, pp. 17–18, 23, 38. See also Valois, *Le Pape*, I, 9, 13, 23, 67, 69.

4(I,137:8). Franciscus Piccolpassus (d. 1443) had just been appointed bishop of Dax, in France, in March 1423 (see Chevalier, *Bio-bibliographie*, Vol. II, col. 3663). He was extremely active in humanist scholarship and correspondence: see Cosenza, *Dictionary*, IV, 2832–2834. During his tenure at Dax, he acquired Cod. Ambrosianus L. 53 sup. (See Angelo Paredi, *La bibliotèca del Pizolpasso* [Istituto nazionale di Studi sul Rinascimento, Sezione Lombarda. Milan: Ulrico Hoepli, 1961], pp. 127–128), containing works of Seneca and Sallust (see also Remigio Sabbadini, "Storia e critica di alcuni testi latini," *Museo italiano di antichità classica*, III [1888–1890], 401–424). Poggius' letter fits Piccolpassus' interests very well. He quotes a long passage from Seneca and then dwells at length on Petrarch and his wisdom in withdrawing from political activity and court life, despite many honors, to a life of study and contemplation.

5(I,137:9–10). The letter to Antonius Luscus is Tonelli Bk. II, ltr. 13; I, 112–119. Luscus had been an apostolic secretary since 1406, with an interlude during the Council of Constance which lasted into 1421. Da Schio, *Loschi*, pp. 103–106. In 1423 or early in 1424, Antonius Luscus had been sent in vain by Martin V to try to persuade Philippus

Maria de Vicecomitibus to give up his belligerence. See Poggius, *Historia Florentina*, Book V (*Poggii Opera Omnia*, Vol. II), pp. 211–212.

6(I,137:19). Presumably Caecilius Statius (d. 168 B.C.), a Roman comic dramatist slightly older than Terence. See *OCD*, p. 187; *The Oxford Companion to Classical Literature*, Sir Paul Harvey, ed. (Oxford: Clarendon Press, 1962), p. 84.

See Chevalier, *Topo-bibliographie*, col. 805. The Cosentines were the inhabitants of Cosenza in Calabria.

7(I,137:19). Cicero *De finibus* 1.3.7.

8(I,137:23). On Nicolaus' visit to Rome, see Letter XXVII, note 10 (Tonelli Bk. II, ltr. 7; I, 99:5–100:4).

9(I,137:23–25). Terence *Phormio* 246.

10(I,137:28–31). See Poggius, *Historia Florentina*, Book V, on the missions and fighting of the year 1424 (*Opera Omnia*, Vol. II), pp. 214–224. Braccius de Montone was killed before Aquila, 5 June 1424.

11(I,138:6–12). For Poggius' brother, see Letter X, note 3 (Tonelli Bk. I, ltr. 10; I, 42:13–14).

12(I,138:13–15). On Poggius' mother, see Letter X (Tonelli Bk. I, ltr. 10; I, 42:13–14). She was Jacoba, daughter of Michaelle Frutti, and was married to Guccius Poggii about 1372. (See Walser, *Poggius*, pp. 5–6, 327.)

13(I,138:30–31). The use of the second person singular is no indication of intimacy in Poggius' correspondence. He used it regularly with his friends, as well as with dignitaries such as Pope Nicolaus V (Bk. XI, ltr. 2); Cardinal Beaufort (Bk. IX, ltr. 7); the Emperor Frederick III (Bk. XIII, ltr. 14); King Alphonsus of Aragon (Bk. IX, ltr. 6); Johannes Franciscus Gonzaga, Marquis of Mantua (Bk. VII, ltr. 1); and Prince Henry of Portugal (Bk. IX, ltr. 35). Ambrosius Traversarius also addressed all his single correspondents in the second person singular.

LETTER XXIX

1(I,145:4). Florentine statesman, 1350–1433 (Chevalier, *Bio-bibliographie*, Vol. II, col. 3356). At the end of his life, Nicolaus de Uzano was active in Florentine politics against the faction favoring the war with Lucca and the expulsion of the Medici. See Machiavelli, *History of Florence*, Book IV, chaps. 2, 3, 4, and 6, pp. 167, 170, 180, 191–193.

For his activities at the beginning of Poggius' career and especially in relation to Pope Gregory XII and the Council of Pisa, see Martines, *Lawyers and Statecraft*, pp. 237, 292–295, 320, 322, where he is also described as a merchant and diplomat. In the *catasto* of 1427, he was recorded as the wealthiest man in the S. Spirito quarter. See Martines, *Social World*, p. 375; on Nicolaus de Uzano's taxes, pp. 102–103, 215.

On what was for many years believed to be his appearance, see Horst W. Janson, *The Sculpture of Donatello* (Princeton: Princeton University Press, 1957), under "Rejected Attributions," I, 237–240.

2(I,145:6–12). Antonius Luscus had been partly responsible for the discovery of Salutatus' great ms. (Vercellensis) of Cicero's *Epistolae ad Familiares*. See Sabbadini, *Scoperte*, I, 34. It is now Cod. Laurentianus Plut. XLIX, 9. (See Bandini, Vol. II, cols. 465–468.) It is an eleventh century ms. that had belonged to Petrarch. See also Novati, *Epistolario di Coluccio Salutati*, Vol. II, pp. 336, 339–342, 390–391. Ullman, in his *Humanism of Coluccio Salutati*, p. 146, says that Cod. Laur. XLIX, 7 was copied for Salutatus in Milan in 1392 from Cod. Laur. XLIX, 9, which he says Salutatus did not own.

3(I,145:14). At the time of his death, Poggius owned a Lactantius bound in white leather (Walser, *Poggius*, p. 420, Inventory No. 32). On p. 108 (note 6), Walser calls attention to this letter and to the book Poggius owned but acknowledges that there may be no connection between them.

4(I,145:19–20). On the library of Coluccius Salutatus, see Ullman, *Humanism*, chap. 9, pp. 129–209. Ullman says (p. 137) that Nicolaus de Niccolis bought the major part of Salutatus' library after his death from his sons but had not finished paying for it at the time of his own death in 1437.

Cod. Laur. XLI, 10: Petrarch's *Canzoniere* belonged to Salutatus (Ullman, p. 145). Cod. Vat. Ottob. lat. 1883: Petrarch's *De viris illustribus* belonged to Salutatus (p. 193). Ullman rejected Cod. Laur. XXXIII, 35: Petrarch's *Africa* as having belonged to Salutatus (pp. 206, 208).

LETTER XXX

1(I,148:6). The church is probably S. Iacopo sopr' Arno, which dates from the twelfth century. It is close to the S. Spirito quarter. The remark about Nicolaus de Uzano's being poor is odd, since he was known to be one of the richest men in Florence (see Martines, *Social World*, p. 375).

2(I,148:10). The archbishop of Florence from 16 July 1411 until his death on 18 March 1435 was Aimericus de Corsinis, Archdeacon of Curavada, who had previously served at Bayeux. (See Eubel, *Hierarchia*, I, 251; II, 154.) On the Corsini, see Martines, *Social World*, pp. 221–229. See also Chevalier, *Bio-bibliographie*, Vol. I, col. 1053.

3(I,148:15–18). The Nicolaus who is mentioned twice without a surname in the same sentence must have been Nicolaus de Medicis. See Letter III, note 31 (Tonelli Bk. I, ltr. 1; I, 10:25).

4(I,148:19–22). Poggius found a text of Lucretius' *De rerum natura* at Fulda in 1417, which would fit the time mentioned in this letter. He later described it as imperfect "et item Lucretii partem." Sabbadini, *Scoperte*, I, 80, 82; II, 233. *Poggii Opera Omnia*, I, 394, from "disputatio . . . de infelicitate principum."

5(I,148:19–22). Poggius had sent a ms. of Nonius Marcellus which he found in Paris directly from there to Nicolaus de Niccolis while on his way to England. See Sabbadini, *Scoperte*, I, 83.

6(I,148:25–28). On the *De oratore, Orator,* and *Brutus,* see Ullman, *Origin and Development*, pp. 35–37; Poggius' ms. is now Cod. Laur. 50, 31.

7(I,149:7–13). This ms. is now Berlin, Hamilton 166. See Ullman, *Origin and Development*, pp. 27–30. See also Helmut Boese, *Die lateinischen Handschriften der Sammlung Hamilton zu Berlin* (Wiesbaden: Harrassowitz, 1966), pp. 87–88.

8(I,149:13–14). On the Livy, see Ullman, *Origin and Development*, pp. 45–48. There is no indication of the identity of this Lactantius ms. Ambrosius Traversarius (*Epist.* VIII, 2, col. 352) speaks of reading Lactantius' *De ira Dei*, which evidently belonged to Nicolaus. At least one ms. of Livy in the San Marco library (no. 822) is known to have belonged to Nicolaus de Niccolis (Ullman-Stadter, *Public Library*, p. 220). Nicolaus is known to have copied a text of Lactantius' *De ira Dei* and to have owned two others as well, one of which was read and annotated by Ambrosius Traversarius. See *Public Library*, p. 75.

9(I,149:17–19). In his account in *Humanism*, pp. 129–209, of Coluccius' library, Ullman lists no books which once belonged to Petrarch, though he lists a number of owners subsequent to Coluccius for many of the books. The friend who was seeking to buy books was doubtless Nicholas Bildeston; see Letter XLIII, note 3 (Tonelli Bk. II, ltr. 35; I, 170:10).

LETTER XXXI

1(I,149:7; 150:1). Nicolaus de Medicis.

2(I,150:3). In me tamen haec cuditur faba. This is a quotation from Terence. See "Istaec in me *cudetur faba*," Terence *Eun.* 381.

3(I,150:5). Poggius mentions the severe heat in August 1433 in Letter LXXXIX (Tonelli Bk. V, ltr. 8; II, 33:8–9).

4(I,150:7–12). Poggius had mentioned Cosmus' volume of Cicero's *Letters to Atticus* as well as the Lucretius and the Nonius Marcellus in his previous letter, written on the fourteenth of April. The Lucretius was copied by Nicolaus de Niccolis, and this copy is now Cod. Laur. 35, 30. See Ullman, *Origin and Development*, pp. 64–66. Poggius, not

Nicolaus, copied Cicero's Orations (the Philippics and the Catilinarians) in 1425 which survive in Cod. Laur. 48,22 (*Origin and Development*, p. 33). Poggius found the text of Silius Italicus' *Punica* in either Constance or Fulda in 1417 (Sabbadini, *Scoperte*, II, 252).

5(I,150:13). This is an unfair attack on Nicolaus, who was always ready, according to Vespasiano da Bisticci, to copy in his own "lettera corsiva o formata" any text that was needed (*Vite*, p. 474).

6(I,150:17). Maiorem in modum. For *in maiorem modum*, meaning "very much, greatly," see Cicero *Q. Fr.* 2.12.3. Coluccius Salutatus owned these letters, now Cod. Laur. 49.18. Poggius also saw a very fine text of them at Fulda in 1417 (Sabbadini, *Scoperte*, II, 213–214). Cod. Hamilton 166 in Berlin, copied by Poggius in 1408 from Coluccius' ms., contains *Ad Q. Fr.* I–III (Boese, *Sammlung Hamilton*, pp. 87–88).

7(I,150:21). Cosmus and Nicolaus de Medicis. All but four (Cod. Vat. Ottob. lat. 2035, Vat. Lat. 11458 and Madrid, Bibl. Nac. M 31, now Cod. 3678, and Bibl. Nac. X, 81, now Cod. 8511) of the mss. known or believed to have been copied by Poggius are on parchment. See Ullman, *Origin and Development*, pp. 27–51.

LETTER XXXII

1(I,151:2). Traversarius mentions Benvenuta several times in his correspondence with Nicolaus de Niccolis: *Epist.* VIII, 2, col. 354 "Benvenutam fidelissimam feminam meo nomine saluta"; VIII, 3, col. 358; VIII, 5, col. 362; VIII, 35, col. 394; VIII, 36, col. 397; VIII, 38, col. 401.

2(I,151:3). No help in Alessandro Chiapelli, "Della Vita di Filippo Brunelleschi attribuita ad Antonio Manetti . . .," *Archivio storico italiano*, Ser. 5, Vol. XVII (1896), pp. 241–278. All that is said of the prior when Brunelleschi began work on San Lorenzo early in the 1420s is "Cosi medesimamente murandosi la chiesa di S. Lorenzo di Firenze principato per i popolani di quella, e fattone capo maestro el Priore della chiesa che vi era in quei tempi," in relation to the hiring of Brunelleschi as architect (pp. 267–268).

See also Antonio di Tuccio Manetti, *The Life of Brunelleschi*, translated by Catherine Enggass, edited by Howard Saalman (University Park: Pennsylvania State University Press, 1970), pp. 102–109.

3(I,151:10–152:5). The Florentines were defeated by the army of the Duke of Milan near Zagonara, where they were attempting to relieve their ally, Count Alberigo. See Poggius, *Historia Florentina*, Book V (*Poggii Opera Omnia*, II, 224), and Machiavelli, *History of Florence*, pp. 163–164, See also Baron, *Crisis*, pp. 374–384 and notes, pp. 544–

546 for a modern examination of the popular views of the period. There is also a reference to the disastrous defeat and the loss to the Florentines of the services of Nicolò Piccinino as their general in Leonardus Brunus Aretinus' *La historia universale de suoi tempi,* with additions by Francesco Sansovino (Venice, n.d.), pp. 227–228.

4(I,151:17–19). A quotation of a fragment from Euripides, quoted in ancient times: *Putnam's Quotations,* col. 476 a. For an account of Nicolaus' ms. of eight plays of Euripides which had belonged to Boccaccio, see Ullman-Stadter, *Public Library,* pp. 62, 82, 90–92. It is not listed in the San Marco catalogue but is catalogued in the Laurentiana as having been San Marco 226 (*Public Library,* p. 120).

5(I,151:20). tantam vecordiam inesse iis. For a similar thought, see "*tanta vecordia* innata cuiquam," Terence *Andr.* 626.

6(I,151:26). ad punienda peccata nostra. See *peccata punimus,* Cicero *Inv.* 2.22.66. Sabbadini says that the *De inventione* was commonly known among the humanists (*Scoperte,* II, 209).

7(I,151:28). post plagam inflictam. For *plagam infligere,* see Cicero, *Vatin.* 8.20: mortiferam *plagam infligere.* On Cicero's oration against Vatinius, see Letter XVI, note 8 (Tonelli Bk. I, ltr. 12; I, 59:18).

8(I,152:7). Vergil *Aeneid* 3.395.

LETTER XXXIII

1(I,152:2, 18). Bartholomeus de Bardis (ca. 1397–1429) was made head of the Rome branch of the Medici Bank very young, in the early 1420s (De Roover, *Rise and Decline,* p. 49). For some of his responsibilities, see pp. 90, 198, 203–211. See also Lunt, *Financial Relations,* p. 203. Bartholomeus de Bardis also appears in Poggius' *Facetiae,* as do many of his acquaintances. See *The Facetiae or Jocose Tales of Poggio,* 2 vols. (Paris: Liseux, 1879), I, 40–42.

2(I,152:12). There is evidence that Nicolaus bought and sold books for profit. See Martines, *Social World,* p. 116.

3(I,152:14–15). The text of Suetonius, *De XII Caesaribus,* was well known during the Middle Ages (Sabbadini, *Scoperte,* II, 253–254). So were the comedies of Terence (p. 255). Quintus Curtius Rufus' *History of Alexander the Great* was not rare, but was less common than the other two (p. 218).

4(I,152:16). Perhaps Piero di Antonio di Piero di Antonio Parigi, cartolaio, who was born 1403 and died between 1443 and 1450, a stationer like his father. See Mirella Lévi d'Ancona, *Miniatura e miniatori a Firenze dal XIV al XVI secolo: Documenti per la storia della miniatura* (Florence: Leo S. Olschki, 1962), pp. 223–224.

LETTER XXXIV

1(I,153:7–10). The orations are not among the texts listed by Ullman as having been copied by scribes and having belonged to Poggius (*Origin and Development*, pp. 49–51).

2(I,153:19–20, 154:12–14). See Clark, *Vetus Cluniacensis*, pp. i–v.

3(I,153:21–22). For Nicolaus de Medicis' activities in the early 1420s, see Partner, *Papal State*, p. 122, note 3, and p. 123, note 4. Ambrosius Traversarius comments on Cosmus de Medicis' activities in Rome "de re nostra . . . cum summo Pontifice" of which he had learned from Nicolaus de Niccolis during Nicolaus' visit to Rome in 1424. His comment suggests that Cosmus was in frequent communication with the Curia (*Epist.* VIII, 8; col. 367).

4(I,154:14). The abbot of Monte Cassino at this time was Pirro Tomacelli of Naples, who had been appointed in 1414, imprisoned in 1422, released in 1427, and was deposed and excommunicated in 1437. See *Dizionario di erudizione storico-ecclesiastico*, Vol. 46, p. 179.

LETTER XXXV

1(I,155:3). in exequendis mandatis meis. For *exsequi mandata*, see Cicero *Phil.* 9.4.9. Poggius copied the *Philippics* in November–December 1425 (Ullman, *Origin and Development*, p. 33). Salutatus' text was probably incomplete (Ullman, *Humanism*, pp. 222–223).

2(I,155:17). See Ullman's analysis of Poggius' copying of the *Verrines* (*Origin and Development*, pp. 37–40), which he identifies as Florence, Cod. Riccardianus 499. See also Walser, *Poggius*, p. 418 (Inventory No. 3 and p. 104, note 3).

3(I,155:18). For a discussion of Cod. Ricc. 504 and other possibilities, see Ullman, *Origin and Development*, pp. 41–42. Walser, *Poggius*, pp. 418–419, records two copies of the *De finibus*, one in Inventory No. 1 with other Ciceronian texts, and the other alone: Inventory No. 12, bound in green leather. There is no identification by Ullman or Walser of a ms. of the *Tusculan Disputations* in Poggius' hand.

4(I,155:19). Ullman identifies Cod. Laur. 49, 24 as the copy of Cicero's *Letters to Atticus*, which Poggius made in 1425 (*Origin and Development*, pp. 43–45). A ms. of this text was in Poggius' library at the time of his death: see Inventory No. 6 (Walser, *Poggius*, p. 418).

5(I,156:4). On various maneuvers concerning Rinucius, Nicolaus de Niccolis, Ambrosius Traversarius, and Franciscus Barbarus, see Franciscus Barbarus, *Diatriaba praeliminaris*, pt. 1, chap. 4, Sec. 7, pp. clxxx–clxxxv. See also Ambrosius Traversarius, *Epist.* VIII, 22, col. 382; VIII, 28, col. 385. Rinucius was one of Poggius' intimate friends and one of the guests at his fiftieth birthday party. On Rinucius and his friendship with Poggius, see Dean Putnam Lockwood, "De Rinucio Aretino Graecarum Litterarum Interprete," *Harvard Studies in Classical Philology*, XXIV (1913), 51–109. For his dedications to Poggius, see pp. 52, 84–86.

Rinucius translated many Greek works, including Plato's *Crito* but not the *Gorgias*, which was translated into Latin by Leonardus Brunus Aretinus in 1409. See Vittorio Rossi, ed., *Il Quattrocento*, Storia Letteraria d'Italia, Vol. V (Milan: Vallardi, 1933), p. 94. Rinucius dedicated his translation of the *Decreta Atheniensia* to Poggius. This was a section of Demosthenes' oration *De corona*. Rinucius later, in 1434, dedicated to Poggius his translation of a selection of letters of Diogenes, Hippocrates, and Euripides. (See Lockwood, "De Rinucio," p. 52.)

6(I,156:6, 15). Antonius Corbinellus (ca. 1377–1425): see Martines, *Social World*, pp. 319–320 and *passim*. He was a very distinguished humanist who was often mentioned in the correspondence of Franciscus Barbarus, Guarinus, and Traversarius. See Cosenza, *Dictionary*, II, 1096–1097. There is further corroborative information about him in Rosmini, *Vita di Guarino*, II, 56–59, 174. See especially p. 59 for Antonius Corbinellus' residence in Rome to avoid frequent Florentine tax levies. See also Letter XXXVII, note 4.

7(I,156:10–11). in quo fons est irriguus. For *irriguus fons*, see Vergil *Georg.* 4.32.

8(I,156:11). On Numa Pompilius, the second King of Rome, and the nymph Egeria, See *Plutarch's Lives*, Langhorne, trans., I, 153–154.

9(I,156:18). Tonelli (note 1) refers to Ammirato, *Storie fiorentine*, Lib. XIX. See also Poggius, *Historia Florentina*, Book V (*Poggii Opera Omnia*, Vol. II), p. 231. Tonelli used Poggius' reference to the Florentine victory over the Ligurians as corroboration of the date 1425.

LETTER XXXVI

1(I,157:10, 14–15). For an account of Cosmus de Medicis' love of books and his responsible attitude toward his own and other people's, as well as his generosity with his own books, see Ullman-Stadter, *Public Library*, pp. 3–5, 12–17, 19–27, 60–61, and throughout the San Marco catalogue, pp. 125–248 (Latin mss.).

2(I,157:26). Poggius had been agitating from May 12 (Letter XXXI; Tonelli Bk. II, ltr. 23: I, 149) to July 7 (for dates, see Charles E. Bennett, *A New Latin Grammar*, 2nd edition [New York: Allyn and Bacon, 1963]), p. 247, about Nicolaus Mediceus' dilatory habits but not always about the same book.

3(I,158:9). Poggius had mentioned Rinucius' departure for Florence in Letter XXXV (Tonelli Bk. II, ltr. 27; I, 156:4–5), dated June 23, two weeks earlier than this letter. Cosenza (*Dictionary,* IV, 3060) refers to Rinucius' trip to Florence in 1424 in the service of Cardinal Gabriel Condulmerius, who was at that time Papal Legate in Bologna.

4(I,158:14). Not the "Ser Loisio" for whom Poggius prepared his second collection of letters. See the dedicatory epistle, Tonelli, I, xi–xii, where he is identified as the Archbishop of Florence, whom Tonelli thought to be Ludovicus Scarampus. There is no confirming evidence.

LETTER XXXVII

1(I,158:3–7). On Poggius' Florentine citizenship and consequent tax payments, see Walser, *Poggius,* Documents 7, 8, 15; pp. 327–328, 330–331. On taxes, see Gutkind, *Cosimo,* pp. 17–34; for Cosmus de Medicis' connection with them, see p. 31, note 1, and pp. 31–32, See also Bayley, *War and Society,* pp. 86–90, and Machiavelli, *History of Florence,* Book IV, chap 3, pp. 172–174.

2(I,158:9). Vespasiano da Bisticci, in his life of Nicolaus de Niccolis (*Vite,* p. 474), reports that Nicolaus heard of a complete text of Pliny at Lübeck in Germany and arranged with Cosmus de Medicis to import it to Florence, which was accomplished. Only a fragmentary text had hitherto been known. The imported text of the *Historia Naturalis* may now be Cod. Laur. 82, 1 and 2, according to Sabbadini (*Scoperte,* II, 241).

The Bishop of Winchester's Pliny cannot be identified, despite much research and many inquiries. Poggius does not indicate what text the volume contained, which would be helpful. It is known from Cardinal Beaufort's will, which is preserved in the archiepiscopal registry at Lambeth Palace: "Registr. Stafford and Kemp, fol. III a.b. 112 a.b. 113 a.b." that he left legacies of money and plate to the "Colleges of the Blessed Mary at Eton near Windsor and of Saint Nicholas of Canterbury." There is no mention of books. See [John Nichols], *A collection of all the wills, now known to be extant, of the Kings and Queens of England, Princes and Princesses of Wales, and every branch of the Blood Royal, from the reign of William the Conqueror, to that of Henry the Seventh Exclusive* (London: J. Nichols, Printer to the Society of Antiquaries, 1780), pp. 321–341.

There is no Pliny that can be ascribed to Beaufort in the catalogues of either library compiled by Montague Rhodes James. See *A Descriptive Catalogue of the Manuscripts in the Library of Eton College* (Cambridge: Cambridge University Press, 1895) and *The Ancient Libraries of Canterbury and Dover* (Cambridge: Cambridge University Press, 1903).

There is a tantalizing note in the Harvard copy of the Tonelli edition of *Poggii Epistolae* in the margin of Vol. I, p. 158, in the handwriting of Niccolò Anziani, director of the Biblioteca Laurenziana in 1878 and owner of the set of three volumes, which says: "Plinio del vescovo vintonense ora Laur." but with no number. No ms. from the library of Cardinal Beaufort is identified by Bandini or by Ullman and Stadter. Perhaps Anziani was thinking of Cod. Laur. 81, 1 and 2.

3(I,159:5). See Mallett, *Florentine Galleys,* pp. 38–39.

4(I,159:11–29). See Rudolf Blum, *La biblioteca della badia fiorentina e i codici di Antonio Corbinelli,* Studi e testi, 155 (Città del Vaticano: Biblioteca Apostolica Vaticana, 1951). For Antonius Corbinellus' life and relationships with other humanists, see chap. 5, pp. 39–47. On the development of his library, see chap. 6, pp. 48–55. There is a review of this book by Curt F. Buhler in *Speculum,* XXVI, No. 4 (October 1951), 707–709.

5(I,159:15). Matthaeus de Bardis was a member of the Florentine banking family in Rome. See Martines, *Social World,* p. 320, and De Roover, *Rise and Decline,* p. 208. Many members of the Bardi family, including Matthaeus' sons, are included in the property list for the S. Spirito quarter, made for the *catasto* of 1427, but not Matthaeus himself; see Martines, *Social World,* pp. 375–378, especially No. 59. Matthaeus was also a captain of the Guelf party, allied with the Albizzi and hostile to the Medici in the early 1430s. See Bayley, *War and Society,* p. 144.

6(I,159:14). The *Palatium Apostolicum* was restored by Martin V, see Ferdinand Gregorovius, *History of the City of Rome in the Middle Ages,* translated from the fourth German edition by Annie Hamilton, Vol. VII (1421–1496) (London: George Bell & Sons, 1900), pt. 2, p. 660. For Nicolaus V's plan for a new Borgo and palace, see pp. 666–671.

7(I,159:15–29). Medical treatment killed Antonius Corbinellus. This should be compared with the opening of Poggius' *Utra artium medicinae an iuris civilis praestent, secunda convivialis disceptatio,* in *Poggii Opera Omnia,* I, 37, written, according to Walser, *Poggius,* pp. 248–258, in 1450. See Blum, *Biblioteca,* pp. 44–46. See also Guarinus' two letters mourning the death of Antonius Corbinellus and praising him (*Epist.* 327–328; *Epist. di Guar. Ver.,* I, 484–487).

8(I,159:21). expectans eventum. For *expectare eventum,* see Caesar *B.G.* 7.49 fin.

9(I,159:29). For an analysis of Poggius' plan to copy the *Verrines* and the *Philippics,* see Ullman, *Origin and Development,* pp. 37–40 and his discussion of Cod. Ricc. 499, copied by Poggius.

10(I,160:11). Poggius mentions this secretary in his *Liber facetiarum* No. 98. See *The Facetiae,* I, 152–154.

LETTER XXXVIII

1(I,160:3–10). See Lockwood, *Ugo Benzi,* pp. 144–145, and Lynn Thorndike, *Science and Thought in the Fifteenth Century* (New York: Hafner Publishing Co., 1963), p. 43.

2(I,160:11–13). Poggius' sources of information on Epicurus probably were Cicero, Plutarch, Lucretius, and Diogenes Laertius (see Sabbadini, *Scoperte,* I, 49–50).

3(I,161:2–12, 16). See Arturo Castiglioni, *A History of Medicine,* translated and edited by E. B. Krumbhaar, second revised edition (New York: Alfred A. Knopf, 1947), pp. 364–407, esp. pp. 365–366, p. 381 (cupping), p. 382 (diet, laxatives). See also George Sarton, *Introduction to the History of Science,* Vol. III, pt. 2: *Science and Learning in the Fourteenth Century* (Baltimore: Williams & Williams Company, 1948), pp. 1234–1247 (eye diseases, diets, baths, Papal physicians, etc.).

4(I,161:24). Ser Loisio is mentioned also in Letter XXXVI (Tonelli Bk. II, ltr. 28; I, 158:13). Martines *(Lawyers and Statecraft)* mentions no one in his long list of lawyers, which includes Poggius and Leonardus Brunus Aretinus, to whom this name belongs.

LETTER XXXIX

1(I,162:4–5). volo omnem moerorem te deponere. See *deponere maerorem* atque luctum, Cicero *Phil.* 14.13.34. On the *Philippics,* see Letter XXXV, note 1; Tonelli Bk. II, ltr. 27 (I, 155:3).

2(I,162:12–13). See *Ambr. Trav. Epist.* VIII, 12, col. 376, where Ambrosius tells Nicolaus de Niccolis that Antonius Corbinellus "antequam magistratum suum intret" asked Ambrosius to try to arrange an exchange of texts between him and Nicolaus. See also Mehus, "Vita Ambrosii," p. ccclxxxiii, where he quotes a considerable section of Antonius Corbinellus' will, made in 1424, leaving his books to Jacobus Nicolai de Corbiziis and upon his death to "the monks, chapter, and monastery of St. Mary, the Florentine Abbey of the Order of St. Benedict" or Badia Fiorentina. The books were still there in 1759, when Mehus published his life of Ambrosius Traversarius.

Ambrosius Traversarius in a letter to Franciscus Barbarus (VI, 12, cols. 289–290) mentions Antonius Corbinellus' long illness and slow recovery. See also the note on the same page describing Guarinus' grief at Antonius' death.

In his "Praefatio," p. xx, Mehus refers to Vespasiano da Bisticci's life of Pallas de Strozzis, where Antonius is listed among the pupils of Manuel Chrysoloras during his teaching in Florence. Mehus repeats this information in his "Vita Ambrosii," p. ccclx.

3(I,162:20–22). Cicero *Att.* 1.10.4.3–4. See *The Correspondence of M. Tullius Cicero*, Robert Y. Tyrrell and Louis C. Purser, eds., Vol. I, Dublin University Press Series, 3rd edition (Dublin: Hodges, Figgis & Co., Ltd., 1904), p. 138.

4(I,163:1–2). Vergil *Aeneid* 7.609–610.

5(I,163:6). Sentio enim aetatem ingravescentem. For *ingravescens aetas*, see Cicero *De sen.* 2.6. This text, according to Sabbadini (*Scoperte*, II, 212), was "molto divulgata." It is impossible to identify the ms. Poggius knew in 1425. His volume of the *Opere tuliane*, including the *De senectute*, is No. 1 of his inventory (Walser, *Poggius*, p. 418).

6(I,163:6–7). Vergil *Georgics* 3.67.

7(I,163:17–18). Poggius' mother may have been preparing to visit him. Walser prints a safe conduct issued to her the following summer: dated 9 June 1426 (*Poggius*, pp. 337–338, Doc. 23).

LETTER XL

1(I,163:2–6). See Blum, *Biblioteca*, pp. 15–18, on the intellectual level of the Badia at the time of Corbinellus' bequest. His library contained about 200 Latin mss. and 80 Greek ones (p. 18). For authors and titles, see pp. 74–79, 88–94. "105 of his Latin mss. and 65 of the Greek contained works of classical authors" (p. 97). On the Greek mss. see pp. 102–105. On the value assigned to the Greek mss. see p. 65 and Appendix IV, pp. 183–184.

2(I,164:4–11). The tragedies of Seneca were, as Sabbadini says (*Scoperte*, I, 23), "alla portata di tutti" even before the time of Petrarch. Poggius' fourteenth century ms. is now Cod. Laur. 37, 11, bound in red leather. See Walser, *Poggius*, p. 420 Inventory No. 22; see also p. 106, note 3.

Either Bartholomeus de Montepolitiano, who had been Poggius' companion during the search for mss. in St. Gall in 1416, or more probably Bartholomeus de Bardis is meant here. See Letter XXXIII (Tonelli Bk. II, ltr. 25; I, 152). Cosmus de Medicis was, according to Vespasiano da Bisticci, always ready to assist any project connected with books and learning (*Vite*, pp. 255–256, 258, 263–267).

Nicolaus de Medicis was at this time also connected with his family's banking enterprise.

At the time of his death, Poggius owned a text of Lactantius (Walser, *Poggius*, p. 420, No. 32; see also p. 108, note 6).

3(I,164:18). If Poggius here means the text of the works of Sulpitius Severus (d. ca. A.D. 425), they were not well known or highly regarded in the early fifteenth century. Bandini records a fifteenth century ms. of some of them in the Biblioteca Laurentiana: Plut. LXXXIX inf. cod.

XXVII, Vol. III, cols. 390–391, "ab aquis pluvialibus maculatus" ["damaged by rain spots"]. See also Sandys, *History*, I, 247. According to Sabbadini, Gregorius Corrarius found a text during his service at the Council of Basel (*Scoperte*, I, 119).

4(I,164:20). Poggius mentions Cardinal Branda Castellioneus several times in connection with Monte Cassino: Letter LXXIII (Tonelli Bk. III, ltr. 37); Letter LXXXIII (Tonelli Bk. IV, ltr. 11). For his life, see Ciacconius, *Vitae*, Vol. II, cols. 801–803. Branda de Castillione (1350–1443), Bishop of Placentia, 1404–1411, was a very important figure at the Papal court, according to Vespasiano (*Vite*, pp. 118–120). He was promoted to Cardinal tit. S. Clementis on 6 June 1411. He founded a library open to all literary men in Lombardy and, Vespasiano says: "Fu molto vôlto a prestar favori agli uomini dotti."

5(I,104:24). Identified by Tonelli (p. 164, note 1) as possibly Angelottus Fuscus Romanus, later Cardinal tit. S. Marci, with whom Poggius and Ambrosius Traversarius had some correspondence: see *Poggii Epistolae* Bk. IV, ltr. 23; I, 352–364, a letter of congratulation and moral warning, dated by Tonelli 8 October 1431 and *Ambr. Trav. Epist.*, II, 13. See also Shepherd, *Vita di Poggio*, I, 186–189. The references collected by Shepherd about Angelottus are far from complimentary, though Poggius' letter purports to be admiring. See also Ciacconius, *Vitae*, Vol. II, col. 895.

6(I,164:25–29). See Walser, *Poggius*, p. 101, note 5, and Sabbadini, *Scoperte*, I, 110–111.

LETTER XLI

1(I,165:14). Bartholomeus de Montepolitiano's financial condition and attitude are confirmed both by his remarks in Poggius' *De avaritia* and by Leonardus Brunus Aretinus' disagreeable letter about his extravagant tomb (*Epistolae*, VI, 5; pt. 2, pp. 45–48). See also Pope-Hennessy, *Italian Renaissance Sculpture*, pp. 290–291 and plates 39 and 40. See also Cosenza, *Dictionary*, I, 439–440, and Sabbadini, *Scoperte*, I, 49–50, 76–80; II, 203, 252.

But Poggius could just as well be referring here to Bartholomeus de Bardis, whom he calls *pecuniosus* in Letter XXXIII; Tonelli Bk. II, ltr. 25 (I, 152: 18).

LETTER XLII

1(I,166:2). *Sodo* here means dense. See Garzanti, *Comprehensive Italian-English, English-Italian Dictionary*, Mario Hazon, ed. (New

York: McGraw-Hill Book Co., Inc., 1961), p. 875. *Marochiuto* probably stands for *malochiuto:* evil-eyed or cross-eyed.

2(I,166:8). Presumably Seneca's *Tragedies;* see Walser, *Poggius,* p. 106, especially note 3, and p. 420 (Inventory No. 22). See also Bandini, Vol. II, col. 251.

3(I,166:15). Terence *Eun.* 415.

4(I,166:19). For other references to the moon in Capricorn, see Letter XXV (Tonelli Bk. II, ltr. 4; I, 91:8–9) and Letter XLVII (Tonelli Bk. III, ltr. 1; I, 188:5).

5(I,167:2). opinari aliquid. For *opinari aliquid,* see Cicero *Mur.* 30.62. The *Pro Murena* was new to the humanists in 1415, when Bartholomeus de Montepolitiano and Poggius saw Cod. Cluniacensis 496, now lost, in Constance. Bartholomeus copied large sections of the ms., after which Poggius sent it to Florence. See Sabbadini, *Scoperte,* II, 72–74, 211.

6(I,167:14). On Aelius Spartianus, see "Historia Augusta," *Oxford Companion to Classical Literature,* p. 210. Two handsome mss. of the text which belonged to Petrus de Medicis are recorded by Bandini, Vol. II, cols. 704 and 805. Poggius still owned a text of Aelius Spartianus when he died; see Walser, *Poggius,* p. 420, Inventory No. 30, and p. 106, note 4.

7(I,167:16). On Justinus see *Oxford Companion,* pp. 232–233, and Sabbadini, *Scoperte,* II, 227 and *passim.* Cosmus de Medicis owned a ms. of the *Epitome* written for him by Joannes Aretinus (Tortellius?); see Bandini, Vol. II, cols. 787–789.

8(I,167:17–19). In the inventory made at the time of Poggius' death, No. 12 is the *De finibus,* Nos. 29, 30, 36, 46, 48, 49, 50 are all historical texts and Nos. 19–21 and probably No. 22 are mss. of various works of Seneca.

9(I,168:1). According to Sabbadini, *Scoperte,* I, 101, 104, II, 235, Martial's *Epigrams* had been known to a few literary men beginning with Richard de Bury, a century earlier; an ancient codex containing the text had lately been found by Bartholomeus Capra. Ullman and Stadter (*Public Library,* p. 87) credit Nicolaus with owning the Martial ms. in *litteris longobardis,* which was No. 947 of the San Marco catalogue and is now lost (p. 236). Poggius quoted Martial twice in his letters to Nicolaus, in Letter I and in Letter LXVII; both quotations are "quicquid in buccam ven[er]it," *Epigr.* 12.24.5.

10(I,168:4–7). Perhaps Poggius was using the text which had belonged to Leonardus Brunus Aretinus since 1407; see Sabbadini, *Scoperte,* I, 75: II, 210.

11(I,168:8). On Poggius' friend, the monk from Hersfeld, see Walser, *Poggius,* p. 101, note 7, and Sabbadini, *Scoperte,* I, 107–109.

12(I,168:14). Joannes Andreae (1275–1348) was an Italian canonist of high reputation during the fifteenth century, during which sixty-four editions of his various works, including four editions of his two *Novellae*, were printed. (See Hain, *Repertorium*, Vol. I, Nos. 1018–1082.)

13(I,168:14–15, 22). Because of the bulk which Poggius mentions, it seems probable that he is referring to the *Speculum Maius* of Vincent of Beauvais (ca. 1190–ca. 1264). See Jacobus Quétif and Jacobus Echard, *Scriptores Ordinis Praedicatorum*, 2 vols., Burt Franklin Bibliographical and Reference Series, No. 16 (New York: Burt Franklin, 1959, a reprint of the Paris edition, 1719–1723), Vol. I, pt. 1, pp. 212–240. An indication of the rarity of Vincent of Beauvais' great work in the fifteenth century is the rarity of printed editions. It is not listed by Hain but only by Copinger in his *Supplement to Hain's Repertorium Bibliographicum*, Vol. II, 2 (Milan: Görlich, 1950), Nos. 6241–6257.

See also Frederick R. Goff, *Incunabula in American Libraries: A Third Census of Fifteenth Century Books Recorded in North American Collections* (New York: Bibliographical Society of America, 1964), nos. V-277–V-294.

14(I,168:26–29). On the list of desiderata, see Sabbadini, *Scoperte*, I, 107–109, and "Notizie storico-critiche di alcuni codici latini," *Studi italiani di filologia classica*, VII (1899), 125–129.

15(I,169:2). On Nicolaus de Medicis, who is mentioned by Poggius as the owner of this text and of the *De oratore, Brutus*, and *Orator*, see Letter XXIII (Tonelli Bk. II, ltr. 2; I, 88:29). In Letter XLVIII (Tonelli Bk. III, ltr. 5; I, 195:20) Poggius asks for his own autograph text of Caesar's *Gallic* and *Civil Wars*, now belonging to Nicolaus de Medicis. The Biblioteca Laurenziana owns a text of Leonardus Brunus Aretinus' translation of certain orations of Demosthenes and Aeschines (Plut. LXXXII, cod. 8), dedicated to Nicolaus de Medicis (Vol. III, col. 192), as well as Plut. LXXXX, cod. 61 (Vol. III, col. 643). See also Ludwig Bertalot's articles on Leonardus Brunus.

LETTER XLIII

1(I,169:10). Antium is the ancient name for Anzio, but that is much too far from Rome for Poggius to have lived there. It is possible that Poggius knew the identification of the Roman tribe of Antium with that of Quirina and was thereby indicating that he lived on the Quirinal Hill. See Lily Ross Taylor, *The Voting Districts of the Roman Republic: The Thirty-Five Urban and Rural Tribes* (American Academy in Rome, Papers and Monographs, Vol. XX, 1960), pp. 319–321.

See Gregory Martin, *Roma Sancta* (1581), George Bruner Parks, ed.

(Rome: Edizioni di Storia e Letteratura, 1969), Plate 2, Antoine Lafrery, "Le Sette Chiese di Roma," 1575; and Plate 3, Pirro Ligorio's map of the monuments of ancient Rome, 1552. In the first life of Martin V given by Muratori (*R.I.S.*, Vol. III, pt. 2, col. 859) is the statement: "Martinus . . . miserabiliter in Palatio apud Sanctos Apostolos vixit" ["Martin lived wretchedly in his palace near the Church of the SS. Apostoli"]; but perhaps that was later in his reign. According to *Roma e dintorni*, p. 257, the present Palazzo Colonna, built in 1730, is on the property which has belonged to the family since Martin V; it is "adjacent" to the SS. Apostoli, on the lower slope of the Quirinal.

2(I,169,14–18). For Rinucius' knowledge of Greek, see Cosenza, *Dictionary*, IV, 3056–3060.

3(I,170:10). Poggius wrote a delightful letter to Nicolaus Bildeston, in 1436, about his bride, Vaggia de Bondelmontis. For Nicolaus in his official and scholarly capacities, see Weiss, *Humanism in England*, p. 19; Josephine Waters Bennett, "Andrew Holes: A Neglected Harbinger of the English Renaissance," *Speculum*, XIX, No. 3 (1944), 331–332; and *Register of Henry Chichele*, I, xlii.

4(I,170:14–18). See Pierre de Nolhac, *Pétrarque et l'humanisme* (Turin: Bottega d'Erasmo, 1959), Chap. II: "Les livres de Pétrarque après sa mort," pp. 87–123. See also p. 270 with ref. to Novati, *Epistolario di Coluccio Salutati*, Vol. IV, p. 126 sqq.

5(I,170:17–18). Poggius is referring to Ammianus Marcellinus, *De imperatoribus*, which, according to Ullman, *Origin and Development*, p. 63, Nicolaus had finished copying in 1423. Poggius had found the text at Fulda in 1417. See Poggius, Letter XXVII (Tonelli Bk. II, ltr. 7; I, 97:6).

LETTER XLIV

1(I,171:23). Foedus ictum. For *foedus icere*, see Cicero *Pis.* 12.28; *Balb.* 15.34. The *Pro Balbo* was in the ms. discovered by Leonardus Brunus in 1407 or 1408 (Sabbadini, *Scoperte*, I, 75; II, 210). The *In Pisonem* was discovered by Poggius in the summer of 1417 in Germany (*Scoperte*, I, 81–82, 84; II, 191–192).

2(I,171:23–172:6). For Poggius' own account of the Florentine attempts to obtain a peace treaty and of their disappointments, see his *Historia Florentina* V (*Opera Omnia*, II, 226–231). See also Baron, *Crisis*, pp. 387–393.

3(I,172:6–173:4–7). Nicolaus' friend was Antonius Gentilis Siculus, to whom Poggius wrote (Tonelli Bk. II, ltr. 37; I, 173–174) a formal letter of goodwill. There is a certain amount of historical material recorded about the humanist Antonius Siculus whose surname was

Cassarinus but none on Antonius *Gentilis* Siculus. See Cosenza, *Dictonary*, I, 919. See also Gianvito Resta, ed., *L'epistolario del Panormita: Studi per una edizione critica*, Università degli Studi di Messina, Facultà di lettere e filosofia, 3 (Messina, 1954), p. 189.

4(I,172:24). See Machiavelli, *History of Florence*, Book IV, chap. 1–2, pp. 158–169.

5(I,172:29–30). Probably not Demosthenes but Xenophon, *Memorabilia* 2.1.31. (See Putnam's *Quotations*, 472b.)

6(I,173:1 and note 1). Tonelli dates this letter 1425 because Poggius mentions the treaty recently made between the Florentines and the Venetians, which was signed on the fourth of December of that year. He refers to Ammirato, *Storie fiorentine*, Lib. 19.

LETTER XLV

1(I,174:3). Poggius' trip to England must have been connected with his friend Nicholas Bildeston's mission to Martin V as "king's orator"; see Weiss, *Humanism*, p. 19. Perhaps Poggius was to be sent to England with or instead of Julianus Caesarinus, auditor of the Camera, whom Martin V sent as nuncio on 5 April 1426 to dispel the trouble which had developed between the papal collector, Simon de Teramo, and Humphrey, Duke of Gloucester; see Lunt, *Financial Relations*, pp. 420–425. See also Walser, *Poggius*, Document 22, pp. 336–337.

2(I,174:7–175:2, 15–16). For Nicolaus de Medicis' position at this time, see De Roover, *Rise and Decline*, pp. 37, 204.

3(I,175:3–8). For Poggius' taxes under the *catasto* of 1427, see Walser, *Poggius*, pp. 140 and 339–341 (Document 27). See also the clear analysis of the *catasto*, its cause and effect in Molho, *Florentine Public Finances*, pp. 79–87. For an analysis of the *catasto* of 1427, see also De Roover, *Rise and Decline*, pp. 23–26, and Machiavelli, *History of Florence*, Book IV, chap. 3, pp. 172–174. Neither text states, as Poggius does, that the *catasto* would last only one year, but De Roover indicates that it was subject to revision each time it was levied.

4(I,175:10). In Letter XV (Bk. I, ltr. 11; I, 49:2) Poggius very firmly contradicted the impression that he had become a priest, although he did indeed hold two benefices (see Walser, *Poggius*, pp. 333–335 [Documents 18–19]).

5(I,175:19). Nicolaus de Niccolis' plea to the officials of the 1430 *catasto* to reduce his tax is preserved. See Martines, *Social World*, p. 116 and note 104. For the officials of the *catasto* in 1427, see Otto Karmin, *La legge del catasto fiorentino del 1427* (Florence: Bernardo Seeber, 1906). There is a list of *catasto* officials on p. 11, note 1, and a different one on p. 41. None of the men listed were Poggius' friends.

6(I,175:20–23). Rinaldus de Albizis (1370–1442, according to Cosenza, *Dictionary*, I, 97; 1452, according to Chevalier, *Bio-bibliographie*, I, 120) was a leading Florentine statesman who promoted the war waged by the Florentines against Milan. The *catasto* was a consequence of the expense of the war, and this was patriotically recognized by the Medici, who were Poggius' usual patrons and protectors. (See Machiavelli, *History of Florence*, Book IV, chaps. 2–3, pp. 164–175.) Rinaldus was forced to support the *catasto*, which he and the other oligarchs would ordinarily have opposed, because of his warlike posture (see Schevill, *History of Florence*, pp. 345–346). Rinaldus belonged to the faction which imprisoned Cosmus de Medicis in 1433 and drove him into exile. On Cosmus' return in 1434, he was exiled in his turn and never readmitted to Florence. He died in Ancona. See Cosenza, *Dictionary*, I, 97, for bibliography. Poggius is perhaps referring here to Rinaldus' normal opposition to a tax like the *catasto*.

7(I,176:1). Poggius has previously asked Nicolaus for works of Seneca. He also asked Leonardus Brunus Aretinus if he did not possess "a certain volume of the works of Seneca which used to belong to our Coluccius, the father shared by all scholarly men" (Tonelli Bk. II, ltr. 39; I, 176–177). Poggius again reminded Nicolaus to urge Leonardus to send him the volume of Seneca in Letter XLVIII (Tonelli Bk. III, ltr. 5; I, 195:16–17). See also Ullman, *Humanism*, for works of Seneca, pp. 150, 166, 169–170, 171 (this ms. belonged to Nicolaus de Niccolis), p. 197. See also Poggius' direct request for this work to Leonardus Brunus Aretinus himself in *Poggii Epistolae* Bk. II, ltr. 39 (Tonelli, I, 179). See Ullman, *Humanism*, p. 136. For books from Coluccius' library that belonged to Leonardus, see p. 147 (Cicero), pp. 195–196 (Pliny). On Coluccius' use of the works of Seneca which he owned, see pp. 250–251.

LETTER XLVI

1(I,85:5–6). Nicolaus de Niccolis must have been an effective speaker in discussions, since he is so often one of the speakers in his friends' dialogues: Poggius, *An seni uxor sit ducenda;* Poggius, *De infelicitate principum;* Poggius, *De nobilitate;* Leonardus Brunus Aretinus, *Dialogi ad Petrum Histrum.* Laurentius Valla also made Nicolaus a speaker in his dialogue, *De voluptate* or *De vero bono*, at least in one version of it (see Girolamo Mancini, *Vita di Lorenzo Valla* [Florence: G. C. Sansoni, 1891], pp. 48–49).

Nicolaus also appears as a speaker in a dialogue by Johannes Arretinus Physicus, identified by Bandini as Johannes Lippius Arretinus, a friend of Laurentius de Medicis and Hieronymus Aliottus. The dialogue

294 Notes: Letter XLVI

is *De medicinae et legum praestantia* (see Bandini, *Catal. cod. lat.*, Vol. III, cols. 141–143, Plut. 77, cod. 22). Johannes Aretinus' dialogue was published by Eugenio Garin in *La disputa delle arti nel Quattrocento: Testi editi ed inediti* (Florence: Vallechi, 1947), pp. 36–101, in Latin and Italian.

2(I,85:7–8). Vergil *Aeneid* 1.409.

3(I,85:8; 86:9). Ambrosius Traversarius seems to refer to Nicolaus de Niccolis' too short trip to Rome and to Cosmus de Medicis' activities there at the same time in his *Epist.* VIII, 8, written on the twenty-fifth of May, which agrees with Poggius' reference to the recent severe winter.

4(I,85:5–86:32). Nicolaus de Niccolis' trip to Rome is corroborated by letters to him from Ambrosius Traversarius, Vol. II, VIII, 1, 3, 4, 5, 6, 8. See also Remigio Sabbadini, *Guarino Veronese e gli archetipi di Celso e Plauto* (Livorno: Raffaello Giusti, 1886), pp. 1–11, where he dates and puts the letters in a different order:

Sabbadini   I: Mehus VIII, 4
Sabbadini   II: Mehus VIII, 5
Sabbadini   III: Mehus VIII, 6
Sabbadini   IV: Mehus VIII, 3
Sabbadini VIII: Mehus VIII, 1
Sabbadini   IX: Mehus VIII, 8

Sabbadini changed the year given by Mehus, 1432, to 1424 and dates all the other letters 1423–1424. The same letters appear in Martène and Durand, *Amplissima Collectio*, III, 486–516, with no year given.

There seems to be no reason to doubt that Nicolaus made a visit to Rome in 1424, with Cosmus de Medicis. Letter XXVII (Tonelli Bk. II, ltr. 7; I, 97–100) testifies to that. The question is whether Nicolaus ever made a second visit to Rome, to which this letter (XLVI) is a pressing invitation but belongs, because of its reference to the Jubilee, to a later year.

5(I,85:11). asperitas hiemis. See ob *asperitatem hiemis*, Tacitus *Annales* 4.56.

6(I,86:3–5). According to Zippel, *Nicolò Niccoli*, p. 38, Benvenuta went to Rome with Nicolaus de Niccolis in 1424.

7(I,86:6–7). omnia sunt parata. See "omne paratum est," Plautus *Men.* 2.3.13; see Cicero *Verr.* 2.4.27, paragraph 62. Leonardus Brunus had had the complete text of the *Verrines* since 1407 (see Sabbadini, *Scoperte*, I, 75; II, 210). Plautus' *Menaechmi* was not known until Nicolaus Cusanus brought the Codex containing twelve lost comedies of Plautus to Cardinal de Ursinis in 1429. See Sabbadini, *Scoperte*, II, 17, 241, and Ullman, *Origin and Development*, pp. 50–51.

8(I,86:11). A mule would be a suitably modest means of transportation for a scholar, a horse luxurious. Vespasiano da Bisticci says of

Cardinal Branda, "Teneva alcune mule non molte in casa; cavalli no," *Vite*, p. 119.

9(I,86:13–14). in utramvis aurem licet dormire. See the idiom, *in utramvis* or in dextram *aurem dormire*, "to sleep soundly." Terence *Heaut.* 342.

10(I,86:15–19). According to Ciacconius, *Vitae*, II, 818, Martin V celebrated a Jubilee year in Rome 1425, amidst a vast throng of visitors.

11(I,86:22). Many of Nicolaus' circle had recently died of plague: Cardinal Pisanus in September 1422 (see Eubel, *Hierarchia*, I, 32) and Lorenzo di Marco Benvenuti in 1423 (see Zippel, "L'invettiva," pp. 166–186).

12(I,86:27). fac periculum. See *fac periculum* in litteris, Terence *Eun.* 476.

13(I,87:4). This letter presents serious complications in the date. It is *Epist.* 21 in Cod. Riccard. 759, ff. 18v–19r, where it is clearly dated "Rome XII Februarii 1423." This is the ms. text which Tonelli followed, as he indicated in note 3 on p. 10. This manuscript sometimes records other dates incorrectly, notably the date of Poggius' account of his fiftieth birthday, given on f. 29v as 1420. The real question hinges on whether Martin V proclaimed a Jubilee and in what year. No proclamation of such a celebration survives in the Papal registers, according to Pastor, *History of the Popes*, I, 232, who used this letter of Poggius' as evidence that the Jubilee was "proclaimed for the year 1423." Walser also accepted this evidence (*Poggius*, pp. 84–85), and Fubini did not alter the date printed by Tonelli. See *Poggii Opera Omnia*, IV, 733. Tonelli has a long note on p. 87 expressing doubt and some evidence against the date 1423. It should be noted that Poggius' letter is also dated February 12 and that he says in it that the Jubilee is over, which consequently would put the Jubilee in 1422 if the letter were correctly dated 1423. In Appendix 17, Vol. I, pp. 393–394, Pastor discusses the arguments in favor of 1423 or 1425 as the date of the Jubilee, if one accepts the fact that there was one. It seems to me that 1425 is by far the more likely date. Martin V's most dangerous enemy, Braccius de Montone, had died in June 1424, leaving the roads to Rome safe for pilgrims. Martin had had a little time to repair the city and to assure the stability of his government. If, therefore, his Jubilee took place in 1425 and was over by the time Poggius wrote this invitation to Nicolaus to make a second visit to him in Rome, the letter should be dated 1426.

LETTER XLVII

1(I,186:4). Probably Rocca di Papa (see *Roma e dintorni*, p. 659), which in 1425 became a possession of the Columna family to which Martin V belonged.

2(I,186:11–12). Terence *Adelphi* 98–99.

3(I,187:4). Vespasiano da Bisticci says of Nicolaus: "Avendo messo in libri tutto quello che aveva potuto, le sua sustanze non gli bastavano a poter vivere parcissimamente" (*Vite*, p. 475), which is why he probably criticized Poggius' expenditures.

4(I,187:10). This must be a reference to Nicolaus' visit to Rome in 1424.

5(I,187:19–20). On the formation of Niccoli's library, see Ullman-Stadter, *Public Library*, pp. 89–104.

6(I,87:23). On the text of Aulus Gellius' *Noctes Atticae* and Nicolaus de Niccolis' copy of it, see Sabbadini, *Scoperte*, I, 92; II, 225–226.

7(I,187:26). Poggius begged repeatedly and vainly for the return of the Lucretius he had discovered in 1417, perhaps in Fulda (Sabbadini, *Scoperte*, II, 233).

8(I,187:30–32). According to Sabbadini, the text of Caesar's *Commentaries* was not widely known in the early fifteenth century (*Scoperte*, II, 208). The ms. mentioned in Poggius' letter is not one which has survived.

9(I,188:4). Coluccius Salutatus had owned a ms. of Cato's *De agricultura* (see Sabbadini, *Scoperte*, I, 34; II, 206), but it has not survived (Ullman, *Humanism*, p. 222). Sabbadini speculates on which ms. of Varro's *De re rustica* Poggius could have been seeking from Nicolaus (*Scoperte*, I, 87; II, 257–258). Nicolaus also owned a volume containing both agricultural works. See Ullman-Stadter, *Public Library*, pp. 74 and 217 (no. 794).

LETTER XLVIII

1(I,192:2). Poggius mentioned Bartholomeus de Bardis often at this period in his letters to Nicolaus and also to other friends, e.g., in Tonelli Bk. II, ltr. 8 (I, 103:12) to Leonardus Brunus Aretinus and in Tonelli Bk. II, ltr. 19 (I, 144:18) to Petrus Donatus, Episcopus Castellanus.

2(I,192:4). Tonelli printed this letter between two letters addressed to Leonardus Brunus, one on September 28 and one (though obviously written later) on September 26 [1426]. In the earlier letter, Bk. III, ltr. 4, Poggius spoke of his earnest desire and Franciscus Barbarus' constant effort to accomplish a reconciliation between Leonardus and Nicolaus. Their quarrel was first mentioned in a letter from Poggius to Nicolaus from London, 17 December [1420], Letter XVI, Tonelli Bk. I, ltr. 12; I, 60:16–17.

3(I,192:7–13). Tonelli Bk. II, ltr. 11 (I, 108–110) is largely devoted by Poggius to an effort to reconcile Leonardus, to whom it is addressed, with Nicolaus. In his letter (Tonelli Bk. II, ltr. 41; I, 178–180) to Leonardus, Poggius again mentions the importance both he and Franciscus Barbarus attach to such a reconciliation.

4(I,192:14). Poggius wrote to Franciscus Barbarus on the same day, 26 September [1426], as he had written to Leonardus, to thank him enthusiastically for accomplishing the reconciliation (Tonelli Bk. III, ltr. 7; I, 197–199). See also Gothein, *Francesco Barbaro*, pp. 110–121.

5(I,193:9). Terence *Andria* 555.

6(I,193:13–15). Epistle of James 1.22.

7(I,193:15). See note 13 on Letter II; Tonelli, I, xv:6.

8(I,193:17–18). vel diffidere prudentiae tuae. For *diffidere prudentiae tuae*, see Cicero *Fam.* 4.5.6.

9(I,194:2). For Poggius' earlier, adverse comment on the English interest in banquets, see Letter XI (Tonelli Bk. I, ltr. 13; I, 61:31–62:3).

10(I,194:4). On Zucharus, see Tonelli, I, 101, note 1, and p. 194, note 1. In his note (p. 194) Tonelli says that, according to the *Facetiae,* Zucharus was the most amusing and worldly man imaginable and that, once he had sold his family property, he used up his whole inheritance in feasting and gambling. See *Poggii Opera Omnia,* I, 424 and 458. He is mentioned in a letter to Petrus Donatus (Tonelli Bk. II, ltr. 14; I, 124:20–22) and in a letter to Julianus Caesarinus (Tonelli Bk. VI, ltr. 2; II, 80:26) both times in connection with his interest in food. In a letter to Franciscus Barbarus (Tonelli Bk. III, ltr. 26; I, 262:6) Poggius mentions Zucharus' fondness for women.

11(I,194:6–7). omnibus aliis rebus posthabitis. For *omnibus rebus posthabitis,* "neglecting everything," see Cicero *Tusc.* 5.1.2.

12(I,194:7). Gnatho is a character, the parasite, in Terence's *Eunuchus.* Poggius here refers to 255–264.

13(I,194:11). fructum studiorum suorum. For *fructus studiorum,* see Quint. 8, praef., paragraph 26.

14(I,194:14–15). vel exercendi ingenii causa. For *exercere ingenium,* see Quint. 2.4.20.

15(I,194:15–195:10). Poggius mentions Nicolaus' severity and irritability in his funeral oration (*Opera Omnia,* I, 271 and 275) and also occasionally in his letters, e.g., to Leonardus Brunus Aretinus (Bk. II, ltr. 11; I, 109), and to Nicolaus himself, Letter VII (Tonelli Bk. I, ltr. 7; I, 36:15–23), Letter IX (Tonelli Bk. I, ltr. 9; I, 41:5–23), and Letter XXV (Tonelli Bk. II, ltr. 4; I, 91:1–93;7).

16(I,194:21). nullam servans legem. For *servare legem,* see Cicero *Fam.* 2.17.2.

17(I,194:25–26). a teneris, ut aiunt, unguiculis: *a teneris unguiculis* is a translation of the Greek ἐξ ἁπαλῶν ὀνόχων. See Cicero *Fam.* 1.6.2.

18(I,195:5). Erras tota via. For *errare via,* see Vergil *Aen.* 2.731.

19(I,195:14). On the text of Cornelius Tacitus, see Walser, *Poggius*, p. 107, note 7, where Nicolaus' Tacitus is identified as Cod. Mediceus II, found by Boccaccio at Monte Cassino. See Bandini, Vol. II, cols. 834–836 (Plut. LXVIII, Cod. 2).

20(I,195:15). On both the Spartianus and the Seneca that belonged to Leonardus Brunus Aretinus, see Tonelli Bk. II, ltr. 39; I, 176–177, to Leonardus.

LETTER XLIX

1(I,207:3). On the monk from Hersfeld, see Sabbadini, *Scoperte*, I, 106–109. On Nicolaus' list of desiderata, see his "Commentarium," published by Sabbadini, *Storia e critica*, pp. 1–7.

2(I,207:14). At this time Nicolaus apparently already owned a text of some of the works of Tacitus. See Letter XLVIII, note 19, (Tonelli Bk. III, ltr. 5; I, 195:14). This may have been Cod. Med. Laur. LXVIII, 2 (Bandini, *Catal. cod. lat.*, Vol. II, col. 834).

3(I,208:5). In Letter XXVII (Tonelli Bk. II, ltr. 7; I, 97:6, 16) Poggius praises Nicolaus for having finished copying the *Res Gestae* of Ammianus Marcellinus. According to Sabbadini, *Scoperte*, II, 200–201, Poggius acquired two mss. of Ammianus Marcellinus from the monastery of Fulda during his stay at Constance; one of these is now Cod. Vat. Lat. 1873. "Another ms. was discovered at Hersfeld in 1427."

Nicolaus already had at least some of the text of Livy and was copying it; see Letter XXX, note 8 (Tonelli Bk. II, ltr. 22; I, 149:14). Poggius had already discovered, acquired, and copied numerous orations of Cicero by this time; it is not clear in this letter what orations he hoped to receive from Hersfeld. He had already lent one ms. of Cicero's orations to Franciscus Barbarus, who was very dilatory about returning it. See Ullman, *Origin and Development*, pp. 33–35, 37–40.

4(I,208:11). Some two years earlier, in 1425, Poggius and the monk of Hersfeld were already arranging shipments of books, via Nuremberg.

5(I,208:16). qui me a teneris unguiculis nosti. For *a teneris unguiculis*, see Cicero *Fam.* 1.6.2. See Letter XLVIII, note 17 (Tonelli, I, 194:25–26).

6(I,208:22–23). On Bartholomeus de Aragazzis de Montepolitiano's research activities, mostly in Poggius' company, see Sabbadini, *Scoperte*, I, 49–50, 76–80. The reason Bartholomeus was seeking another Lucretius for his friends is unclear. The ms. which Poggius discovered and copied while at Constance was closely and selfishly retained by Nicolaus.

7(I,203:28–29). Nicolaus Treverensis was the celebrated scholar and philosopher Nicolaus Cusanus (1401–1464). See Chevalier, *Bio-biblio-*

graphie, Vol. II, cols. 3328–3330. See also Cosenza, *Dictionary*, III, 2450–2455, and Ludwig Pralle, *Die Wiederentdeckung des Tacitus: Ein Beitrag zur Geistesgeschichte Fuldas und zur Biographie des jungen Cusanus. Quellen und Abhandlungen zur Geschichte der Abtei und der Diözese Fulda XVII* (Fulda: Parzeller & Co., 1952), pp. 65–101.

On the discoveries of Nicolaus of Trier, especially in the Cathedral library at Cologne, and on the exaggerated hopes and expectations of his Italian scholarly friends, see Paolo Rotta, *Il Cardinale Nicolò di Cusa*, Publicazioni della Università cattolica del Sacro Cuore, Serie Prima, Vol. XII (Milan: Società Editrice "Vita e Pensiero," 1928).

On Nicolaus Cusanus and the humanists' knowledge of Pliny, the Elder and the Younger, see Sabbadini, *Scoperte*, II, 16–27, 241–243.

The supposed *De republica* turned out to be merely Macrobius' commentary on the *Somnium Scipionis*. See Rotta, *Nicolò di Cusa*, p. 18.

8(I,209:12–13). According to William R. Shepherd, *Historical Atlas*, 4th edition (New York: Henry Holt and Co., 1927), pp. 98–99, there was, during the Middle Ages, a regular commercial land route that led from Frankfurt, via Nuremberg and the Brenner Pass, to Venice.

9(I,209:15–24). According to Sabbadini, *Scoperte*, II, 246, Propertius was known in France earlier in the fourteenth century than in Italy. The text was acquired by Petrarch and owned by Salutatus. It was known to Antonius Luscus and to Antonius Beccadellius Panormita. This is the first time it is mentioned by Poggius.

10(I,209:24). in domo casta. For *casta domus*, see Catullus 64.385. Salutatus owned Cod. Vat. Ottob. 1829 and perhaps Paris: Bibl. Nat. 14137. See Sabbadini, *Scoperte*, II, 207, and Ullman, *Humanism*, pp. 192–193, 196, 222.

11(I,209:26–31). The fragmentary text of Valerius Flaccus' *Argonautica* was one of the discoveries made by Poggius and Bartholomeus de Montepolitiano at St. Gall in 1416. See Sabbadini, *Scoperte*, II, 257. See also Poggius' announcement of the discovery to Guarinus from Constance in December 1416 (Tonelli Bk. I, ltr. 5; I, 29:12–13). Poggius announced his discovery of Asconius Pedianus' commentaries on eight of Cicero's orations in the same letter; see Sabbadini, *Scoperte*, II, 202–203. For the letter to Guarinus, see Appendix, Letter III.

12(I,209:27). Poggius refers to Varro's *De agricultura* in Letter XLVII (Tonelli Bk. III, ltr. 1; I, 188:4), but it is unclear whether here he is referring to that text or to the *De lingua latina*.

13(I,209:29). On the ruin and destruction of Rome in this time, see Poggius, *Historia de varietate fortunae*, Bk. I (*Opera Omnia*, II, 503–541).

14(I,210:2–6). See Russell Meiggs, *Roman Ostia* (Oxford: Clarendon

Press, 1960). He mentions Poggius' visit (p. 103) but does not attempt
to identify the sarcophagus which Poggius saw (see pp. 469–470). For
the inscription on the sarcophagus at Ostia, see Ludovicus Antonius
Muratori, *Novus Thesaurus Veterum Inscriptionum,* Vols. I, II (Milan:
Ex Aedibus Palatinis, 1740), perhaps Vol. II, p. mlxvi, No. 1 or No. 2.
For the inscriptions at Tivoli, see *Novus Thesaurus:* Vol. I, p. cxc,
No. 7; p. cxci, No. 1; p. dxxiii, No. 6; Vol. II, p. cmlxxiv, No. 2; p. mlxxxvi,
Nos. 3, 4, 5. Poggius might mean one of these or none of them.

15(I,210:6–11). On Cosmus' office and responsibilities, see Nicolai
Rubinstein, *The Government of Florence under the Medici: 1434–1494,*
Oxford-Warburg Studies (Oxford: Clarendon Press, 1966), pp. 48–52.
On the war against Milan and Lucca in 1427, see Poggius, *Hist. Flor.*
(*Opera Omnia,* Vol. II), pp. 247–253. On Cosmus' stay in Rome, see
Gutkind, *Cosimo,* p. 251, under 1426. For an explanation of Cosmus'
responsibilities, see Schevill, *History of Florence,* pp. 342, 351.

16(I,210:12). Tonelli, in his note 1, dates this letter 1427, because
Poggius mentions his excursion with Cosmus de Medicis to see the port
of Ostia as a recent event. "Cosmus was in Rome at the beginning of the
year and stayed for several months, according to Ammirato, *Storie
fiorentine,* lib. 19, and Fabronius, *Vita Cosmi,* p. 15."

17(I,210:14). Carolus Marsuppinus Aretinus, humanist, scholar, and
poet (1399–1453) was succeeded by Poggius as Chancellor of Florence.
See Chevalier, *Bio-bibliographie,* Vol. II, col. 3094, and Cosenza,
Dictionary, I, 268–271. See also Tonelli's note 2 (I, 213).

LETTER L

1(I,210:5). Poggius was constantly hoping and searching for the
missing Decades of Livy. Decades I, III, and IV were known to Poggius
and had been known during the Middle Ages, but the humanists were
constantly seeking additional texts, mostly in vain. See Sabbadini,
Scoperte, II, 231–233.

2(I,211:6–7). Nuremberg is mentioned repeatedly as a shipping point
in the letters. On its commercial and political importance, see *CMH,*
VIII, 143–144: "The Close of the Middle Ages."

Nicolaus of Trier was in Rome in 1425 as a layman and again visited
Rome in holy orders from May to September 1427. See Rotta, *Nicolò
di Cusa,* pp. 12–18.

3(I,211:12). This is undoubtedly a deliberate pun on the republican
government and the *De republica.*

4(I,211:16). Ullman and Stadter believe that the Propertius listed
as Cod. 922 in the San Marco catalogue came from Nicolaus' library
(*Public Library,* pp. 87, 234).

LETTER LI

1(I,212:4). Comessatio. See *Thesaurus Linguae Latinae*, III, 1788, "Comissatio a comedendo satis" = "Luxuria convivia."

2(I,212:8). Laurentius de Medicis (1395–1440), son of Johannes Bicci de Medicis and brother of Cosmus, was a friend of many of the humanists. He seems to have been a particular friend of Poggius' at this time. In 1429, Poggius entrusted the text of his *De avaritia* to Laurentius de Medicis to deliver to Nicolaus de Niccolis. See De Roover, *Rise and Decline*, p. 385. See also Cosenza, *Dictionary*, III, 2272. Franciscus Barbarus dedicated his *De re uxoria* to Laurentius de Medicis. See Letter III, note 32.

3(I,212:11–12). "If you didn't gorge or guzzle so, you wouldn't be in such a rush for the nozzle."

4(I,212:20). On the whole question of Poggius, Nicolaus de Niccolis, and the lost texts of Tacitus, see P. Hochart, *De l'authenticité des annales et des histoires de Tacite* (Bordeaux: Imprimerie G. Gounouilhou, 1889). See also Sabbadini, *Scoperte*, II, 254. For a modern and scholarly approach to the matter, including the order and dating of Poggius' letters on the subject, see Pralle, *Wiederentdeckung*.

5(I,212:25). cum commodum erit. See *Cum erit* tuum *commodum*, "when it shall be convenient for you," Cicero *Att.* 12.28.3.

6(I,212:26). Paulus de Marganis was, like Poggius, a *scriptor apostolicus*. His name appears frequently in the registers of the Roman years of Martin V's reign, not in the earlier years of Constance or Florence. See *Reg. Vat.* 349, 350, 352, 353, 355. It often appears on documents in conjunction with Cincius' and twice with Poggius' (*Reg. Vat.* 350: f. 200v. "anno octavo" [1425]).

7(I,213:2). All that is left of this is Books XXI–XXV. See *OCD*, pp. 614–615.

8(I,213:4). It is impossible to identify Marinus among all the Marini listed by Kristeller in his *Iter.*

9(I,213:4). It is not clear what text of Varro Poggius was copying; both were known at this time, more or less complete. See Sabbadini, *Scoperte*, II, 257–258. In September, 1426, Poggius asked Nicolaus de Niccolis to send him Varro's *De agricultura*. (*Scoperte*, I, 87.)

10(I,213:6). See Ullman, *Origin and Development*, pp. 45–47.

LETTER LII

1(I,213:2). For Poggius' autograph copy of Seneca's *Epistles*: Cod. Vat. Lat. 2208, see Ullman, *Origin and Development*, pp. 40–41. It may have been No. 19 in the inventory of his library (Walser, *Poggius*, p. 419). In Bandini, Vol. II, col. 252, the twelfth century ms. of Seneca's

Tragedies (Plut. XXXVII, Cod. XIII) belonged to Nicolaus de Niccolis. See Ullman-Stadter, *Public Library*, p. 232, No. 912.

2(I,213:2–6). Bandini describes Vol. II, cols 834–835 (Plut. LXVIII, Cod. II), the volume as containing (ff. 1–104v) "Cornelii Taciti ab excessu Divi Augusti Libros XI. ab undecimo nimirum usque ad vigesimum primum" and says it is "codex membranacceus ms. in fol. Saec. XI charactere Longobardico conscriptus" and bears the notation ". . . Conventus S. Marci de Florentia Ordinis Praedicatorum de hereditate Nicolai Nicoli Florentini viri doctissimi." Bandini says nothing here about Boccaccio and Monte Cassino; Sabbadini, in *Scoperte*, I, 29–30, identifies this ms. with both. It does, however, fit the description in Poggius' letter. See also Cornelia C. Coulter, "Boccaccio and the Cassinese Manuscripts of the Laurentian Library," *Classical Philology*, XLIII (October 1948), 217–230.

The evidence of Coluccius' letters indicates that the Tacitus was not his. See Novati, ed., *Epistolario di Coluccio Salutati*, Vol. II, p. 297; Vol. III, pp. 81–82. Perhaps Poggius was thinking of the ms. of *Annales* XI–XVI and *Historiae* I–V, taken by Boccaccio from Monte Cassino and now Cod. Laur. 68.2. See Sabbadini, *Scoperte*, I, 29–30; II, 254.

3(I,214:3). si volueris nervos intendere. See digna res est ubi tu *nervos intendas* tuos, Terence *Eun.* 312.

4(I,214:4–5). The moon should be in the Ram in January. (I am grateful to Richard Korn, an amateur astronomer in New York, for this information.)

On Poggius' copying of Seneca's *Epistles*, see Ullman, *Origin and Development*, pp. 40–41; on Seneca's *Tragedies*, p. 49; on Tacitus, p. 46. In an earlier letter, XXV (Bk. II, ltr. 4; I, 91:8–9 of II, 4), Poggius says: "nisi luna ascendisset Capricornum" ["unless the moon had risen in Capricorn"]. There must have been a significance attached to the position of the moon in relation to the signs of the Zodiac.

5(I,214:9). Ullman tentatively identified the Livy with Codices Vat. Lat. 1843, 1849, 1852 (*Origin and Development*, pp. 45–47).

6(I,214:10). There is no other mention anywhere of a trip taken by Nicolaus de Niccolis to Siena. Zippel gives evidence for Nicolaus' trips to Rome, 1424, and to Verona and Venice, 1430–1431 (*Nicolò Niccoli*, p. 38).

7(I,214:12–14). For Nicolaus de Niccolis' financial condition at this time, see Martines, *Social World*, p. 115. Nicolaus was more prosperous,, apparently, in 1427 than later (see Ullman-Stadter, *Public Library*, pp. 292–299, for his two wills and p. 90 for his financial decline and the sale of his famous ancient jewel). It was in 1427 that Coluccius Salutatus' son Arrigo "declared to the *catasto* that Nicolaus still owed him 100 florins for books bought in 1406 from Coluccius' library" (*Public Library*, p. 98, and Novati, *Epistolario*, Vol. IV, pt. 2, p. 544).

8(I,214:18–22). According to Vespasiano, Nicolaus was an enthusiastic collector of antiquities of all sorts, including marble heads (*Vite*, p. 476). Mehus, in his life of Nicolaus in *Ambr. Trav. Epist.*, Vol. I (p. li), also mentioned Nicolaus' love of ancient art, as recorded by Bartholomaeus Facius in his *De viris illustribus* (edited by Mehus) (Florence: Joannes Paulus Giovannellus, 1745), p. 11.

9(I,214:23). The "academia" must have been the house Poggius bought on 18 April 1427 in Terranuova. See Walser, *Poggius*, Doc. 24, p. 338.

LETTER LIII

1(Wilmanns, pp. 305–306; 305:6). Poggius is probably speaking here of his mss. of Livy. See Ullman, *Origin and Development*, pp. 45–48, which deals largely with the Livy in Poggius' hand: Codices Vat. Lat. 1843, 1849, 1852.

2(305:9–10). See Walser, *Poggius*, p. 420, Poggius' inventory No. 23 "in uno vol. copertum corio rubeo."

3(305:10). scriptorem rudis ingenii. For *Rudis ingenium*, see Horace *Ars Poet.* 410. See Walser, *Poggius*, p. 421, inventory No. 42.

4(305:12). Vereor ne litus arem. For the proverbial phrase *litus arare*, "to bestow useless labor," see Ovid *Heroides* 5.116; *Tristia* 5.4.48; see Juvenal 7.49. The works of Ovid and Juvenal do not appear in Poggius' inventory. Coluccius Salutatus had owned a volume of Ovid's *Heroides*, now in New York (Pierpont Morgan 810). The texts of these works were easily available in the fifteenth century. Bandini lists nineteen texts of Juvenal in the Bibliotheca Laurenziana (Vol. II, cols. 146, 153–159), four of Ovid's *Heroides* (Vol. II, cols. 237–238), and two of his *Tristia* (Vol. II, cols. 228, 239).

5(305:12). This is probably Cod. Laur. 63, 26. See Ullman, *Origin and Development*, p. 50. It belonged to the Medici and does not appear in Poggius' inventory.

6(305:16). Leonardus Brunus Aretinus (see Letter II, note 22) succeeded Paolo Fortini as Chancellor of Florence on 27 November 1427. He was elected provisionally then and definitely on 10 December 1427. See Leonardus Brunus Aretinus, *Epistolae* V, 8. See also Poggius' letter of congratulation and sympathy, in Guglielmo Shepherd, *Vita di Poggio*, 2 vols. (Florence: Gaspero Ricci, 1825), I, 148, note b. For a complete account see Marzi, *Cancelleria*, pp. 190–191.

7(305–306). See Flavius Blondus, *Roma instaurata* (Basel: Froben, 1531), p. 222. In his dedication to Eugenius IV, Blondus admits the current state of dilapidation in Rome but still sees the city as the center of spiritual and intellectual life. In dedicating his book to the Pope, many years after Poggius wrote Letter LIII, Blondus echoed his feelings and at the same time urged the Pope to return Rome to her former physical glory.

8(306:6–7). Poggius was probably thinking of St. Jerome, *Epist.* 125.20, "Satis dives qui pane non indiget," and Cicero *Paradoxa* 6.1, [Dives est] "cui tanta possessio est ut . . . nihil optet amplius."

9(306:10). frenumque inieci. For *frenum inicere*, see Cicero *Phil.* 13.9.20. Wilmanns proposed the date 1427 for this letter. Poggius had copied the *Philippics* "in the last two months of 1425." See Ullman, *Origin and Development*, pp. 33–35.

LETTER LIV

1(I,104:5). The first, third, and fourth Decades of Livy's *Ab urbe condita* were known in the Middle Ages and throughout the Renaissance. A few fragments were added in 1495 and 1615. Poggius and his fellow humanists were constantly searching for additional text and constantly pursuing vain hopes. Sabbadini, *Scoperte*, II, 231–232.

2(I,104:11). The cardinal must have been a recognized book collector, for in 1429 he acquired a codex containing 20 comedies by Plautus, 12 of them unknown. He refused to allow scholars to see or copy the ms. Jordanus de Ursinis, Archbishop of Naples, 13 February 1400, was appointed Cardinal, tit. S. Martini, by Innocent VII on 12 June 1405 and translated to tit. S. Laurentii in Damaso, 23 September 1412, when he became Cardinal Episcopus Albanensis. According to Richenthal, *Concilium*, f. 70, Jordanus de Ursinis had the title of SS. Petrus et Marcellinus at the time of the Council of Constance.

He became Cardinal Episcopus Sabinensis 14 March 1431; he died 29 May 1438. See Eubel, *Hierarchia*, I, 26, 35, 38, 56, 360. He played an extremely important part at the Council of Constance (see Loomis, *Council, passim*). He was the chief supporter of the election of Gabriel Condulmarius as Pope Eugenius IV and remained with him and faithful to his cause in Rome, Florence, Bologna, etc., during the Council of Basel up to the time of his death. (See Valois, *Le Pape, passim*). He presided at some sessions of the Council of Ferrara (see Gill, *Council of Florence*, pp. 96–97, 104, 107). For a general account of his life, see Ciacconius, *Vitae*, Vol. II, cols. 719–720.

Professor Kristeller has called my attention to a work devoted to Cardinal de Ursinis: Erich Koenig, *Kardinal Giordano Orsini: Ein Lebensbild aus der Zeit der grossen Konzilien und des Humanismus* (Freiburg im Breisgau: Herdersche Verlagshandlung, 1906).

3(I,104:18). For Cosmus de Medicis' book collecting, see Gutkind, *Cosimo*, pp. 223–233. See also Bandini, II, 79, 147, 237, 275, 438, 456–457, 519, 523, 658, 687, 793 for mss. that belonged to Cosmus. On

Cosmus' collecting and gifts to the library in San Marco, see Ullman-Stadter, *Public Library,* pp. 20–21 and 310–313.

4(I,104:20–27). For Soroe, a Cistercian monastery in the diocese of Roeschild (Roskilde) on the island of Zeeland near Copenhagen, founded 15 July 1162, see Chevalier, *Topo-bibliographie,* col. 2990. Poggius' geography seems to be in error. The direct distance from Lübeck to Roskilde is approximately 125 miles of combined land and water travel. The distance entirely by water is greater. See *Encyclopaedia Britannica World Atlas* (New York: C. S. Hammond and Co., 1943), pp. 32–33.

5(I,104:23). iter diei unius, "a day's journey." See Cicero *Fam.* 15.4.8.

6(I,104:23). Terence *Andria* 933.

7(I,105:1). Gherardus de Bueris was a Florentine who resided in Lübeck from 1413 until his death in 1449. He was connected with the Medici by marriage and transacted business for them in Lübeck independently with his partners, not as a partner or an employee of the Medici Bank. See De Roover, *Rise and Decline,* pp. 63–64, 422.

8(I,105:4–5). Cardinal de Ursinis was a great traveler and ambassador, having been to Constance and France by 1423–1424. In 1425 he was sent as Papal Legate into Hungary and Bohemia. See Ciacconius, *Vitae,* Vol. II, col. 719.

9(I,105:5–6). Terence *Heaut. Tim.* 673.

10(I,105:15). Vespasiano, in his life of Nicolaus de Niccolis, says: "Se di Firenze si partiva persona che andasse o in Grecia o in Francia o altrove, gli dava note di libri che non fussino in Firenze; e col mezzo di Cosimo de' Medici, ch'era tutto suo, ne trasse di più luoghi" ["If anyone left Florence to go to Greece or France or some other place, Nicolaus gave him a memorandum of books that did not exist in Florence and with the help of Cosmus de Medicis who was in complete accord with him, he brought books from many sources"]. See *Vite,* p. 474.

11(I,105:19). Tonelli's note says that Leonardus Brunus Aretinus had just been appointed chancellor. Garin says he was chancellor 1410–1411 and *1427-1444.* See Eugenio Garin, "I cancellieri umanisti della repubblica fiorentina da Coluccio Salutati a Bartolomeo Scala," *Rivista storica italiana,* Vol. LXXI (1959), fasc. 2 p. 199. See also Letter II, note 22, and Letter LIII, note 6, on Leonardus' recent election as chancellor. The letter is not dated in Cod. Riccard. 759. Tonelli chose the wrong year, 1424, and Fubini made no change. From internal evidence the letter should be dated 8 January 1428.

LETTER LV

1(Wilmanns, 307:1). Cicero *ad Quintum fratrem* 1.4.12. Ullman assigns this text to Poggius' volume listed as inventory No. 6 (Walser,

Poggius, p. 418) and identifies it as Vat. Ottob. lat. 2035 (Ullman, *Origin and Development*, p. 51).

2(307:7). Joannes Aurispa (1369–1459) was, according to Sabbadini (*Scoperte*, I, 46), "the most illustrious bibliophile of his century." He claimed, in a letter to Ambrosius Traversarius (27 August [1424]), to have brought back to Italy from his travels to Constantinople 238 volumes of pagan, i.e., classical, Greek authors. See Sabbadini, *Carteggio di Giovanni Aurispa*, p. 11. Aurispa made at least two trips to Greece, in 1405–1413 and in 1423. In 1417, according to Cosenza (*Dictionary*, I, 338), Aurispa sold a ms. of Thucydides to Nicolaus de Niccolis. Later, during the Council of Basel, Aurispa searched for Latin texts in Aachen, Cologne, Mainz, and Basel, and discovered Donatus' *Commentary on Terence* in Mainz and Pliny's *Panegyricus* in Cologne in 1433 (Cosenza, *Dictionary*, I, 338). See also *Ambr. Trav. Epist.* V, 34, cols. 268–269 and VI, 8, col. 285.

There is a bull of Nicolaus V legitimatizing three of Aurispa's children, dated 21 July 1453 (see Cosenza, *Dictionary*, I, 340, and Sabbadini, *Carteggio*, p. 126, note 2).

Only one letter (Tonelli Bk. XII, ltr. 11; III, 139–140) from Poggius to Aurispa is known. It was written late in their lives; Sabbadini (*Carteggio*, pp. 137–138) dates it 1454. It is fairly friendly in tone and introduces Bartholomeus Bucinensis to Aurispa as a "socius studiorum." No letter from Aurispa to Poggius is known.

In his *Biografia documentata*, p. 82, note 2, Sabbadini records evidence from a letter of Zeno Amidanus to Petrus Candidus Decembrius that Poggius and Aurispa were friendly and often together during the Council of Florence, in 1439. In his dedication to Thomas de Parentucellis, later Pope Nicolaus V, of his translation made in 1439 of Plutarch's *Convivium septem sapientium*, Aurispa spoke warmly of Poggius: "Cum superiore hebdomada me et Poggium, virum doctum et eloquentia praeditum, invitasses . . ." ["When last week you invited Poggius, who is so learned and expresses himself so well, and me . . ."]. (Sabbadini, *Biografia documentata*, pp. 82–83.)

3(307:9). According to Mazzuchelli *Scrittori d'Italia*, Vol. I, pt. 2, p. 1279, Aurispa had been accused before the Emperor of despoiling the city, but instead of punishing him, the Emperor gave him mss. of Procopius and Xenophon and a sum of money. Aurispa's great friend and frequent correspondent, Franciscus Philelphus, accused him of being a bookseller, not a reader, and of not returning borrowed books. Much later, in 1448, Philelphus wrote to Aurispa: "Te uno, mi Aurispe, nemo est in accipiendo liberalior, in dando autem nemo rursus avarior" ["No one is more generous than you, my dear Aurispa, in accepting gifts, but no one is stingier about returning them"]. (Sabbadini, *Carteggio*, p. 118.)

4(307:10–16). For the parts played in Aurispa's appointment to teach in Florence, 1425–1426 and 1428, by Ambrosius Traversarius, Nicolaus de Niccolis, and Pallas de Strozzis, see Tiraboschi, *Storia,* VI, 983–985. In his funeral oration for Nicolaus, Poggius praised him, among many other achievements, for bringing to Florence "vir praestans ingenio et doctrina Joannes Aurispa" (*Poggii Opera Omnia,* I, 272). A few months before his own death Poggius wrote a venomous attack on Aurispa, who had just died, in a letter to Franciscus Marescalcus Ferrariensis (Walser, *Poggius,* Inedita 115, pp. 554–555).

5(307:21; 308:2–5). Both Wilmanns (*Briefsammlungen,* pp. 307–309) and Sabbadini (*Carteggio,* pp. 164–165) appear to take this letter seriously and accept it as genuine. It seems very contrived and the accusations involved and incredible. It also indicates an atmosphere of hostility between Poggius and Aurispa which was not consistently maintained. They had many friends in common, while Aurispa also had friends, notably Franciscus Philelphus, whom Poggius later hated.

Sabbadini (*Carteggio,* p. 164, note 1) identified the senator as Simone Bondelmonti, of the same family as Poggius' future wife. See F. A. Vitale, *Storia diplomatica dei senatori di Roma,* II (Rome, 1791), 391–399. Vitale lists at least two other men who were connected with Poggius' circle who might be *the* senator: Joannes Nicolaus Salernus Veronensis (Tonelli Bk. XII, ltr. 9), elected senator 1421, who was a great friend of Guarinus and also of Laurentius Justinianus and of S. Bernardinus, and Valerius de Luschis Vicentinus, confirmed as senator 3 December 1425. Simon de Bondelmontis was elected senator 17 January 1428.

6(307:24). Wilmanns identifies this quotation as coming from Cicero *Pro Flacco* 17.39. For the discovery of this text late in the fourteenth century and Antonius Luscus' commentary on it, see Sabbadini, *Scoperte,* II, 123–124, 211.

7(307:25–27). On Aurispa's large holdings of Greek mss., see Sabbadini, *Scoperte,* I, 46–47. Other letters which seem to apply to Aurispa's bundle of books and to the young man in his employ are in Sabbadini, *Carteggio,* No. 33, pp. 51–52, Nos. 43–44, pp. 57–59, written to Ambrosius Traversarius, in the course of Aurispa's move from Florence to Ferrara, 1427–1428.

8(308:6). Antonius Beccadellius Panormita, born Palermo 1394, died in Naples 1471, according to Chevalier, *Bio-bibliographie,* Vol. I, col. 491. See also Cosenza, *Dictionary,* III, 2577–2588. In 1426, Poggius had written two letters to Panormita (Tonelli Bk. II, ltrs. 40 and 42; I, 177–178 and 180–185). In the first letter, Poggius offered Panormita his friendship and enthusiastic praise of Panormita's recently published (in 1425) obscene verse collection "Hermaphroditus." See Fedele Marletta: "Note all' epistolario del Panormita," *Rinascita,* V, No. 27

(1942), 516–526. In his second letter, Poggius is mildly critical of the collection, which was condemned by San Bernardino of Siena and by Albertus de Sartheano. The work was dedicated to Cosmus de Medicis and brought to Rome by Joannes Lamola (see Remigio Sabbadini, "Notizie di alcuni umanisti," *Giornale storico della letteratura italiana,* V [1885], 170). Sabbadini (p. 171) says that Panormita was in Bologna in 1428, but there is no record of Poggius' having been there then. Antonius Panormita was in Rome rather briefly in late 1428 or early 1429. See Remigio Sabbadini, *Cronologia documentata della vita del Panormita e del Valla* (Florence: Successori le Monnier, 1891), p. 40. See also Sabbadini, *Epist. di Guar. Ver.,* III, 317, for the relationship between Antonius Panormita and Aurispa.

About 1429, Panormita entered the service of Filippo Maria Visconti and taught in Pavia and Milan; in 1436 he moved to the court of Alfonsus of Aragon in Naples and remained there for the rest of his life. (See Tiraboschi, *Storia,* Vol. VI, pt. 2, pp. 736–740.) He was a friend and correspondent of all Poggius' circle and, like Poggius, quarreled with Laurentius Valla. (See Bayle, *General Dictionary* [London, 1739], VIII, 127–131.) Pastor (*History,* I, 25, note 2) mentions a letter of Panormita's rejecting even Poggius' gentle criticism of "Hermaphroditus."

9(308:19–20). difficile est furtum admittere in domo furis. This is introduced as a "vetus proverbium," but checking in the dictionary did not reveal a classical source.

10(308:18, 24–27). According to Sabbadini, Aurispa, while teaching in Florence, suspected Nicolaus de Niccolis and his associates of wanting to drive him out of Florence but trying to retain his books. See "Un biennio umanistico," *Giornale storico della letteratura italiana,* Supplemento No. 6 (1903), p. 78. See also Sabbadini, *Carteggio,* pp. 41–43 and p. 42, note 1.

11(308:35–44). Sabbadini, in his appendix III (*Biografia documentata,* pp. 157–167), gives an inventory of 137 works bequeathed by Aurispa to his heirs. Number 5 (p. 157) reads: "Item Ovidium Epistolarum in membranis cum albis precii ducatorum duorum."

Aurispa had another copy of Ovid's *Epistles,* number 64 (p. 161), "veteres sine albis precii soldorum viginti marchesinorum."

12(308:35–309:6). It is not clear whether Aurispa had lost Ovid's *Heroides* or his *Ex Ponto,* both of which were common in the fifteenth century and often bear the title *Epistolae.* See Sabbadini, *Scoperte,* II, 100 and *passim.*

13(308:45). For other confusions in Aurispa's trade or exchange of books, see his correspondence with Ambrosius Traversarius, in Sabbadini, *Biografia documentata,* pp. 16–27.

14(309:7). At the time of his death, Aurispa also owned a volume of the *Metamorphoses.* See Sabbadini, *Biografia documentata,* p. 158, number 13, "in papiro cum uno fondelo de montanina precii ducatorum trium."

15(309:11, 14, 22). Twenty years after writing this hostile letter, Poggius wrote to Antonius Panormita of Aurispa's arrival in Rome in 1448: "vir doctissimus et utrique nostrum amicissimus Iohannes Aurispa reddidit mihi litteras tuas." (Sabbadini, *Biografia documentata,* p. 102, note 1, and *Poggii Epist.* Bk. IX, ltr. 23; II, 350.)

16(309:12–13). For Panormita's wanderings to Bologna, 1424–1425, to Venice in 1427, to Florence in 1427, to Rome in December 1427 and throughout 1428, and to Pavia in 1429, see Sabbadini, *Epist. di Guar. Ver.,* III, 317.

17(309:18). Theotonicus is possibly Henricus Teutonicus who received two letters in 1425 from Johannes Tuscanella, referring to Nicolaus de Niccolis and to Aurispa with admiration. See Remigio Sabbadini, *Ottanta lettere inedita del Panormita* (Catania: Niccolò Giannetta, 1910), pp. 151–152.

18(309:19). capite nudato incedit. For *nudatum caput,* see Vergil *Aen.* 12.312.

19(309:26–27). For an example of Aurispa's secretiveness at this time, see his letter to Ambrosius Traversarius in Sabbadini, *Carteggio,* pp. 57–58.

20(309:26–30). Presumably the ambassador of the Marquis of Ferrara, for Aurispa moved there in 1427 to become, on Guarinus' recommendation, tutor to Meliadusus Estensis. See Sabbadini, "Biennio umanistico," p. 81. See also Aeneas Silvius Piccolumini's (*sic* in Sabbadini, *Carteggio,* pp. 78–79 and note 2) letter to Aurispa referring to "Nicolaum, illustris marchionis nuntium."

21(309:40–43). Although Nicolaus devoted his energy, thought, and property to bringing scholars, especially those with a knowledge of Greek, to Florence for the general good, he was frequently violently attacked by the very men whose benefactor he had been. See Tiroboschi, *Storia,* Vol. VI, pt. 1, pp. 128–132, and Mehus, *Vita Ambrosii Traversarii,* pp. lx–lxii.

22(309:46–48). Psalms 7:16.

LETTER LVI

1(Wilmanns, 310:2). Poggius was right in his anxiety about Nicolaus' well-known irascibility, because his Letter LV is not in the formal tradition of invective, a direct attack on the enemy. Letter LV is a letter to a friend, attacking a friend of *his.* Poggius did not repeat this practice in later life but took with enthusiasm to the direct attack: four invectives directed at Philelphus, the first a defense of Nicolaus (*Opera Omnia*, I, 164–187), written, according to Walser (*Poggius*, pp. 176–180, 455–484), between 1435 and 1447; and against Laurentius Valla (*Opera Omnia*, I, 188–251 [five separate attacks, of which the fourth was never printed until it appeared in the *Opera Omnia*, edited by Fubini, II, 869–885, in 1966]), written between 1451 and 1453 (Walser, *Poggius*, pp. 273–277).

Just before or just after his confused and confusing attack on Aurispa in 1428, Poggius wrote an extremely detailed and tedious attack on his colleague in the Curia, Franciscus de Vellate. See Tonelli Bk. III, ltr. 23; I, 224–258. See also Wilmanns, *Briefsammlungen*, p. 314 (*Poggii Opera Omnia*, IV, 286), and Walser, *Poggius*, pp. 94–95.

2(310: 10–12, 18–19). Poggius' remarks strengthen the opinion that in Letter LV he was engaging in a stylistic exercise rather than a genuine or justified attack.

3(310:15–16). Nicolaus and Poggius had, by 1428, been friends for almost thirty years. Nicolaus had known Aurispa for at least eleven years and possibly much longer. See Sabbadini, *Biografia documentata*, pp. 11–41. It seems unlikely that he would have been friendly with Antonius Beccadellius Panormita, whose scabrous and thoroughly pagan verse collection, *Hermaphroditus*, probably appeared in 1425 or 1426. It pleased Poggius mightily (see Tonelli Bk. II, ltr. 40; I, 177–178) but would not have pleased Nicolaus, who was "cristianissimo," according to Vespasiano, *Vite*, p. 473.

4(310:20,22). No letter from Aurispa to Nicolaus has survived, but Aurispa was in active correspondence with Nicolaus' great friend, Ambrosius Traversarius, in 1428 and had been for many years and continued to be, at least through 1430. See Sabbadini, *Carteggio*, pp. 197–198.

LETTER LVII

1(I,216:2). On Poggius' autograph text of the *Philippics*, see Ullman, *Origin and Development*, p. 33, on Cod. Laur. 48, 22.

2(I,217:5). Poggius mentioned Bartholomeus de Bardis frequently in his letters of 1425 and 1428. Bartholomeus, through his position as manager of the Rome branch of the Medici Bank, could easily handle the delivery of books and other possessions for his friends; see De Roover, *Rise and Decline*, pp. 203–205.

3(I,217:6). The Livy mentioned here was probably Cod. Laur. 63, 19, an eleventh century ms. which belonged to Nicolaus. See Bandini, Vol. II, cols. 693–694. See also Ullman-Stadter, *Public Library*, p. 220.

LETTER LVIII

1(I,217:6). Presumably Laurentius de Medicis, Cosmus' brother, though there seems to be no record of his being in Rome in June 1428.
2(I,217:10). See the Life of Lucullus in Plutarch's *Lives*, III, 357.
3(I,217:10). Seneca *Epist*. 21.10.
4(I,218:3). totus teretur dies. For the expression, see *Teritur dies*, Plautus *Truc*. 912. The *Truculentus* is one of the comedies unknown to the humanists until Nicolaus Cusanus presented his discovery to Cardinal de Ursinis in November 1429. Poggius was not allowed to see it until 1431. See Letters LXVI, LXVIII, LXIX, LXXV (*Poggii Epist*. Bk. III, ltrs. 29, 31, 32, 39; Vol. I, pp. 267, 270, 274, 288), and Ullman, *Origin and Development*, p. 51.

LETTER LIX

1(I,218:2). On Genezano, see *Roma e dintorni*, p. 676. This village, overlooking Lake Nemi, had been held by the Colonna family, to which Martin V belonged, since 1393.
2(I,218:8). Minias Lucensis received a letter from Panormita commiserating on his illness. See Resta, *L'epistolario del Panormita*, p. 212. The letter is published in full by Janus Gruter in his *Lampas sive Fax Artium Liberalium hoc est Thesaurus Criticus* (Lucca, 1747), III, 304–306; see "Antoni Beccatelli Vulgo Panormitae Epistolarum Gallicarum Libri Quatuor," IV, 25. There is also a letter from Minias Lucensis to Cosmus de Medicis in *Ambr. Trav. Epist*. XXV, 8, cols. 1051–1052, asking for an oration that Cosmus delivered before the Pope.
3(I,218:9). convaluit ex longo morbo. For *convalescere ex morbo*, see Cicero *Fam*. 13.29.4.
4(I,218:17). ut mature redeat. For *mature redire*, see Horace *Ep*. 1.7.97.
5(I,219:2). ne succumbas laboribus variis. For *succumbere labori*, see Caesar *B.G*. 7.86.
6(I,219:6–31). On Ferentino, see *Lazio* (Milan: Touring Club Italiano, 1943), pp. 223–224. See also Karl Baedeker, *Rome and Central Italy*, 16th revised edition (Leipzig: Baedeker, 1930), pp. 549–550.
7(I,219:24–26). On Nicolaus' learning and linguistic proficiency, see Poggius' funeral oration for him (*Opera Omnia*, I, 272–273).
8(I,219:31–32). Vergil *Georgics* 1.145.

LETTER LX

1(I,220:12). The gate is now called the *Porta Sanguinaria*; see *Lazio*, p. 223.

2(I,220:17–221:6, 10–11). For the inscription on the gate at Ferentino, see *Corpus Inscriptionum Latinarum,* Theodor Mommsen, ed. (Editio altera, pars posterior a cura Ernesti Lommatsch; Berlin, 1919), Fasc. 1, pp. 628–629, No. 1522, and Muratori, *Novus Thesaurus,* II, mxlvi, Nos. 6, 7.

3(I,221:13). On Alatri, see *Lazio,* p. 212, and *Rome and Central Italy,* p. 530.

4(I,221:20). Poggius owned a Josephus, *De bello Judaico* at the time of his death; it is in his inventory as No. 36. See Walser, *Poggius,* p. 107, note 2, and p. 421.

5(I,221:21). Poggius had been agitating about the text of the *Noctes Atticae* for two years: see Letter XLVII (Tonelli Bk. III, ltr. 1; I, 187). This text is No. 26 in his inventory. See Walser, *Poggius,* p. 106, note 7, and p. 420. No letter from Poggius to Leonardus Aretinus written close to this date survives; see Tonelli Bk. III, ltr. 16 (1427), which contains no reference to Aulus Gellius. Hans Baron in his *Leonardo Bruni Aretino,* p. 133, gives evidence that at least once Leonardus paraphrased a passage from the *Noctes Atticae.*

LETTER LXI

1(I,222:6). On the Stoics, see J. M. Rist, *Stoic Philosophy* (Cambridge: Cambridge University Press, 1969), and A. A. Long, ed., *Problems in Stoicism* (London: University of London, The Athlone Press, 1971).

2(I,222:18–19). ad lenitatem et familiaritatem propensior. For *ad lenitatem propensior,* see Cicero *Mur.* 31.64. On Cicero's *Pro Murena,* see Letter XLII, note 5 (*Poggii Epist.* Bk. II, ltr. 34; I, 167:2).

3(I,222:24–28). See Muratori, *Novus Thesaurus,* I, lxxxv, No. 10: "Tibure, extra Portam Cornutam . . .," and another on p. cxxv, No. 7.

4(I,223:11). On H.A.I.R. see John Edwin Sandys, *Latin Epigraphy: An Introduction to the Study of Latin Inscriptions,* 2nd edition, revised by S. G. Campbell (Cambridge: Cambridge University Press, 1927), p. 110: H.A.I.R. *Honore accepto impensam remisit.*

5(I,223:13). Poggius refers to Oedipus here as a solver of riddles. Presumably he knew this story from Seneca's tragedy. See his Inventory No. 22 (Walser, *Poggius,* p. 106, note 3, and p. 420). See also Lucius Annaeus Seneca, *Tragoediae* (Lyons: Antonius Lambillon and Marinus Saracenus, 1491). "Oedipus," f. 108v. There are frequent mentions of Seneca and his tragedies in Poggius' letters.

LETTER LXII

1(,223:4). On the three volumes of Livy copied by Poggius' secretary, see Ullman, *Origin and Development,* pp. 45–47, where they are identified as Mss. Vat. Lat. 1843, 1849, 1852.

2(I,223:4). According to Ullman (*Origin and Development,* p. 66), Nicolaus himself had copied the text of Aulus Gellius' *Noctes Atticae* some time before July 1431. See also Ullman-Stadter, *Public Library,* pp. 84, 86, 88, and 231 (ms. 900).

3(I,223:6). The text of Josephus' *Contra Appionem grammaticum* does not appear among the mss. in the Biblioteca Laurenziana, but it was printed twice in the fifteenth century, in 1480 (Hain, Vol. II, 1, No. 9452) and in 1481 (No. 9453) in volumes which also contain the *Libri antiquitatum Judaicarum* and the *De bello Judaico.*

4(I,223:10; 224:4). Antonius Luscus' visit is confirmed by Nicolaus' report of it mentioned in Letter LXIII (Tonelli Bk. III, ltr. 25; I, 260).

5(I,224:7). For Poggius' home and garden in Terranuova, bought in 1427 and 1428, see Walser, *Poggius,* Documents 24, 27, 28, pp. 338–342.

6(I,224:13). See *Poggius,* Document 27 (p. 339), where Poggius is specifically called *cittadino fiorentino.*

LETTER LXIII

1(I,260:2). Bartholomeus de Bardis died not long after this letter was written, in January or February 1429; see De Roover, *Rise and Decline,* p. 211.

2(I,260:7). This Garsia may have been Alphonsus Garsia de Cartagena (1396?–1456) appointed Bishop of Burgos in 1435. See Nicolaus Antonius Hispalensis, *Bibliotheca Hispana vetus,* II (Madrid, 1788), 261–265, and Sabbadini, *Storia e critica,* pp. 224–241. He may also have been Ludovicus de Garsiis, clericus camerae apostolicae (see Baix, *Chambre apostolique,* II, 534). His name appears frequently on documents surviving from 1427–1429 (*Chambre apostolique,* I, 225–226, 256, 285, 287–288, 290, 326).

3(I,260:10; 261:4). During the 1420s Antonius Luscus was sent by Martin V on embassies to Milan and Budapest, where in 1429 he was made Count Palatine by the Emperor Sigismund. His visit to Nicolaus in Florence probably took place in the course of his diplomatic journey. See Luigi Pàstine, "Antonio Loschi umanista vicentino," *Rivista d'Italia,* XVIII (1915), 870. Da Schio dates this embassy 1426 (*Antonio Loschi,* p. 109).

LETTER LXIV

1(I,263:2). Aut aures nimis delicatae sunt. For *delicatae aures,* see Quint., 3.1.3.

2(I,263:5–6). Letters of Poggius in Italian are extremely rare. Riccardo Fubini printed three in Poggius Bracciolini, *Opera Omnia,* Vol. IV: pp. 213–215 and 611–613, to Cosmus de Medicis, and p. 647, to Johannes Cosmi de Medicis.

3(I,263:12). On Poggius' humor, see Walser, *Poggius,* pp. 262–266.

4(I,264:14-17). It is hard to identify the dead friend who is mentioned here. The letter is too late for Antonius Corbinellus and too early for Bartholomeus de Montepolitiano. Perhaps Poggius was referring to Bartholomeus de Bardis, whose illness he had mentioned about two weeks earlier. Poggius was able to express his grief and fright at the death of friends in a way that still carries conviction.

5(I,264:28-265:2, 9-11). See Ullman, *Origin and Development*, pp. 45-47. Poggius must have been using a much damaged text of the fourth Decade, because in print the text of Books 31-32 runs to 92 pages. See Titus Livius, *Ab urbe condita libri*, G. Weissenborn and M. Mueller, eds. (Leipzig: Teubner, 1938), Vol. III.

6(I,265:6-8). Poggius was still waiting hopefully but doubtfully six weeks later. The book did not come before Christmas, if ever.

LETTER LXV

1(I,265:2-3). There had so far been a delay of more than two months. Poggius had meantime reminded Nicolaus of his request a month earlier.

2(I,266:5-7). Poggius accomplished perhaps more than he realized: see Ullman, *Origin and Development*, pp. 21-57, and *Mostra della biblioteca di Lorenzo nella biblioteca Medicea Laurenziana* (Florence, 1949), pp. 59, 157-158, 177-182, 186, 188.

3(I,266:12-16). This sounds like the same Petrus Chartularius mentioned in Letter XXXIII (Tonelli Bk. II, ltr. 25; I, 152:16).

LETTER LXVI

1(I,266:6-7). For an account of the early life of Nicolaus Treverensis (Cusanus) and his studies at Deventer, Heidelberg and Padua, see Rotta, *Nicolò di Cusa*, pp. 3-18. The books which Nicolaus had announced in his letter were in the library of the Cathedral of Cologne (p. 17). See also Edmond Vansteenberghe, *Le Cardinal Nicolas de Cues (1401-1464)* (Paris: Honoré Champion, 1920), pp. 3-32.

2(I,267:3-4). Poggius himself had discovered the lost texts of the *De lege agraria* and the *In Pisonem* during the Council of Constance. See Sabbadini, *Storia e critica*, pp. 43-46, and Albert C. Clark, *Inventa Italorum*, in Anecdota Oxoniensia, Classical Series, XI (Oxford: Clarendon Press, 1909), pp. 9-15. The relation between Poggius' discoveries and Cusanus' later ones is discussed by Clark, pp. 24-32.

Guarinus owned a ms. of the *De legibus* at this time and was asking to borrow a *De fato* from one of his pupils to copy it. See Sabbadini, *Storia e critica*, p. 179. Another *De fato* belonged to Modestus Decembrius. Poggius at the time of his death owned his autograph copy of the *De legibus* (Walser says "perhaps Cod. Vat. Lat. 3245"). See No. 13 of the inventory of Poggius' library (Walser, *Poggius*, p. 419).

3(I,267:5–9). Cod. Laur. Lat. XVI, 22 contains works of Cyprian of Carthage. It is a fifteenth century ms. which belonged to Petrus de Medicis, Cosmus' son. See Bandini, *Cat. cod. lat.*, Vol. I, cols. 267–269. For other mss. of Cyprian's works in the Laurentiana, see *Cat. cod. lat.*, Vol. V, cols. 568–569. These were apparently not very rare works. Sabbadini (*Scoperte*, II, 27, note 137) suggests that the codex mentioned by Poggius may still exist as no. 29 of the hospital in Cues.

Although two large sections of the text of Aulus Gellius' *Noctes Atticae* had been known in Italy at least since the time of Petrarch, the humanists were always, as here, hoping for a complete text. See Sabbadini, *Scoperte*, I, 25, 91–92; II, 24, 225–226. The imperfect text of Quintus Curtius Rufus' *History of Alexander the Great* was fairly widely known in fourteenth century Italy. See Sabbadini, *Scoperte*, II, 218.

Nicolaus Cusanus offered a Quintus Curtius containing the first book but did not mention the end. Poggius thought the end would be there if the beginning was. There is no trace of this ms. now (see Sabbadini, *Scoperte*, II, 27). Poggius found it disappointing when it was delivered (Sabbadini, *Scoperte*, I, 111). See also Letter LXXXI (*Poggii Epistolae* Bk. IV, ltr. 4; I, 305: 4–10).

4(I,267:12–25). According to Rotta, *Nicolò di Cusa* (p. 18), this twelfth century manuscript is now Cod. Vat. Lat. 3870. Sabbadini (*Storia e critica*, p. 327) says that eight of Plautus' comedies were known throughout the Middle Ages. The twelve lost comedies, found by Nicolaus Cusanus, are those listed in Poggius' letter from the *Bacchides* through the *Trinummus*. Sabbadini collected most of the humanist correspondence (Poggius, Traversarius, Guarinus) dealing with this thrilling find in his *Guarino Veronese e gli archetipi di Celso e Plauto*. See also Sandys, *History*, II, 34.

For a very interesting account of the text of the comedies see Georgius Merula Alexandrinus' preface to the *editio princeps*, printed by Joannes de Colonia and Windelinus de Spira in Venice, 1472. Merula refers to "duodecim Comoedias quadraginta abhinc annis repertas" (Beriah Botfield, ed., *Prefaces to the First Editions of the Greek and Roman Classics and of the Sacred Scriptures* [London: H. G. Bohn, 1861], pp. 141–145).

"Dum bellum gereret" is the beginning of the second line of *Argumentum I* of the *Amphitruo*. "Amanti argento filio" is part of the first line of the *argumentum* of the *Asinaria*.

5(I,267:27). The *De republica* was finally found by Angelo Mai in a palimpsest in the Vatican Library (Cod. Vat. Lat. 5757) and published by him in 1822. (Sandys, *History*, III, 241.) See also Gianni Gervasoni, *Angelo Mai* (Bergamo: Edizioni Orobiche, 1954), pp. 24, 33–35; and see Sabbadini, "Storia e critica di alcuni testi latini," *Museo italiano di antichità classica,* III (1890), 401–424.

6(I,268:5). Cardinal de Ursinis was by this time the senior member of the College of Cardinals, having been promoted by Innocent VII in 1405 when Poggius was new to the Curia. Poggius had been associated with the Cardinal at the Council of Constance as well as in Rome. See Eubel, *Hierarchia,* I, 26, and Letter LIV, note 2. The only other survivor of the same promotion was Pope Martin himself.

7(I,268:15–21). For a detailed account of Heinrich von Grebenstein, the monk from Hersfeld, see Pralle, *Wiederentdeckung,* pp. 29–39.

8(I,268:24). On Joannes Bicci de Medicis, see Gutkind, *Cosimo, passim;* De Roover, *Rise and Decline, passim,* and especially pp. 51–52; and Machiavelli, *History of Florence,* Book IV, chaps. 1–4. Poggius in his funeral oration for Laurentius de Medicis (d. 1440) also praised Joannes de Medicis: "Patrem habuit eum quo neque iustior vir, neque humanior, neque melior quisquam, neque charior patriae civis fuit" ["He had a father who was unsurpassed in fairness, and in culture; there was no one better than he and no citizen dearer to the state"]. (*Opera Omnia,* I, 283.) Tonelli in note 2 on page 268 points out that the date, 1428, given in Cod. Riccard. 759, either is wrong and should read 1429 or Poggius was using the Florentine style of dating with the year beginning in March. However, it is certain that Joannes de Medicis died on the twentieth of February according to the inscription on his tomb and the statement of Ammirato, *Storie fiorentine,* p. 1, t. 2, pag. 1046.

Baron reports (*Crisis,* p. 327) that Joannes de Medicis was one of the strongest adherents of peace in the discussions leading to war with Milan in 1423–1424. See also Schevill, *History of Florence,* p. 344; Machiavelli, *History of Florence,* Book IV, chap. 2; and Zannoni, "Letteratura: Della Carcere . . . e del trionfal ritorno di Cosimo padre della patria . . . Ms. di Giovanni Cavalcanti," *Antologia,* V (January–March, 1822), 44–51. See Joannes de Medicis' deathbed advice to his sons, *Antologia,* pp. 48–50. For further contemporary praise of Joannes de Medicis, see "Leonardi Bruni Aretini Praefatio in Libros Oeconomicorum [Pseudo] Aristotelis," in Baron, *Leonardo Bruni Aretino,* p. 120.

9(I,268:29–269:3). Cosmus and Laurentius de Medicis had the Sagrestia Vecchia in San Lorenzo in Florence rebuilt by Brunelleschi as a family chapel to contain their father's tomb. See L. V. Bertarelli, *Firenze e dintorni,* 3rd edition (Milan: Guida d'Italia del Touring Club Italiano, 1937), p. 248.

For the monuments in Florence connected with Joannes de Medicis, especially after his death, see Eugene Müntz, *Histoire de l'art pendant la Renaissance,* I (Paris: Hachette, 1889), 54, 414, 427–429, 448, 518, 540.

For "the Burial Chapel of the Medici," see Maud Cruttwell, *Donatello* (London: Methuen, 1911), pp. 95–101.

LETTER LXVII

1(I,269:4–270:5). Poggius' letter of sympathy to Cosmus must not have satisfied Nicolaus, for it has not been preserved, whereas his later condolences (1433) on Cosmus' exile were recopied often and were printed in Poggius' *Opera* (Strasburg, 1513) ff. 118v–120r, and *Opera Omnia,* I (Basel, 1538, and Turin, 1964), 312–317, and by Tonelli (Florence, 1859), II, 37–46: Book V, *Epist.* 12. Poggius also wrote a funeral oration for Cosmus' brother Laurentius (d. 1440) which is published in his *Opera Omnia,* I, 278–286.

2(I,269:10). sumpto calamo. For *sumere calamum,* see Cicero *Att.* 6.8.1. quicquid in buccam venit: for the colloquial phrase, see Cicero *Att.* 1.12.4; 7.10 fin.; 14.7.2; Martial 12.24.5. By the date of this letter, Poggius had copied Cicero's *Letters to Atticus* at least twice, which would naturally result in phrases from them coming readily to mind. See Ullman, *Origin and Development,* pp. 27–28, 43–45.

3(I,269:13). aliquid perfectius. For *aliquid perfectius,* see Cicero *De or.* 1.2.5; *Brut.* 18.69; Horace *Epod.* 5.59; Quint. 12.1.21. Poggius had copied Cicero's *De oratore* and *Brutus* beginning in 1425; there are many references to this activity in his letters. See Ullman, *Origin and Development,* pp. 35–37. He had copied the text of Quintilian when he found it, as he told Guarinus (*Poggii Epist.* Bk. I, ltr. 5; I, 29: 16–18).

4(I,270:5). Stirring up Cardinal de Ursinis seems to have been a favorite humanist activity. See Ambrosius [Traversarius] Camaldulensis, *Epistolarum Liber XVI, Epist.* 14 (Martène and Durand, *Amplissima Collectio,* Vol. III, cols. 542–543): "Scripsi hortatu tuo Cardinali Ursino, orans Plauti Comoedias, quas apud se haberi compereram, mitteret ad me, sed profeci nihil." This letter is VIII, 35 in Mehus' edition (cols. 393–394).

5(I,270:7). In 1429, Easter fell on March 27 (see A. Cappelli, *Cronologia, cronografia e calendario perpetuo,* 2nd edition revised (Milan: Hoepli, 1930; anastatic reprint, 1960).

6(I,270:10). The *"opusculum"* which Poggius had just finished was his *De avaritia.* See Helene Harth, "Niccolò Niccoli als literarischer Zensor. Untersuchungen zur Textgeschichte von Poggios 'De avaritia,'" *Rinascimento,* Second Series, VIII (1967), 29–53. See also Walser, *Poggius,* pp. 126–134, on the dating, content, and reception of the essay.

7(I,270:note 2). Tonelli notes that there is no date on this letter but that its ending shows it to be earlier than Bk. III, ltr. 32, which is dated 6 May 1429.

LETTER LXVIII

1(I,270:8-10). Poggius had already listed the comedies in the Plautus codex in his letter of 26 February 1428, nearly two months earlier (Letter LXVI; Tonelli Bk. III, ltr. 29; I, 266-269). Tonelli indicates in a note that Bk. III, ltr. 29 is wrongly dated in the ms. Both letters clearly belong to 1429 after the death of Joannes Bicci de Medicis, who died on 20 February 1429.

2(I,271:4). Poggius does not divulge to whom Nicolaus Treverensis wrote. To Cardinal de Ursinis who later acquired the Plautus ms.?

3(I,271:14). Laurentius de Medicis was a younger brother of Cosmus and dear friend of Poggius, who wrote a very elaborate but sincerely mournful funeral oration some time after Laurentius' death in 1440 (see Gutkind, *Cosimo*, p. 73) which strangely is addressed to Carolus (Marsuppinus?) and not to Cosmus de Medicis. See *Poggii Opera Omnia*, I, 278-286. Poggius mentions Laurentius' grief also in Letter LXVI (Tonelli Bk. III, ltr. 29), dated 26 February 1428 wrongly in the ms. Tonelli (I, 268, note 2) corrects the date to 1429. It seems probable that Laurentius de Medicis was in Rome in April 1429 after the death of his father because Bartholomeus de Bardis, head of the Medici Bank in Rome, had also died early in 1429. See De Roover, *Rise and Decline*, p. 53.

4(I,271:20). Rinucius was in the service of Gabriel Condulmarius, Cardinal (1408) tit. S. Clementis, (1426) S. Mariae trans Tib., later Pope Eugenius IV, beginning in 1423. See Lockwood, "De Rinutio Aretino," p. 52.

5(I,271:29). Rinucius' most important Greek work was on Aesop's *Fables*. See Lockwood "De Rinutio Aretino," pp. 61-68. See also B. E. Perry, "The Greek Source of Rinuccio's Aesop," *Classical Philology*, XXIX, No. 1 (1934), 53-62, and Thomas O. Achelis, "Die hundert äsopischen Fabeln des Rinucci da Castiglione," *Philologus*, LXXXIII (1927-1928), 55-88. Cosenza, *Dictionary*, I, 3056-3060, mentions at least a dozen other translations from the Greek by Rinucius, especially of Lucian. Rinucius dedicated his translation of the "Decreta Atheniensia" from Demosthenes' *De corona* to Poggius to whom he was teaching Greek. (See Lockwood, *loc. cit.*)

6(I,272:1-2). This is a veiled reference to Martin V, about whom Poggius is more outspoken in Letter LXXII (Tonelli Bk. III, ltr. 35), where (I, 277: 20-27) he clearly mentions the Pope's reputation for stinginess.

7(I,272:6). Poggius' most recent mention of Ciceronian orations was in Letter LVII (Tonelli Bk. III, ltr. 17), where he was using an ancient codex to emend his copy of the *Philippics* which he promised to bring with him when he came to Florence.

8(I,272:8-9). It should be noted that the following autumn Poggius was "home" himself in Terranuova; see Letter LXXVIII (Tonelli Bk. IV, ltr. 1).

9(I,272:13). Joannes de Toscanella was a rhetorician in Bologna in 1431, according to Chevalier, *Bio-bibliographie*, Vol. II, col. 2501. See also Cosenza, *Dictionary*, IV, 3495-3496. This is a strange attitude for Poggius to take about another literary man who was a pupil of Guarinus and a friend of Aurispa, Philelphus, and Antonius Beccadellius Panormita unless Poggius wished to emphasize his distrust of Joannes de Toscanella's friends.

LETTER LXIX

1(I,273:1). On Cincius, see Letter XXIII, note 6 (Tonelli Bk. II, ltr. 2; I, 88: 14) and Letter LXXXII (Tonelli Bk. IV, ltr. 5; I, 308). See also Cincius' letter to Poggius, congratulating him on the birth of a son, giving advice on his upbringing, and reporting toasts and good wishes from a convivial gathering (*Poggiana, ou la vie, le caractère, les sentences, les bons mots de Pogge florentin avec son histoire de la république de Florence*, 2 vols. [Amsterdam: Pierre Humbert, 1720], II, 322-326). For a long account of Cincius' career and writings, and his relationship with Poggius, Antonius Luscus, Bartholomeus de Montepolitiano, and with the popes he served, see Max Lehnerdt, "Cencio und Agapito de' Rustici," *Zeitschrift für vergleichende Litteraturgeschichte*, N. F. XIV (1900), 149-172, 289-318. See also Cincius' very eloquent account of his expedition to St. Gall with Poggius and their discoveries there, in a letter written to his teacher Franciscus de Fiano, which also includes a diatribe against those who engage in or permit the destruction of ancient monuments in Rome. The letter appears in *Diatriba Praeliminaris*, pp. 8-11, and as Letter I in the Appendix, above. On Cincius' avarice, see Letter LXXII, note 11 (Tonelli Bk. III, ltr. 35; I, 278: 20-26), referring to Ludwig Bertalot. Ludwig Bertalot edited all of Cincius' known letters in his article "Cincius Romanus und seine Briefe," in *Quellen und Forschungen*, Vol. XXI (1929-1930), especially pp. 220-251.

2(I,273:5). Andreas de Petra Constantinopolitanus, a Dominican who became Archbishop of Colossus or Rhodes in 1431 and of Nicosia in 1447 and died in, probably, 1457. See Chevalier, *Bio-bibliographie*, Vol. I, cols. 225-226. See also Cosenza, *Dictionary*, I, 172-173, and Quétif-Echard, *Scriptores*, I, 801-803. In the *Dictionnaire d'histoire*, Baudrillart ed., Vol. II, there are four separate biographies: cols. 1654, 1688, 1692–1693, and 1696–1700, all of which may apply partly or wholly to the same man.

3(I,273:8–9). avaritie crimen. For *avaritiae crimen,* see Cicero *Verr.* 2.2.78, paragraph 192. See Letter XXXV, note 2 (Tonelli Bk. II, ltr. 27; I, 155: 17).

4(I,273:18–28; 274:10–11). For Nicolaus' opinion of the *De avaritia,* see Letter LXXII (Tonelli Bk. III, ltr. 35), where it is reflected in Poggius' reply to him. For a reflection of Ambrosius Traversarius' opinion, see Poggius' letter to him about it: Tonelli Bk. III, ltr. 36 (I, 282–283). See also Walser, *Poggius,* pp. 133–134.

5(I,273:30–274:3). Poggius wrote later to Leonardus Brunus, who apparently did take offense, defending his dialogue. See Walser, *Poggius,* pp. 429–430, "Inedita" No. 3.

6(I,274:7–10). Neither of the two letters (Bk. III, ltrs. 24 and 26; I, 259–263) which Poggius wrote to Franciscus Barbarus to alert him to the forthcoming *De avaritia* seems to be the one Poggius intended Nicolaus to forward with the text. For Barbarus' and his friends' reaction to the dialogue, see Petrus Thomasius' letter to Franciscus Barbarus, published by Walser, *Poggius,* pp. 432–435, "Inedita" No. 6.

7(I,274:12–15). On Nicolaus' irascible disposition, see Letters IX (Tonelli Bk. I, ltr. 9), XXV (Tonelli Bk. II, ltr. 4), XLII (Tonelli Bk. II, ltr. 34), and XLVIII (Tonelli Bk. III, ltr. 5), all to Nicolaus, and Tonelli Bk. II, ltr. 11 to Leonardus Brunus Aretinus. See also *Ambr. Trav. Epist.* VIII, 30, col. 388, urging an improvement in Nicolaus' disposition.

8(I,274:14–15). Horace *De arte poetica* 169. See No. 42 in Poggius' inventory: Horace's works on vellum bound in white leather (Walser, *Poggius,* p. 421).

9(I,274:15). nimis es difficilis ac morosus. *Difficilis* and *morosus* are found together elsewhere: see "usque eo *difficiles ac morosi* sumus, ut nobis non satisfaciat ipse Demosthenes," Cicero *Orator* 29.104. On Nicolaus' copying of this newly discovered text and Poggius' copying of his copy, see Ullman, *Origin and Development,* pp. 35–37, 61–63. See also Horace *Sermones* 2.5.90.

10(I,274:31–32). nimis es delicatus. For a similar thought, see *nimium ego te habui delicatam,* Plautus *Men.* 1.2.10. It is curious to find that both here and in Letter LXXIII (Tonelli Bk. III, ltr. 37; I, 284: 26) Poggius used phrases from newly discovered comedies which he had not been allowed to see.

LETTER LXX

1(I,275:11–12). Evidently Nicolaus could not supply the name of the man who praised Dionysius and censured Plato, because in the text of the *De avaritia* he is merely *quemdam* (see *Poggii Opera Omnia,* I, 17). Poggius probably refers to the Syracusan historian Philistus (see Plutarch, "Life of Dion," VI, 10). Philistus is mentioned several times by Cicero (see *Correspondence*, II, 135–136, in *Epistolae ad Quintum fratrem* II.11 or 13) and in the *Brutus*, Martin Kellogg, ed. (New York: Ginn and Co., 1889), pp. 33, 144.

LETTER LXXI

1(I,276:4–5, 12–13). For some of the changes in the text of the *De avaritia* made to satisfy Nicolaus, see Helene Harth, "Niccolò Niccoli," pp. 47–49.

Tonelli Bk. III, ltr. 36 (I, 282–283) in which Poggius discusses his dialogue with Ambrosius Traversarius has to be omitted from a collection of letters only to Nicolaus de Niccolis.

LETTER LXXII

1(I,277:3). Nicolaus' reaction to Poggius' dialogue *De avaritia* was quite negative. Poggius wrote to Ambrosius Traversarius: "Nonnulla ei displicent; multa non placent; ornatum vero dicendi deesse arbitratur" ["Some parts of it he does not like; quite a bit he actively dislikes and he thinks the whole work lacks style"]. (Tonelli Bk. III, ltr. 36; I, 282).

2(I,277:8). See Da Schio, *Antonio Loschi*, pp. 115–116.

3(I,277:12). iudicium tuum acre. For *acre iudicium*, see *"acri iudicio perpende,"* Lucretius 2.1041. Poggius discovered the lost text of Lucretius' *De rerum natura* in the spring of 1417, probably at Fulda (Sabbadini, *Scoperte*, I, 80; II, 192, 233). He repeatedly and plaintively asked Nicolaus de Niccolis to send him the book which he had himself returned to the scholarly world, so that he might read and copy it. See *Poggii Epist*. Bk. II, ltrs. 22, 26; Bk. III, ltr. 1; Bk. IV, ltrs. 2, 4; I, 148, 154, 187, 294–295, 303–304. See also Ullman, *Origin and Development*, pp. 64–66: Cod. Laur. 35.30, the text of Lucretius in the hand of Nicolaus de Niccolis.

4(I,277:12). iudicium exquisitum. For *exquisitum iudicium*, see Cicero *Off.* 1.37.133: *exquisitum iudicium litterarum.*

5(I,277:20–25). See *Vitae Romanorum Pontificum: De Martino V.* "Martinus vero avarissimus fuit; miserabiliter in Palatio apud Sanctos Apostolos vixit" ["Martin was truly terribly stingy; he lived in squalor in his palace near the Santissimi Apostoli"]. In Muratori, *R.I.S.*, Vol. III, pt. 2, col. 859. See also *loc. cit.*, a second life of Martin V, which reports: "Erat supra modum humilis, gratus et dilectus hominibus" ["He was humble beyond measure, kindly and well loved"].

Martin V had earned a reputation for touchiness in Florence. See Vespasiano's life of Leonardus Brunus Aretinus, *Vite*, p. 430.

6(I,277:24). naturae sit facilis et beneficae. For *benefica natura*, see Cicero *Fam.* 3.8.8.

7(I,277:25). Poggius must have had a very clear recollection of the trouble recently (February 1427) brought by detractors upon Henry Chichele, Archbishop of Canterbury. See *Register of Henry Chichele*, I, xlv–xlvii.

8(I,278:3–6). Although Poggius maintained that he was keeping his tract unpublished, he sent it with a dedicatory epistle to Franciscus Barbarus in November and December [of 1428?]. See *Poggii Epistolae* Bk. III, ltrs. 24 and 26 (Tonelli, I, 259–263). It is hard to establish the date of publication, since none of the sixteen mss. studied by Helene Harth is dated.

9(I,278:6–12). Apparently Nicolaus must have objected to Poggius' introduction of contemporaries and friends as speakers in the dialogue, though this was often done by the humanists. Nicolaus, who was so devoted to antiquity that he always ate out of "vasi antichi bellissimi" (see Vespasiano, *Vite*, p. 480), must have wanted the speakers disguised with classical names.

10(I,278:15). Antonius Luscus, Bartholomeus de Montepolitiano, and Cincius Romanus were scholars and good friends of Poggius who were all serving in the Curia in the early summer of 1429. Bartholomeus died of the plague in July 1429, to Poggius' horror and distress. Cincius and Poggius had to go to Ferentino with Pope Martin V; Antonius Luscus managed to escape this boring and uncomfortable period of service. See Letter LXXIII (Tonelli Bk. III, ltr. 37; I, 283–285). The same group attended a party given by Poggius several years earlier and described in a letter to Leonardus Brunus Aretinus (Tonelli Bk. II, ltr. 8; I, 101–103). Poggius had known both Antonius Luscus and Bartholomeus de Montepolitiano for more than twenty years when this letter was written. They had served in the Curia together, starting about 1409, and had been at the Council of Constance together. See Luigi Pàstine, "Antonio Loschi," *Rivista d'Italia*, XVIII, pt. 1 (1915), 864–866. Both Bartholomeus de Montepolitiano and Cincius de Rusticis were Poggius' companions in Constance and on his search for mss. in St. Gall. See Sandys, *History*, II, 26.

11(I,278:20–26). According to Ludwig Bertalot, it was accepted in Cincius' circle that he was a miser. Bertalot so interprets Ambrosius Traversarius' remark to Nicolaus de Niccolis in his *Epistolae* VIII, 8 (col. 370). See Bertalot, "Cincius Romanus," in *Quellen und Forschungen*, XXI (1929–1930), 215. It is interesting that one of Cincius' few surviving letters is a request addressed to the Medici brothers asking them to make payment as managers of the Florentine State debt of sums owed to him and Antonius Luscus (28 September 1436 or 1437) (p. 239).

There is no indication in the correspondence of Guarinus or Philelphus, with or about Cincius, that they regarded him as a miser, nor is he so depicted in Laurentius Valla's *De voluptate.* Perhaps the abrupt treatment of his life by Vespasiano, *Vite,* p. 517, indicates that he was an unsatisfactory customer.

12(I,278:28–29). What Poggius means here is not clear. Each of the interlocutors — Antonius Luscus, Cincius de Rusticis, Bartholomeus de Montepolitiano, and Andreas Constantinopolitanus — speaks a considerable section of the dialogue.

13(I,279:1). Nicolaus was right. The discussion of S. Bernardinus and his effectiveness as a preacher, at the beginning of the dialogue, seems unrelated to the stated subject of avarice. On p. 4 of the 1538 text of the *De avaritia* (in *Poggii Opera Omnia,* Vol. I) is the statement that S. Bernardinus' diatribe against usury ". . . magis [movet] populum ad risum, quam ad ad [sic] horrorem tanti criminis" [". . . he moves the populace more to laughter than to horror of such a sin"]. On St. Bernardinus' preaching, see Origo, *World of San Bernardino,* especially the bibliography and notes, pp. 258–297.

Tonelli's note 1, p. 279, identifies Bernardinus de Albizeschis de Senis, of the Minorite Order of the Observants. It refers also to Tiraboschi, *Storia,* Vol. VI, Lib. 3, cap. 6, sec. 3, and Shepherd, *Vita di Poggio,* I, 157.

14(I,279:4). hos molestos latratores ac rabulas. *Rabula* and *latrator* are connected elsewhere. See a viro bono in *rabulam latratoremque* converti: Quintilian 12.9.12.

15(I,279:4). The Council of Constance granted a certain amount of independence to the French Observants but did not succeed in thereby securing their obedience to the Provincial Ministers. See John Moorman, *A History of the Franciscan Order* (Oxford: Clarendon Press, 1968), p. 445, and Loomis, *Council,* pp. 260–261 (Fillastre's Diary: Session XIX).

16(I,279:11). Eugenio Garin, *Prosatori latini del quattrocento,* La Letteratura Italiana, Storia e Testi, Vol. XIII (Milan: R. Ricciardi, 1952), p. 288, note 2: "Isidoro, *De summo bono,* 3." Poggius refers to Isidore of Seville, d.636.

17(I,279:16–17). Poggius refers to St. Paul (p. 27), St. Augustine (pp. 12, 22, 27, 29), and St. John Chrysostom (pp. 19, 24, 26, 28) in the *De avaritia* printed in his *Opera Omnia,* Vol. I.

18(I,279:23–28). Poggius named and quoted not only the three saints mentioned but also St. Ambrose as well as three ancient Greek and eight ancient Roman authors and Petrarch, in the *De avaritia.*

19(I,280:1). See, for instance, Cicero's *Tusculan Disputations,* Book

I, or his *De finibus bonorum et malorum,* Book I (Zurich: Artemis Verlag, 1966 and 1964).

20(I,280:7–10). See Walser, *Poggius,* pp. 418–423. At the time of his death, Poggius owned the following works of Cicero:

1. De finibus. De amicitia. De senectute. Topica. Rhetorica. Framentum academicorum. Somnium Scipionis.
2. De natura deorum. De divinatione.
3. Verrines.
4. Philippics and Catilinarians.
5. De oratore. Paradoxa; Brutus; Orator.
6. Epistolae ad Atticum.
7. Epistolae ad Lentulum.
8. Orationes XXXI.
9–11. De officiis.
12. De finibus.
13. De legibus.
14. Tusculanae.
15–16. Rhetorica.
18. Orationes.
73. Orationes tullii V.

21(I,280:12–24). Poggius, in his dedication of the *De avaritia* to Franciscus Barbarus, praises no one specifically except the dedicatee. In the letter, he quotes his exact words in the second sentence of the dedication: "Magnam laudem consecuti sunt, et nomen multis seculis duraturum" ["They have achieved great glory and a name that will last through the ages"]. In praising especially writers who were competent in Greek, he may have had Leonardus Brunus Aretinus in mind, as he says in the letter, but he does not mention Leonardus by name in the dedication. (*Poggii Opera Omnia,* I, 1.)

22(I,280:11–13). On the question of "publication," see Helene Harth, "Niccolò Niccoli," pp. 50–51. Nicolaus, according to Tonelli, was Nicolaus Mediceus.

23(I,281:13–16). Tonelli, in note 2 on p. 281, says: "Albertus of Sarteano near Clusium was a member of the Friars Minor and the Observants and a pupil of Guarinus, as well as the most celebrated preacher of the Gospel in his time. Franciscus Barbarus, in a letter to Leonellus Estensis, referred to him as a 'holy man and the finest preacher of Christ.' On his life, habits, works, and pilgrimages, see Tiraboschi, *Storia,* Vol. VI, lib. 2, cap. 1, sec. 15, and Shepherd, *Vita di Poggio,* Vol. I, pp. 162–166; Vol. II, appendix XV, p. xxxviii."

For the life and learning of Albertus Sarthianensis, see Martène and Durand, *Amplissima Collectio,* Vol. III, cols. 753–756, and his courteous letters to Nicolaus de Niccolis and to Poggius, cols. 755–775.

The letter to Nicolaus is dated 1430. For a more detailed life, see De Sérent's article in *Dictionnaire d'histoire ecclésiastique,* edited by A. Beaudrillart, A. Vogt, U. Rouzies, I (1912), 1554–1556. For his works and a fuller account of his life, see Franciscus Haroldus, *Beati Alberti a Sarthiano Ord. Min. Reg. Observ. Opera Omnia* (Rome: Joannus Baptista Bussottus, 1688).

24(I,281:15–16). vitaeque ut puto integerrimae. For *integerrima vita,* see Cicero *Planc.* 1.

25(I,281:16–21). The General of the Minorites in 1429 was Antonius de Massa who that year gave up his position as "Minister Generalis" to Guillelmus Casalensis. See Luke Wadding, *Annales Minorum,* edited by P. J. M. Fonseca, 2nd edition, 25 vols. (Rome: Typis Rachi Bernabò, 1731–1886), X, 141–142. Wadding also discusses (pp. 80–200, 506–507) the problems within the Franciscan order which might have led to the interdict threatened by Poggius.

26(I,281:20). splendor bonorum virorum. For a similar expression, see summorum *hominum splendor,* Cicero *De orat.* 1.45.200. Again one of the three newly discovered rhetorical works of Cicero copied by Poggius in Cod. Laur. 50.31. See Ullman, *Origin and Development,* pp. 35–36.

27(I,281:19). perstringit enim aciem oculorum. See *praestringere aciem oculorum,* Plautus *Miles* 1.1.4. This adaptation of a phrase in the *Miles Gloriosus* occurs in a letter presumably written by Poggius in June 1429. Nicolaus Cusanus did not bring the twelve hitherto lost comedies, including the *Miles,* to Rome until December 1429 (Sabbadini, *Scoperte,* I, 112). Poggius was not allowed to have it copied until 1431, when his scribe wrote Cod. Vat. lat. 1629 (Ullman, *Origin and Development,* pp. 50–51).

LETTER LXXIII

1(I,283:6–7). Bartholomeus de Montepolitiano had been associated with all Poggius' major activities. He had gone with Pope John XXIII to the Council of Constance in 1414. He had been with Poggius and Cincius to St. Gall in June–July 1416 and had discovered and copied classical texts there; he took the ms. of Silius Italicus' "Punica" with him to Italy. In 1417 he discovered and copied the text of Festus' *De significatione verborum* in St. Gall. See Cosenza, *Dictionary,* I, 439–440, and Sabbadini, *Scoperte,* I, 78–80; II, 252. See also Sandys, *History,* II, 26–29, and *Ambr. Trav. Epist.,* Vol. II, *Epist.* XXIV, 9, cols. 981–985, Bartholomeus' own account in a letter to Ambrosius. For this letter, see Appendix, Letter VII. He was also a papal secretary under Martin V and Poggius' companion in archeological research, see Letter LIX

(Tonelli Bk. III, ltr. 19; I, 219:6–31) in September 1428. Two months before Bartholomeus' death, Poggius wrote of substituting him for Cincius as a speaker in the *De avaritia*, see Letter LXIX (Tonelli, Bk. III, ltr. 32; I, 273:4). For a very unfriendly attack on Bartholomeus and his tomb, see Leonardus Brunus Aretinus, *Epist.*, VI, 5; pt. 2, pp. 45–48. For an account of the tomb, see Pope-Hennessy, *Italian Renaissance Sculpture*, pp. 290–291 and plates 39–40.

2(I,284:1;285:2–5). At Ferentino, Martin V was close to his familiar, ancestral land holdings, all around Genazzano, which had belonged to the Colonna family since 1292 and even earlier. See Partner, *Papal State*, pp. 197–198 and 205, note 3.

3(I,284:7). The Cardinal Placentinus was Branda de Castiglione, who was a great supporter of the search for books. See Sandys, *History*, II, 28, note 13.

4(I,284:9,14). Poggius had been trying for a long time to locate the text of Frontinus' *De aquaeductu urbis*. In two letters written a few months after this one, Poggius was still concerned with copying the text. This text has survived through the ms. discovered at Monte Cassino by Poggius and that discovered in 1425 by the monk of Hersfeld and described by Nicolaus de Niccolis in his *Commentarium*. See Sabbadini, *Scoperte*, I, 85, 88, 108; II, 192, 224. Poggius' discovery of the text was hailed by Ambrosius Traversarius in his letter to Nicolaus: *Epist.* VIII, 43, col. 409. See especially note 2, where Mehus discusses the difference between Frontinus and Fronto.

5(I,284:10). This exemplar, according to Sabbadini, *Scoperte*, II, 223, note 3, is lost but Cod. Harleian. 2766 may be a copy of it.

6(I,284:16–24). See Walser, *Poggius*, p. 147, and Poggius' description of a visit by Nicolaus de Niccolis and Laurentius de Medicis to his garden full of sculpture at the beginning of the *De nobilitate* (*Poggii Opera Omnia*, I, 65).

7(I,284:26). secundo vento se in portum contulit. See *in portum vento secundo*, velo passo pervenit, Plautus *Stich.* 2.3.45.

8(I,285:2). On Anagni, see *Lazio*, pp. 425–429, and on Ferentino, pp. 430–433.

LETTER LXXIV

1(I,285:6–12). Poggius' surviving letter, written from Rome about the structure of the *De avaritia* is Letter LXXII (Tonelli Bk. III, ltr. 35). His recent letter (LXXIII, Tonelli Bk. III, ltr. 37) was from Anagni and told of the Frontinus. On Santo Germano, a tiny refuge near Cassino, see *Lazio*, p. 477.

2(I, 285:12,22). On the Livy, see Ullman, *Origin and Development*, pp. 45–48. The Livy is now Cod. Vat. Lat. 1843, 1849, 1852, bound separately, as Poggius directed, and "illuminated, just as Poggio wished his set to be."

3(I,285:12;286:14). Poggius wrote constantly to Nicolaus during 1428 and 1429 about parchment to copy the text of Aulus Gellius, which was to be done by a scribe and which was finally carried to Nicolaus by Laurentius de Medicis.

4(I,286:7–8). Poggius did not in fact give up his interest in copying texts. His letters during 1430 are full of his desire to study and copy the Plautus ms. brought by Nicholaus Treverensis to Cardinal de Ursinis and he also had a scribe copying the letters of St. Jerome.

5(I,286:10). There is no Pliny in the inventory of Poggius' books made after his death in 1459 (see Walser, *Poggius*, pp. 418–423) or any record of his having copied the text.

LETTER LXXV

1(I,287:3). Poggius' letter from Anagni dated 9 July 1429 is LXXIII (Tonelli Bk. III, ltr. 37).

2(I,287:5,19–20). There is still an incomplete permit issued to "Dilecto filio francisco de Pistorio ordinis minorum professori sacre theologie magistro" on record in *Reg. Vat.* 356, f. 32v, dated "Ferentini X Kal. Septembris Anno XI," which fits in well with the text of this letter.

3(I,287:9). The "Sultan" at this time was Murad II. For his relations with Venice and other Western governments, see Franz Babinger, *Maometto il conquistatore e il suo tempo*, translated by Evelina Polacco, Biblioteca di Cultura Storica No. 54 (Sancasciano: Giulio Einaudi, 1957), pp. 32–33.

4(I,287:11–15). For Friar Felix Fabri's journey to Alexandria, Cairo, and Jerusalem in 1483, see Hilda F. M. Prescott, *Once to Sinai* (London: Eyre and Spottiswoode, 1957), pp. 17–29, 139–172, 190–218, and bibliography of books on similar pilgrimages: pp. 287–290. For a voyage to Jerusalem, Alexandria, and Cairo taken very shortly before that of Franciscus Pistoriensis, probably between 1419 and 1425, see H. Moranvillé, "Un pèlerinage en Terre Sainte et au Sinaï au XVe siècle," *Bibliothèque de l'école des chartes*, LXVI (1905), 70–106. It contains detailed accounts of Cairo and Alexandria. See also M. Margaret Newett, *Canon Pietro Casola's Pilgrimage to Jerusalem in the Year 1494* (Manchester: Manchester University Press, 1907). For details about pilgrimages from Venice to the Holy Land between 1400 and 1430, see pp. 48–64. For a journey to Jerusalem and Egypt made by Gilbert de Lannoy in 1421, see Hilda F. M. Prescott, *Jerusalem Journey: Pilgrim-*

age to the Holy Land in the Fifteenth Century (London: Eyre and Spottiswoode, 1954), pp. 23–25 and bibliography, pp. 219–221, and Michel Join-Lambert, *Jérusalem, Isréalite, Chrétienne, Musulmane* (Paris: Albert A. Guillot, 1956), pp. 84–92, 136–143. See also Moorman, *Franciscan Order*, p. 437.

On Cairo, see A. R. Guest and E. T. Richmond, "Misr in the Fifteenth Century," *Journal of the Royal Asiatic Society* (1903), pp. 791–816 and map.

5(I,287:21). On Franciscan financial interests at this time, see Moorman, *Franciscan Order*, pp. 501–503.

6(I,287:24–288:1). The General of the Franciscan Order in 1424–1430 was Antonius de Massa. See Moorman, *Franciscan Order*, p. 446. At the beginning of his pontificate, while still in Florence, Martin V had sent "Frater Antonius de Massa," later General of the Franciscan Order, to Constantinople to explore the Emperor's attitude toward the unification of the Eastern and Western Churches. (Muratori, *R.I.S.*, Vol. III, pt. 2, col. 864.) Ciacconius, *Vitae*, Vol. II, col. 827, also lists many embassies dispatched by Martin V.

The procurator was "Guglielmo da Casale di Monferrato, gia procuratore cismontano nella Curia romana, fornito di dottrina e di molti pregi, che morì in Firenze passati dodici anni di governo prudente." (*Dizionario di erudizione storico-ecclesiastica*, XXVI, 99.)

The *Bullarium Franciscanum*, Nova Series, Vol. I, p. 83, No. 165, contains a document addressed by Eugenius IV to Guillelmus de Casali, instructing him to permit Franciscus de Pistorio to undertake "ministrum provinciae Orientis." Dated Florence, 13 June 1435. From *Reg. Vat.* 359, f. 248, the document records the Pope's high opinion of Franciscus' piety, character, and intellectual attainments.

7(I,288:6,11–12). On Poggius' acquisition of Julius Firmicus' *Matheseos Libri VIII*, see Letter LXXIII (Tonelli Bk. III, ltr. 37; I, 284:10). According to Sabbadini, *Scoperte*, II, 223, the text of Book I was fairly available in France and Italy by this time. Petrarch had it (*Scoperte*, I, 25–26); so did Jean de Montreuil (II, 66).

8(I,288:8). The abbot of Monte Cassino at this time was still Pirro Tomacelli of Naples.

9(I,288:9). Poggius probably here means Branda de Castillione, Bishop and Cardinal of Placentia (Piacenza) 1350–1443.

10(I,288:15–16). Poggius had mentioned the solitude in Letter LXXIII (Tonelli Bk. II, ltr. 37; I, 285:2), and it seems to be confirmed by the paucity of curial names in *Reg. Vat.* 356.

11(I,288:18). Nicolaus Cusanus returned to Rome with the Plautus ms., now Cod. Vat. Lat. 3870, in December 1429 (Rotta, *Nicolò di Cusa*, p. 18). It is an interesting coincidence that Nicolaus Cusanus is mentioned here in a letter that also mentions a mission from the Pope to the Sultan because he was one of the few Western churchmen able to regard Islam with any sympathy, which was indicated in treatises that he wrote many years later, in 1453 and 1460. See R. W. Southern, *Western Views of Islam in the Middle Ages* (Cambridge, Mass.: Harvard University Press, 1962), pp. 86–94; Raymund Klibansky and Hildebrand Bascour, *Nicolai de Cusa De pace fidei* (London: The Warburg Institute; Mediaeval and Renaissance Studies, Supplement III, 1956); and Nicolaus Cusanus, *Cribratio Alchorani*, in his *Opera* (Basel, 1565).

12(I,288:20). Here Poggius refers to Cardinal Jordanus de Ursinis.

13(I,289:2–7). Bartholomeus' devoted service to Martin V is confirmed by the vast number of documents bearing his name in the Vatican and Lateran registers 1418–1429. See *Reg. Vat.* 349, 350, 351, 353, 355, 356; *Reg. Lat.* 209, 210, 212, 231, etc. His name occurs in the documents in the first six months of Martin V's twelfth year: January–June 1429: *Reg. Vat.* 351: ff. 8, 107v, 113v, 119r, 128v.

14(I,289:12–14). For Poggius' position and property in 1429, see Walser, *Poggius*, pp. 339–342, Documents 26–29.

15(I,289:16–17). Horace *Epistles* I.2.47–48.

16(I,289:22). nulla ambitione laboro. For *ambitione laborare*, see aut ab avaritia aut misera *ambitione laborat*, Horace *Satires* 1.4.26.

17(I,289:29–30). On Albertus de Sarteano's friendship with Nicolaus de Niccolis and on his visit to Florence in 1429, see Haroldus, *Beati Alberti*, pp. 23–25, 200.

Carolus here may be Carolus de Ricasolis, a citizen of Florence who donated land to the Observants for a new monastery which was opposed by Poggius. See Letter LXXX (Tonelli Bk. IV, ltr. 3) and Haroldus, *Beati Alberti*, p. 19.

18(I,290:4). In a later letter, Bk. III, ltr. 41 (LXXVII) dated 8 September 1429, Poggius was still hoping to visit Arpinum a day or two later after the Pope's departure for Rome. After that it is not mentioned again.

19(I,290:6–7). Ser Angelus was the notary who attended to Poggius' affairs in Florence. (See Walser, *Poggius*, pp. 338, 341, 343, 346, 351–355, 357, 359.) Poggius' will, dated 19 October 1443 (Walser, pp. 359–370), lists only his sister Caterina and her son Raffaelus as Poggius' relatives in addition to his wife Vaggia and his children.

LETTER LXXVI

1(I,290:3). Ambrosius Traversarius, in a letter to Nicolaus de Niccolis, says that he wrote him earlier from Venice about meeting a man there who had met Magister Franciscus Pistoriensis in Syria, where Franciscus was spending money lavishly and acquiring fine ancient gold coins (Martène and Durand, *Amplissima Collectio*, Vol. III, cols. 686–687 [Lib. XX, *Epist.* 26] and *Ambr. Trav. Epistolae*, Vol. II, *Epist.* VIII, 48, col. 417). Dated by Mehus 1433. In Letter LXXXIV, which is Tonelli's Bk. IV, ltr. 12, Poggius reports to Nicolaus on the ancient sculpture which Franciscus has promised to bring him from Chios. In Tonelli's Bk. IV, ltr. 15, Poggius responds to a letter written to him from Chios by Franciscus and mentions his own letter to Andreas (Andreolus) Justinianus of Chios (Tonelli Bk. IV, ltr. 18) seeking further ancient sculpture as a gift in return for Poggius' letters, an indication of the high value in which they were held. There is another letter, to Suffretus of Rhodes (Tonelli Bk. IV, ltr. 21), seeking further ancient sculpture to be brought back to Italy by Franciscus, who ultimately disappointed Poggius by disposing of the sculpture and pretending that it had been stolen. He apparently made two trips, one which Poggius was arranging in 1429 and the second to which Poggius refers in his letter to Andreolus Justinianus (Tonelli Bk. VII, ltr. 14; II, 174–177), dated Ferrara, 15 May [1438].

2(I,290:7–8). For background material on the proposed journey, see Stephen Runciman, *A History of the Crusades,* Vol. III: *The Kingdom of Acre* (Cambridge: Cambridge University Press, 1954), pp. 444–449, which deals with the sack of Alexandria in 1365 and the sack of Cyprus in 1426. See *Encyclopaedia Britannica,* 11th edition, IX, 102, on Barsbai, the anti-European *and* anti-Turkish Sultan of Egypt 1422–1438.

3(I,290:10). Chios was a Genoese outpost 1346–1566 and a dependency of the diocese of Rhodes. According to R. Janin, "C'est peut-être dans l'île de Chios que les relations furent les meilleures entre grecs et latins." *Dictionnaire d'histoire et de géographie ecclésiastiques,* edited by Alfred Baudrillart, A. de Meyer, and E. van Cauwenbergh, XII (Paris: Librairie Letouzey et Ané, 1953), 743–746.

4(I,290:14). recusare hunc laborem. For *recusare laborem,* see Caesar *B.C.* 1.68 fin.; Quintilian 2.3.26; 12.11.10. On Quintilian, see Letter XXIII, note 3 (Tonelli Bk. II, ltr. 2; I, 87:9) and Letter LXVII, note 3 (Tonelli Bk. III, ltr. 30; I, 269:13).

5(I,290:30;291:1). Magister Franciscus' assignment to travel on a mission to the Sultan for the Pope is recorded by Luke Wadding in his *Annales Minorum,* X, 141. Perhaps the Procurator, whom Poggius describes as "mihi amicissimus," was Jordanus Cardinalis Ursinus, described by Wadding (*Annales,* X, 159) as "ordinis protector."

6(I,291:6). expansurum vela. For *pandere vela,* see Quint. 6.1.52.

7(I,291:29). Poggius was closely involved with Antonius Luscus at this period. They had explored the ruins of ancient Rome together (see *De varietate fortunae,* Book I), and Luscus was both a speaker in and a critic of the *De avaritia:* see Letter LXXII (Tonelli Bk. III, ltr. 35; I, 277–282). Before joining the Curia, Luscus had been secretary to the Duke of Milan and had written an invective against Florence (see Baron, *Humanistic and Political Literature,* pp. 9, 38–52, and *Crisis,* pp. 76, 90, 99–100). There is no evidence given by da Schio, *Antonio Loschi,* of Luscus' being in Florence or anywhere with the Medici brothers and Nicolaus de Niccolis in 1429 or 1430.

LETTER LXXVII

1(I,292:4). Poggius seems to have obtained permission to go to Florence, because the next letter, LXXVIII (Tonelli Bk. IV, ltr. 1), was written in Terranuova when Poggius was preparing to return to Rome.

2(I,292:7). lateri adheret. For *lateri adhaerere,* see Livy 39.25.11. Poggius was copying the three Decades of Livy's *Ab urbe condita* which are now Cod. Vat. Lat. 1843, 1849, and 1852 between April 1425 and early 1429. In July 1429, shortly before this letter was written, Poggius had already sent them to Nicolaus de Niccolis to be illuminated and bound. See Letter LXXIV, note 2 (*Poggii Epist.* Bk. III, ltr. 38; I, 285:12–13), and Ullman, *Origin and Development,* pp. 45–47.

3(I,292:15). Gregorovius (*History of Rome,* Vol. VII, pt. 1, p. 12) says that Martin V built himself a castle at Genazzano for a summer residence and also spent summers at Gallicano, Tivoli, Frascati, and Molara. See also Muratori, *R.I.S.,* Vol. III, ii, 858, for Martin V's repairs in Rome and to the palace of the Sancti Apostoli, where he lived. On Martin's wealth and on his country residences, see Andreas Billius, *Historiae Patriae Libri IX* in Muratori, *R.I.S.,* Vol. XIX, cols. 141–144.

4(I,292:17). Whether Poggius ever saw them or not, the remains of ancient buildings are there. For Arpino and Ferentino, see *Lazio, attraverso l'Italia,* 3rd edition (Milan: Touring Club Italiano, 1943), XI, 224, 228–229.

5(I,292:19). According to Mancini, Poggius was in Ferentino with Martin V when Laurentius Valla's uncle Scribanus, also an apostolic secretary, died of the plague early in September on his way from Ferentino to Rome. Valla applied for his position, but Poggius and Antonius Luscus persuaded Martin V to refuse him, ostensibly because of his youth. (Girolamo Mancini, *Vita di Lorenzo Valla* [Florence: Sansoni, 1891], pp. 20–21.) Valla told this story himself in his "In Pogium Antidotum Liber IV," *Opera Omnia,* with a Preface by Eugenio Garin (Monumenta Politica et Philosophica Rariora, Ser. I, No. 5, 2 vols. [Turin: Bottega d'Erasmo, 1962], an anastatic reprint of the Basel 1540 edition), I, 352.

LETTER LXXVIII

1(I,293:5). Poggius' letters in July, August, and September 1429 are dated from Ferentino as are letters from Martin V (*Reg. Vat.* 356, ff. 34v–35r). On f. 38v there is a document ending with a whole sentence in Poggius' handwriting which includes the words "per me Poggium de mandato domini nostri papae vii Novembris 1429." These dates help to assign Letter LXXVIII (IV, 1) to October 1429 when Poggius arranged for the building of a chapel and also bought land in Terranova (Walser, *Poggius,* Doc. 30–31, pp. 342–343; 4 and 11 October 1429).

2(I,293:11–15). Coluccius Salutatus' ms. of Pliny's *Naturalis historia,* now Paris: Bibl. Nat. lat. 6798 passed into the possession of Leonardus Brunus Aretinus (Sabbadini, *Scoperte,* I, 75; II, 241).

3(I,294:1–9). According to Bandini, Vol. II, cols. 744–749, and Vol. III, cols. 356–357, 370, 421–422, 628, Leonardus Brunus Aretinus translated Plutarch's lives of Demosthenes, Marcus Antonius, Pyrrhus, Paulus Aemilius, Tiberius and Gaius Gracchus, Sertorius and Marcus Cato. Two codices in the Bibliotheca Laurentiana, Plut. LXV Cod. 28 (Vol. II, cols. 748–749) and Plut. LXXXIX Cod. IX (Vol. III, col. 356), contain most of these lives collected in one volume. Both codices are fifteenth century. Leonardus' original work, a life of Cicero called "Cicero Novus," is dedicated to Nicolaus de Niccolis. Poggius' inventory No. 35 lists "Vite Prutarchi [*sic*] VIII a Leonardo traducte . . . " (Walser, *Poggius,* p. 420).

The text Poggius wanted may now be Laurentianus: Plut. XXIX, Inf. Cod. XIII, containing numerous translations of Plutarch's *Lives of Illustrious Men,* with a dedication to Cosmus de Medicis. For a detailed discussion of Leonardus Brunus Aretinus' translations of Plutarch's *Lives,* see Baron, *Leonardo Bruni Aretino,* pp. 102–104, 113–114, 123–125, 161–163, 167, 187.

4(I,294:11). Carolus (Tonelli, I, 294:11) is identified as Carolus Marsuppinus Aretinus in Tonelli's note 1.

LETTER LXXIX

1(I,294:2). ut obsequar voluntati tue. For *obsequi voluntati* alicuius, see Cicero *De finibus* 2.6.17. Poggius' scribe was copying the *De finibus* for him in November 1425. See Letters XXXV and XLII (*Poggii Epist.* Bk. II, ltrs. 27 and 34; I, 155 and 169). See also Walser, *Poggius,* pp. 106 and 419 (inventory No. 12).

2(I,294:3). There is evidence for Petrus Candidus Decembrius' (1399–1477) being in Rome and being given assignments by Martin V in 1425 but not in 1429. There is also no evidence to corroborate a visit by him to Florence that year. See Mario Borsa, "Pier Candido Decembrio e l'umanesimo in Lombardia," *Archivio storico lombardo*, X, Ser. 2 (1893), 12. Tonelli (I, 294, note 2) refers the reader, for information on Petrus Candidus Decembrius' life, studies, and works, to Tiraboschi, *Storia della letteratura italiana*, Vol. I, Lib. 3, cap. L, sec. 48–49, and Shepherd, *Vita di Poggio*, Appendix XXII. For further bibliography on Decembrius, see Chevalier, *Bio-bibliographie*, Vol. I, col. 1160, and Cosenza, *Dictionary*, II, 1196–1204.

Decembrius was one of the most energetic and successful of the humanists. He was secretary to the Duke of Milan 1419–1447 and traveled widely on embassies for him during which he met humanists, courtiers, and clerics from other parts of Italy and Europe. See Borsa, pp. 5–75. His father Ubertus was a pupil of Manuel Chrysoloras and collaborated with him on translating Plato's *Republic*. Decembrius himself made many translations from the Greek which were standard texts during the fifteenth century, as evidenced by the frequency with which they were printed. He was one of the important figures in the introduction of Greek literature into England, with the translation which he made of Plato's *Republic* for Humphrey, Duke of Gloucester. See Weiss, *Humanism*, pp. 54–60, 134, and Mario Borsa, "The Correspondence of Humphrey Duke of Gloucester and Pier Candido Decembrio," *English Historical Review*, XIX (1904), 509–526, XX (1905), 484–498. Poggius' letters to him (VIII, 2 and XII, 12) date from much later in their lives. The first (1438) praises the style and sentiments of a letter which Decembrius wrote officially for Philippus Maria de Vicecomitibus to send to Cosmus de Medicis; Poggius' letter also contains interesting details of his own domestic life. The second letter, written around 1453, is merely an introduction for a young humanist, Bartholomeus de Bucino, seeking work. At this time Poggius and Decembrius were collaborating on a translation of Diodorus Siculus' *Bibliotheca historica*, at the request of Pope Nicolaus V. Although, according to Borsa ("Pier Candido," pp. 15–16), Decembrius' letters were passed around like gazettes, they seem never to have been published. A careful analysis of them was made by Vittorio Zaccaria, "L'epistolario di Pier Candido Decembrio," *Rinascimento*, III (1952), 85–118, who says, pp. 85–86, that Decembrius himself prepared them for publication. Zaccaria's list, pp. 114–118, of the recipients of Decembrius' letters includes a sizable number of Poggius'. In another article, "Sulle opere di Pier Candido Decembrio," *Rinascimento*, VII (1956), 13–74, Zaccaria discusses the 127 works for which Decembrius was given credit on his handsome tomb in Sant' Ambrogio in Milan. Ernst Ditt gives a considerable analysis of Petrus Candidus Decembrius' classical knowledge and literary output but deals only briefly and incidentally with his travels and personal activities, omitting the 1420s almost completely. See his "Pier Candido Decembrio: Contributo alla storia dell' umanesimo italiano," *Memorie del r. istituto lombardo di scienze e lettere,* Classe di lettere, scienze morali e storiche, XXIV, Ser. III, 15 (1931), 21–106. There is also little biographical information in Paul Oskar Kristeller's "Pier Candido Decembrio and His Unpublished Treatise on the Immortality of the Soul," in *The Classical Tradition: Literary and Historical Studies in Honor of Harry Caplan,* Luitpold Wallach, ed. (Ithaca: Cornell University Press, 1966), pp. 536–558.

3(I,294:2–295:3). Presumably the codex of Cicero's orations found by Poggius at Cluny.

4(I,294:10). Poggius found a large fragment of Asconius Pedianus' commentary on five of Cicero's orations while at St. Gall in 1416. Sabbadini, *Scoperte,* II, 202–203, and *Poggii Epistolae,* Bk. I, ltr. 5 to Guarinus Veronensis (Tonelli, I, 29). It was copied immediately by Bartholomeus de Montepolitiano and sent to Nicolaus de Niccolis. The Cod. Laur. Lat. LIV, 5 bears the date 25 July 1416. Poggius himself made a copy of Asconius Pedianus also in 1416 which was Madrid, Bibl. Nac. X, 81 and is now Cod. 854 (Ullman, *Origin and Development,* p. 48). In the light of Poggius' Letter LII (Tonelli Bk. III, ltr. 15) it is interesting that the Madrid ms. is on paper.

5(I,294:11). Poggius must mean here the fragment of Petronius which he found in England, more than seven years earlier. (Sabbadini, *Scoperte,* I, 83.) The fragment found in Cologne on Poggius' return journey from England could not have been in Nicolaus' possession so many years.

6(I,294:7). On Poggius and the text of Lucretius which he discovered see Laurentius Mehus' "Praefatio" to his *Vita Ambrosii,* I, xxxviii, and Schanz-Hosius, *Geschichte der römischen Literatur,* Handbuch der Altertumswissenschaft, edited by Muller, VIII, 1, 4th edition (Munich: Beck'sche, 1927), Vol. I, p. 281.

Poggius' letter suggests that Nicolaus was keeping either the original manuscript found by Poggius or a copy made by him. The archetype of the text as known now is the copy made by Nicolaus: Cod. Laurentianus XXXV, 30.

7(I,295:12). Poggius, in his funeral oration for Nicolaus de Niccolis, says that Nicolaus collected more than 800 books "summo labore et diligentia" (*Poggii Opera Omnia,* I, 276). The inventory of Poggius' library at the time of his death lists only 95 books. Nonius Marcellus is No. 39 of the inventory of Poggius' books made when he died (Walser, *Poggius,* p. 421). For a discussion of the number of manuscripts in Nicolaus' library, see Ullman-Stadter, *Public Library,* pp. 59–76.

8(I,295:26). Carolus Marsuppinus Aretinus was a good friend of the Medici brothers. In the Bodleian Library ms. Rawlinson A no. 402, among other works by Marsuppinus there is a long (ff. 26v–50r) letter from him to Cosmus and Laurentius offering sympathy on the death in 1433 of their mother: Piccarda de' Bueri (see *Firenze e dintorni,* p. 248). The letter was published by Pier Giorgio Ricci, "Una consolatoria inedita del Marsuppini," *Rinascità,* III (1940), 363–433. The text of the letter fills pp. 389–433. Ricci does not mention the ms. in the Bodleian but lists twelve others.

LETTER LXXX

1(I,296:2–4). See Moorman, *Franciscan Order,* pp. 444–447, especially p. 446, note 4.

2(I,296:10). Cicero *Ad fam.* 1.6.2.

3(I,296:22–26). See Origo, *San Bernardino,* chap. IX, "The Reform of the Observants," pp. 205–228 and pp. 290–293.

4(I,296:27–297:2). Poggius must have ascribed this saying to the wrong Father of the Church. No experts on St. Augustine who have been consulted could identify it and it does not appear in David Lenfant, *Concordantiae Augustinianae, sive Collectio omnium sententiarum quae sparsim reperiuntur in omnibus S. Augustini operibus,* 2 vols. (Brussels: Culture et civilization, 1963).

5(I,297:5). St. Bernardinus: Bernardino degli Albizzeschi of Siena (1380–1444). Canonized by Pope Nicholas V, 1450. (Origo, *San Bernardino,* pp. 1–2.) His sermons were printed eight times in the fifteenth century (Hain, *Repertorium,* Vol. I, pt. 1, nos. 2827–2834). See Remigio Sabbadini, "Briciole umanistiche," *Giornale storico della letteratura italiana,* XLVI (1905), 70–71.

Cod. Ambros. D.113 sup., f.18 contains a caricature of S. Bernardinus Senensis by Modestus Decembrius, brother of Petrus Candidus Decembrius (see Borsa, "Pier Candido Decembrio," *Archivo storico lombardo,* X, Ser. 2 [1893], 1–75, 358–422, 423–441).

6(I,297:10–14). Origo, *San Bernardino,* pp. 11–42, chap. I: "The False and the True Vocation." See also the account of S. Bernardinus in Antoninus Florentinus, *Chronicon,* III, f. CCXXXIV–f. CCXXXV. For criticism of preaching friars other than S. Bernardinus, see the opening section of Poggius' *De avaritia* in *Poggii Opera Omnia,* I, 2–3.

7(I,297:15–32). Moorman, *Franciscan Order,* pp. 446–447.

8(I,298:3–7). In Beaudrillart, *Dictionnaire,* Vol. I, cols. 1554–1555, Antoine de Sérent reports that a meeting of the Chapter General of the Italian Observants was held at Bologna at Pentecost 1431 and was requested by Pope Eugenius IV to choose six churchmen to be used to summon the Council at Basel and to preach a crusade against the Turks. Albertus was among the six chosen.

9(I,298:8–17). Moorman, *Franciscan Order,* pp. 446–447, deals with the decrees of the "Chapter General of 1430, called 'Martinianae.'" On p. 465 Moorman mentions the vast increase in the number of Observant communities during San Bernardino's active life.

10(I,298:20–22). At this time, Poggius was also engaged in correspondence with Albertus Sartheanensis, whose letter to Poggius appears in Martène and Durand, *Amplissima Collectio,* Vol. III, cols. 757–775. Poggius replied. See Tonelli Bk. IV, ltr. 7 (I, 310–315). Poggius and Albertus Sartheanensis were each trying to win Nicolaus de Niccolis to his side of the controversy in 1430. Albertus' letter to Nicolaus (Martène and Durand, *Amplissima Collectio,* Vol. III, cols. 755–757) is distinctly critical of Poggius for using language unbecoming to a Christian (col. 756).

11(I,299:1–9). In his life of St. Bernardinus, his recent biographer mentions Poggius' resentment of lands being given to the Observants in 1425–1426 by Carolus de Ricasolis in San Giovanni in Valdarno. See Vittorino Fachinetti, *San Bernardino da Siena* (Milan: Casa editrice S. Lega Eucaristica, 1933), pp. 364–370. Wadding (*Annales,* X, 146) indicates that Martin V in two documents issued in May of 1429, more than six months earlier than the date of this letter, had given the Observants permission to move and/or to build. In an unpublished Ph.D. thesis, John W. Oppel, in his second chapter, pp. 27–77, "Lay Society and the Reform of the Church: The Dialogue *On Avarice* and Poggio's Attack on the Mendicants," points out that Poggius had a well-developed hostility to the followers of St. Bernardinus when he started to write his *De avaritia,* which was finished and published in 1429. See "The Moral Basis of Renaissance Politics: A Study of the Humanistic Political and Social Philosophy of Poggio Bracciolini (1380–1459)" (Ph.D. dissertation, Princeton University, 1972).

12(I,299:7–10). In this letter to Poggius, also written in 1430 (submitted to Nicolaus in a letter of that date), Albertus says: "Peto abs te praeterea...apud pontificem maximum hoc iustum negotium non impedias" ["I beseech you furthermore not to interfere between us and the Pope in this honorable business"]. (Martène and Durand, *Amplissima Collectio,* Vol. III, col. 773.)

See Eubel, *Hierarchia,* I, 249. The Bishop of Fiesole was Benotius (Federighi), an apostolic notary who died in 1450.

13(I,299:13–15–300:8). On new building by the Observants, see Wadding, *Annales,* X, 132–136.

"Antonius Nerius Aretinus, sacrae Theologiae Magister, qui Parisiis circa annum MCCCCV florebat, et docte scripsit in Magistrum Sententiarum, aliaque scripsit opera, quae in Conventu Sergiani, ubi pie obiit, asservabantur" ["Antonius Nerius Aretinus, master of sacred theology, who was active in Paris around 1405 and who wrote learned comments on the *Sententia Magistrum* and wrote other works which are preserved in the monastery of Sergianus where he died in piety"]. *Annales*, X, 120.

14(I,300:5). For the Chapter General in 1430 and the "chapter held by the Observants of Bologna at Whitsuntide 1431," see Moorman, *Franciscan Order*, pp. 447–449.

15(I,300:18). Seneca *De beneficiis* 1.10.3. (*Moral Essays*, III [Loeb Classical Library, London, 1935], 32.)

16(I,301:5–7). Wadding, *Annales*, X, 142, used almost the same language: "Locus est amoenus, et pietati colendae opportunus, hortis, et aquis abundans" ["The place is pleasant and suitable for cultivating a pious spirit, and full of gardens and of water"].

17(I,301:10). According to tradition, Plato intentionally set up his Academy in an unhealthy spot: an uncomfortable body would strengthen the mind. See Paul Shorey, *What Plato Said* (Chicago: University of Chicago Press, 1933), pp. 29 and 449, where Shorey quotes Porphyry *De abstin.* 1.36 and Aelian 9.10. Shorey describes the traditional theory of Plato's choice of site as "fantastic."

18(I,301:22). "Ambrosius Traversarius Generalis Camaldulensium" (Tonelli, note 1).

LETTER LXXXI

1(I,302:7,15). See Tiraboschi, *Storia della letteratura italiana*, Vol. VI, pt. 2, pp. 717–721. This introductory passage suggests a much longer period of time than do the dates of the letters if they are to be believed. Letter LXXIX sent through Candidus with the books is dated December 1429; the letter about the Observantia, Letter LXXX, which Poggius here says he sent first, is dated 16 December 1429. Poggius says he then sent three more short letters and is rather hurt not to have received an answer, but he appears to be expecting much more rapid service than is ever the case elsewhere in his correspondence. All this suggests some error in the date of Letter LXXXI.

2(I,303:3–7). In his funeral oration for Nicolaus, Poggius says: "Communes erant libri sui omnibus etiam ignotis, praesto aderant aut legere volentibus, aut transcribere ... " ["His books were freely available to everyone, even people he did not know. They were readily available to all who wanted to read or copy them . . ."]. (*Poggii Opera Omnia*, I, 271.)

3(I,303:7–10). According to Vespasiano, *Vite*, p. 476, at the time of Nicolaus' death, 200 of his books were out on loan to a variety of people, including a number of his Greek books which had been borrowed by Frater Franciscus de Pietrapane. See also Ullman-Stadter, *Public Library*, pp. 59–60.

4(I,303:14–16). Poggius is exaggerating here. In Letter LXXIX

(Tonelli Bk. IV, ltr. 2), dated 13 December 1429, he complains that Nicolaus has kept the Lucretius *twelve* years and the Asconius Pedianus *seven*. For an analysis of Poggius' discovery of Statius' *Silvae* and the Madrid ms. X 31 which once belonged to him, see Albert C. Clark, "The Literary Discoveries of Poggio," *Classical Review*, XIII (1899), 127–128. For Petronius, see Letter LXXIX, note 5 (Tonelli Bk. IV, ltr. 2; Vol. I, 294:11).

5(I,303:24–28). Vespasiano, *Vite*, p. 474, describes Nicolaus' passion for copying newly found or rare texts, but says nothing about his employing copyists, as Poggius often did.

6(I,303:31–304:6). In Letter LXXIII (Tonelli Bk. III, ltr. 37) Poggius describes finding the text of Julius Frontinus, *De aquaeductu urbis* and Firmicus, *Matheseos Libri VIII* at Monte Cassino and borrowing them to copy them. At the time that Letter LXXXI was written, depending on the reading of the date, Poggius could not have had the text more than six months at most.

There seems to be no documentation for "the fragment of Aratus."

7(I,304:8–12). There is no surviving evidence that Poggius was able to obtain the Lucretius, Asconius, or Petronius at this time. See Ullman, *Origin and Development*, pp. 21–57.

8(I,304:18–26). On Nicolaus Cusanus (Treverensis) and the ms. of Plautus' *Comedies*, 8 known and 12 hitherto unknown, see Letter LXVI (Tonelli Bk. III, ltr. 29; I, 266:5; 267:17–22). See also Sabbadini, *Scoperte*, II, 240–241. In Letter LXVI, Poggius mentions 20 comedies; in Letter LXXXI, only 16. He omits 4 which were already known.

9(I,304:29–30). In describing his discovery of Quintilian to Guarinus Veronensis (Tonelli Bk. I, ltr. 5; I, 27–29), Poggius says nothing about the text being in "an ancient and corrupt hand"; rather the contrary, for he speaks of copying it "velociter." See Appendix, Letter III.

10(I,304:30–305:1). Poggius was finally permitted, in 1431, to have a copy of the Plautus made which is now Cod. Vat. Lat. 1629. See Ullman, *Origin and Development*, pp. 50–51.

11(I,305:9). This suggests that Poggius was capitulating to pressure on behalf of the Observants.

12(I,305:18). ut demulceam tibi caput: a quotation from Terence *Heaut.* 762.

13(I,305:19). repugnante natura. See adversante et *repugnante natura,* Cicero *Off.* 1.31.110.

14(I,305:22). The date as expressed by Tonelli presents a problem unless one takes the view that Poggius was using the Florentine style of dating and would not date his letters 1430 until March. That does not seem to be consistent with his practice in other years. It is clear from internal evidence that this letter follows Letters LXXIX and LXXX, both dated December 1429. For this letter to be rightly dated in the right order it should bear the date VI Kalendas Januarii 1430 and not 1429, since 6 days before the first of January 1429 would set it back into 1428; and all the events mentioned in it, especially the arrival of Nicolaus Cusanus with the Plautus ms., are believed to have taken place in December 1429. See Sabbadini, *Storia e critica*, pp. 327–328, and Rotta *Nicolò di Cusa*, p. 18.

LETTER LXXXII

1(I,305:2). Poggius was born 11 February 1380 (Walser, *Poggius*, p. 6).

2(I,305:5–6). Poggius could have known the text of Censorinus' *De die natali*, a major source of information on birthdays in antiquity, which had belonged to Petrarch and, among Poggius' contemporaries, to Bartholomeus Capra and to Petrus Candidus Decembrius (Sabbadini, *Scoperte*, II, 208). He must have known the reference to birthdays in Vergil (*Ecl.* 3.76), Horace (*Odes* 3.17; 4.11), Propertius (*Carmina* 3.10), and Ovid (*Tristia* 3.13.2; 5.5.1). He had recently been working on Aulus Gellius, and there is a reference to birthdays in the *Noctes Atticae* 15.7. There are many references to birthdays in Martial's *Epigrams*, which Poggius owned at the time of his death (inventory No. 58 in Walser, *Poggius*, p. 421) but which he very seldom quoted in his letters to Nicolaus. There are also references to birthdays in Plautus: *Pseudolus*, 165, *Curculio*, 653, *Epidicus*, 640, none of which Poggius is believed to have read by February 1430.

3(I,306:1). According to Cosenza, *Dictionary*, IV, 3149, Coluccius Salutatus was born on 16 February, 1331. See Poggius' Letter II, to Nicolaus, mourning the death of Coluccius, "patrem quem posthac non facile reperiemus ... portum ac refugium omnium eruditorum, lumen patriae, Italiae decus," in *Poggii Epistolae* (edited by Tonelli), Vol. I, xiii–xvi, esp. xiv (*Poggii Opera Omnia*, Vol. III).

4(I,306:3). If this letter is correctly dated, and it appears to have been dated by Poggius himself, he was beginning his fifty-first year, or else was born in 1381.

5(I,306:6–12). Leviticus 25:8–13.

6(I,307:11–13). Plato *Protagoras* 339 B. (See *Platonis Opera*, John Burnet, ed., Vol. III [Oxford: Clarendon Press, 1909].)

7(I,307:15–16). Vergil *Aeneid* 6.129.

8(I,307:16–18). Terence *Andria* 189, and a common proverb in many languages. See Putnam's *Complete Book of Quotations*, col. 823b.

9(I,308:13–15). Nicolaus de Niccolis, born 1363, was older by almost a decade than Antonius Luscus, the senior guest at Poggius' party. He was also his own master and reputed to be wealthy.

10(I,308:18). Ludovicus Orcanus is the mysterious guest at the party. He is not mentioned anywhere in Poggius' works or correspondence, or in the correspondence of other humanists. He does not appear in the Vatican Registers that bear the names of Poggius and his friends. He is almost the only person whom Poggius mentions by his full name who cannot be identified.

LETTER LXXXIII

1(I,319:5). Nicolaus was in Rimini, Verona, and Venice in the autumn of 1430 to avoid the plague in Florence. See Zippel, *Nicolò Niccoli*, pp. 54–55, and Gutkind, *Cosimo*, p. 70.

2(I,319:8–9). Perhaps Poggius here refers to the severe plague of 1423, mentioned in his Letter XXVII (Tonelli Bk. II, ltr. 7; I, 97) and in his *Historia Florentina*, V, 209 (*Poggii Opera Omnia*, Vol. II).

3(I,320:2–10). Laurentius Mehus, in his "Praefatio" to *Ambrosii Traversarii Epistolae*, pp. lxii–lxiii, quotes from a will made by Nicolaus on 11 June 1430 and preserved "in Tabulario Florentino," in which he left *all his books* "Sanctissimo Coenobio S. Mariae de Angelis" and made Poggius one of the twelve executors. For Nicolaus' two wills and his twelve executors, see Ullman-Stadter, *Public Library*, pp. 7–15 and 292–299.

4(I,320:12–17). Grottaferrata is a monastery of the Greek rite founded in the ninth century. It was suitable for Martin V to visit it, since he was beginning to send the missions to Constantinople which led to the Council of Florence and the Union of the Churches in 1439.

The plain of Tusculum is very close to Grottaferrata, about 6 kilometers away. See Bernard de Montfaucon, *Diarium Italicum* (Paris: Apud Joannem Anisson, 1702), pp. 334–338. See also *Roma e dintorni*, 6th edition (Milan: Touring Club Italiano, 1962), pp. 653–654, 657–659, and map, pp. 664–665.

Campania: see Flavius Blondus, *Italia illustrata* (Verona: Boninus de Boninis, 1482), "Regio tertiadecima," ff. Li(v)–M(iv–r).

5(I,320:22). ut somnum excuterent. See *excutior somno*, Vergil *Aeneid* 2.302.

6(I,320:22–31). Not too long after this, in June 1431, Laurentius de Medicis succeeded in borrowing the Plautus from Cardinal de Ursinis and taking it to Florence, where Nicolaus copied it. See Sabbadini, *Storia e critica*, pp. 329–330. Cod. Vat. Lat. 1629 was copied for Poggius by a scribe at an unspecified date. See Ullman, *Origin and Development*, pp. 50–51.

Mehus reports that Ambrosius Traversarius copied the ms. of Plautus when Laurentius de Medicis brought it to Florence and that Nicolaus copied his copy. (*Ambr. Trav. Epist.*, "Praefatio," p. xxxix.)

7(I,321:3). There is no indication of the number of letters of St. Jerome in the mss. listed by Andrea Caravita, *I codici e le arti a Monte Cassino*, I (Monte Cassino: Della Badia, 1869), 87: St. Jerome's *Epistolae*, tenth century. No St. Jerome listed pp. 88–93 in section on Lombard script:

p. 102: No. 295: *Hier. epist.*
p. 166: No. 91: *Hier. epist.* Vol I (11th C.)
p. 167: No. 296: *Hier. epist. et Aug. epist.*

The edition of St. Jerome's *Epistolae*, printed in Rome by Sweynheym and Pannartz in 1468, contains 281 tracts and letters, in two volumes. It is hard to tell from Poggius' text whether he differentiated between the letters and tracts, Vol. I, f. 2r: "In hoc volumine sunt tractatus sive epistole numero centum et Vigintiuna, non omnes tamen Sancti Hieronymi: sed ad opus presens necessarie." Vol. II contains 160 letters and tracts.

The colophon reads: "Eusebii Hieronymi doctoris eximii secundum epistolarum explicit volumen. Anno christi MCCCCLXVIII."

On Lombard script, see Edward Maunde Thompson, *An Introduction to Greek and Latin Paleography* (Oxford: Clarendon Press, 1912), pp. 348–355. Thompson illustrates with examples still in the library of Monte Cassino. On Lombard script, see also Elias Avery Loew, *The Beneventan Script: A History of the South Italian Minuscule* (Oxford: Clarendon Press, 1914), pp. 22–29.

8(I,321:12–15). According to Sabbadini, *Scoperte*, I, 75; II, 241, the ms. of Pliny the Elder's *Naturalis Historia*, which belonged to Coluccius Salutatus, was afterward the property of Leonardus Brunus Aretinus and is now in Paris: Bibl. Nat. Cod. Lat. 6798.

Poggius might also have had access to the mss. of the *Natural History* which belonged to Gasparinus Barzizius (*Scoperte*, I, 36) and Thomas Fregosus (I, 184).

9(I,321:16–20). For the opposition to the war with Lucca in the circle of Cosmus de Medicis, see Gutkind, *Cosimo*, pp. 69–72.

10(I,321:18–19). obductis prioribus cicatricibus. See *obducta cicatrix*, Cicero *Agr.* 3.2.4. Poggius discovered the lost text of the *De lege agraria* during his travels in France and Germany in 1417 (Sabbadini, *Scoperte*, I, 81).

11(I,321:20–22). Cicero: "In M. Antonium Oratio Philippica XI," 34 in *M. Tullii Ciceronis Orationes*, Albert C. Clark, ed., Vol. VI (Oxford: Clarendon Press, 1900).

12(I,321:23–24). Non enim consilia ab eventu laudari oportet. For a similar thought, see etiam amplissimorum virorum *consilia ex eventu, non* ex voluntate a plerisque *probari solent*, Cicero *Att.* 9.7.

13(I,321:27–28). Aristotle, *Politics* VI C.1–3, VIII C.2–3, 1317–1320, 1338.

14(I,321:31–322:3). Identified by Tonelli I, 322, note 1, as Paulus Guinigius. See Chevalier, *Bio-bibliographie,* Vol. I, col. 1991, for bibliography of studies about him and his fortune. He ruled from 1400 to 1430. See also Poggius, *Historia Florentina,* Book VI (*Poggii Opera Omnia,* Vol. II), pp. 273–280. Poggius also gives (pp. 256–273) an account of the events and speeches leading up to the disastrous war. See also Schevill, *Hist. of Florence,* pp. 350–351.

15(I,322:3–4). Vergil *Aeneid* 10.467.

16(I,322:8–9). Cosmus and Laurentius de Medicis and Carolus Marsuppinus Aretinus, with whom Nicolaus was traveling. Sibylla is another name used for Nicolaus' housekeeper-mistress, Benvenuta.

17(I,322:note 1). Tonelli assigns the date 1430 because of Poggius' mention of the fall of Paulus Guinigius. According to a document published by E. Lazzareschi, "Francesco Sforza e Paolo Guinigi" (extract from *Miscellanea di studi storici in onore di Giovanni Sforza,* Turin, n.d., p. 416), the people of Lucca rose against Paulus Guinigius in the middle of August. This fits precisely with Poggius' letter, which is dated September 3.

LETTER LXXXIV

1(I,322:2). For Franciscus Pistoriensis, see Letter LXXVI (Tonelli Bk. III, ltr. 40; I, 290–291). See also Tonelli Bk. IV, ltr. 18 (I, 341–343) to Andreolus Justinianus; Bk. IV, ltr. 21 (I, 347–349) to Suffretus of Rhodes; and Bk. IV, ltr. 15, Poggius' letter to Franciscus himself in answer to one written from Chios. Poggius expressed his delight over the statues Franciscus had promised him. Ambrosius Traversarius wrote to Nicolaus that Poggius' letter to Suffretus had been reported to him by Julianus Beninus; see *Ambr. Trav. Epist.,* VIII, 38, col. 400.

2(I,322:10). Chios at this time was under Genoese rule. See Barker, *Manuel II Paleologus,* p. 336.

3(I,322:12). On the medieval tradition of Polycleitus and Praxiteles, see Müntz, *Histoire de l'art,* I, 217–218.

4(I,323:7–8). See *Ambr. Trav. Epist.,* VIII, 38, col. 400 on another vast discovery, or the same one with the account slightly changed.

5(I,323:11). Andreolus Justinianus (ca. 1400–ca. 1455, warrior, according to Chevalier, *Bio-bibliographie,* Vol. I, col. 1804) had two letters addressed to him by Poggius. The first, ca. 1430, is Tonelli Bk. IV, ltr. 18 (I, 341–343); the second is Tonelli Bk. VII, ltr. 14 (II, 174–177). The later letter, ca. 1437, deals with Poggius' disappointment and rage over the fact that Franciscus Pistoriensis had defrauded him of the works of art which he had promised to bring him from Andreolus and from Suffretus of Rhodes. Franciscus had, however, delivered gifts to the Pope. An account of the siege of Chios by Andreolus Justinianus survives in Ms. Barb. lat. 3210, ff. 108–115. Ambrosius Traversarius also wrote Andreolus a letter which survives (*Epist.* XXIII, 11, col. 970) and mentions him in a letter to Nicolaus (*Epist.* VIII, 35, cols. 393–394).

6(I,324:3). See Janson, *Donatello*, II, 99–101: Donatello was in Rome, not in 1430, the date which Tonelli proposed for this letter, but in 1432–1433. The letter does not actually say that Donatello saw Poggius' treasure *in Rome*, but suggests it. Janson discusses Donatello's earlier visit to Rome in 1400 or in 1403–1404. See also pp. 102 and 110 for Donatello's work in Rome July 1432–1433.

On Donatello's interest in the art of antiquity see Fritz Burger, "Donatello und die Antike," *Repertorium für Kunstwissenschaft*, XXX (1907), 1–13. Burger does not place Donatello's second visit to Rome earlier than 1432 (p. 3).

7(I,324:note 2). Tonelli dates this letter 23 September 1430, with the explanation that it clearly belongs long after Bk. III, ltr. 40 and is certainly earlier than Bk. IV, ltr. 16.

LETTER LXXXV

1(I,324:1–5). Poggius refers to the arrogance of the Florentines, who insisted on continuing the war against Lucca after they had gained their announced purpose: the defeat of Paulus Guinigius. The Florentines' ill-considered belligerence brought the Milanese into the war on the side of Lucca. See Poggius, *Historia Florentina* (*Poggii Opera Omnia*, II, 274–275).

2(I,324:8–9). Poggius refers to Letter LXXXIV, his letter of September 23 [1430], which is Tonelli Bk. IV, ltr. 12.

3(I,325:1–10,23–32). Much of what Poggius describes is still visible. See *Roma e dintorni*, p. 654. See also the opening lines of Poggius' *De varietate fortunae*, where he refers to this trip and to the awakening of his interest in the ancient ruins of Rome itself.

4(I,325:13–16). This description fits the caves of Marino, like Tusculum about 6 kilometers from Grottaferrata, and the home of Martin V's nephew, Cardinal Prosperus de Columnis. See *Roma e dintorni*, p. 667, and *Lazio, attraverso l'Italia*, p. 58.

5(I,325:16–19). See Tenney Frank, *An Economic History of Rome*, 2nd edition revised (Baltimore: The Johns Hopkins Press, 1927), chap. 17, "The Laborer," pp. 324–346. See also Tenney Frank, *Aspects of Social Behavior in Ancient Rome*, Martin Classical Lectures, Vol. II (Cambridge, Mass.: Harvard University Press, 1932), chap. 3, "Farmers or Peasants," pp. 64–91.

6(I,325:22). No explanation of *capociae* has been found in any Latin or Italian dictionary.

7(I,326:1). Poggius quotes directly from Cicero *Pro Milone* 20.53:

"propter insanas illas substructiones." This oration, although already known, was among those found by Poggius at Cluny (Walser, *Poggius*, pp. 49–50).

On Lucullus' villa in Tusculum, see "Lucullus" in *Plutarch's Lives*, translated by John Langhorne and William Langhorne, 6 vols., 5th edition, corrected (London: For C. Dilly, 1792), III, 364. On Cicero's villa, see "Cicero" in *Plutarch's Lives*, V, 279, 316, 323.

Blondus, *Italia illustrata*, ff. (C vii, v–C viii, r). These pages contain a description of Tusculum, Grottaferrata, Marino, Frascati, and Albano, which accords well with Poggius'. Flavius Blondus also mentions "etiam Tusculo propinquum olim lucullanum Lucii luculi villa."

8(I,326:11–17,23–26). The wall, cistern, and amphitheater still exist: see *Roma e dintorni*, p. 672. So does the water-regulating system of the Alban Lake (p. 666). See also *Lazio*, pp. 61–62, 64.

9(I,326:20). Livy *Ab urbe condita* 1.5.15.

10(I,326:32–327:1). Borghetto is now a ruin, 1.2 kilometers from Grottaferrata (*Roma e dintorni*, p. 657).

11(I,327:24,28). Nicolaus de Niccolis, with the Medici brothers and Carolus Marsuppinus Aretinus, was in Rimini in the autumn of 1430, avoiding the plague in Florence. See Zippel, *Niccolò Niccoli*, p. 54, and *Ambr. Trav. Epist.*, VIII, 34 (cols. 391–392), where Ambrosius describes the severity of the plague and sympathizes with the inconveniences met by the travelers, about which he had learned from Cosmus "ornamentum saeculi nostri." He also sends greetings to "fidelissimam illam famulam tuam," the Sibylla of Letter LXXXIII (Tonelli Bk. IV, ltr. 11; I, 322:9). Traversarius' letter was written in late October (1430).

12(I,327:27). Poggius again refers to his letter of September 23 (Letter LXXXIV; Tonelli Bk. IV, ltr. 12). Tonelli dates this letter 1430 from the preceding letter and from internal evidence.

LETTER LXXXVI

1(I,333:5). multa nobis incommoda pepererunt. See ne quicquam nobis *pariant* ex se *incommodi*, Plautus *Most.* 418. Perhaps it was only by chance that Poggius was using the language of one of the newly discovered comedies which in his next letter (Letter LXXXVII [Tonelli Bk. IV, ltr. 17; I, 339:6–7]) he complained that he had not yet seen.

2(I,333:6). belli molem. For *moles belli*, meaning munitions of war, see Tacitus *H.* 1.61. For Poggius' familiarity with this text, which belonged to Nicolaus de Niccolis, see Letter LII, note 2 (Tonelli Bk. III, ltr. 15; I, 213:2).

3(I,333:3–6;334:1–10). See Poggius, *Historia Florentina*, Book VI, in *Poggii Opera Omnia*, II, 255–280.

4(I,333:14–20;334:12–18). On the extent of the war and its participants, see Dorothy E. Muir, *A History of Milan under the Visconti* (London: Methuen and Co., 1924), pp. 149–157. These matters were handled rather sketchily by Petrus Candidus Decembrius in his "Vita Philippi Mariae Vicecomitis" in Muratori, *R.I.S.*, Vol. XX, cols. 985–1020, especially cols. 991–994. They are annotated in great detail in the new edition of *R.I.S.*, edited by Giosue Carducci and Vittorio Fiorini (Bologna: Zanichelli, 1925), Vol. XX, fasc. 203–204, pp. 33–43. The military action of the period is also covered by Leonardus Brunus Aretinus in his "Rerum suo tempore in Italia gestarum Commentarius," in *R.I.S.*, Vol. XIX, cols. 913–942, especially 932–936. See also *R.I.S.*, Vol. XIX, edited by Carmine di Pierro (Bologna: Zanichelli, 1926), pp. 403–469, especially pp. 446–451.

5(I,334:3–4). quantum in Italia incendium excitavit bellum. For *incendium excitare*, see Cicero *Phil.* 7.1.3. Poggius made a copy of the *Philippics* late in 1425 and owned it for the rest of his life. It is now Cod. Laur. 48.22. See Ullman, *Origin and Development*, pp. 33–34.

6(I,334:26–335:9). On the Florentine Wars of 1425–1430 and their management, see Schevill, *History of Florence*, pp. 349–351. Those especially in favor of the war against Lucca were Averardus de Medicis, Rinaldus de Albizzis, and Nerus de Capponis, all of whom were wisely opposed by Nicolaus de Uzano. See, on these men, Martines, *Lawyers and Statecraft*, pp. 105, 158, 160, 178, 187, 208–209, 238, 241, 292–296, 320–323, 351, 363, 378.

7(I,334:30–32). in extremum ferme discrimen rempublicam deduxerunt. For the thought, see adducta est res in maximum periculum et *extremum* pene *discrimen*, Cicero *Phil.* 7.1.

8(I,335:11). suis viribus freti. For *freti viribus*, see Plautus *Am.* 1.1.60. According to Sabbadini, *Storia e critica*, p. 327, Plautus' *Amphitruo* was one of eight of his comedies known throughout the Middle Ages and available before Nicolaus Cusanus' great discovery.

9(I,335:10–17). Poggius suggests that the kings were situated outside of Italy, but he may have been referring to Alphonsus of Aragon and Naples, who at this time was not quite thoroughly established in Italy, and to the Emperor Sigismund, who yearned to have influence, if not power, in Italy.

10(I,335:19–29). See Machiavelli, *History of Florence*, Book IV, chaps. 4–5, pp. 175–189.

11(I,336:1–14). Florentine dependence on mercenaries is well documented by Machiavelli, (*History of Florence*, Book IV, chaps. 4–5, 175–189), who also describes the disappointments suffered by the Florentines at their hands. See also Molho, *Florentine Public Finances*, pp. 119–121, 136–138, 143–148.

12(I,336:16). *Inertia* here seems to mean lack of skill rather than lack of energy. See *A Latin Dictionary,* revised and enlarged by Charlton T. Lewis and Charles Short (Oxford: Clarendon Press, 1966), p. 941.

13(I,337:1-4). Poggius probably felt the *"aliorum stultitia ac iniquitate"* more forcefully since, although the Medici, of whom Poggius was a follower, supported the war with Lucca, they were not completely in charge of the running of it and could not control decisions (see Machiavelli, *History of Florence,* chap. VI, pp. 189–190).

14(I,337:6). On Democritus (ca. 460–370 B.C.) see *OCD,* pp. 327–328. He wrote a work, *On Cheerfulness,* among many others, all lost except for fragments.

15(I,337:9). Horace *Odes* 1.9.9.

16(I,337:17). Poggius' reference seems to be to Terence *Phormio* 246.

17(I,337:26). On Poggius' Greek studies, see Walser, *Poggius,* pp. 228–234. His ability to translate was doubtful; see p. 230, note 1, and his letter to Petrus Thomasius about his method (Tonelli Bk. IX, ltr. 26; II, 358–360).

LETTER LXXXVII

1(I,338:2-3). superatis . . . difficultatibus. For *superare difficultates,* see Velleius Paterculus 2.120.4. According to Sabbadini (*Scoperte,* II, 258), the text of Velleius Paterculus' *Historiae Romanae* was not known until discovered at Murbach in 1515 by Beatus Rhenanus and published in 1521. For the use of the text by later Roman and medieval authors, see Schanz-Hosius, pt. 2, sec. 422a.

2(I,338:2-5). Ambrosius Traversarius' letters VIII, 35 and 36 indicate that Nicolaus was traveling toward Venice, because of the plague raging in Florence. According to Zippel, *Nicolò Niccoli,* pp. 54–55, Nicolaus' trip to Rimini (August 1430), Verona, Venice (October 1430), and Verona (January 1431) on the way back to Florence was carried out in the company of the Medici family and Carolus Marsuppinus Aretinus.

In the Bibliotheca Laurentiana: Cod. Lat. XXXIV, 53 and Cod. Lat. XXXIV, 55 (see Bandini, Vol. II, cols. 179–193 and 197–199) contain numerous poems by Carolus Marsuppinus Aretinus, including two to and about Poggius (published in *Carmina illustrium poetarum italorum,* VI [Florence: Apud Joannem Cajetanum Tartinium, 1720], 278–280 and 282–284) but apparently none to or about Nicolaus de Niccolis.

Poggius here refers to either the tenth labor of Hercules, "Geryon," or more probably the twelfth, "The Hesperides," both of which involved long journeys westward and partly in Africa. See Herbert Jennings Rose, *A Handbook of Greek Mythology,* 6th edition (New York: E. P. Dutton and Co., 1958), pp. 214–216.

3(I,338:14-15). Poggius had visited Monte Cassino in 1425 and thereafter corresponded with the abbot about borrowing mss. to copy. See Walser, *Poggius*, pp. 100, 107, 109.

4(I,338:19). For the miniaturists in Florence in 1430–1431, see Levi d'Ancona, *Miniatura e miniatori a Firenze*. See especially Battista di Biagio Sanguigni, pp. 54–56, Matteo di Filippo Torelli, pp. 186–191, and Niccolò Rosselli, pp. 214–216, all connected with the monastery of S. Maria degli Angeli, of which Nicolaus de Niccolis' friend Ambrosius Traversarius was abbot.

5(I,338:21–25). Very probably, especially since Poggius refers to France in the next sentence, Petrus de Sacco of Verona (1379?–1430), librarian to Jean Duc de Berry. See Millard Meiss, *French Painting in the Time of Jean de Berry: The Late Fourteenth Century and the Patronage of the Duke*, Kress Foundation Studies in the History of European Art, No. 2, 2 vols. (London: Phaidon, 1967), I, 63–67. Petrus seems to have been a resident of Verona again in 1430, after many years in France, since he is mentioned as executor of a will in Doc. 10 (1430) in Meiss, p. 67. See also Julian Brown, "French Painting in the Time of Jean de Berry: A Review," *The Book Collector*, XVIII, No. 4 (1969), 470–488. This identification is confirmed by Tino Foffano in "Niccoli, Cosimo, e le ricerche di Poggio nelle biblioteche francesi" *Italia medioevale e umanistica*, XII (1969), 117, 125.

6(I,339:11–15). The only Plautus ms. recorded by Elisabeth Pellegrin in *La bibliothèque des Visconti et des Sforza, ducs de Milan au XVe siècle*, Publication de l'Institut de Recherche et d'Histoire des Textes, 5 (Paris: Vente au Service des Publications du C.N.R.S., 1955), is Cod. Vat. Urb. Lat. 655, a fourteenth century ms. containing nine comedies. It did not belong to Philippus Maria (p. 404).

For Guarinus' and Leonellus Estensis' efforts to obtain the ms. of Plautus and for Guarinus' copy of eight of the newly discovered comedies, see Sabbadini, *Storia e critica*, pp. 330–339. There is no record of Leonellus Estensis' copy of Plautus in Domenico Fava's *La biblioteca estense nel suo sviluppo storico* (Modena: G. T. Vincenzi e Nipoti di Dante Cavallotti, 1925), nor can it be identified in Giulio Bertoni's *La biblioteca estense e la coltura ferrarese ai tempi del duca Ercole I (1471–1505)* (Turin: Ermanno Loescher, 1903).

Once Cardinal de Ursinis let the Plautus codex out of his hands he seems not to have recovered it, at least not for some time. It was copied by Poggius in 1431, then by Guarinus in 1432. After that most of the correspondence relating to the text and its emendation centers around the copy made by Guarinus, carried off by Antonius Beccadellius Panormita to the court of Alphonsus Aragonensis in 1434, and not returned to Guarinus until 1445. See Sabbadini, *Storia e critica*, pp. 330–347. Another copy of the cod. Orsiniano is also known (*Storia e critica*, pp.

350–352), Cod. Vat. Barber. lat. 146. See also Guarinus' letters to Leonellus Estensis commenting on Plautus (*Epist. di Guar. Ver.*, II, 96–97, 140–141.

7(I,339:17–22). None of the codices of Plautus' comedies listed by Bandini, Vol. II, cols. 242–246, are described as containing Antonius Luscus' verses. Da Schio, *Antonio Loschi*, p. 154, Op. LI, says that they introduced each of Plautus' comedies in the copies given by Cardinal de Ursinis to the Duke of Milan and the Marquis of Este.

8(I,340:1,6). It is not clear whether Poggius means the elder or the younger Pliny. He and Nicolaus had access to the copy of the Letters of the younger Pliny which had perhaps belonged to Coluccius Salutatus and is now in the Laurentian Library. See Ullman, *Origin and Development*, pp. 16–19.

9(I,340:4). credo in spongiam incubuit. See "Ajax in spongiam incubuit," Augustus apud Macrobium *Saturnalia* 2.4; see Suetonius *Aug.* 85.2.

10(I,340:6). "Col ghiribizzare" means "to be whimsical or to indulge in fancies." *The Cambridge Italian Dictionary* (Cambridge University Press, 1962), I, 336.

11(I,340:10–12). For the history of Poggius' texts of Livy and of Cicero's *Letters to Atticus*, see Ullman, *Origin and Development*, pp. 43–47.

12(I,340:14–25). Poggius, in his *Historia Florentina*, Book VI, edited by Joannes Baptista Recanatus (Venice: Joannes Gabriel Hertz, 1715), pp. 255–280, gives an account of the war with Lucca, its cause, and the the Duke of Milan's part in it.

13(I,340:23). Terence *Andria* 480.

14(I,340:27). See Tonelli, note 1. He dates letter 17 in Book IV 1431 and points out that Bk. IV, ltr. 11 must be earlier than this letter, in which the war with Lucca is dragging on, although in Bk. IV, ltr. 11, the tyrant of Lucca, Paulus Guinigius, has been defeated. See also E. Lazzareschi, "Francesco Sforza e Paolo Guinigi," an extract from *Miscellanea di studi storici in onore di Giovanni Sforza*. Tonelli says that Poggius must have used the Florentine style of dating here, beginning the year in March. However, he forgets the Florentine style with the very next letter, Bk. IV, ltr. 18, which is dated January 22, and which he assigns to 1431.

LETTER LXXXVIII

1(II,15:5). omni laude digna. For a similar thought, see summa *laude digni*, Cicero *Rep.* 3.4 and 3.17.

2(II,15:11–14). Poggius was doubtless referring to the ancient historians whose works he owned: Caesar, Tacitus, Eusebius, Macrobius, Plutarch, Josephus, Livy, Sallust, Q. Curtius Rufus, Suetonius, Cassiodorus. (Walser, *Poggius,* pp. 420–421.)

3(II,15:15–19). Leonardus Brunus Aretinus and Flavius Blondus were writing histories at this time; Poggius had not yet begun. See Rossi, ed., *Il Quattrocento,* pp. 169–174. See also Wilcox, *Historiography.*

4(II,15:23). pristinae imaginem gloriae. For *pristina gloria,* see Vergil *Aeneid* 10.143.

5(II,15:24). duplici fruor voluptate. For *frui voluptate,* see Seneca *Vit. Beat.* 10 fin. Coluccius Salutatus owned and annotated this text. His ms. is now in Florence, Naz. Conv. Soppr. I, iv.2 (No. 53) according to Ullman, *Humanism,* pp. 169–170, 250. The works of Seneca were widely known among the humanists (Sabbadini, *Scoperte,* II, 250).

6(II,15:26). altera complectens cogitatione. For the idiom "aliquid complecti cogitatione," see Cicero *Orator* 2.8; see *Fam.* 5.17.4. Poggius copied the *Brutus, Orator,* and *De oratore* in Cod. Laur. 50,31 (Ullman, *Origin and Development,* p. 35).

7(II,15:23–27). See Wilcox, *Historiography,* chap. 6: "Narrative technique in the *Historia fiorentina,*" pp. 154–176.

8(II,16:1). Sigismund (1368–1437). For his long and varied career, as ruler of Hungary, Germany, the Holy Roman Empire, Bohemia, etc., as vanquished crusader (1396), as instigator of the Council of Constance, 1414 and of Basel, 1431; for his four coronations: in Hungary, 1387; in Aachen, 1414; in Milan, 1431; and in Rome, 1433, see *Encyclopaedia Britannica,* 11th edition, XXV, 66–67. For the difficulties related to his coronation in Rome, see Gregorovius, *History of Rome,* Vol. VII, pt. 1, pp. 35–37.

9(II,16:5). No one alive in 1433 was likely to have seen the last coronation in Rome, which was that of Charles IV (1316–1378) in 1354. He was crowned not by the Pope but by the Bishop of Ostia. See James Bryce, *The Holy Roman Empire* (New York: The Macmillan Co., 1932), p. xlvi.

10(II,16:6–9). Nicolaus was well known for despising the learning of his own time and of the previous century. See Arnoldo della Torre, *Storia dell' accademia platonica di Firenze* (Florence: G. Carnesecchi, 1902), pp. 191–194, and Leonardus Brunus Aretinus, *Ad Petrum Paulum Istrum Dialogus,* edited by Theodor Klette in *Beiträge zur Geschichte und Literatur der italienischen Gelehrtenrenaissance,* II, 48–55.

11(II,16:11–12). The gate was the Porta Collina. The whole ancient ceremony is described in Ludovicus Antonius Muratorius, *Antiquitates Italicae Medii Aevi, sive Dissertationes,* 6 vols. (Milan: Ex typographia Societatis Palatinae, 1738–1742), Vol. I, cols. 99–110.

For the Porta Collina, see "The Topography of Rome." "A summary collected by *John Bartholomew Marlianus,* a Gentleman of *Millain,* touching the Topography of Rome in ancient time." In *The Romane Historie Written by T. Livius of Padua,* translated by Philemon Holland, pp. 1078, 1112.

According to the map of Rome made by Pirro Ligorio in 1552, the gate behind the tomb of Hadrian is the *Porta Castelli.* See Gregory Martin, *Roma Sancta,* George B. Parks, ed., Plate 3.

Ascension Sunday must be the Sunday following Ascension Day, which is forty days after Easter and is always a Thursday. See *Encyclopaedia Britannica,* 11th edition, II, 716–717. Sigismund entered Rome on May 21. (Creighton, *History of the Papacy,* II, 223.)

12(II,16:12–14). omnis multitudo se ad conspiciendum effudit. For the expression, see "omnis sese multitudo ad cognoscendum effudit," Caesar *B.C.* 2.7.3.

13(II,16:14–15). On the 13 districts into which Rome was divided, see Gregorovius, *History of Rome,* Vol. VII, pt. 2, chap. 7, sec. 5: "Aspect of the city surveyed according to its regions about the year 1500," pp. 726–793.

14(II,16:18). The equestrian order was reestablished in Rome in the twelfth century. *CMH,* V, 373 and note 1: Otto Frising, *Gesta Friderici I imperatoris,* I, 28, edited by Waitz-Simson (Hanover: Scriptores rerum Germanicarum in usum scholarum, 1890–1920), p. 44.

For an account of the public games see Flavius Blondus, *Roma Triumphans* (Mantua: Petrus Adam, de Michaelibus, about 1473), Book II.

15(II,16:31). Joseph Gill, in two books, mentions the presence of the Byzantine envoys in Rome at the time of Sigismund's coronation, but in neither book does he give their names. See Raymond H. Schmandt, general editor, *The Popes through History,* Vol. I: *Eugenius IV, Pope of Christian Union,* by Joseph Gill (Westminster, Maryland: Newman Press, 1961), p. 51, and Gill, *Council of Florence,* p. 52.

See figures 30 and 31 in Barker, *Manuel II Palaeologus.* These depict the Emperor's attendants as shown in *Les très riches heures du Duc de Berry* (Musée Condé, Chantilly), ff. 51v–52r. See also the well-known portrait medal of the Emperor John VIII Palaeologus by Pisanello, in William L. Langer, general editor, *The Rise of Modern Europe: The Dawn of a New Era 1250–1453,* by Edward P. Cheyney (New York: Harper and Brothers, 1936), illustration no. 48.

16(II,17:8). aures adstantium replentes. For *aures replere,* see Plautus *Rud.* 4.6.22. By 1433, when Poggius wrote this letter, he owned Cod. Vat. lat. 1629, which contains twenty comedies by Plautus, twelve newly discovered and eight long known. See Ullman, *Origin and Development,* pp. 50–51, and Letter LXXXI (*Poggii Epist.* Bk. IV, ltr. 4; I, 304: 18–26). The *Rudens* was one of the twelve new plays.

17(II,17:12). See Edward Gibbon, *The Decline and Fall of the Roman Empire,* III (New York: The Heritage Press, 1946), 2374–2375, 2383.

18(II,17:17–25). See Mantegna's "Triumph of Caesar," especially the elephant section, in Erika Tietze-Conrat, *Mantegna: Paintings, Drawings, Engravings* (London: The Phaidon Press, 1955), Plate 112. See also G. B. Bellissima, "Analisi archeologica dell'Arco di Traiano in Benevento," *Classici e neo-latini,* II, No. 2 (1906), 101–113, especially p. 108.

Perhaps Poggius meant the trophies which appear in ancient reliefs. See Ernest Nash, *Pictorial Dictionary of Ancient Rome,* 2 vols., 2nd edition (New York: Praeger, 1968). Vol. I, p. 112, "the Arch of Constantine." Vol. I, p. 129, "the Arch of Septimius Severus."

19(II,17:27–31). See *Monumenta Germaniae Historica,* Georg Heinrich Pertz, ed. (Hanover: Hahn, 1837), *Legum Tomus II,* pp. 528–537. "Ordo coronationis." The coronation of the Emperor Henry VII by Pope Clement V closely resembles Poggius' account, but there is no mention of a youth in purple, scattering money. Muratori says that the scattering of money was an essential part of imperial coronations from early times (Muratori, *Antiquitates Italicae,* Vol. I, col. 108). See also the description of the coronation of the Emperor Berengarius in *De laudibus Berengarii Augusti,* Liber IV in Muratori, *R.I.S.,* Vol. II, pt. 1, pp. 403–414.

On the Emperor, see Muratori, *Antiquitates Italicae,* Vol. I, col. 99.

20(II,18:3–7). There is a portrait of the Emperor Sigismund in Cheyney, *Dawn of a New Era,* Figure 33.

21(II,18:10). See Muratori, *Antiquitates Italicae,* Vol. I, cols. 101–102.

22(II,18:12–13). inter dissonas voces. For *dissonae voces,* see Livy 30.34.1. See Ullman, *Origin and Development,* pp. 45–48, on Poggius' set of Livy in three codices.

23(II,18:17–18). Sigismund was crowned on 31 May 1433 (Creighton, *History of the Papacy,* II, 223).

24(II,18:21). Giuseppe Billanovich, in his "Gli umanisti e le cronache medioevali," *Italia medioevale e umanistica,* I (1958), 103–137, presents convincing reasons why the humanists, probably including Poggius, could have learned this history of the eighth and ninth centuries from the *Liber Pontificalis.*

25(II,18:22). According to Vasiliev, *L'Empire byzantin,* I, 353–354, the Byzantine Emperor Constantine VI was dethroned in A.D. 797 by his mother, the Empress Irene, who had ruled during his minority. His father was Leo IV, who died in 780 (p. 349). Vasiliev mentions no son named Leo as Constantine's co-ruler.

26(II,18:28–31). In Einhard, *Vita Karoli Magni,* edited by Georg Heinrich Pertz and G. Waitz, Scriptores rerum germanicarum in usum

scholarum ex Monumentis Germaniae Historicis separatim editi 6th
edition (Hanover: Impensis Bibliopolii Hahniani, 1927), Poggius could
have found the following events:

p. 8 (773–774): Charlemagne's war against the Lombards and his
victory.

p. 24: Death (796) of Pope Adrian. Charlemagne's grief.

pp. 32–33: Charlemagne's coronation in Rome by Pope Leo on Christmas Day, A.D. 800.

See also Gerhard Seeliger, "Conquests and Imperial Coronation of
Charles the Great," in *CMH*, Vol. II, chap. 19, especially pp. 619–624.

27(II,19:5). See Suetonius Tranquillus, *De XII Caesaribus Libri
VIII*, Isaac Casaubon, ed. (Paris: Apud Jacobum Chouët, 1545). "Tiberius Nero Caesar," chap. 17, p. 70. For a lengthy description of a
triumph see "Life of Paulus Aemilius" in *Plutarch's Lives*, translated
by Langhorne, II, 299–302. This life was translated from Greek into
Latin by Leonardus Brunus Aretinus in 1407.

See Suetonius Tranquillus, *De XII Caesaribus*, "Divus Julius
Caesar," chap. 45, p. 14.

28(II,19:16–19). Poggius suggests that a custom dating back to
Charlemagne and the year 800 is sufficiently venerable.

29(II,19:20). See Bryce, *Holy Roman Empire*, pp. 237–250. Perhaps
one reason for this is that most of the candidates for the imperial crown
of the Holy Roman Empire were already kings of France or some German or Austrian territory before their election. See "Germany" in the
Encyclopaedia Britannica, 11th edition, XI, 833–850, especially pp.
839–840.

This view is confirmed by *The Oxford Universal Dictionary on Historical Principles*, revised and edited by C. T. Onions, 3rd edition (Oxford: Clarendon Press, 1955), p. 601. "Emperor .... The sovereign of
an Empire: a title considered superior in dignity to that of 'king.'"

Livy *Ab urbe condita* 2.1.9–10.

30(II,19:30). C. Julius Caesar *De bello civili* 2.26.1; 3.71.3; 3.31.1.
Livy *Ab urbe condita* 27.9.4.

31(II,19:31). See "Cicero" in *Plutarch's Lives*, V, 312.

32(II,20:4). Suetonius *Iulius* 41.

33(II,20:6–11). This sentence is worded almost exactly like that in
"Caesar" in *Plutarch's Lives*, IV, 391. Plutarch's life of Caesar was
translated by Guarinus before 1416 (see Sabbadini, *Scuola*, p. 130).

34(II,20:13–15). See Lily Ross Taylor, *Party Politics in the Age of
Caesar*, Sather Classical Lectures, Vol. XXII (Berkeley: University of
California Press, 1949), pp. 30–33.

35(II,20:17). Suetonius *Aug.* 26; *Calig.* 17; *Claud.* 14.

36(II,20:20–23). mos erat consalutari imperatorem. For *consalutare* aliquem *imperatorem,* see Tacitus *Agri.* 12.69; Sueton. *Nero* 8. Ludwig Pralle, after reviewing the correspondence of Poggius and other humanists 1425–1427 in detail, concludes that in 1427 Poggius received in secret a ms. of the shorter works of Tacitus stolen from the famous monastic library at Fulda (*Wiederentdeckung,* p. 53).

The work of Suetonius was readily available to the humanists (Sabbadini, *Scoperte,* II, 253).

37(II,20:23–25). The practice was certainly common in the fifteenth century. Infessura says: "fu pubblicata la pace de papa Eugenio collo imperadore Sigismondo re delli Romani . . . ." (Infessura, *Diario,* p. 29.)

38(II,20:27). neque verborum vim tenuerunt. For *vis verborum,* meaning the sense or signification of words, see Cicero *Orator* 32.115. See note 6 above.

39(II,20:25–31). See Poggius, *De varietate fortunae,* III (*Poggii Opera Omnia,* Vol. II), pp. 92–93, especially note a, and Antoninus Florentinus, *Chronicon,* Vol. III, tit. XXII, cap. X, sec. 1 (Vol. III, f. CLXVIII v). St. Antoninus gives an explanation for some matters about which Poggius is uncertain.

40(II,21:7–8). iuramentum praestitit. For the idiom *iuramentum praestare,* "to take an oath, to swear," see *Codex* 2.56.4.

41(II,21:7). The Pope was Eugenius IV. He was born Gabriel Condulmarius in Venice, 1383. His maternal uncle was Pope Gregory XII, who made him a cardinal on May 9, 1408, with the title of S. Clement (Eubel, *Hierarchia,* I, 31). He had been Bishop of Siena since 30 December 1407. He attended the Council of Constance but, according to Fillastre, "for a long time had held aloof in the college." See Loomis, *Council,* p. 414. He was elected Pope on 3 March 1431 and died 23 February 1447 (Eubel, *Hierarchia,* II [Regensburg, 1914], 7). His entire reign was a ceaseless battle with the Council of Basel, which tried frequently to depose him and even elected an anti-Pope, Felix V. See Valois, *Le Pape, passim,* and Pastor, *History of the Popes,* Vols. I and II, *passim.* For the most recent account of him see R. Aubert and E. van Cauwenbergh, eds., *Dictionnaire d'histoire,* Vol. XV (Paris: Letouzey et Ané, 1963), cols. 1355–1359.

42(II,21:5–6). According to Mapheus Vegius, the silver door, which had deteriorated badly, was replaced by order of Eugenius IV by the bronze door designed by Filarete and still in use. See Eugene Müntz, *Les arts à la cour des papes,* Bibliothèque des écoles françaises d'Athènes et de Rome, fasc. 4, 9, and 28, 3 vols. (Paris: Ernest Thorin, 1878), I, 42–43.

43(II,21:10, 17, 22–26). See Bryce, *Holy Roman Empire,* p. 112, and Muratori, *Antiquitates Italicae,* Vol. I, col. 18. The Cardinal Bishop of Ostia at this time was Antonius Corrarius, translated 1431, died 1445

(Eubel, *Hierarchia,* II, 60). It must have been customary for the Bishop of Ostia to have an important role in the coronation ceremony; see note 9 above.

44(II,21:13). augurio consecrata. Servius makes the comment "augurio consecrata" on Vergil *Aeneid* 7.153 (moenia augusta). According to Sabbadini, Servius' *Commentarii in Vergilium* were "abbastanza noti" to the humanists (*Scoperte,* II, 251). See also Ovid *Fasti* I. 609–611.

45(II,21:14). Suetonius *Aug.* 58.

46(II,21:19–31). These details are all mentioned in the Chronicle of Cornelius Zantfliet (Martène and Durand, *Amplissima Collectio,* V, 433–434). See also Bryce, *Holy Roman Empire,* p. 305, note.

47(II,21:29; 22:2–8). This episode in the coronation ceremony is described by Infessura, *Diario,* p. 30.

LETTER LXXXIX

1(II,31:8–9). In Letter LXXXVIII (Tonelli Bk. V, ltr. 6), Poggius did indeed refer to the coronation and not the election. Charlemagne was not elected.

2(II,31:9). exordium sumpsisse. For *exordium sumere,* see Ammianus Marcellinus 26.1.9: tertius (annus) a prima vigilia *sumens exordium.* Poggius owned two mss. of Ammianus Marcellinus, acquired during the Council of Constance, 1414 and 1417 (Sabbadini, *Scoperte,* II, 200–201).

3(II,32:1–2). It does not appear that the election was a matter of primary interest to Gregory VII, but rather Papal authority over the Emperor. See Bryce, *Holy Roman Empire,* pp. 158–163. It was generally believed during the Renaissance that "the elective constitution had been established . . . by a decree of Gregory V" (p. 235). Gregory V was the first German pope and reigned 996–999. (*New Century Cyclopedia of Names,* Clarence L. Barnhart, ed., II [New York: Appleton-Century-Crofts, Inc., 1954], 1830–1831.) Poggius had the right Pope in his *Historia Florentina,* Book VII (*Poggii Opera Omnia,* II, 298–299).

4(II,32:3–5). There are no books in the inventory made after Poggius' death that would have provided this information (Walser, *Poggius,* pp. 418–423).

5(II,32:6). Sigismund did not succeed in seeing Florence. St. Antoninus recorded: "Cum primum Sigismundus Romam dimisisset: . . . per Tudertinum agrum ac Perusinum transiens Ariminum petiit. Optaverat satis ac postularat per Florentiam iter agere; sed non acquieverunt cives, formidantes ex ingressu eius novitates exurgere" ["When Sigismund first left Rome, he traveled by way of Todi and Perugia to Rimini. He had very much hoped and even asked to go through Florence but the citizens had refused, fearing that his visit might bring on rebellions"]. *Chronicon,* pars III, titulus XXII, cap. X, sec. 1; f. CLXIX.

It is ironic that nine years earlier, in 1424, the Florentines had sent ambassadors to Sigismund, their protector against the Duke of Milan, to urge him to travel to Italy to be crowned. See Poggius, *Historia Florentina,* Book V (*Poggii Opera Omnia,* II, 223).

6(II,32:11). On the conflicts within the Franciscan Order, especially at the Chapter General in Bologna in 1433, see Moorman, *Franciscan Order,* p. 449. Pastor, *History* (I, 33) mentions Eugenius IV's "zealous support" for the preaching friars, and this is confirmed by the decrees and *bullae* issued by him at this time. See *Bullarium Franciscanum . . . Eugenii IV . . . 1431–1455,* pp. 1–57.

7(II,32:13). committendum negotium. For *committendum negotium,* see nec illi (Catoni) *committendum* illud *negotium,* sed inponendum putaverunt, Cicero *Sest.* 28.60. Leonardus Brunus found a ms. of Cicero's orations, including the *Pro Sestio,* in Lucca in 1408 (Sabbadini, *Scoperte,* I, 75; II, 210). Leonardus sent it to Nicolaus de Niccolis.

8(II,32:14–18). Both Cosmus de Medicis, a great friend of Nicolaus, and Franciscus Cathanius were supporters of the Observants in Florence (see Wadding, *Annales,* X, 180). Eugenius IV's favor toward them was obtained by Frater Franciscus Francisci Florentinus. See Lynn Thorndike, "Franciscus Florentinus or Paduanus," in *Mélanges Mandonnet: Etudes d'histoire littéraire et doctrinale du moyen age,* II, (Paris: J. Vrin, 1930), 353–369.

The General of the Order in 1433 was Guillelmus Casalensis (Wadding, *Annales,* X, 141–142).

9(II,32:23). Repair work was being done on the ruined Porta Pinciana in September 1433, according to Müntz (*Les arts,* I, 51).

10(II,32:28–31). The collector might possibly have been the Florentine priest Christophorus Bondelmontius who moved to Rhodes in 1414 and lived for sixteen years in the Greek islands. See Roberto Weiss, *The Renaissance Discovery of Classical Antiquity* (Oxford: Basil Blackwell, 1969), pp. 135–138. See also Cosenza, *Dictionary,* I, 651, and Martines, *Social World,* pp. 322–323.

11(II,32:29–33:4). The traveler may have been Ciriacus de Pizzicollis Anconitanus (ca. 1391–ca. 1455); see Chevalier, *Bio-bibliographie,* Vol. I, col. 1092, and Weiss, *Renaissance Discovery,* pp. 138–141. Tiraboschi, *Storia,* Vol. VI, pt. 1, p. 183, says that Ciriacus first became acquainted with Cardinal Gabriel Condulmarius, later Pope Eugenius IV, in Ancona in 1421 and (pp. 187–188) that he was in Rome during the coronation of the Emperor Sigismund and in great favor with both the Emperor and the Pope.

12(II,33:8–9). For another comment on the heat of the Roman summer, see Letter XXXI (Tonelli Bk. II, ltr. 23; I, 150: 5), written in May 1425.

LETTER XC

1(II,36:2). This letter must represent Poggius' first reaction to the arrest and exile of Cosmus de Medicis, which took place between September 7 and 3 October 1433. See Gutkind, *Cosimo*, pp. 77–88. This letter precedes Letter XCI (Tonelli Bk. V, ltr. 3) and Letter XCII (Tonelli Bk. V, ltr. 4), which were written in January *1434* (misdated or dated in Florentine style by Tonelli), whereas this letter, written two weeks after Cosmus was banished from Florence, is correctly dated 1433. For an account of the feelings of Cosmus' friends in Florence which would have been quickly transmitted to Poggius, see Ambrosius Traversarius, *Hodoeporicon*, Nicolaus Bartholini Bargensis, ed. (Florence, 1680), pp. 41–44.

2(II,36:5–11). A contemporary account of the factions (a word actually used in his text) and the agitation was given by St. Antoninus Florentinus, *Chronicon*, Vol. III, Tit. XXII, cap. X, sec. 3, f. CLXIX r-v. One of St. Antoninus' remarks may explain the anxiety felt by Nicolaus and other friends of Cosmus': "Ac etiam qui com eo exulati fuerant amici" ["And even his friends had been exiled with him"].

3(II,36:5–6). popularium iactationum. For *iactatio popularis*, meaning a striving after popular applause, see Cicero *Clu.* 35.95. According to Ullman and Stadter, *Public Library*, p. 99, Nicolaus owned Cod. Laur. 51.10, which contained Varro's *De lingua latina* and Cicero's *Rhetorica ad Herennium*, and *Pro Cluentio*, which had belonged to Boccaccio. The *Pro Cluentio* was also among the texts found by Poggius at Cluny. See Clark, *Vetus Cluniacensis*, p. 111.

4(II,36:9–10). impetum repentinum. For *repentinus impetus*, see *repentino* quodam *impetu* animi incitatus, Cicero *De off.* 1.15.49. See note 9 on Letter XI (Tonelli Bk. I, ltr. 13; I, 62:30). There is no secure evidence that either Coluccius or Nicolaus owned this text, although it was owned and prized by Petrarch (see Sabbadini, *Scoperte*, II, 120).

5(II,36:11–21). At this time Ambrosius Traversarius wrote: "Postridie requisiti, ut Pontifici summo Antonium Arretinum commendaremus (petebatur enim ad Episcopatum Arretinum)" ["The next day we were asked to recommend Antonius of Arezzo to the Pope, for he was sought after for the see of Arezzo"]. See *Hodoeporicon*, p. 44. Vespasiano da Bisticci also indicates (see "Vita di Eugenio IV Papa," sec. VI, p. 9) that at this time Eugenius IV "attendeva con ogni diligenza a riformare la Chiesa," including some congregations in Arezzo.

6(II,36:21). salva conscientia. For the ablative *salva conscientia*, see nec consentire *salva conscientia* possum, Seneca *Ep.* 117.1. It is not surprising that Poggius quoted several times from Seneca's letters. Coluccius had owned a volume of them, now Cod. Laur. Edili 161. Poggius made a great effort to obtain that text from Leonardus Brunus in order to copy it in 1426–1427 but finally had to be content with another. Poggius' copy is Vat. lat. 2208 (Ullman, *Origin and Development*, pp. 40–41).

7(II,36:22). In contrast to the wisdom which Poggius ascribes to Eugenius IV in this passage, Platina (*Vitae*, f. cc 3) says: "Principio enim pontificatus sui malis consiliis ductus, divina humanaque omnia perturbavit" ["At the beginning of his reign he was influenced by bad advice and upset everything, both spiritual and mortal"]. But he also says (Platina, *Vitae*, f. cc 3): "Nam Leonardum Aretinum, Carolum, Poggium, Aurispam, Trapezuntium, Blondum, viros doctissimos secretis suis admisit" ["For he welcomed Leonardus, Carolus, Poggius, Aurispa, Trapezuntius, and Blondus, all great scholars, to his intimate circle of associates," or "he opened his secret councils to them"].

8(II,37:1–3). Since Poggius and Eugenius IV had been in the Curia together since the time of Eugenius' uncle, Pope Gregory XII (1406–1415), the distrust was probably of long standing and compounded by his "oversevere action against the House of Colonna, the relatives of his predecessor," Martin V, whom Poggius had served. See Hans Kühner, *Encyclopedia of the Papacy*, translated by Kenneth J. Northcott (New York: Philosophical Library, 1958), pp. 112–113, 115, and Valois, *Le Pape*, I, 96–98.

9(II,37:13–16). Ambrosius Traversarius (*Hodoeporicon*, p. 11), in describing his trip to Grottaferrata, mentions Poggius among other members of the Curia who were kind to him. None of the others was from Florence, which doubtless contributed to Poggius' sense of isolation.

LETTER XCI

1(II,11:3; 12:3). The letter Poggius had written to Cosmus was published by Tonelli as Bk. V, ltr. 12 (II, 37–46). Tonelli (p. 46, note 1) says that it was obviously written in the same month and year as Letter XC (Tonelli Bk. V, ltr. 11; II, 36–37), which was clearly written in the year of Cosmus' arrest and banishment, 1433. Within its text Letter XC contains the date "the seventeenth day of October." This makes Letter XCI (Tonelli Bk. V, ltr 3) subsequent to Letter XC (Tonelli Bk. V, ltr. 11) and, since it contains within the text the words "the ninth day of January," it should bear the date 1434 and not Tonelli's proposed date 1433.

2(II,11:9–11). Nicolaus de Niccolis was seventy years old at this time; Poggius' tone is much ruder than his usual approach to Nicolaus, who was his senior by seventeen years. Nicolaus, who was deeply involved with and financially dependent on Cosmus, had good reasons in 1433 to be *"immutatus . . . vel temporum vitio vel rerum privatarum cura"* ["completely changed by the evils of our time or by worry over his private affairs"]. See Gutkind, *Cosimo,* pp. 77–95.

3(II,11:14). It is not clear from the contents whether Tonelli Bk. V, ltr. 12, Poggius' letter to Cosmus, was the one he had written earlier or a second one written in January. It is clear that he knew a great deal about Cosmus' high-minded actions and motives, which he praises, and about the conditions of his exile. Walser (*Poggius,* p. 158) points out that it was courageous of Poggius to write and publish a letter to Cosmus at the time of his downfall. Strangely, Poggius did not mention Cosmus' reverse of fortune anywhere in his *De varietate fortunae.*

LETTER XCII

1(II,12:2). Carolus Marsuppinus Aretinus was closely associated with both Nicolaus de Niccolis and Cosmus de Medicis. He had traveled with them both to Venice and Verona in 1431, and it was to him that Poggius wrote to express his grief at the death of Nicolaus (Tonelli Bk. VI, ltr. 12).

2(II,12:19–13:3). It is difficult to identify which *"protervus"* Poggius means here, since he wrote numerous letters attacking people who annoyed him, such as Tonelli Bk. III, ltr. 23 (I, 224–258) to Franciscus Bianchi de Vellate. It was also customary for Poggius to submit his letters to eminent men and his other writings to Nicolaus and other friends for approval before delivery or publication. See, for instance, Letter LXXII (Tonelli Bk. III, ltr. 35) on his *De avaritia* and Tonelli Bk. VII, ltr. 1, his long letter to Joannes Franciscus Gonzaga, first submitted to Victorinus Feltrensis (see Bk. VII, ltr. 2) in 1437.

3(II,13:5–12). Poggius' fears were soon realized: Eugenius IV was forced to flee from Rome in June, 1434 (see Pastor, *History of the Popes,* I, 292–295). Here Poggius was probably referring to the activities of the Emperor Sigismund and the Duke of Milan, both hostile to Florence and unfriendly to Eugenius IV. See Valois, *Le Pape,* I, 147.

4(II,13:8). Acts 1:16.

5(II,13:15). This letter, like the preceding one, should be dated 1434, since it was written during the month of January after Cosmus de Medicis' exile in October 1433.

LETTER XCIII

1(Wilmanns, 289:3). See Letter I (Tonelli, I, x): the dedicatory letter to Franciscus Marescalcus of Ferrara gives much of this same information. The notes on that letter give what little biographical information exists about him. According to Haroldus, *Beati Alberti*, p. 25, Franciscus Marescalcus was an admirer and companion of Albertus de Sartheano during his stay in Ferrara in the late 1420s.

2(289:5–6). Only one letter from Poggius to Nicolaus written in Rome, Germany, or France prior to 1416 is known to have survived. It is Letter II (Tonelli, I, xiii–xvi), about the death of Coluccius Salutatus written in 1406 (see Walser, *Poggius*, p. 37). We have no letters written either on his way to England via Paris in 1418 or on his return trip to Italy via Cologne in 1423. See Sabbadini, *Scoperte*, I, 83.

3(289:9–10). Poggius' extant letters about his discoveries were written to Guarinus (Tonelli Bk. I, ltr. 5; I, 25–29) in December 1417 and to Franciscus Barbarus (see Clark, "Literary Discoveries of Poggio" *Classical Review*, XIII, No. 2 [1899], 119–130, especially p. 125). Franciscus Barbarus replied with a most enthusiastic letter of praise (*Francisci Barbari . . . Epistolae*, I), pp. 1–8. Poggius' discoveries were also praised by Leonardus Brunus Aretinus (*Epistolae*, IV, 4). For Poggius' earliest discoveries in France, see Clark, *Vetus Cluniacensis*, p. lxiv. For these letters, see Appendix, Letters II, III, IV, and VIII.

Poggius also announced both his French and his "German" discoveries to Franciscus Piccolpassus in 1417 in two letters published by Wilmanns, *Briefsammlungen*, pp. 459–461. See Appendix, Letters V and VI. See also Remigio Sabbadini, "Poggio scopritore di codici latini in Germania," *Rendiconti del r. istituto lombardo di scienze e lettere*, XLVI (1913), 905–908.

For a complete list of the texts discovered by Poggius 1413–1418 see Sabbadini, *Scoperte*, I, 76–82.

4(290:3). See, for instance: Tonelli Bk. VI, ltr. 6 to Fernandus Didax; Tonelli Bk. VII, ltr. 3 to Franciscus Piccolpassus, Archbishop of Milan; Tonelli Bk. VII, ltr. 12 to Joannes Spelimbergensis dating from 1437–1438.

BIBLIOGRAPHY

MANUSCRIPT SOURCES

Registri Vaticani: Nos. 115, 117, 170, 192, 272, 285, 292, 333, 349, 350, 351, 352, 353, 355, 356, 359.
Registri Laterani: Nos. 209, 210, 212, 231.

PRINTED SOURCES

Agostini, Giovanni degli. *Notizie istoriche-critiche intorno la vita, e le opere degli scrittori viniziani.* 2 vols. Venice: Occhi, 1752–1754.

Ambrose, St. *Expositio evangelii Lucae,* Book VII (Commentary on Luke X.35). Edited by Carolus Schenkl. Corpus Scriptorum Ecclesiasticorum Latinorum, Vol. XXXII, pt. 4. Vienna: F. Tempsky, 1902.

Antoninus Florentinus. *Chronicon,* Partes I–III. Nuremberg: Anton Koberger, 1484.

Antonius Hispalensis, Nicolaus. *Bibliotheca Hispana Vetus sive Hispani Scriptores Qui ab Octaviani Augusti Aevo ad Annum Christi MD Floruerunt.* 2 vols. Madrid: Iberra, 1788.

Aubert, R., and E. van Cauwenbergh, eds. *Dictionnaire d'histoire èt de géographie ecclésiastiques.* 17 vols. Paris: Letouzey et Ané, 1912–1970.

Augustinus, St. *De Baptismo contra Donatistas* IV, 5, in Jacques Migne, ed., *Patrologiae Cursus Completus; sive, Biblioteca Universalis . . . omnium SS. Patrum, Doctorum Scriptorumque Ecclesiasticorum Augustini,* Series Prima (Latina), Vol. XLIII: *S. Aurelii Augustini Opera Omnia,* T. IX. Paris: J. P. Migne, 1844–1865.

—— *Contra Faustum Libri Triginta Tres,* etc. Joseph Zycha, ed. Vienna: F. Tempsky, 1891.

Babinger, Franz. *Maometto il conquistatore e il suo tempo.* San Casciano: Giulio Einaudi, 1957.

Baedeker, Karl. *Rome and Central Italy.* 16th revised edition. Leipzig: Karl Baedeker, 1930.

Baix, François. *La Chambre apostolique et les "Libri Annatarum" de Martin V (1417–1431).* Première partie: Introduction et textes. Analecta Vaticano-Belgica, Vol. XIV. Brussels and Rome: L'Institut historique belge de Rome, 1942.

Bandinius, Angelus Maria, ed. *Catalogus Codicum Graecorum Bibliothecae Mediceae Laurentianae.* 3 vols. Florence: Typis Caesareis, 1764–1770.

—— *Catalogus Codicum Latinorum Bibliothecae Mediceae Laurenti-anae.* 5 vols. Florence, 1774–1777.

Barbarus, Franciscus. *Diatriba Praeliminaris in duas partes divisa ad Francisci Barbari et aliorum ad ipsum Epistolas.* 2 vols. Brescia: Joannes-Maria Rizzardi, 1741.

Barker, John W. *Manuel II Paleologus (1391–1425): A Study in Late Byzantine Statesmanship.* Rutgers Byzantine Series. New Brunswick: Rutgers University Press, 1969.

Baron, Hans. *The Crisis of the Early Italian Renaissance.* 2 vols. Princeton: Princeton University Press, 1955.

—— *From Petrarch to Leonardo Bruni.* Chicago and London: Published for the Newberry Library by the University of Chicago Press, 1968.

—— *Humanistic and Political Literature in Florence and Venice at the Beginning of the Quattrocento.* Cambridge, Mass.: Harvard University Press, 1955.

—— *Leonardo Bruni Aretino: Humanistisch-philosophische Schriften.* Leipzig: Teubner, 1928.

Barozzi, Luciano, and Remigio Sabbadini. *Studi sul Panormita e sul Valla.* Remigio Sabbadini, *Cronologia documentata della vita di Antonio Beccadelli, detto il Panormita.* Florence: Istituto di Studi Superiori Practici e di Perfezionamento in Firenze, Successori Le Monnier, 1891.

Bayle, Pierre. *A General Dictionary, Historical and Critical.* 10 vols. London, 1734–1741.

Bayley, Charles. *War and Society in Renaissance Florence: The De militia of Leonardo Bruni.* Toronto: University of Toronto Press, 1961.

Bellissima, G. B. "Analisi archeologico dell' arco di Traiano in Benevento," *Classici e neo-latini,* II, No. 2 (1906), 101–113.

Benedictus, St. *Regula.* Gregorio Penco, O.S.B., ed. Biblioteca di studi superiori XXXIX. Florence: La Nuova Italia, 1958.

Bennett, Charles E. *New Latin Grammar.* 3rd edition reprinted. New York: Allyn and Bacon, 1928.

Bennett, Josephine Waters. "Andrew Holes: A Neglected Harbinger of the English Renaissance," *Speculum,* XIX, No. 3 (1944), 314–335.

Bertalot, Ludwig. "Cincius Romanus und seine Briefe," *Quellen und Forschungen aus italienischen Archiven und Bibliotheken,* herausgegeben vom preussischen historischen Institut in Rom, XXI (Rome: W. Regensberg, 1929–1930), 209–255.

—— "Forschungen über Leonardo Bruni Aretino," *Archivum Romanicum,* XV, 1931 (1932), 284–323.

—— "Rezension von Leonardo Bruni Aretino: Humanistisch-philosophische Schriften," H. Baron, ed., *Historische Vierteljahrschrift,* XXIX (1934), 385–400.

—— "Zur Bibliographie der Überzetzungen des Leonardus Brunus Aretinus," *Quellen und Forschungen aus italienischen Archiven und Bibliotheken,* herausgegeben von preussischen historischen Institut in Rom, XXVII (1937), 178–195.

—— "Zur Bibliographie des Leonardus Brunus Aretinus," *Quellen und Forschungen aus italienischen Archiven und Bibliotheken,* herausgegeben von preussischen historischen Institut in Rom, XXVIII (1938), 268–285.

Bertarelli, L. V. *Firenze e dintorni.* Milan: Guida d'Italia del Touring Club Italiano, 1937.

Bertoni, Giulio. *La biblioteca estense e la coltura ferrarese ai tempi del duca Ercole I (1471–1505).* Turin: Ermanno Loescher, 1903.

—— *Guarino da Verona fra letterati e cortegiani a Ferrara (1429–1460).* Geneva: L. S. Olschki, 1921.

Billanovich, Giuseppe. "Dal Livio di Raterio (Laur. 63,19) al Livio del Petrarca (B. M. Harl, 2493)," *Italia medioevale e umanistica,* II (1959), 103–178.

—— "Giovanni del Virgilio, Pietro da Moglio, Francesco da Fiano," *Italia medioevale e umanistica,* VI (1963), 203–234.

—— "Gli umanisti e le cronache medioevali. Il 'Liber Pontificalis,' le 'Decadi' di 'Tito Livio' e il primo umanesimo a Roma," *Italia medioevale e umanistica,* I (1958), 103–137.

—— "Petrarch and the Textual Tradition of Livy," *Journal of the Warburg and Courtauld Institutes,* XIV (1951), 137–208.

Billius, Andreas. *Historiae Patriae Mediolanensis,* in Ludovicus Antonius Muratorius, *Rerum Italicarum Scriptores,* Vol. XIX, cols. 1–158. Milan: Societas Palatina, 1731.

Blondus, Flavius. *Italia illustrata.* Verona: Boninus de Boninis, 7 February 1482.

—— *Roma triumphans.* Mantua: Petrus Adam, de Michaelibus, ca. 1473.

Blum, Rudolf. *La biblioteca della badia fiorentina e i codici di Antonio Corbinelli.* Studi e testi, 155. Città del Vaticano: Biblioteca Apostolica Vaticana, 1951.

Boese, Helmut. *Die lateinischen Handschriften der Sammlung Hamilton zu Berlin.* Wiesbaden: Harrassowitz, 1966.

Böhmer, J. F., ed. *Regesta Imperii,* Vol. XI. *Die Urkunden Kaiser Sigmunds (1410–1424),* Vol. I, Wilhelm Altmann, ed. Hildesheim: Georg Olms, 1968.

Borsa, Mario. "The Correspondence of Humphrey Duke of Gloucester and Pier Candido Decembrio," *English Historical Review,* XIX (1904), 509–526; XX (1905), 484–498.

—— "Pier Candido Decembrio e l'umanesimo in Lombardia," *Archivio storico lombardo,* X, Ser. 2 (1893), 5–75, 358–441.

Botfield, Beriah. *Prefaces to the First Editions of the Greek and Roman Classics and of the Sacred Scriptures.* London: H. G. Bohn, 1861.

Brown, Alison M. "The Humanist Portrait of Cosimo de' Medici, Pater Patriae," *Journal of the Warburg and Courtauld Institutes*, XXIV (1961), 186–221.

Brown, Julian. "French Painting in the Time of Jean de Berry: A Review," *The Book Collector*, XVIII, No. 4 (1969), 470–488.

Brunet, Jacques-Charles. *Manuel du libraire et de l'amateur de livres.* 8 vols. Paris: Firmin Didot, 1860–1880.

Brunus Aretinus, Leonardus. *Epistolarum Libri VIII.* 2 vols., edited by Laurentius Mehus. Florence: Paperinius, 1741.

—— *Historia fiorentina.* Venice, 1561.

—— *La historia universale de suoi tempi,* with additions by Francesco Sansovino. Venice: n.p., n.d.

—— "Ad Petrum Paulum Istrum Dialogus." Theodor Klette, ed., in *Beiträge zur Geschichte und Litteratur der italienischen Gelehrtenrenaissance*, Vol. II. Greifswald: Julius Abel, 1889.

—— *Rerum suo tempore in Italia gestarum Commentarius ab anno MCCCLXXVIII usque ad annum MCCCCXL,* in Ludovicus Antonius Muratorius, *Rerum Italicarum Scriptores*, Vol. XIX. Milan: Societas Palatina, 1731. Also XIX 3, Carmine di Pierro, ed., Fasc. 128, 130, 207–208. Bologna: Zanichelli, 1926; and Città di Castello: Lapi, 1914–1926.

Bryce, James. *The Holy Roman Empire.* New York: The Macmillan Company, 1932.

Buhler, Curt F. Review of Rudolf Blum, "La biblioteca della badia fiorentina e i codici di Antonio Corbinelli (Studi e testi 155)," *Speculum*, XXVI, No. 4 (October, 1951), 707–709.

Bullarium Franciscanum continens Constitutiones, Epistolas, Diplomata Romanorum Pontificum Eugenii IV et Nicolai V ad tres Ordines S.P.N. Francisci Spectantia. Nova Series, Vol. I. Ulricus Hüntemann, ed. Quaracchi: Collegium S. Bonaventurae, 1929.

Burger, Fritz. "Donatello und die Antike," *Repertorium für Kunstwissenschaft*, XXX (1907), 1–13.

Calendar of Inquisitions post mortem Edward III. Vol. XIV. London: Her Majesty's Stationery Office, 1952.

Calendar of the Register of John de Drokensford, Bishop of Bath and Wells (A.D. 1309–1329). Right Rev. Bishop Hobhouse, ed. Vol. I. Somerset Record Society, 1887.

The Cambridge Medieval History. Vol. V, pp. 672–691, chap. XX, Alexander Hamilton Thompson, "The Monastic Orders." Cambridge: Cambridge University Press, 1929.

—— Vol. VII, pp. 368–392, chap. XIII, A. Coville, "France: Armagnacs and Burgundians (1380–1422)," and pp. 632–663, chap. XXII, Cecil

Roth, "The Jews in the Middle Ages." Cambridge: Cambridge University Press, 1949.

Cammelli, Giuseppe. *I dotti bizantini e le origini dell' umanesimo.* Vol. I: *Manuele Crisolora.* Florence: Vallechi Editore, 1941.

Caplan, Harry. *The Classical Tradition: Literary and Historical Studies in Honor of Harry Caplan.* Luitpold Wallach, ed. Ithaca: Cornell University Press, 1966.

Cappelli, A. *Cronologia, cronografia e calendario perpetuo.* 2nd edition revised. Milan: Hoepli, 1930; anastatic reprint, 1960.

Caravita, Andrea. *I codici e le arti a Monte Cassino.* 3 vols. Monte Cassino: Della Badia, 1869.

Carcopino, Jerome. *Daily Life in Ancient Rome.* Henry T. Rowell, ed., E. O. Lorimer, trans. New Haven: Yale University Press, 1940.

Carmina illustrium poetarum italorum. 10 vols. Florence: Apud Joannem Cajetanum Tartinium, 1720.

Castiglioni, *A History of Medicine.* Trans. and ed., E. B. Krumbhaar. 2nd edition, revised. New York: Alfred A. Knopf, 1947.

Catalano-Tirrito, M. *Nuovi documenti sul Panormita tratti dagli archivi palermitani.* Catania: Niccolò Giannotta, 1910.

Catalogue of Books Printed in the XVth Century Now in the British Museum. 9 vols. London and The Hague: Martinus Nijhoff, 1908–1962.

Chevalier, Ulysse. *Répertoire des sources historiques du moyen age: Bio-bibliographie.* 2 vols. Paris: Alphonse Picard, Nouvelle édition refondue, 1905–1907.

—— *Répertoire des sources historiques du moyen age: Topo-bibliographie.* Montbéliard: Imprimerie Montbéliardaise, 1894–1899.

Cheyney, Edward P. *The Dawn of a New Era, 1250–1453.* William L. Langer, gen. ed., The Rise of Modern Europe. New York: Harper and Brothers, 1936.

Chiappelli, Alessandro. "Della vita di Filippo Brunelleschi attributa ad Antonio Manetti ... ," *Archivio storico italiano,* Ser. 5, XVII (1896), 241–278.

[Chichele, Henry.] *The Register of Henry Chichele, Archbishop of Canterbury 1414–1443.* Ernest F. Jacob, ed. 4 vols. Oxford: Clarendon Press, 1943–1947.

Ciacconius, Alphonsus. *Vitae et Res Gestae Pontificum Romanorum et S.R.E. Cardinalium ab initio nascentis Ecclesiae usque ad Clementem IX P.O.M.* 4 vols. Rome: De Rubeis, 1677.

[Cicero, M. Tullius.] *The Correspondence of M. Tullius Cicero.* Robert Yelverton Tyrrell and Louis Claude Purser, eds. 7 vols. Dublin University Press Series. London: Longmans, Green and Co., 1901–1934. Vol. I, 3rd edition; Vols. II–VI, 2nd edition; Vol. VII, Index.

Clark, Albert Curtis. *Inventa Italorum.* Anecdota Oxoniensia, Classical
    Series, XI. Oxford: Clarendon Press, 1909.
—— "The Literary Discoveries of Poggio," *The Classical Review*, XIII
    (1899), 119–130.
—— *The Vetus Cluniacensis of Poggio.* Anecdota Oxoniensia, Classical
    Series, X. Oxford: Clarendon Press, 1905.
[Commines, Philippe de.] *The Historie of Philip de Commines.* Lon-
    don: Ar. Hatfield, for I. Norton, 1596.
Cook, Olive. *English Abbeys and Priories.* London: Thames and
    Hudson, 1962.
Copinger, W. A. *Supplement to Hain's Repertorium Bibliographicum,
    or Collections toward a New Edition of That Work,* in 2 parts. Milan:
    Görlich, 1950.
Corpus Inscriptionum Latinarum. Theodor Mommsen, ed. Editio altera,
    pars posterior a cura Ernesti Lommatsch. Berlin, 1919.
Cosenza, Mario Emilio. *Biographical and Bibliographical Dictionary
    of the Italian Humanists and of the World of Classical Scholarship
    in Italy, 1300–1800.* 6 vols. Boston: G. K. Hall & Co., 1962–1967.
Coulter, Cornelia C. "Boccaccio and the Cassinese Manuscripts of the
    Laurentian Library," *Classical Philology*, XLIII (October, 1948),
    217–230.
Coulton, George G. *Medieval Panorama: The English Scene from Con-
    quest to Reformation.* New York: The Macmillan Company, 1938.
Coville, A. "France: Armagnacs and Burgundians, 1380–1422," in *The
    Cambridge Medieval History*, Vol. VII. Cambridge: The Cambridge
    University Press, 1949.
Cox, John Charles. *Hampshire.* Revised by Philip M. Johnston. The
    Little Guides, 6th edition revised. London: Methuen and Co., 1929.
Craig, Katherine Taylor. *Stars of Destiny: The Ancient Science of
    Astrology and How to Make Use of It Today.* London: Kegan Paul,
    Trench, Trubner and Co., Ltd., 1916.
Creighton, Charles. *A History of Epidemics in Britain.* Vol. I: A.D.
    664–1666. 2nd edition. London: Frank Case and Co., Ltd., 1965.
Creighton, Mandell. *A History of the Papacy during the Period of the
    Reformation.* London: Longmans, Green and Co., 1899.
Cruttwell, Maud. *Donatello.* London: Methuen, 1911.
Cusa, Nicolaus de. *De pace fidei, cum epistula ad Ioannem de Segobia.*
    Raymund Klibansky and Hildebrand Bascour, eds., Mediaeval and
    Renaissance Studies, Supp. III. London: The Warburg Institute,
    1956.
Decembrius, Petrus Candidus. *Vita Philippi Mariae Vicecomitis, Tertii
    Ligurum Ducis,* in Ludovicus Antonius Muratorius, *Rerum Italicarum
    Scriptores,* Vol. XX, cols. 985–1020. Milan: Societas Palatina, 1731.

Also Vol. XX, 1 in Giosue Carducci and Vittorio Fiorini, eds., Fasc. 203–204, 210, 217, 221. Bologna: Zanichelli, 1925–1935.

Dictionnaire d'histoire et de géographie ecclésiastiques. Alfred Baudrillart, A. de Meyer, and E. van Cauwenbergh, eds. 17 vols. Paris: Librairie Letouzey et Ané, 1912–1970.

Diller, Aubrey. "The Library of Francesco and Ermolao Barbaro," *Italia medioevale e umanistica,* VI (1963), 253–262.

Ditt, Ernst. "Pier Candido Decembrio: Contributo alla storia dell' umanesimo italiano," *Memorie del R. Istituto Lombardo di scienze morale e lettere,* Classe di lettere, scienze morali e storiche, XXIV, Ser. III, 15 (1931), 21–105.

Dizionario biografico degli italiani, Vol. XIII. Rome: Istituto della Enciclopedia Italiana, 1971.

Dizionario di erudizione storico-ecclesiastico. 103 vols. Gaetano Moroni, ed. Venice, 1840–1879.

Du Cange, Charles Du Fresne. *Glossarium mediae et infimae latinitatis.* 10 vols. Paris: Librairie des sciences et des arts, 1938.

Duff, J. Wight. *A Literary History of Rome in the Silver Age.* 3rd edition. New York: Barnes and Noble, 1964.

Dunbar, Archibald. *Scottish Kings: A Revised Chronology of Scottish History, 1005–1625, with Notices of the Principal Events, Tables of Regnal Years, Pedigrees, Calendars, etc.* Edinburgh: D. Douglas, 1899.

Einhard. *Vita Karoli Magni.* Georg Heinrich Pertz and G. Waitz, eds. Scriptores rerum germanicarum in usum scholarum ex Monumentis Germaniae Historicis separatim editi. 6th edition. Hanover: Impensis Bibliopolii Hahnaiani, 1927.

Eubel, Conrad. *Hierarchia catholica medii aevi.* Vols. I and II. Munster: Regensberg. Vol. I, 1913. Vol. II, 1914; reprinted, Rome, 1960.

Fabricius, Joannes Albertus. *Bibliotheca latina mediae et infimae aetatis.* Florence: Thomas Baracchi, 1858.

[Fabyan, Robert.] *Fabyans cronycle.* London: Wyllyam Rastell, 1533.

Fachinetti, Vittorino. *San Bernardino da Siena.* Milan: Casa editrice S. Lega Eucaristica, 1933.

Facius, Bartholomeus. *De viris illustribus.* Laurentius Mehus, ed. Florence: Giovanelli, 1745.

Fava, Domenico. *La biblioteca estense nel suo sviluppo storico.* Modena: G. T. Vincenzi e Nipoti di Dante Cavellotti, 1925.

Ficinus, Marsilius. *Opera Omnia.* 2 vols. Basel: Henricus Petrus, 1576. Reproduced photographically in *Monumenta Politica et Philosophica Rariora,* Luigi Firpo, ed., Ser. I, Nos. 7–8. Turin: Bottega d'Erasmo, 1962.

—— *Supplementum Ficinianum: Marsilii Ficini Philosophi Florentini*

Opuscula inedita et dispersa. Paul Oskar Kristeller, ed. 2 vols. Florence: L. S. Olschki, 1937.

Firenze e dintorni. 3rd edition. Milan: Touring Club Italiano, 1937.

Foffano, Tino. "Niccoli, Cosimo, e le ricerche di Poggio nelle biblioteche francesi," *Italia medioevale e umanistica,* XII (1969), 113–128.

Fowler, James E. *A History of Beaulieu Abbey, A.D. 1204–1539.* London: The Car Illustrated, 1911.

Fowler, W. Warde. *The Religious Experience of the Roman People from the Earliest Times to the Age of Augustus.* London: Macmillan and Co., 1933.

Frank, Tenney. *Aspects of Social Behavior in Ancient Rome.* Martin Classical Lectures, II. Cambridge, Mass.: Harvard University Press, 1932.

—— *An Economic History of Rome.* 2nd edition revised. Baltimore: The Johns Hopkins Press, 1927.

Galen, Claudius. *Opera Omnia.* 20 vols. Carolus Gottlob Kühn, ed. Leipzig: Car. Cnobloch, 1830.

Garin, Eugenio. "I cancellieri umanisti della republica fiorentina da Coluccio Salutati a Bartolomeo Scala," *Rivista storica italiana,* LXXI, Fasc. 2 (1959), 185–208.

—— *La cultura filosofica del Rinascimento italiano.* Florence: Sansoni, 1961.

—— *La disputa delle arti nel Quattrocento: Testi editi ed inediti.* Florence: Vallechi, 1947.

—— *L'educazione in Europa (1400–1600) problemi e programmi.* Bari: Laterza, 1957.

—— *Prosatori latini del Quattrocento.* La Letteratura Italiana, Storie e Testi, Vol. XIII. Milan: R. Ricciardi, 1952.

Garin, Eugenio, ed. Coluccius Salutatus, *De nobilitate legum et medicinae* and *De verecundia.* Edizione nazionale dei classici del pensiero italiano VIII. Florence: Vallechi, 1947.

Gervasoni, Gianni. *Angelo Mai.* Bergamo: Orebiche, 1954.

Gibbon, Edward. *The Decline and Fall of the Roman Empire.* 3 vols. New York: The Heritage Press, 1946.

Gill, Joseph. *The Council of Florence.* Cambridge: The Cambridge University Press, 1959.

—— *Eugenius IV, Pope of Christian Union.* Raymond H. Schmandt, gen. ed., The Popes Through History, Vol. I. Westminster, Md.: Newman Press, 1961.

Giuliari, Giambattista Carlo. "La letteratura veronese al cadere del secolo XV, e le sue opere a stampa," *Il Propugnatore,* V, pt. 2 (1872), 105–128.

Glasfurd, Alec. *The Antipope (Pedro de Luna, 1342–1423), A Study in Obstinacy.* London: Barrie and Rockliff, 1965.

Goff, Frederick R. *Incunabula in American Libraries: A Third Census of Fifteenth-Century Books Recorded in North American Collections.* New York: Bibliographical Society of America, 1964.

Gothein, Percy. *Francesco Barbaro, Früh-Humanismus und Staatskunst in Venedig.* Berlin: Verlag die Runde, 1932.

Graham, Rose, gen. ed. Canterbury and York Series. Vol. XLV: *The Register of Henry Chichele.* Ernest F. Jacob, ed. 4 vols. Oxford: Oxford University Press, 1943.

Gregorovius, Ferdinand. *A History of the City of Rome in the Middle Ages.* Translated from the 4th German edition by Annie Hamilton. 8 vols. in 13. London: T. Bell & Sons, 1894–1902.

Gruter, Janus. *Lampas sive fax artium liberalium, hoc est Thesaurus Criticus.* Vol. III. Lucca, 1747.

Guest, A. R., and E. T. Richmond. "Misr in the Fifteenth Century," *Journal of the Royal Asiatic Society* (1903), pp. 791–816 and map.

Gutkind, Curt S. *Cosimo de' Medici: Pater Patriae, 1389–1464.* Oxford Studies in Modern Languages and Literature. Oxford: Clarendon Press, 1938.

Hain, Ludwig. *Repertorium Bibliographicum.* 2 vols., 4 pts. Milan: Görlich Editore, 1948.

Haller, Johannes. *England und Rom unter Martin V.* In *Quellen und Forschungen aus italienischen Archiven und Bibliotheken.* Vol. VIII, pt. 2 (1906).

Hampshire, Extracted from Domes-Day Book. Edited and translated by Richard Warner. London: Faulder, 1789.

[Harleian Manuscripts.] *A Catalogue of the Harleian Manuscripts in the British Museum.* 4 vols. London: Eyre and Strahan, 1808.

Haroldus, Franciscus, ed. *Beati Alberti a Sarthiano Ord. Min. Reg. Observ. Opera Omnia.* Rome: Joannes Baptista Bussottus, 1688.

Harth, Helene. "Niccolò Niccoli als literarischer Zensor. Untersuchungen zur Textgeschichte von Poggios 'De avaritia,'" *Rinascimento,* XVIII (1967), 29–53.

Herlihy, David. *Medieval and Renaissance Pistoia: The Social History of an Italian Town, 1200–1430.* New Haven: Yale University Press, 1967.

—— *Pisa in the Early Renaissance.* Yale Historical Publications, Miscellany No. 68. New Haven: Yale University Press, 1958.

Hieronymus Foroliviensis, Frater. *Chronicon Foroliviense,* in Ludovicus Antonius Muratorius, *Rerum Italicarum Scriptores,* Vol. XIX, cols. 873–906. Milan: Societas Palatina, 1731.

Higden, Ranulf. *Polychronicon.* [Westminster]: William Caxton [1482].

Hind, Arthur M. *An Introduction to a History of Woodcut, with a De-*

tailed Survey of Work Done in the Fifteenth Century. 2 vols. New York: Dover Publications, 1963.

Hochart, P. *De l'authenticité des annales et des histoires de Tacite.* Bordeaux: Imprimerie G. Gounouilhou, 1889.

Hofmann, Georgius. *Epistolae Pontificiae ad Concilium Florentinum Spectantes.* Vol. I, 3 pts. Rome: Pontificium Institutum Orientalium Studiorum, 1940–1946.

Holinshed's Chronicles: Richard II 1398–1400, Henry IV and Henry V. Oxford: Clarendon Press, 1923.

IIürlimann, Martin. *English Cathedrals.* Boston: Houghton Mifflin Co., 1950.

Hutchison, Harold F. *Henry V: A Biography.* London: Eyre and Spottiswoode, 1967.

Infessura, Stefano. *Diario della Città di Roma.* Oreste Tommasini, ed. Rome: Istituto Storico Italiano, 1890; reprinted, Turin: Bottega d'Erasmo, 1960.

Italia centrale: Guida breve. Vol. II. Milan: Touring Club Italiano, 1952.

Jacob, Ernest F. *The Fifteenth Century: 1399–1485.* The Oxford History of England, Sir George Clark, ed., Vol. VI. Oxford: Clarendon Press, 1961.

—— "Two Lives of Archbishop Chichele, with an appendix containing an early book list of All Souls College, Oxford," *The Bulletin of the John Rylands Library,* Vol. 16, No. 2, July, 1932.

Jacob, Ernest F., ed. *The Register of Henry Chichele.* 4 vols. Rose Graham, gen. ed., Canterbury and York Series, Vol. XLV. Oxford: Oxford University Press, 1943–1947.

James, Montague Rhodes. *The Ancient Libraries of Canterbury and Dover.* Cambridge: Cambridge University Press, 1903.

—— *A Descriptive Catalogue of the Manuscripts in the Library of Eton College.* Cambridge: Cambridge University Press, 1895.

Janson, Horst W. *The Sculpture of Donatello.* Princeton: Princeton University Press, 1957.

John Chrysostom, St. "Sermon before His Exile," Vol. III. Paris: Edited by Bernard de Montfaucon, 1837.

Join-Lambert, Michel. *Jérusalem, Isréalite, Chrétienne, Musulmane.* Paris: Albert A. Guillot, 1956.

Jusserand, Jean Adrien Antoine Jules. *English Wayfaring Life in the Middle Ages.* Translated by Lucy T. Smith, 4th edition. London: Ernest Benn, 1950.

Karmin, Otto. *La legge del catasto fiorentino del 1427.* Florence: Bernardo Seeber, 1906.

Ker, Neil R. *Medieval Libraries of Great Britain: A List of Surviving*

Books. Royal Historical Society Guides and Handbooks, No. 3. London: The Royal Historical Society, 1941.

Klette, Theodor. *Beiträge zur Geschichte und Litteratur der italienischen Gelehrtenrenaissance.* 3 vols. Greifswald: Julius Abel, 1888–1890.

Klibansky, Raymund, and Hildebrand Bascour, eds. *Nicolaus de Cusa, De Pace Fidei, cum Epistula ad Ioannem de Segobia.* Mediaeval and Renaissance Studies, Supp. III. London: The Warburg Institute, 1956.

Knowles, Dom David. *The Religious Orders in England.* 3 vols. Cambridge: Cambridge University Press, 1955.

Knowles, David, and R. Neville Hadcock. *Medieval Religious Houses: England and Wales.* London: Longmans, Green and Co., 1953.

Koenig, Erich. *Kardinal Giordano Orsini: Ein Lebensbild aus der Zeit der grossen Konzilien und des Humanismus.* Freiburg im Breisgau: Herdersche verlagshandlung, 1906.

Kristeller, Paul Oskar. *Eight Philosophers of the Italian Renaissance.* Stanford: Stanford University Press, 1964.

—— *Iter Italicum: A Finding List of Uncatalogued or Incompletely Catalogued Humanistic Manuscripts of the Renaissance in Italian and Other Libraries.* 2 vols. London: The Warburg Institute, and Leiden: E. J. Brill. Vol. I, 1963; Vol. II, 1967.

—— "Ludwig Bertalot," *Scriptorium,* XVI, 1 (1962), 102–104.

—— "Pier Candido Decembrio and His Unpublished Treatise on the Immortality of the Soul," in *The Classical Tradition: Literary and Historical Studies in Honor of Harry Caplan,* Luitpold Wallach, ed. Ithaca: Cornell University Press, 1966. Pp. 536–558.

Kühner, Hans. *Encyclopedia of the Papacy.* New York: Philosophical Library, 1958.

Labalme, Patricia H. *Bernardo Giustiniani: A Venetian of the Quattrocento.* Uomini e Dottrine, 13. Rome: Edizione di Storia e Letteratura, 1969.

Lane, Frederic C. *Venice and History: The Collected Papers of Frederic Chapin Lane.* Baltimore: The Johns Hopkins Press, 1966.

Langer, William L., gen. ed., The Rise of Modern Europe. *The Dawn of a New Era, 1250–1453* by Edward P. Cheyney. New York: Harper and Brothers, 1936.

Lazio. 3rd edition. Milan: Guida d'Italia del Touring Club Italiano, 1964.

Lazio, attraverso l'Italia. Vol. XI. Milan: Touring Club Italiano, 1943.

Lazzareschi, E. "Francesco Sforza e Paolo Guinigi," extract from *Miscellanea di studi storici in onore di Giovanni Sforza.* Turin, n.p., n.d.

Lehnerdt, Max. "Cencio und Agapito de' Rustici," *Zeitschrift für vergleichende Litteraturgeschichte*, N.F. XIV (1900), 149–172, 289–318.

Lenfant, David. *Concordantiae Augustinianae, sive Collectio omnium sententiarum quae sparsim reperiuntur in omnibus S. Augustini operibus*. 2 vols. Brussels: Culture et civilization, 1963.

Lenfant, Jacques. *Histoire de la Guerre des Hussites et du Concile de Basle*. 2 vols. Amsterdam: Pierre Humbert, 1731.

Levi d'Ancona, Mirelle. *Miniatura e miniatori a Firenze dal XIV al XVI secolo: Documenti per la storia della miniatura*. Florence: Leo S. Olschki, 1962.

Livius, Titus. *The Romane Historie written by T. Livius of Padua. Also, The Breviaries of L. Florus: with a Chronology to the whole Historie and the Topography of Rome in the old time*. Translated out of Latine into English, by Philemon Holland, Doctor in Physick. London, Printed by W. Hunt, for Gabriel Bedell, at the Middle Temple Gate, 1659.

Lockwood, Dean Putnam. "De Rinucio Aretino Graecarum litterarum interprete," *Harvard Studies in Classical Philology*, XXIV (1913), 51–109.

—— *Ugo Benzi: Medieval Philosopher and Physician 1376–1439*. Chicago: University of Chicago Press, 1951.

Loew, Elias Avery. *The Beneventan Script: A History of the South Italian Minuscule*. Oxford: Clarendon Press, 1914.

Long, A. A., ed. *Problems in Stoicism*. London: University of London, The Athlone Press, 1971.

Loomis, Louise Ropes. "The Greek Studies of Poggio Bracciolini," in *Medieval Studies in Memory of Gertrude Schoepperle Loomis*. Roger Sherman Loomis, ed. New York: Columbia University Press, 1927. Pp. 489–512.

Loomis, Louise Ropes, trans. *The Council of Constance: The Unification of the Church*. John H. Mundy and Kennerly M. Woody, eds. Records of Civilization: Sources and Studies, Vol. LXIII. New York: Columbia University Press, 1961.

Lunt, William E. *Financial Relations of the Papacy with England*. Vol. II: 1327–1534. Studies in Anglo-Papal Relations during the Middle Ages, II. Cambridge, Mass.: The Mediaeval Academy of America, 1962.

Mabillon, Jean, O.S.B. *De re diplomatica Libri VI*. 2 vols. Paris: Louis Billaine, 1681.

Machiavelli, Niccolo. *History of Florence and of the Affairs of Italy from the Earliest Times to the Death of Lorenzo the Magnificant*. New York: Harper Torchbooks, 1960.

Macrobius. *In Somnium Scipionis ex Ciceronis VI Libro de Rep. Erudi-tissima explanatio. Eiusdem Saturnaliorum Libri VII.* Venice: Aldus et Andreas Asulanus, 1528.

Mallett, Michael E. *The Florentine Galleys in the Fifteenth Century with the Diary of Luca di Maso degli Albizzi, Captain of the Galleys 1429-1430.* Oxford: Clarendon Press, 1967.

Mancini, Girolamo. "Alcune lettere di Lorenzo Valla," *Giornale storico della letteratura italiana*, XXI (1893), 1-48.

—— *Vita di Leon Battista Alberti.* Florence: Sansoni, 1882.

—— *Vita di Lorenzo Valla.* Florence: Sansoni, 1891.

Manetti, Antonio di Tuccio. *The Life of Brunelleschi.* Translated by Catherine Enggass, edited by Howard Saalman. University Park: Pennsylvania State University Press, 1970.

Mare, A. C. de la. *The Handwriting of Italian Humanists.* Vol. I, fasc. I. The Association Internationale de Bibliophilie. Oxford: Oxford University Press, 1973.

Marletta, Fedele. "Note all' epistolario del Panormita," *Rinascita*, V, No. 27 (1942), 516-526.

Martène, Edmond, and Ursin Durand. *Veterum Scriptorum et Monumentorum Historicorum, Dogmaticorum, Moralium Amplissima Collectio.* 9 vols. Paris: Montalant, 1724-1733.

—— *Voyage littéraire de deux religieux de la congrégation de Saint Maur.* 2 vols. Paris: Delaulne, 1717 and 1724.

Martin, Gregory. *Roma Sancta (1581).* George Bruner Parks, ed. Rome: Edizioni di Storia e Letteratura, 1969.

Martines, Lauro. *Lawyers and Statecraft in Renaissance Florence.* Princeton: Princeton University Press, 1968.

—— *The Social World of the Florentine Humanists, 1390-1460.* Princeton: Princeton University Press, 1963.

Marzi, Demetrio. *La cancelleria della repubblica fiorentina.* Rocca S. Casciano: Licinio Cappelli, 1910.

Mazzuchelli, Giammaria. *Gli scrittori d'Italia cioe notizie storiche, e critiche intorno alle vite, e agli scritti dei letterati italiani.* 6 vols. Brescia: Giambatista Bossini, 1753-1763.

McCormick, P. J. "Two Catholic Medieval Educators. II. Guarino da Verona," *Catholic University Bulletin*, XIII (1907), 232-249.

Meiggs, Russell. *Roman Ostia.* Oxford: Clarendon Press, 1960.

Mercati, Angelo. *Una corrispondenza fra curiali della prima metà del Quattrocento.* Sudi e testi, 157. Città del Vaticano: Biblioteca Apostolica Vaticana, 1951.

Molho, Anthony. *Florentine Public Finances in the Early Renaissance, 1400-1433.* Cambridge, Mass.: Harvard University Press, 1971.

Monumenta Germaniae Historica. Georg Heinrich Pertz, ed. Legum Tomus II. Hanover: Impensis Bibliopolii Aulici Hahniani, 1837.

Moorman, John. *A History of the Franciscan Order.* Oxford: Clarendon Press, 1968.

Moranvillé, H. "Un Pélerinage en Terre Sainte et au Sinai au XVᵉ siècle," *Bibliothèque de l'école des chartes,* LXVI (1905), 70–106.

Müllner, Karl. *Reden und Briefe italienischer Humanisten: Ein Beitrag zur Geschichte der Pädagogik des Humanismus.* Vienna: Alfred Holder, 1899.

Müntz, Eugene. *Histoire de l'art pendant la Renaissance.* 3 vols. Paris: Hachette, 1889–1895.

Muratorius, Ludovicus Antonius. *Antiquitates Italicae Medii Aevi, sive Dissertationes.* 6 vols. Milan: Societas Palatina, 1738–1742.

—— *Novus Thesaurus Veterum Inscriptionum.* Vol. II. Milan: Ex Aedibus Palatinis, 1740.

—— *Rerum Italicarum Scriptores ab anno aerae Christianae quingentesimo ad millesimumquingentesimum.* 25 vols. in 28. Milan: Societas Palatina in Regia Curia, 1723–1751.

Mynors, Roger Aubrey Baskerville. *Catalogue of the Manuscripts of Balliol College, Oxford.* Oxford: Clarendon Press, 1963.

Nash, Ernest. *Pictorial Dictionary of Ancient Rome.* 2 vols. 2nd edition. New York: Praeger, 1968.

Negrier, Paul. *Les bains à travers les ages.* Paris: Librairie de la construction moderne, 1925.

Newett, Margaret. *Canon Pietro Casola's Pilgrimage to Jerusalem in the Year 1494.* Manchester: Manchester University Press, 1907.

Niceron, Jean Pierre de. *Mémoires pour servir à l'histoire des hommes illustres dans la république des lettres, avec un catalogue raisonné de leurs ouvrages.* 43 vols. Paris: Chez Briasson, 1729–1745.

[Nichols, John.] *A collection of all the wills, now known to be extant, of the Kings and Queens of England, Princes and Princesses of Wales, and every branch of the Blood Royal, from the reign of William the Conqueror, to that of Henry the Seventh Exclusive.* London: J. Nichols, Printer to the Society of Antiquaries, 1780.

Nolhac, Pierre de. *Pétrarque et l'humanisme.* Turin: Bottega d'Erasmo, 1959.

Oman, Charles, gen. ed. A History of England. Vol. III: *England in the Later Middle Ages,* by Kenneth H. Vickers. London: Methuen & Co., 1914.

Oppel, John W. "The Moral Basis of Renaissance Politics: A Study of the Humanistic Political and Social Philosophy of Poggio Bracciolini (1380–1459)." Ph.D. dissertation, Princeton University, 1972.

Origo, Iris. *The Merchant of Prato, Francesco di Marco Datini.* London: Jonathan Cape, 1957.

—— *The World of San Bernardino.* New York: Harcourt, Brace & World, Inc., 1962.

[Ottenthal, E. von.] Review by O. T. of E. von Ottenthal, *Die Bullenregister Martins V und Eugens IV* (Innsbruck, 1885), in *Archivio della r. società romana di storia patria,* VIII (1885), 285–289.

The Oxford Classical Dictionary. N. G. L. Hammond and H. H. Scullard, eds. 2nd edition. Oxford: Clarendon Press, 1970.

The Oxford Companion to Classical Literature. Compiled and edited by Sir Paul Harvey. Oxford: Clarendon Press, 1937.

The Oxford Universal Dictionary on Historical Principles. Revised and edited by C. T. Onions. 3rd edition. Oxford: Clarendon Press, 1955.

Paredi, Angelo. *La biblioteca del Pizolpasso.* Istituto nazionale di Studi sul Rinascimento, Sezione Lombarda. Milan: Ulrico Hoepli, 1961.

Parks, George Bruner. *The English Traveler to Italy.* 2 vols. Rome: Edizioni di Storia e Letteratura, 1954.

Partner, Peter. *The Papal State under Martin V: The Administration and Government of the Temporal Power in the Early Fifteenth Century.* London: The British School at Rome, 1958.

Pàstine, Luigi. "Antonio Loschi umanista vicentino," *Rivista d'Italia,* XVIII, pt. 1 (1915), 831–879.

Pastor, Ludwig. *The History of the Popes, from the Close of the Middle Ages. Drawn from the Secret Archives of the Vatican and Other Original Sources.* Frederick Ignatius Antrobus, ed. London: Kegan Paul, 1938 [Vol. I, 6th edition], 1949 [Vols. II, III . . . 7th edition].

Pegolotti, Francesco Balducci. *La pratica della mercatura.* Allen Evans, ed. Cambridge, Mass.: The Mediaeval Academy of America, 1936.

Pellegrin, Elisabeth. *La bibliothèque des Visconti et des Sforza, ducs de Milan au XVᵉ siècle.* Publication de l'Institut de Recherche et d'Histoire des Textes, 5. Paris: Vente au Service des Publications du C.N.R.S., 1955.

Platina, Bartholomaeus. *Vitae summorum pontificum.* [Venice]: Johannes de Colonia and Johannes Manthen, 1479.

Plutarch's Lives. Translated from the original Greek and edited by John Langhorne and William Langhorne. 6 vols. 5th edition. London: C. Dilly, 1792.

Poggio Bracciolini, Giovanni Francesco [Johannes Franciscus]. *The Facetiae or Jocose Tales of Poggio, Now first translated into English with the Latin Text, in two volumes.* Paris: Isidore Liseux, 1879.

—— *Historia Florentina.* Johannes Baptista Recanatus, ed. Venice: Apud Jo. Gabrielem Hertz, 1715.

—— *Historiae de varietate fortunae. Libri Quatuor.* Dominicus Georgius, ed. Paris: Antonius Urbanus Coustelier, 1723.

—— *Opera Omnia.* A cura di Riccardo Fubini, ed. 4 vols. Turin: Bottega d'Erasmo, 1964–1969.

—— *Opera.* Basel: Henricus Petrus, 1538.

—— *Poggiana, ou la vie, le caractère, les sentences, les bons mots de Pogge florentin, avec son histoire de la république de Florence* .... 2 vols. Amsterdam: Pierre Humbert, 1720.

Pope-Hennessy, John. *Italian Renaissance Sculpture.* London: Phaidon Press, 1958.

Pralle, Ludwig. *Die Wiederentdeckung des Tacitus: Ein Beitrag zur Geistesgeschichte Fuldas und zur Biographie des jungen Cusanus. Quellen und Abhandlungen zur Geschichte der Abtei und der Diözese Fulda XVII.* Fulda: Parzeller & Co., 1952.

Prescott, Hilda F. M. *Jerusalem Journey: Pilgrimage to the Holy Land in the Fifteenth Century.* London: Eyre and Spottiswoode, 1954.

—— *Once to Sinai: The Further Pilgrimage of Friar Felix Fabri.* London: Eyre and Spottiswoode, 1957.

Putnam's Complete Book of Quotations, Proverbs and Household Words. W. Gurney Benham, ed. New York: G. P. Putnam's Sons, 1927.

Quétif, Jacobus, and Jacobus Echard. *Scriptores Ordinis Praedicatorum.* 2 vols. Burt Franklin Biographical and Reference Series, No. 16. New York: Burt Franklin, 1959; a reprint of the Paris edition, 1719–1723.

Radford, Lewis Bostock. *Henry Beaufort: Bishop, Chancellor, Cardinal.* London: Sir Isaac Pitman & Sons, Ltd., 1908.

Rashdall, Hastings. *The Universities of Europe in the Middle Ages.* A New Edition in Three Volumes. F. M. Powicke and A. B. Emden, eds. Oxford: Clarendon Press, 1936.

Recanatus, Johannes Baptista. *Poggii Vita,* in Ludovicus Antonius Muratorius, *Rerum Italicarum Scriptores,* Vol. XX, cols. 163–190. Milan: Societas Palatina, 1731.

Resta, Gianvito, ed. *L'epistolario del Panormita: Studi per una edizione critica.* Università degli Studi di Messina, Facultà di lettere e filosofia, 3. Messina, 1954.

Ricci, Pier Giorgio. "Una consolatoria inedita del Marsuppini," *Rinascità,* III (1940), 363–433.

Richenthal, Ulrich von. *Das Concilium so Zu Constanz gehalten.* Augsburg: Heinrich Stainer, 1536.

Rist, J. M. *Stoic Philosophy.* Cambridge: Cambridge University Press, 1969.

Roma e dintorni. 6th edition. Milan: Touring Club Italiano, 1962.

Roover, Raymond de. *The Rise and Decline of the Medici Bank, 1397–1494.* Cambridge, Mass.: Harvard University Press, 1963.

Rose, H. J. *A Handbook of Greek Mythology.* New York: E. P. Dutton and Company, 1929.

Rosmini, Carlo de'. *Vita e disciplina di Guarino Veronese e de'suoi discepoli*. 3 vols. in one. Brescia: Nicolò Bettoni, 1805–1806.

[Ross, John Wilson.] *Tacitus and Bracciolini: The Annals Forged in the XVth Century*. London: Diprose & Bateman, 1878.

Rossi, Vittorio, ed. *Il Quattrocento*. Storia Letteraria d'Italia, Vol. V. Milan: Vallardi, 1933.

Roth, Cecil. *The Jews in the Renaissance*. Philadelphia: The Jewish Publication Society of America, 1959.

Rotta, Paolo. *Il Cardinale Nicolò di Cusa*. Publicazioni della Università Cattolica del Sacro Cuore, Serie Prima, Vol. XXI. Milan: Società Editrice "Vita e Pensiero," 1928.

Rubinstein, Nicolai. *The Government of Florence under the Medici: 1434–1494*. Oxford-Warburg Studies. Oxford: Clarendon Press, 1966.

Runciman, Steven. *A History of the Crusades*. Vol. III: *The Kingdom of Acre*. Cambridge: Cambridge University Press, 1954.

Sabbadini, Remigio. "Un biennio umanistico," *Giornale storico della letteratura italiana*, Supplemento No. 6 (1903).

—— *Biografia documentata di Giovanni Aurispa*. Noto: Zammit, 1890.

—— "Briciole umanistiche," *Giornale storico della letteratura italiana*, XLVI (1905), 70–71.

—— *Centotrenta lettere inedite di Francesco Barbaro*. Salerno: Tipografia Nazionale, 1884.

—— *Cronologia documentata della vita di Antonio Beccadelli, detto il Panormita*. See Luciano Barozzi and Remigio Sabbadini, *Studi sul Panormita e sul Valla*.

—— *Guariniana*. 1. *Vita di Guarino Veronese*. 2. *La scuola e gli studi di Guarino Veronese*. Mario Sancipriano, ed. Turin: Bottega d'Erasmo, 1964.

—— *Guarino Veronese e gli archetipi di Celso e Plauto*. Livorno: Coi Tipi di Raffaello Giusti, 1886.

—— "Notizie di alcuni umanisti," *Giornale storico della letteratura italiana*, V (1885), 175–177.

—— "Notizie storico-critiche di alcuni codici latini," *Studi italiani di filologia classica*, VII (1899), 125–129.

—— *Ottanta lettere inedite del Panormita tratte dei codici milanesi*. Biblioteca della Società di Storia Patria per la Sicilia Orientale, Vol. I. Catania: Niccolò Giannotta, 1910.

—— "Poggio scopritore di codici latini in Germania," *Rendiconti del r. istituto lombardo di scienze e lettere*, XLVI (1913), 905–908.

—— *Le scoperte dei codici latini e greci ne' secoli XIV e XV*. 2 vols. Florence: Sansoni, 1905 and 1914. Revised by Eugenio Garin. Anastatic reprint, 1967.

—— *Storia e critica di testi latini.* Biblioteca di Filologia Classica, 10. Catania: Battiato, 1914.

—— "Storia e critica di alcuni testi latini," in *Museo italiano di antichità classica,* III (1888–1890), 401–424.

Sabbadini, Remigio, ed. *Carteggio di Giovanni Aurispa.* Fonti per la Storia d'Italia. Rome: Tipografia del Senato, 1931.

—— *Epistolario di Guarino Veronese.* 3 vols. Venice: R. Deputazione Veneta di Storia Patria, 1915–1919.

[Salutati, Coluccio.] *Epistolario di Coluccio Salutati.* Francesco Novati, ed. 4 vols. Fonti per la Storia d'Italia. Rome: Istituto Storico Italiano, 1891–1905.

Sandys, John Edwin. *A History of Classical Scholarship.* 3 vols., 3rd edition. Cambridge: Cambridge University Press, 1908–1921.

—— *Latin Epigraphy: An Introduction to the Study of Latin Inscriptions.* 2nd edition, revised by S. C. Campbell. Cambridge: Cambridge University Press, 1927.

Sarton, George. *Introduction to the History of Sciences.* Vol. 3, pt. 2: *Science and Learning in the Fourteenth Century.* Baltimore: Williams & Williams Company, 1948.

Schanz, Martin, and Carl Hosius. *Geschichte der römischen Literatur bis zum Gesetzgebungswerk des Kaisers Justinian.* 2 pts., 4th edition. Vol. VIII of *Handbuch der Altertumswissenschaft.* Munich: C. H. Beck'sche, 1927–1935.

Schevill, Ferdinand. *History of Florence from the Founding of the City through the Renaissance.* New York: Harcourt, Brace and Co., 1936.

Schio, Giovanni da. *Sulla vita e sugli scritti di Antonio Loschi vicentino.* Padua: Tipi del Seminario, 1858.

Schirmer, Walter F. *Der englische Frühhumanismus: Ein Beitrag zur englischen Literaturgeschichte des 15. Jahrhunderts.* 2nd edition. Tubingen: Max Niemeyer Verlag, 1963.

Schmandt, Raymond H., gen. ed. The Popes through History. Vol. I: *Eugenius IV, Pope of Christian Union,* by Joseph Gill. Westminster, Md.: Newman Press, 1961.

A School Atlas of English History. Samuel Rawson Gardiner, ed. London: Longmans, Green, and Co., 1902.

Seznec, Jean. *The Survival of the Pagan Gods: The Mythological Tradition and Its Place in Renaissance Humanism and Art.* New York: Harper Torchbooks, 1961.

Shepherd, William. *The Life of Poggio Bracciolini.* Liverpool and London: Longman, Rees, Orme, Brown, Green & Longman, 1837.

—— *Vita di Poggio Bracciolini.* Scritta in inglese e tradotta dell' Tommaso Tonnelli. 2 vols. Florence: Gaspero Ricci, 1825.

Shepherd, William R. *Historical Atlas.* 6th edition. New York: Henry Holt and Company, 1927.

Shorey, Paul. *What Plato Said.* Chicago: University of Chicago Press, 1933.

Southern, R. W. *Western Views of Islam in the Middle Ages.* Cambridge, Mass.: Harvard University Press, 1962.

Southern Italy with Sicily and Sardinia. L. Russell Muirhead, ed. The Blue Guides, 3rd edition. London: Ernest Benn, Ltd., 1959.

Strickland, Agnes. *Lives of the Queens of England.* London: George Bell & Sons, 1859.

Switzerland. L. Russell Muirhead, ed. The Blue Guides, 3rd edition. New York: Rand McNally & Company, 1952.

Taylor, Henry Osborn. *The Medieval Mind.* 2 vols., 4th edition. Cambridge, Mass.: Harvard University Press, 1959.

Taylor, John. *The Universal Chronicle of Ranulf Higden.* Oxford: Clarendon Press, 1966.

Taylor, Lily Ross. *Party Politics in the Age of Caesar.* Sather Classical Lectures. Berkeley: University of California Press, 1949.

—— *The Voting Districts of the Roman Republic: The Thirty-five Urban and Rural Tribes.* American Academy in Rome, Papers and Monographs, Vol. XX, 1960.

Thompson, Edward Maunde. *An Introduction to Greek and Latin Paleography.* Oxford: Clarendon Press, 1912.

Thorndike, Lynn. "Franciscus Florentinus or Paduanus," in *Mélanges Mandonnet: Etudes d'histoire littéraire et doctrinale du moyen age,* II. Paris: J. Vrin, 1930.

—— *A History of Magic and Experimental Science.* 3 vols., sixth printing. New York: Columbia University Press, 1964.

—— "Sanitation, Baths, and Street Cleaning in the Renaissance," *Speculum,* III, No. 2 (April, 1928), 192–203.

—— *Science and Thought in the Fifteenth Century: Studies in the History of Medicine and Surgery, Natural and Mathematical Science, Philosophy and Politics.* New York: Columbia University Press, 1929.

Tietze-Conrat, E. *Mantegna: Paintings, Drawings, Engravings.* London: The Phaidon Press, 1955.

Tiraboschi, Girolamo. *Storia della letteratura italiana.* 9 vols. Florence: Molini Landi, 1805–1813.

Torre, Arnaldo della. *Storia dell' accademia platonica di Firenze.* Florence: G. Carnesecchi, 1902.

Toscana (non compresa Firenze). L. V. Bertarelli, ed. 2nd edition. Milan: Guida d'Italia della Consociazione Turistica Italiana, 1935.

Traube, Ludwig. *Vorlesungen und Abhandlungen.* Franz Boll, ed. Vol. I. Munich: C. H. Beck'sche, 1909.

[Traversarius, Ambrosius.] *Ambrosii Traversarii Generalis Camaldulensium . . . Latinae Epistolae.* Laurentius Mehus, ed. 2 vols. Bologna:

Forni Editore, 1968; a photostatic reprint of the Florence edition, 1759. Vol. I, "Praefatio" and "Vita"; Vol. II, Epistolae.

—— *Hodoeporicon.* Nicolaus Bartholinus. ed. Florence: Vincentius, 1680.

Trevelyan, George Macaulay. *Illustrated English Social History.* Vol. I. London: Longmans, Green and Co., 1949.

Ullman, Berthold Louis. *The Humanism of Coluccio Salutati.* Medioevo e Umanesimo, 4. Padua: Antenore, 1963.

—— *The Origin and Development of Humanistic Script.* Rome: Storia e Letteratura, 1960.

—— *Studies in the Italian Renaissance.* Rome: Edizioni di Storia e Letteratura, 1955.

Ullman, Berthold Louis, ed. Coluccius Salutatus, *De laboribus Herculis.* 2 vols. Zurich: Thesaurus Mundi, 1951.

—— Coluccius Salutatus, *De seculo et religione.* Florence: L. S. Olschki, 1957.

Ullman, Berthold Louis, and Philip A. Stadter. *The Public Library of Renaissance Florence.* Medioevo e Umanesimo, 10. Padua: Antenore, 1972.

Valla, Laurentius. *Opera Omnia.* With a Preface by Eugenio Garin. Monumenta Politica et Philosophica Rariora, Ser. I, No. 5. 2 vols. Turin: Bottega d'Erasmo, 1962; an anastatic reprint of the Basel edition, 1540.

Valois, Noël. *Le Pape et le concile (1418–1450).* 2 vols. Paris: Alphonse Picard, 1909.

Vansteenberghe, Edmond. *Le Cardinal Nicola de Cues (1401–1464).* Paris: Honoré Champion, 1920.

Vasiliev, A. A. *Histoire de l'empire byzantin.* 2 vols. Paris: A. Picard, 1932.

[Vergerio, Pier Paolo.] *Epistolario di Pier Paolo Vergerio.* Leonard Smith, ed. Fonti per la Storia d'Italia. Rome: Istituto Storico Italiano, 1934.

Vespasiano da Bisticci. *Vite di uomini illustri del secolo XV.* Florence: Barbèra, Bianchi e Comp., 1859.

Vickers, Kenneth H. *England in the Later Middle Ages.* 7th edition. London: Methuen & Co., Ltd., 1950.

Vitale, F. A. *Storia diplomatica dei senatori di Roma.* Vol. II. Rome, 1791.

Vocabulario degli accademici della Crusca. Vol. V, 5th edition. Florence, 1886.

Voigt, Georg. *Die Wiederbelebung des classischen Alterthums.* 2 vols., 4th edition. Berlin: De Gruyter, 1960.

Wadding, Luke. *Annales Minorum*. P. J. M. Fonseca, ed. 2nd edition, 25 vols. Rome: Typis Rachi Bernabà, 1731–1886. Vol. X.

Walser, Ernst. *Poggius Florentinus: Leben und Werke*. Beiträge zur Kulturgeschichte des Mittelalters und der Renaissance, XIV. Leipzig: Teubner, 1914.

Weiss, Robert [Roberto]. *Humanism in England during the Fifteenth Century*. Medium Aevum Monographs, 4. 3rd edition. Oxford: B. Blackwell, 1967.

—— *The Renaissance Discovery of Classical Antiquity*. Oxford: Basil Blackwell, 1969.

—— Review of Deno John Geanakoplos, *Greek Scholars in Venice: Studies in the Dissemination of Greek Learning from Byzantium to Western Europe, Speculum*, XXXVIII, No. 2 (April 1963), 351–353.

Wilcox, Donald J. *The Development of Florentine Humanist Historiography in the Fifteenth Century*. Harvard Historical Studies, LXXXII. Cambridge, Mass.: Harvard University Press, 1969.

William of Malmesbury. *Gesta Regum Anglorum, atque Historia Novella*. Thomas Duffus Hardy, ed. Vol. I. London: The English Historical Society, 1840.

Williams, Ethel Carleton. *My Lord of Bedford*. London: Longmans, Green and Co., 1963.

Wilmanns, A. "Über die Briefsammlungen des Poggio Bracciolini," in *Poggius Bracciolini, Opera Omnia*, Vol. IV, *Epistulae miscellaneae*. Riccardo Fubini, ed. Reprinted from *Zentralblatt für Bibliothekswesen* (Leipzig: Otto Harrassowitz, 1913). Turin: Bottega d'Erasmo, 1969.

Wood-Legh, Kathleen L., ed. *A Small Household of the XVth Century, being the Account Book of Munden's Chantry, Bridport*. Manchester: Manchester University Press, 1956.

Wormald, Francis, and C. E. Wright, eds. *The English Library before 1700. Studies in Its History*. London: University of London, The Athlone Press, 1958.

Zaccaria, Vittorio. "L'Epistolario di Pier Candido Decembrio," *Rinascimento*, III (1952), 85–118.

—— "Sulle opere di Pier Candido Decembrio," *Rinascimento*, VII (1956), 13–74.

Zannoni, ——. "Letteratura: Della carcere, del iniusto esilio e del trionfal ritorno di Cosimo padre della patria: narrazione genuina tratta dall' istoria Fiorentina Ms. di Giovanni Cavalcanti ... ," *Antologia*, V (January–March, 1822), 44–51.

Zantfliet, Cornelius. "Chronicon S. Jacob Leodiensis Monachus Ab Anno MCCXXX ad MCCCCXI," in Edmond Martène and Ursin

Durand, *Veterum Scriptorum et Monumentorum Historicorum, Dogmaticorum, Moralium, Amplissima Collectio*, Vol. V, cols. 67–504. Paris: Montalant, 1729.

Zenus, Jacobus. *Romanorum Pontificum, regum atque illustrium virorum testimonia de beato Nicolao Albergato*. Rome: Franciscus de Comitibus, 1744.

Zippel, Giuseppe. "L'invettiva di Lorenzo di Marco Benvenuti contro Nicolò Niccoli," *Giornale storico della letteratura italiana*, XXIV (1894), 166–186.

—— *Nicolò Niccoli*. Florence: Bocca, 1890.

INDEX

NOTE: The reader will notice that many pages are listed in the index under classical and patristic authors and under the Old and New Testaments although those names do not in fact appear on the pages listed. The references are to quotations from such authors and sources embedded in the text and can be traced only by the use of the appropriate footnotes.